Gun Control in the United States

Recent Titles in the
CONTEMPORARY WORLD ISSUES
Series

Date: 4/23/18

363.33 CAR
Carter, Gregg Lee,
Gun control in the United
States : a reference

Books in the **Contemporary World Issues** series address vital issues in today's society such as genetic engineering, pollution, and biodiversity. Written by professional writers, scholars, and nonacademic experts, these books are authoritative, clearly written, up-to-date, and objective. They provide a good starting point for research by high school and college students, scholars, and general readers as well as by legislators, businesspeople, activists, and others.

Each book, carefully organized and easy to use, contains an overview of the subject, a detailed chronology, biographical sketches, facts and data and/or documents and other primary source material, a forum of authoritative perspective essays, annotated lists of print and nonprint resources, and an index.

Readers of books in the Contemporary World Issues series will find the information they need in order to have a better understanding of the social, political, environmental, and economic issues facing the world today.

Gun Control in the United States

A REFERENCE HANDBOOK

Second Edition

Gregg Lee Carter

An Imprint of ABC-CLIO, LLC

Santa Barbara, California • Denver, Colorado

Library of Congress Cataloging-in-Publication Data

Names: Carter, Gregg Lee, 1951– author.
Title: Gun control in the United States : a reference handbook / Gregg Lee Carter.
Description: Second edition. | Santa Barbara, California : ABC-CLIO, [2017] | Series: Contemporary world issues | Includes bibliographical references and index.
Identifiers: LCCN 2016042008 (print) | LCCN 2016056897 (ebook) | ISBN 9781440835667 (alk. paper) | ISBN 9781440835674 (ebook)
Subjects: LCSH: Gun control—United States. | Firearms—Law and legislation—United States. | Firearms—Social aspects—United States. | Violent crimes—United States.
Classification: LCC HV7436 .C36 2017 (print) | LCC HV7436 (ebook) | DDC 363.330973—dc23
LC record available at https://lccn.loc.gov/2016042008

ISBN: 978-1-4408-3566-7
EISBN: 978-1-4408-3567-4

21 20 19 18 17   1 2 3 4 5

This book is also available as an eBook.

ABC-CLIO
An Imprint of ABC-CLIO, LLC

ABC-CLIO, LLC
130 Cremona Drive, P.O. Box 1911
Santa Barbara, California 93116-1911
www.abc-clio.com

This book is printed on acid-free paper ∞

Manufactured in the United States of America

Portions of this book have been updated from various entries in *Guns in American Society: An Encyclopedia of History, Politics, Culture, and the Law* (Santa Barbara, CA: ABC-CLIO, 2002; © 2002 by Gregg Lee Carter), as well as from the Second Edition of this work (Santa Barbara, CA: ABC-CLIO, 2012, © 2012 by ABC-CLIO, LLC); used by permission from the publisher.

The second edition of *Gun Control in the United States: A Reference Handbook* is the result of two decades of my thinking and writing on the controversial topic of gun control. My goal is to provide a well-organized and readable reference that makes this complex subject more accessible to a variety of audiences: researchers, teachers, students, public officials, law-enforcement personnel, journalists, and interested members of the general public. To enhance accessibility, I have broken down gun control in the United States along its key dimensions: its current and proposed regulations, its effectiveness, its chronology, its similarities and differences to gun control in other industrialized democracies, important legislation and court rulings, individuals who have had a notable impact on it through political action or academic research, prominent organizations and agencies involved on both sides of the gun control debate, and those print and electronic resources that use valid data and skilled analysis to pursue each of these areas in more depth.

I propose no easy solutions to the problem of gun violence, and I take seriously the arguments and data supporting both sides of the gun debate. This is unusual. The vast literature on guns control is biased—strongly so. Popular writers and academics alike generally begin their books and essays with either a pro- or anti-gun slant and then proceed to line up the evidence to correspond with it—ignoring or discounting or misinterpreting any studies that do not fit. In contrast, I try to present enough information and logical reasoning, based on the best scholarly research to date, for each reader to make up his or her own mind on the benefits or harms that the strict control of guns might incur, as well as the obstacles facing those who would like to strengthen or weaken the current level of control. Everyone agrees that some control is necessary; the debate is over how much and what kind. All of this said, I must admit that over the years I have come to change my outlook from a fairly strong gun rights to a fairly strong gun control inclination. At heart, I am an empiricist, and though the logical reasoning of both sides of the gun debate have their strengths and moments of shining glory, in the end I find the scientific data to favor gun control. These data and their interpretations are complex, but I have struggled with them long enough to realize that comprehensive gun control can both reduce the economic costs and human suffering involved in the enormous amount of gun violence that the United States presently endures on a daily basis, while still protecting the right of individuals to own and use guns for lawful purposes, including hunting, target shooting, and self-defense.

I am grateful to the following scholars for the assistance noted: Stephen P. Halbrook, for clarification of federal gun control laws relating to domestic violence; David Hemenway (Harvard University), for sharing some of the unpublished data that was amassed in early the 2000s by the National Violent Injury Statistics System Workgroup; Harry L. Wilson (Roanoke College) for his communications with me on how the mass media portrays the gun debate; Glenn L. Pierce (Northeastern University) for his thoughtful conversations with me on ways to curb illegal gun trafficking, which is high on the agenda of gun control advocates; Robert J. Spitzer (State University of New York, Cortland), for his review of the topics covered in the *Handbook*—to make sure that they fairly represent the range and complexity of the gun control issue; and Garen J.

Wintemute (University of California, Davis) for updating me on California's attempts to control the manufacture of cheap handguns. I want to also thank the scholars contributing position papers on gun control as presented in Chapter 3 (Perspectives): David B. Kopel (Independence Institute; Denver University), Lawrence Southwick (*emeritus*, University of Buffalo), and Robert J. Spitzer (State University of New York, Cortland). Professors Kopel, Spitzer, and Wilson have also been generous in sharing their opinions with me over the years on selected key topics that surround the gun debate, as has Professor James P. Beckman of the University of Central Florida. Those familiar with the relevant literature will recognize all of the above named individuals as high-profile analysts and commentators on the current debate over gun control in the United States.

My research benefited greatly from the reference library staff at Bryant University, with research librarians Collen Anderson, Mackenzie Dunn, Laura Kohl, and Allison Papini being particularly helpful. Joanne Socci performed many valued clerical services, as did my research assistant Alex Evans; Mr. Evans did especially outstanding research in helping to update and organize Chapters 4 and 5. The Bryant University administration supported my research with course releases and a sabbatical, and I particularly thank former College of Arts & Sciences dean Dr. David S. Lux, as well as current dean Wendy Samter and associate dean Bradford Martin. My acquisition editor at ABC-CLIO, Catherine Lafuente, was encouraging from the start to the end of this endeavor, while managing editor David Paige was critical in helping me to formulate and launch this project during its early stages. ABC-CLIO project editor Robin Tutt was similarly enthusiastic and helpful.

I have updated and used portions of selected entries in *Guns in American Society: An Encyclopedia of History, Politics, Culture, and the Law*, 2nd ed. (© 2012 by ABC-CLIO, LLC). I thank the authors for the use of this material, all of which has been done by permission from the publisher.

Finally, on a personal note, I want to thank my wife, Lisa, for her constant encouragement, and my children—Travis, Kurtis, Alexis, and Davis—for their love and forbearance.

Gregg Lee Carter
North Smithfield, Rhode Island

Gun Control in the United States

Introduction

Public and private debate on gun control is generally only minimally informed by the relevant social science research. Based on personal experiences—such as being introduced to hunting at a young age or being revolted by the television images of an act of gun violence—individuals talk themselves into either a pro– or anti–gun control position. There is good reason why most people sidestep the research—as much of it relies on complex, arcane statistical analyses, and it is generally not well organized into a coherent whole.

The primary aim of this book is to rectify this situation—to help policymakers, academics, and average citizens understand the research and to reach the point where each one can make an informed decision on whether to support stricter or more lenient gun control, as well as on which types of control have the best chances for success. The book draws on the most recent and scientifically sound research on the various aspects of gun control. It illuminates gun control efforts in the United States by putting them into both cross-national and historical contexts.

National Guard troops at a camp in Harpers Ferry, West Virginia, during WWI. The 1916 National Defense Act subsumed state Guard units under national military rules, organization, and authority. The units become a dual enlistment system, whereby a guard member is simultaneously part of the relevant state National Guard and the U.S. National Guard. (Library of Congress)

Gun Prevalence, Gun Control, and Violence

Of the many aspects surrounding the issue of gun control, none is more important than whether there exists a causal link between gun prevalence and violence; and if it exists, what its nature is. Many people assume that such a link exists: that gun prevalence is the independent variable (cause), that violence is the dependent variable (effect), and that the relationship is linear and strongly positive (more guns yields more violence). The social policy implication is that if we reduce the number of guns in our society, we will reduce the amount of violence. Yet establishing the validity of the guns-leads-to-violence link is much more difficult to confirm than the ordinary person might think. The same can be said for supposed effects of gun control in reducing violence. This chapter will review the social science research that speaks to these issues. To anticipate its conclusion, there *is* a causal link between gun prevalence and several kinds of violence (deaths resulting from murder, suicide, and accidents), but it is complex and modified by a number of social contexts. Furthermore, even though gun control in the United States has produced few of the benefits its proponents have alleged, lessons from the experiences of some U.S. states, as well as from our peer nations (economically developed, industrialized democracies), reveal that this needn't be the case—that there are indeed some approaches to gun control cohering with both the cultural unwillingness in the United States to give up guns and the laudable societal goal of reducing gun-related violence.

The United States has a huge number of guns, many more guns than people—an estimated 350–360 million guns as of 2016, in the context of a total population of approaching 325 million by the end of that year (Ingraham, 2015; U.S. Census Bureau, 2016a). It also has weak national gun laws in comparison with almost all other economically developed, democratic nations. And compared with these countries, U.S. gun violence is very high. For example, Krug's analysis of firearm-related deaths in the United States and 25 other high-income countries found that the age-adjusted rate of firearm death (homicide, suicide, accident) "in the U.S. (14.24 per 100,000) is eight times the pooled rate for the other H[igh]-I[ncome] countries (1.76)" (Krug, Powell, and Dahlberg, 1998; data are from the 1990s). In the same article, Krug reports that the U.S. crude homicide rate is six times higher than that for the typical economically developed country. Hemenway and Miller (2000) confirm Krug's analysis, examining all high-income countries (as designated by the World Bank) with populations greater than one million. More recent United Nations (2016) homicide data reveal that this cross-national pattern in gun violence has remained quite stable for decades—despite a significant drop in the homicide rate of the United States in recent years. For example, Carter's (2016) analysis of these data reveals that the U.S. homicide rate is five times greater than its average peer nation, and, even more dramatically, the U.S. gun-homicide rate is almost 10 times greater (raw data available at United Nations, 2016). He also reports that the per capita number of guns in the United States is five times the rate of its average peer nation (raw data available from GunPolicy.org, 2016).

To gun control advocates, these social facts are causally connected: the more firearms circulating in a society and the weaker the regulations governing their possession and use, the greater the likelihood of the occurrence of violent crime, suicide, and accidental firearm-related death. Guns are not just another weapon: assault with a gun, whether inflicted by another or self-inflicted, is many times more likely to result in death or serious injury than with any other weapon (Lindgren and Zimring, 1983). However, gun control opponents—who have come to label themselves as "gun rights" proponents—argue that the United States would be a bloody society with or without the 350–360 million or so rifles, shotguns, and pistols currently in circulation. This argument is not groundless: if the gun homicides are removed from the U.S. total number of homicides, the rate of 1.8 per 100,000 people is still one and two-thirds greater than the entire murder rate (gun-related and non–gun-related) of 1.1 of the typical high-income country (raw data from United Nations, 2016; the comparison year here is 2008, when the total rate for the United States was 5.4; note that as of 2014, this rate had dropped to 4.5). Moreover, even though the suicide rate in the United States is higher than that of its average peer nation (12.1 per 100,000 people, age standardized, for the United States vs. a mean of 10.0 for its 23 peers), it is lower than that of Belgium, Finland, France, and Japan—all four of which have significantly lower rates of gun prevalence. Indeed, for the high-income democratic nations of Western Europe, plus Australia, Canada, Iceland, Japan, New Zealand, and the United States, the correlation between gun prevalence and the total age-adjusted suicide rate is not statistically significant ($r = .22$; $N = 23$; suicide data from WHO, 2016; gun prevalence data from Gunpolicy.org, 2016). Finally, gun rights advocates point out that even though the number of guns in the United States has increased significantly each year over the past two decades (Ingraham, 2015), the homicide rate, including gun-related murders, has dropped significantly (FBI, 2015). In short, at first wash it appears that persuasive data can be marshaled to fit either side of the gun control debate. Ironically, as observed by criminologists James Lindgren and Franklin E. Zimring (1983, 837), the debate over gun control is a war of statistics—but "both sides in the debate often invoke the same statistics."

In actuality, the data do tell a more coherent story when examined more carefully, the process of which will begin in the next section and continue in Chapter 2. But the first point to be made is that even though it might be hard to ascertain which side has the upper hand in the assessment of the guns-leads-to-violence data, it is clear that these varying assessments are at the heart of the gun control debate. Those working for stronger national gun laws, akin to the laws existing in most economically developed democracies, assume that such laws will reduce violence and save lives. As the Brady Campaign to

Prevent Gun Violence states in many of its advertisements and communications with its supporters: "Our goal is to enact a comprehensive federal gun control policy to reduce gun violence." (The Brady Campaign has historically been the largest and most important organization sustaining the movement to control guns; see its website at http://bradycampaign.org/; more recently, Everytown for Gun Safety has taken a leading role in this movement: http://everytown.org/.) Indeed, the Brady organization argues that gun control works. In the fall of 2000, for example, it sent a letter to its supporters contending that the 1993 Brady Handgun Violence Prevention Act, which requires background checks on prospective gun buyers using conventional retail stores, resulted in gun deaths dropping from 37,776 in 1992 to 32,436 in 1997 (Brady, 2000); over the next decade and a half, this message did not change and letters to potential supporters observed that the drop in gun deaths that continued to occur throughout this period was due to the Brady Act "legislation requiring licensed dealers to perform background checks . . . proof that sensible gun laws save lives" (Phillips, 2014); and, finally, several pages on its current homepage (2016) extol "Since 1994, the Brady law has blocked over 2.4 million prohibited purchases. But that's only the beginning. With your help we can cut gun deaths in half by 2025" (http://www.bradycampaign.org/). On the other hand, gun-rights groups challenge the premise that a comprehensive federal gun control policy will reduce gun violence. In the words of the National Rifle Association (NRA), "Guns don't kill; people do." In its flyers and on its web page (https://home.nra.org/), the NRA repeatedly stresses that stricter national gun laws, especially "registration and licensing," would have no effect on criminal violence, "as criminals, by definition, do not obey laws." In the view of gun rights organizations like the NRA, U.S. gun laws are already strict enough, indeed overly strict, and to reduce bloodshed from gun violence, the most important action to be taken is to ensure that these laws are stringently enforced.

Cross-National Comparisons

As noted previously, the United States has an overall murder rate that is five to six times higher than the average economically developed nation. And comparisons of murder-by-gun rates reveal an even more dramatic ratio: the U.S. rate of 3.6 is nearly 10 times higher than the 0.37 average of its peer nations (Carter, 2016; raw data from the United Nations, 2016). Concomitantly, this huge murder rate disparity is accompanied by generally huge differences in gun prevalence: for example, Carter's (2016) analysis of Gunpolicy.org (2016) data reveals a U.S. rate of guns-per-100-civilians that is five times the rate of the average high-income democratic nation (in 2008, 101.1 for the United States vs. 20.2 its peer nations; by 2016, the U.S. rate had risen to 110.5). Killias (1993) reports that in the United States the percentage of households in the early 1990s with any type of gun was 48.0, which is three times greater than that for the typical European country (16.2%) and twice as high as the rate of Australia and Canada (24.3%). (Note that the percentage of U.S. households with a firearm on the premises has dropped significantly in recent years—to 31 percent according to the General Social Survey [GSS]. Why? Hunting has dropped in popularity, and millions of immigrants, relatively few of whom possess guns, have established households in the past two decades. We've also become more urban, and city dwellers are much less likely than their counterparts in rural areas and small towns to own guns [General Social Survey, 2014a, 2014b; Smith and Son, 2015].) Killias's data reveal a strong positive correlation between gun prevalence and homicide. And as noted earlier, Hemenway and Miller (2000) confirm this correlation for high-income countries, as does Carter (2016). On the other hand, Gary Kleck's (1997, 254) analysis of all 36 nations (both high- and upper-middle-income) in the Krug data set reveals a much more modest correlation. Kleck believes that the entire Krug data set is a better indication of the truth, because a careful review of gun prevalence/violent crime studies in U.S. cities and counties shows no consistent relationship (see Kleck, 1991, 185–215). However, Mark Duggan (2001, 1086) believes that "previous research has suffered from a lack of reliable data on gun ownership." Using the level of sales of the magazine *Guns & Ammo* as an indicator of the level of gun ownership, he found that "changes in gun ownership are significantly positively related to changes in the homicide rate, with this relationship driven almost entirely by an impact of gun ownership on murders in which a gun is used" (Duggan, 2001, 1086). Moreover, in an international sample of cities, Altheimer (2010) found strong, independent effects of gun prevalence on assault, gun assault, robbery, and gun robbery rates—even after controlling for unemployment, family disruption, age structure, the sex ratio, and the percentage of residents who go out nightly. Altheimer (2010, 217) emphasizes that "no support was found for Lott's . . . hypothesis that increasing gun availability reduces rates of crime."

Australia, Canada, Japan, New Zealand, and most European countries have much stricter gun regulations than the United States. Most importantly, these countries require that guns be registered, that gun owners be licensed, and that guns be stored with utmost security. To get a license, a potential gun owner must typically pass an exam on gun safety and, quite commonly, must show a "genuine reason" for owning a weapon (e.g., hunting, sport shooting, or a high security need—such as protecting the transportation of cash; this implies that firearm ownership is seen more as a privilege than as a right). Also required are comprehensive background checks of individuals seeking to purchase guns (whether from a retailer or from a private party), including any histories of criminality or mental incapacity (for reviews of cross-national gun regulations, see Parker, 2011; United Nations, 1999). Although in the United States background checks are required by federally licensed firearms dealers when selling guns to their customers, sales between private individuals (including those on the web and at gun shows) are not regulated by federal law, like they are in its peer nations. Of special interest to countries that advocate gun control, *handguns* (because they are considered the most blameworthy weapons of violence) are either outlawed or restricted so severely that ownership of them is extremely rare. This is reflected in the comparatively high percentage of households with a handgun present in the United States (about 22%) and the relatively tiny percentages elsewhere: 0.1 percent in the United Kingdom, 0.2 percent in the Netherlands, 2 percent in Australia, 2.5 percent in Spain, and 7 percent or less in Belgium, Canada, Finland, France, Norway, and Spain (U.S. data are from the General Social Survey, 2014c; data for other countries are dated and come from Killias, 1993; however, because severe restrictions on handgun purchases have remained unchanged in these countries, it is not unreasonable to assume that the older data are still relevant). The striking exception in Europe is Switzerland, which has a laxity in its gun laws comparable to that of the United States and a high prevalence of firearms (46 guns per 100 people according to Gunpolicy .org, 2016). Switzerland is a favorite example of the gun rights maxim that "guns don't kill, people do," because it has low murder rates (both overall and by gun). However, gun control advocates are quick to point out that Switzerland's population is generally better trained in the safe use of firearms than the population of the United States, because most adult Swiss men are members of the national militia. And those on both sides of the U.S. gun debate acknowledge that the civic-minded culture of the Swiss, along with the high level of social and economic homogeneity of their local communities, greatly reduce the potential dangers of having a high prevalence of firearms (e.g., see Kopel and D'Andrilli, 1990).

The case of Switzerland warns us not to oversimplify when making cross-national comparisons. Pro-gun writers and groups have other favorite examples—Finland and Norway have high numbers of firearms but low rates of violence. On the other hand, Mexico and Russia have low numbers of firearms but high rates of violence. In short, there are forces beyond gun availability that influence the level of violence in any particular country. Most importantly, varying combinations of social heterogeneity and economic development have been linked to violence. For this reason, when countries are compared, they should be socioeconomically similar. Simplistic pairwise comparisons are rarely useful, because as Kleck (1991, 188–189) correctly argues, "out of any large number of possible pairings, it is safe to say that at least a few pairs can be found to appear to support either side" of the gun control debate. For example, in recent years, gun-rights writers have liked to point out that Russia is extremely violent, yet has strict gun control and a relatively low percentage of households with guns, whereas in Switzerland, gun prevalence is high but gun violence tends to be low (notwithstanding the massacre in the Swiss Canton of Zug in September 2001, when a gunman broke into a government building and shot 14 people to death).

The Nature of Gun Violence in the United States

Victimization

Gun violence in the United States does not affect all segments of the population equally. For example, African American males in and near their twenties are the most likely to suffer such violence in its criminal form, whereas older white males are most likely to commit suicide with a firearm.

Homicide

In 2014, 14,249 people were murdered in the United States. Of these homicides, the Federal Bureau of Investigation (FBI) had information on 11,911 regarding what type of weapon was used (firearm, knife, hands-fist-or-feet, or other weapon). Of these murders, two out of three (8,124, or 68.2%) were killed with a firearm—with a handgun most often used (5,562 victims, or 68.5%). Seventy-five percent of these victims were under the age of 45. Seventy-seven percent were male. And even though African Americans represent only about 13 percent of the total U.S. population, 51 percent of the victims were black (in contrast, note that Hispanics constitute 17.4% of the population and 17.7% of homicide victims) (FBI, 2015, Tables 1, 19, 20, and Expanded Homicide Data Table 2; U.S. Census Bureau 2016b).

As has been the case for decades, those most at risk for a gun homicide are African American males. Indeed, their risk is many times greater than that of their non-Hispanic white, Hispanic, and Asian counterparts. In 2014, black males had a firearm homicide rate of 26.4 per 100,000, while the rate for non-Hispanic white males was 2.0, for Hispanic males 5.3, and for Asian males 1.3 (see Table 1.1; historical data can be found in Carter, 1997; 2001; 2006, 8–9; and Fox, 2000).

Table 1.1 shows that the most common age range for gun homicide victimization is the early twenties, followed by the late twenties and early thirties. Figure 1.1 graphically displays the rate for these combined age groups, thereby more starkly revealing the hugely disproportionate rate suffered by African American men—and to a much lesser (but still significantly higher than the average) degree by Hispanic men—in their twenties and early thirties. However, the good news for U.S. society is that the rates of homicide, including by firearm, have been falling for two decades (and reaching their peaks in the early 1990s). As displayed in Figure 1.2, for those always at the greatest risk of being murdered by a gun—men in their twenties and early thirties—all saw their rates of firearm homicide drop between 1999 and 2014, no matter what their race and ethnic background.

Suicide

In 2014, there were 42,773 reported suicides in the United States, with 50 percent of these being classified as firearm-related. Males were four times more likely than females to kill themselves, using a gun in 55 percent of the cases (note that the most common method that females use is poisoning—representing 35 percent of female suicide deaths in recent years; see CDC, 2015, 2016).

Table 1.1   U.S. Firearm Homicides in 2014 by Age, Race, Ethnicity, and Sex

Ages	All N**	All Rate	WHITE* Male N	WHITE* Male Rate	WHITE* Female N	WHITE* Female Rate	BLACK* Male N	BLACK* Male Rate	BLACK* Female N	BLACK* Female Rate	HISPANIC Male N	HISPANIC Male Rate	HISPANIC Female N	HISPANIC Female Rate	ASIAN* Male N	ASIAN* Male Rate	ASIAN* Female N	ASIAN* Female Rate
All	10,945	3.5	1,885	2.0	809	0.8	5,607	26.4	596	2.7	1,488	5.3	244	0.8	121	1.3	43	0.4
0–14	225	0.4	48	0.3	33	0.2	61	1.3	30	0.7	19	0.3	24	0.3	3	0.2	1	0.1
15–19	1,230	5.8	96	1.6	33	0.6	738	45.2	74	4.7	231	9.7	32	1.4	9	1.6	2	0.4
20–24	2,357	10.3	228	3.5	58	0.9	1,481	81.1	124	6.9	362	14.5	54	2.4	21	3.0	3	0.4
25–34	3,260	7.4	457	3.6	174	1.4	1,873	64.2	166	5.3	456	9.7	55	1.3	33	2.2	2	0.1
35–44	1,835	4.5	367	3.0	138	1.2	853	34.4	105	3.8	269	6.5	44	1.1	26	1.9	9	0.6
45–54	1,132	2.7	358	2.6	139	1.0	392	15.7	51	1.8	114	3.6	24	0.8	15	1.3	17	1.3
55–64	538	1.4	200	1.4	98	0.7	153	7.3	26	1.1	29	1.5	8	0.4	8	0.9	5	0.5
65+	367	0.8	130	0.8	136	0.7	56	3.0	20	0.8	8	0.5	3	0.1	6	0.6	4	0.4

* Non-Hispanic (note that Hispanic/non-Hispanic is not a racial category—thus even though the majority of Hispanics claim a white racial background, there are also black and Asian Hispanics).

** Because Native Americans and "other" racial categories are not included in this table, the All N's are greater than the sum of the individual cell n's in each row; note, also, that the sum of each column from ages 0–14 through 65+ may not add to the total (All) at the top of the column, as there is missing age information for a small number of cases.

Note that rates are per 100,000 and age adjusted. (Some events occur more often among certain age groups than others. For instance, gun homicides are more common among those in their twenties than among other age groups. Age adjustment enables the comparison of homicide rates without concern that the differences uncovered are because of differences in the age distributions among different populations.)

Source: Raw data from CDC (2016a); 2014 data most recent available.

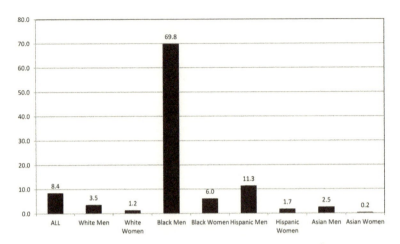

Figure 1.1   U.S. Firearm Homicide Rate (per 100,000 Population) in 2014 for Ages 20–34, by Race, Ethnicity, and Gender.
Source: Raw data from CDC (2016a); 2014 data most recent available.

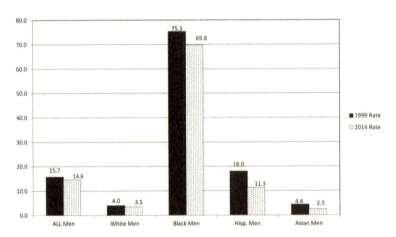

Figure 1.2   U.S. Firearm Homicide Rate (per 100,000 Population): 1999 vs. 2014 for Men Ages 20–34, by Race and Ethnicity.
Source: Raw data from CDC (2016a); 2014 data most recent available.

As shown in Table 1.2, gun-related suicides are associated with white males much more than any other of the racial-ethnic-gender combinations listed. Moreover, although the Rate in the All column reveals a strong positive association with age

Table 1.2 U.S. Firearm Suicides in 2014 by Age, Race, Ethnicity, and Sex

Ages	ALL		WHITE*				BLACK*				HISPANIC				ASIAN*			
			Male		Female		Male		Female		Male		Female		Male		Female	
	N**	Rate	N	Rate	N	Rate	N	Rate	N	Rate	N	Rate	N	Rate	N	Rate	N	Rate
ALL	21,334	6.3	15,925	14.6	2,694	2.5	1,002	5.3	117	0.6	994	4.1	120	0.5	203	2.2	33	0.3
0–14	174	0.3	114	0.7	29	0.2	10	0.2	2	0.0	10	0.1	5	0.1	2	0.1	2	0.1
15–19	755	3.6	539	8.9	63	1.1	46	2.8	6	0.4	62	2.6	9	0.4	13	2.3	2	0.4
20–24	1,515	6.6	966	14.7	147	2.3	176	9.6	9	0.5	139	5.6	20	0.9	32	4.6	3	0.4
25–34	2,829	6.5	1,863	14.7	326	2.6	254	8.8	22	0.7	231	4.9	29	0.7	40	2.7	7	0.4
35–44	2,830	7.0	1,888	15.7	430	3.6	182	7.3	27	1.0	197	4.8	20	0.5	33	2.4	7	0.5
45–54	3,954	9.0	2,845	19.7	722	4.9	128	5.0	21	0.7	143	4.5	19	0.6	33	2.9	5	0.4
55–64	3,910	9.8	3,081	21.6	546	3.7	92	4.4	16	0.7	103	5.3	10	0.5	26	2.9	5	0.5
65+	5,367	11.8	4,629	29.6	431	2.2	114	7.6	14	0.6	109	7.8	8	0.4	24	2.8	2	0.2

* Non-Hispanic (Note that Hispanic/non-Hispanic is not a racial category—thus even though the majority of Hispanics claim a white racial background, there are also black and Asian Hispanics.)

** Because Native Americans and "other" racial categories are not included in this table, the All N's are greater than the sum of the individual cell n's in each row; note, also, that the sum of each column from ages 0–14 through 65+ may not add to the total (All) at the top of the column, as there is missing age information for a small number of cases.

Note that rates are per 100,000 and age adjusted. (Some events occur more often among certain age groups than others. For instance, gun suicides are more common among those 65+ than among other age groups. Age adjustment enables the comparison of suicide rates without concern that the differences uncovered are because of differences in the age distributions among different populations.)

Source: Raw data from CDC (2016a); 2014 data most recent available.

(that is, as age increases, so does the suicide rate), the rate for white males rises with age with much greater consistency than the rates for other racial-ethnic-gender combinations. Despite this positive association between age and the probability of committing gun suicide, other Centers for Disease Control and Prevention (CDC; 2016b) data reveal that suicide does not even make the top 10 list for those over 65, whereas it is a leading cause of death of adolescents and younger and middle-aged adults. More specifically, it is the number 3 cause for those 10 to 14 years of age, the number 2 cause of death for those aged 15 to 34, the number 4 cause for those aged 35 to 44, the number 5 cause for those aged 45 to 54, and the number 8 cause for those aged 55 to 64 (accidents are the number 1 cause of death for those under 45, whereas cancer and heart disease top the list for those aged 45 and older).

Although the overall suicide rate of the United States is below that of its average peer nation (Richardson and Hemenway, 2011), the U.S. youth (ages 5–14) and young adult (15–24) rates are greater. Public health researchers attribute the higher rates for U.S. children, adolescents, and young adults to the much greater availability of firearms in U.S. homes compared to homes in other economically developed nations. For example, Johnson, Krug, and Potter (2000) found in a study of 34 prosperous nations—including those in Western Europe, Canada, and Australia—that only Finland (11.4 per 100,000) had a suicide-by-firearm rate higher than that in the United States (9.3 per 100,000) for those in the age range of 15 to 24, and that the U.S. rate positively dwarfed those of most of these nations. The rate per 100,000 in Canada was 5.9, in Australia 3.9, in New Zealand 2.7, and less than 1.0 in France, Germany, the Netherlands, the United Kingdom, Spain, Italy, and Portugal (note that firearm and suicide rate findings apply almost exclusively to males—as this is their overwhelming choice of method in those nations where firearms are widely available; note that follow-up research by Richardson and Hemenway [2011] confirms the Johnson, Krug, and Potter findings). The human tragedy here is that children, adolescents, and young adults tend to be more impulsive than older adults (25 and older), and scientific study reveals that many suicides are impulsive acts—and are often committed under the influence of alcohol (33.4% of suicide decedents in a recent CDC analysis) and opiates (23.8%; see CDC, 2015). Moreover, many survivors of attempted suicide are glad to be alive when interviewed months and even years later (see Hemenway's [2004, 38–39] review of these studies). Research also reveals that there is more myth than truth in the common assumption that those intent on killing themselves will use whatever means necessary: estimates are that only 10–15 percent of individuals who commit suicide have an "unbreakable determination" to kill themselves. Public health researcher Matthew Miller (2012, e2) provides an excellent illustration of this point when he observes that in "the 1950s, nearly half of all suicides in the United Kingdom were because of carbon monoxide gas from coal burning ovens. As homes replaced coal with detoxified gas over the next two decades, rates of suicide by gas fell in effect to zero without offsetting increases in rates of nongas suicide. Consequently (and critically), overall rates of completed suicide dropped substantially for both men and women [by approximately 30%]." One inference from this kind of finding is that there should be a positive correlation between gun availability and suicide, and indeed there is (where guns are less available—in the home, in the neighborhood, in the community—suicide rates are significantly lower; see Azrael, 2004; Harvard School of Public Health, 2016; and Miller, 2012). The implication is obvious to public health researchers: with the risk period being transient for most potential suicide victims, "reducing the availability of firearms—the most common, lethal, and symbolically resonant instruments—during this period may prevent suicide attempts and would certainly reduce the rate of suicide completions" (Hemenway, 2004, 38–39)—especially for adolescents and younger adults, who are more likely to act impulsively and less likely than their older counterparts to comprehend the absolute finality of death.

As a final note, unlike the rate of gun homicide, which as noted earlier has been falling for the past two decades, suicides by firearm have been on the rise and have more than made up for the lowering rate of gun homicides over the course of the past 15 years (see Figure 1.3)—and thus the absolute number of gun deaths is on the rise, as is the combined rate of gun suicides plus gun homicides.

Accidental Death and Injury

In 2013, emergency rooms in the United States reported a total of 16,864 individuals having been unintentionally shot. The CDC reported that 505 individuals were accidentally killed with a firearm that same year (CDC, 2016a). As indicated in Table 1.3, males between the ages of 15 and 34 are most likely to die or suffer injury from an accidentally fired gun—and that, overall, males account for almost 9 of out 10 accidental firearm deaths and injuries. Because of the small numbers involved, the CDC does not encourage analyses of unintentional firearm

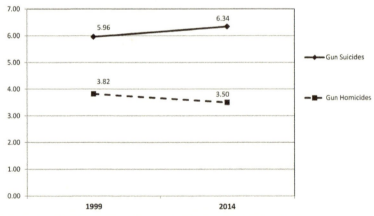

Total gun deaths from these causes in 1999 = 10,868 homicides + 16,599 suicides = 27,467.
Total gun deaths from these causes in 2014 = 10,945 homicides + 21,334 suicides = 32,279.

Figure 1.3   U.S. Firearm Homicide and Suicide Rates (per 100,000 Population): 1999 vs. 2014.
Source: Raw data from CDC (2016a); 2014 data most recent available.

deaths using racial and ethnic breakdowns—but at crude level, the rates for non-Hispanic black males are consistently higher than they are for non-Hispanic white males and Hispanic males. For example, in 2014, the unintentional firearm death rate for black males was 0.60 (involving 124 deaths), which was twice the rate for non-Hispanic white males (0.32, with 329 deaths), and four and a half times the rate for Hispanic males (0.13, 40 deaths).

More than a third of the individuals involved in nonfatal gun accidents require hospitalization (37.9%). Most of their injuries are self-inflicted while cleaning or loading a gun, hunting, or target shooting (Hemenway, 2002). Injury rates in the United States and most other economically developed countries have fallen over the past three decades—mainly owing to the decreasing popularity of hunting and the decreasing proportion of households having a gun. According to the GSS (Smith and Son, 2015), between the early 1970s and 2014, the ratio of U.S. adults who reported keeping a gun at home dropped from 1 in 2 to 1 in 3, while the ratio of having at least one hunter in the house (the respondent or the respondent's spouse) fell from 1 in 3 to 1 in 6.5.

Implied in these social facts is a positive correlation between gun prevalence and gun-related accidents, and, indeed, Miller, Azrael, and Hemenway (2001) found this correlation to be substantial at the state level of analysis: for example, a resident of Alabama, Arkansas, Louisiana, or Mississippi has an eightfold greater chance of being killed in a gun accident than his or her counterpart living in Hawaii, Massachusetts, Rhode Island, or New Jersey. The same relationship holds at the household level: Merrill (2002) and Wiebe (2003a, 2003b), using large-scale national surveys, found that the probability of suffering a gun death was significantly related to having a gun in the house—and, moreover, this relationship holds up under a variety of controls, including race, sex, region, age, marital status, education, family income, military service (veteran vs. nonveteran), and city size. Considering this and related evidence, epidemiologist David Hemenway (2004, 35) reaches the inexorable conclusion that "reduced exposure to firearms should reduce unintentional firearm injuries, all other things being equal. At the extreme, if there are no guns, there certainly can be no gun accidents. States with more guns per capita and less strict handgun control laws appear to have more accident gun fatalities; similarly, high-income nations with more guns seem to have more accidents." More generally, U.S. state-level data clearly support a strong statistical relationship between the percentage of households reporting having at least one gun on the premises and firearms deaths from all causes (Figure 1.4)—including homicide, suicide, and accidental shooting (for more sophisticated—and confirmatory—analyses of this relationship, see Monuteaux et al. 2015; Siegel, Ross, and King, 2013; and Siegel et al., 2014). Finally, per Hemenway's conclusion, the firearm-related death rate also correlates positively and statistically significantly with the strength of gun control laws at the state level of analysis (Figure 1.5; for a more sophisticated—and still confirmatory—analysis of this relationship, including using controls for age, sex, race/ethnicity, poverty, unemployment, college education, population density, and nonfirearm violence, see Fleegler et al., 2013; further confirmatory evidence is presented in Kaleson et al., 2016, and Safavi et al., 2014).

Crime-Related Injury and Assault

In 2013, 62,220 people were treated in emergency rooms after being wounded by a gunshot in a criminal assault (robbery or aggravated assault) in the United States. Eight-nine percent of these victims were males, and 90 percent were also under the age of 45 (Table 1.4). An additional 262,197 individuals were criminally assaulted with a firearm (35.4% of the 345,031 total reported robberies in 2013; 19.3% of the total 724,149 reported aggravated assaults) according to the FBI's 2013 *Uniform Crime Report*. Note that while the rate of firearm-assault injuries has risen in the past decade and a half (Figure 1.6), similar to the rate of firearm-related suicides (Figure 1.3), the rate

Table 1.3   U.S. Firearm-Related Deaths and Unintentional Injuries in 2013 by Age and Sex

	ALL				MALES				FEMALES			
	Deaths		Injuries		Deaths		Injuries		Death		Injuries	
Ages	N	Rate	N	Rate	N	Rate	N	Rate	N	Rate	N	Rate
ALL	505	0.16	16,864	5.37	441	0.28	14,886	9.57	64	.04	1,977	1.20
0–14	69	0.11	538	0.88	55	0.18	424	1.36	14	.05	114	0.38
15–19	55	0.26	2,590	12.24	51	0.47	2,231	20.57	4	.04	359	3.48
20–24	52	0.23	2,754	12.08	49	0.42	2,478	21.22	3	.03	276	2.48
25–34	82	0.19	3,401	7.76	70	0.32	3,037	13.67	12	.06	365	1.70
35–44	48	0.12	3,164	7.85	43	0.21	3,050	15.19	5	.02	115	0.57
45–54	80	0.18	1,381	3.10	69	0.32	1,102	5.06	11	.05	280	1.20
55–64	59	0.15	1,546	3.95	49	0.26	1,208	6.39	10	.05	338	1.68
65+	60	0.13	1,390	3.21	55	0.28	1,267	6.45	5	.02	124	0.54

Note that all rates are per 100,000 and age adjusted. (Some events occur more often among certain age groups than others. For instance, gun accidents are more common among those in their teens and twenties than among other age groups. Age adjustment enables the comparison of injury rates without concern that the differences uncovered are because of differences in the age distributions among different populations.) Note, also, that the sum of each column from ages 0–14 through age 65+ may not add to the total (ALL) at the top of the column, as there is missing age information for a small number of cases.

Source: Raw data from CDC (2016a); 2013 data are the most recent available.

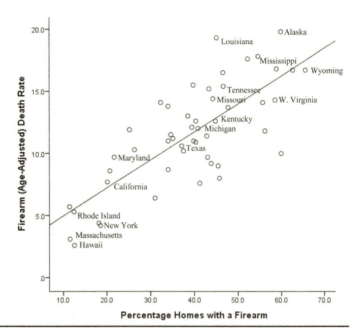

Note: r = .76, p<.0001, N = 50. For those unfamiliar with this statistic, the correlation coefficient r
measures the strength of the straight-line relationship between two variables; if the two
variables are perfectly inversely related, the coefficient equals –1, and if the variables are
perfectly positively related, the coefficient equals +1; in real-world analyses of demographic
and related health and sociological data, the absolute values of correlation coefficients are
always well below 1 (which is to say, no single dependent variable is very full explained by a
single independent variable); the .76 value for r is very strong and highly statistically
significant; for an intuitive introduction to the correlation statistic, see Stockburger (2013:
Chap. 15).

**Figure 1.4   U.S. State-Level Firearm Death Rate (per 100,000 Population) in
2013 by Percentage of Homes with a Firearm, with Selected Example States.**
Source: Raw data from CDC (2016c, 2016d); 2004 is the most recent available
for home firearm data; note that the CDC did not collect this data for Hawaii for
2004, which was subsequently obtained from the Violence Policy Center (2016).
The firearm death rate combines gun-related deaths from homicide, suicide, and
unintentional/accidental shootings.

of firearm-related robberies and aggravated assaults have fallen
significantly (Figure 1.7)—a key fact, along with the steadily
falling rate of firearm homicides (Figure 1.3), that gun rights
advocates point to in support of their position that guns can
be made widely available, with few restrictions, as they currently are, to the law-abiding adult population. Also note that,
as in cases of gun homicides and unintentional gun deaths, the
firearm injury rate for crime-related assaults is much higher for

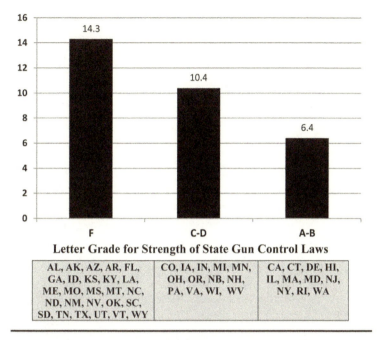

Letter Grade for Strength of State Gun Control Laws

AL, AK, AZ, AR, FL, GA, ID, KS, KY, LA, ME, MO, MS, MT, NC, ND, NM, NV, OK, SC, SD, TN, TX, UT, VT, WY	CO, IA, IN, MI, MN, OH, OR, NB, NH, PA, VA, WI, WV	CA, CT, DE, HI, IL, MA, MD, NJ, NY, RI, WA

Note: The rank-order correlation (Spearman *rho*) between the letter grade for strength of gun control laws and the ranking of firearm death rate (from the highest = Alaska, 19.8 firearm deaths per 100,000 population = 50th; to lowest = Hawaii, 2.6 firearm deaths per 100,000 population = 1st) = –.78, p<.0001, N = 50 (the rank-order correlation coefficient is a variant of the Pearson correlation coefficient described in the Note for Figure 1.4).

Figure 1.5   Average Firearm Death Rate (per 100,000 Population) in 2013 by Strength of State Gun Laws.

Source: Raw data for the firearm death rate is from the CDC (2016c, combines gun-related deaths from homicide, suicide, and unintentional/accidental shootings), while the letter grade (A, B, C, D, or F) is from the strength-of-firearm-legislation grading scale developed by the Law Center to Prevent Gun Violence (2015a). The complex scale weights and combines the number and strength of state gun control laws regarding the curbing of firearm trafficking (e.g., allowing only one gun purchase per month), requiring of background checks for gun sales (e.g., requiring at gun shows), the quality of child safety laws (e.g., requiring guns to be stored in a locked cabinet), the restriction of magazine size for semiautomatic weapons (e.g. allowing a maximum of 15 or less rounds), and the restriction of guns in public places (e.g., not allowing them on college campuses).

young black males than other age-race-gender combinations. For example, in 2013, the criminal assault rate for black males aged 15 to 34 was three times that of their Hispanic counterparts and 19 times greater than the rate for their white counterparts (see Figure 1.8; note that per Table 1.4, the 15–34 age range involves the greatest risk for gun injuries from criminal assault).

The annual National Crime Victimization Survey (NCVS) is the nation's primary source of information on criminal victimization (Bureau of Justice Statistics, 2016). The survey consistently reveals that victims of a robbery in which a gun is used are less likely to be nonfatally injured than when no weapon is used. This is because they are less likely to resist when confronted with a gun. However, victims of gun robberies and gun-related aggravated assaults are much more likely to be killed compared to when no weapon is used (see Alba and Messner, 1995; also see the discussion that follows in the Magnification Hypothesis).

Table 1.4   Firearm-Related Injuries due to Violent Assault by Age and Sex, 2013

Ages	ALL		MALES		FEMALES	
	N	Rate	N	Rate	N	Rate
ALL	62,220	19.8	55,229	35.5	6,984	4.5
0–14	665	1.1	511	1.6	154	0.5
15–19	10,948	51.7	9,754	89.9	1,194	11.6
20–24	17,507	76.8	15,834	135.6	1,673	15.1
25–34	19,009	44.1	16,732	76.9	2,277	10.7
35–44	7,770	19.2	6,944	34.5	826	4.1
45–54	4,276	9.8	3,715	17.2	560	2.5
55–64	1,009	2.6	824	4.4	185	0.9
65+	228	0.5	115	0.5	114	0.4

Note that rates are per 100,000 and age adjusted. (Some events occur more often among certain age groups than others. For instance, gun injuries are more common among those in their teens and twenties than among other age groups. Age adjustment enables the comparison of injury rates without concern that the differences uncovered are because of differences in the age distributions among different populations.) Note, also, that the sum of each column from ages 0–14 through 65+ may not add to the total (ALL) at the top of the column, as there is missing age information for a small number of cases.

Source: Raw data from CDC (2016a); 2013 data are the most recent available.

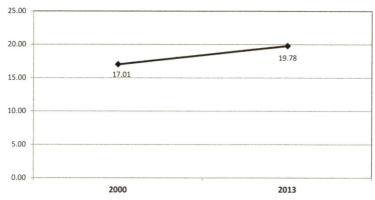

Total injuries from firearm-related violent assault in 2000 = 48,868; in 2013 = 62,220.

Figure 1.6   Rate of Firearm-Related Injuries (per 100,000 Population) due to Violent Assault, 2000 vs. 2013.

Source: Raw data from CDC (2016a); 2013 data most recent available.

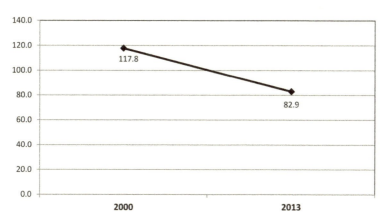

Total gun-related robberies and aggravated assaults in 2000 = 331,652; in 2013 = 262,197. Note that the National Criminal Victimization Surveys (NCVS) of the 2000–2014 era confirm the FBI's Uniform Crime Report (UCR) data displayed in the this figure: In 2000, the NCVS reported a rate of 2.4 firearm victimizations per 1,000 persons of ages 12 and over, which had fallen to 1.3 by 2013. Although the NCVS and UCR data bases use different population definitions and sample techniques, they both yield the same conclusion of a declining rate of gun-related violence.

Figure 1.7   Rate of Firearm-Related Robberies and Aggravated Assaults (per 100,000 Population), 2000 vs. 2013.

Source: Rates calculated from raw data provided by the FBI (2001, 2014a) and the Bureau of Justice Statistics (2010, 2014).

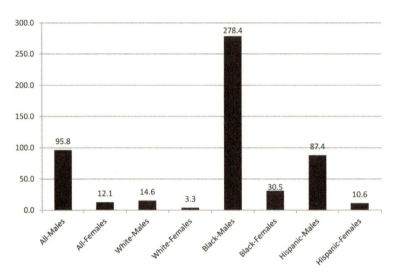

Figure 1.8   U.S. Firearm-Related Injury Rate (per 100,000 Population) in 2013 for Ages 15–34, by Race, Ethnicity, and Gender.
Source: Raw data from CDC (2016a); 2013 data most recent available.

Active-Shooter, Mass-Murder Events

While the overall U.S. homicide rate has been steady falling over the past two decades, including the homicide-by-gun rate, the rise of active-shooter, mass-murder incidents involving three or more victims has been on the rise and, indeed, have been one of the dominant themes in the U.S. public debate over guns since the 1999 mass murder of 12 students and one of their teachers at Columbine High School in Littleton, Colorado. Figure 1.9a reveals the dramatic fall in homicide and gun homicide rates since the early 1990s, when these rates reached their highest peaks in U.S. history, while Figure 1.9b shows the concomitant rise in active-shooter, mass-murder shooting sprees over the same time period (although "active-shooter" incidents often take place in private homes and domestic settings, they are also common in public settings such as schools, workplaces, or shopping areas; note that the operational definition used for an active-shooter, mass-murder event in Figure 1.9b is that it is nongang- and nondrug-related, with at least three homicide victims; this definition differs slightly from the FBI's, which uses four victims murdered in a nongang/nondrug incident; despite the different definitions, the findings in Figure 1.9b are generally similar to those of the FBI's own study of active-shooter incidents—most importantly, the number is on the rise [in its study covering the years 2000 through 2013, the FBI found 6.4 incidents per year between 2000 and 2006, and 16.4 incidents per year between 2007 and 2013; see FBI, 2014b, 8]). As observed earlier in this chapter, this era also witnessed a dramatic rise in the number of guns in the United States (though an overall falling rate of household gun ownership—with the rise in the number of guns being accounted for by current gun owners adding more guns to their collections).

It is important to note that the demographic profiles of the offenders for the overall murder rate versus the offenders in active-shooter/mass-murder events differ in at least one key regard: though for both types of killings the offenders are overwhelming male (90%+), for active-shooter events, African Americans constitute a clear minority of the offenders (e.g., for the events in Figure 1.9b, 22% involved black shooters) while for the overall murder rate African Americans are typically half of the offenders (e.g., for 2014, for those murders for which the race of the offender was known, 53% were blacks; see FBI, 2015, Expanded Homicide Data—Table 3).

The nature of the relationship between gun prevalence and violent crime is currently a hotly debated issue in academic circles, as well as in organizations involved in gun control. Indeed, despite the discussion of how the United States stands out in cross-national analyses of gun violence, as well as the data presented in Figures 1.4 and 1.5, a prestigious panel of social scientists reviewed the empirical studies relating gun ownership and prevalence to criminal violence and suicide and concluded that the data "do not credibly demonstrate" any fundamental causal relationships (National Research Council, 2005, 6). Among the major reasons the panel arrived at this conclusion was the lack of data on gun ownership and the lack of access to the Bureau of Alcohol, Tobacco, Firearms and Explosives' database that tracks guns used in crimes. However, other scholars believe this is an overly conservative conclusion (see, e.g., Cook and Ludwig, 2004; Hemenway, 2004; Monuteaux et al. 2015; Siegel, Ross, and King, 2013; and Siegel et al., 2014). The next

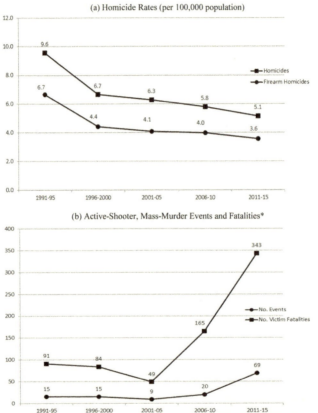

*Note: As defined here, an active-shooter, mass-murder event is one that is nongang- and nondrug-related, with at least three homicide victims. Active-shooter, mass-murder events are a special subcategory of mass murder in which one or more individuals are "actively engaged in killing or attempting to kill people in a confined and populated area. Implicit in this definition is that the subject's criminal actions involve the use of firearms" (FBI, 2014b, 5).

Figure 1.9   Curves Moving in Very Different Directions: U.S. Homicide and Firearm Homicide Rates vs. Active-Shooter, Mass-Murder Events and Fatalities, 1991–2015.

Source: Raw data for (a) from CDC (2016a); for (b) from Stanford Geospatial Center (2016).

section explores more of the contours of this debate and some of its implications for present and future gun control policies.

Establishing Causality—Not an Easy Task

Whether a causal link exists between the high number of firearms in the United States and its relatively lax federal gun laws, on the one hand, and its high rates of violence, on the other hand, represents the heart of the gun control debate. From the mid-1980s through early 1990s, guns spread throughout the inner cities and many suburban communities of the United States. At the same time, these areas experienced growing rates of violence. Between 1984 and 1992, the FBI's *Uniform Crime Reports* revealed that property crime was leveling off; yet violent crime continued to rise—steeply so between 1987 and 1993; and, most significantly, handgun violence catapulted from 589,000 murders, rapes, robberies, and assaults committed with handguns in 1988 to 1.1 million in 1993 (see Bastian and Taylor, 1994; Mackellar and Yanagishita, 1995). That violent and gun-related crime rates have fallen in the past two decades to roughly those levels of the early 1970s does not negate the argument that the influx of guns was connected to the steep rise in violence in the late 1980s and early 1990s (recent and historical crime rates are available from the FBI, 2015, 2016). Just as the riots of the 1960s in African American neighborhoods were self-limiting (one can only burn down a neighborhood so many times), so too was much of the inner-city youth violence in the 1980s and early 1990s. More specifically, the most violence-prone were the first to be cut down; those succeeding them were more mindful of the destructiveness of firearms; they also realized the benefits of a stabilized drug market. Alfred Blumstein (1995, 30–31) offers the following interpretation:

> [Beginning in 1985,] in order to accommodate the increased demand, the drug sellers had to recruit a large number of new sellers. . . . The economic plight of many

young urban African-American juveniles, many of whom see no other comparably satisfactory route to economic success or even sustenance, makes them particularly amenable to the lure of the drug markets. These juveniles, like many other participants in the illicit-drug industry, are likely to carry guns for self-protection, largely because that industry uses guns as an important instrument for dispute resolution. . . . Since the drug markets are pervasive in many inner-city neighborhoods, and the young people recruited into them are fairly tightly networked with other young people in their neighborhoods, it became easy for the guns to be "diffused" to other teenagers who go to the same school or who walk the same streets. . . .

In view of both the recklessness and bravado that is often characteristic of teenagers, and their low level of skill in settling disputes other than through the use of physical force, many of the fights that would otherwise have taken place and resulted in nothing more serious than a bloody nose can now turn into shootings as a result of the presence of guns. This may be exacerbated by the problems of socialization associated with high levels of poverty, high rates of single-parent households, educational failures, and a widespread sense of economic hopelessness. But those factors have been changing gradually over the years, and so they cannot readily provide the explanation for the sharp changes that began to take place in the mid-1980s.

Blumstein also contends that *white* juvenile homicide rates increased during the same era because of a "gun diffusion process" into suburbia (as guns crossed over into suburbia, guns begat guns in close-knit teenage circles). However, because national data, most importantly from the GSS, reveal no increase in the percentages of individuals (including blacks and urban dwellers) or households possessing a gun, some analysts reject the notion that guns spread throughout the inner city and parts of suburbia during this period and accept the simpler "rise-in-gang-activity" interpretation (see, e.g., Kleck, 1997, 72–74 and 256–258). Respondents to the GSS are noninstitutionalized adults willing to take the survey. Not a very social scientific statement—but to those living in the streets of Boston, Chicago, Las Vegas, Los Angeles, Miami, New York, and other urban areas during the 1980s, the GSS data seem unable to detect or speak to the diffusion of guns they witnessed. Indeed, in line with the basic contours of the Blumenstein thesis (that guns generate violence), Duggan's (2001) research reveals that part of the drop in violent crime and murder that occurred in late 1990s reflected a falling proportion of gun-owning households. And consistent with the Blumenstein thesis and Duggan's research is the observation pointed out earlier in this chapter regarding gun ownership: even though the number of firearms afloat in the United States has risen dramatically in recent decades, the proportion of households reporting having a gun on the premises has fallen (from 48.9% in 1989 to 32.5% in 2014; see General Social Survey 2014a).

The Knotty Problems of Causal Direction and Defensive Gun Use

Even if we find intuitive appeal in the Blumstein and Duggan line of reasoning and the correlations contained in the cross-national data cited earlier, correlation itself does not prove causality. Gun rights researchers and writers argue that the causal arrow might very well run the other way—in other words, that rising rates of violence prompt citizens to arm themselves. Indeed, this is the argument of John R. Lott Jr. (1998, 2000; also see Gius, 2014; Lott and Mustard, 1997): that rising criminal violence motivates people to acquire guns for defensive purposes and that when a sufficient number of such people are armed, crime rates actually begin to fall.

Lott's thesis—made popular with the catchy title of his 1998 book, *More Guns, Less Crime*—fueled one of the greatest debates on the effectiveness of gun control, and it is closely linked to Gary Kleck and Marc Gertz's (1995) controversial research on the "good" effects of gun possession—that is, its usefulness in defending against criminal attack. Meta-analyses conducted by Kleck and Lott of both area-level (e.g., cities or counties) and individual-level data reveal no consistent relationship between gun prevalence/ownership and violent crime. Indeed, according to their research, when individuals are freely allowed to carry concealed weapons, rates of violent crime drop. Their interpretation is straightforward and has intuitive appeal: criminals are rational, and they are less likely to rape, rob, or assault when they are fearful that a potential victim might be armed. For example, "in Canada and Britain, both with tough gun-control laws, almost half of all burglaries are 'hot burglaries' [where a resident is at home when a criminal strikes]. In contrast, the United States, with fewer restrictions, has a 'hot burglary' rate of only 13 percent. Criminals are not just behaving differently by accident. . . . The fear of potentially armed victims causes American burglars to spend more time than their foreign counterparts 'casing' a house to ensure that nobody is home" (Lott, 1998, 5).

However appealing, the research of Lott/Mustard and Kleck/Gertz has been assailed on a number of accounts, mainly methodological. Kleck and Gertz's data, based on a 1993 national probability-sample telephone survey, led them to estimate some 2.2–2.5 million defensive uses of guns per year in the early 1990s. However, criminologists Philip J. Cook and Jens Ludwig (2000, 37) question this estimate (as do Hemenway, 2004, Spitzer, 2015, and many other social scientists skilled in quantitative analysis). They do so because it is so far out of line with the estimate of 100,000 defensive gun uses suggested by the NCVS, considered the "most reliable source of information on predatory crime because it has been in the field continuously since 1973 and incorporates the best thinking of survey methodologists." And even though the 1994 National Institute of Justice survey on the "Private Ownership of Firearms" (National Survey of the Private Ownership of Firearms, NSPOF) revealed a very high estimate for defensive gun use, 1.5 million uses (more in line with the Kleck and Gertz's data than with the NCVS's estimate), Cook and Ludwig (1997, 9) still contend the NCVS data are much more reasonable:

> *National Crime Victimization Survey (NCVS), some troubling comparisons*: If the DGU [defensive gun use] numbers are in the right ballpark, millions of attempted assaults, thefts, and break-ins were foiled by armed citizens during the 12-month period. According to these results, guns are used far more often to defend against crime than to perpetuate crime. (Firearms were used by perpetrators in 1.07 million incidents of violent crime in 1994, according to NCVS data.) Thus, it is of considerable interest and importance to check the reasonableness of the NSPOF estimates before embracing them. Because respondents were asked to describe only their most recent defensive gun use, our comparisons are conservative, as they assume only one defensive gun use per defender. The results still suggest that DGU estimates are far too high.
>
> For example, in only a small fraction of rape and robbery attempts do victims use guns in self-defense. It does not make sense, then, that the NSPOF estimate of the number of rapes in which a woman defended herself with a gun was more than the total number of rapes estimated from NCVS. For other crimes . . . the results are almost as absurd.

In the appendix to his *Private Guns, Public Health* (2004, 239–240), David Hemenway zeroes in on why Kleck and Gertz were led so far astray in their survey estimating the frequency of defensive gun use:

> Two aspects of [Kleck and Gertz's] survey combine to create a severe false-positive problem. The first is the likelihood of "social desirability" responses. . . . For example, an individual who acquires a gun for protection and then

uses it successfully to ward off a criminal is displaying the wisdom of his precautions and his capacity to protect himself. His action is to be commended and admired. . . .

Some positive social-desirability bias might not by itself lead to serious overestimation. However, combined with a second aspect of the survey—the attempt to estimate a rare event—it does. . . . Because the survey is trying to estimate the incident of a rare event, a small percentage bias can lead to extreme overestimation. . . . In Kleck and Gertz's (1995) self-defense gun survey, if as few as 1.3 percent of respondents were randomly misclassified, the 2.5 million figure would be thirty-three times higher than the true figure. [In short,] using surveys to estimate rare occurrences with some positive social-desirability bias, will lead to large overestimates.

Since 1993, the percentage of nonfatal violent victimizations involving firearms used in self-defense has been relatively stable—at under 2 percent according the to the NCVS (Planty and Truman, 2013, 12, which would put the absolute numbers in the 40,000–50,000 range in recent years; the actual number of these events reported to the police is much lower, for example, in 2014 it was fewer than 1,600 [DeFilippis and Hughes, 2015]). Hemenway and Solnick's (2015) analyses of the 2007–2011 NCVSs reveal that the typical incident of defensive gun use involves a rural male away from home—against another male who has a gun. Importantly, the data do not indicate any special benefit beyond other protective actions (such as yelling, running, hiding, hitting, kicking, or using a less lethal weapon): when any protective action was taken, 4.2 percent of the victims were injured; when a gun was used defensively (most usually involving simply brandishing it), 4.1 percent of victims were injured. DeFilippis and Hughes (2015) actually contend that the alleged benefits of defensive gun use constitute a "tragic myth": "Despite having nearly no academic support in public health literature, this myth is the single largest motivation behind gun ownership" (according to a 2013 Gallup Poll; see Swift, 2013). Indeed, when individuals actually do fire a weapon in what they think are acts of self-defense, they "are far more likely to end up . . . accidently shooting an innocent person or seeing their weapons harm a family member, than be heroes warding off criminals." Moreover, DeFilippis and Hughes contend the myth of the benefit of defensive gun use is compounded because most people assume that "defensive gun uses [are] good." On the contrary, Hemenway, Azrael, and Miller (2000, 263) found that most "most self-reported self-defense gun uses may well be illegal and against the interests of society."

Franks's (2016) review of stand-your-ground laws, which condone defensive gun use (between 2005 and 2015, 33 states adopted a version of these; stand-your-ground means an individual is not obligated to retreat in the face of a violent threat), coheres with the analyses and conclusions of Hemenway, Azreal and Miller. Franks's review led her to conclude that these laws

> have not only failed to deter crime, but have been instrumental in promoting and defending escalation to deadly force in situations that do not call for it. Homicide rates increased in states after they passed stand-your-ground laws, and states with stand-your-ground laws have higher homicide rates than states without them (Franks 2016). Moreover the laws have encouraged the use of deadly force by those with the least reason to use it. [For example,] . . . the *Tampa Bay Times*'s review of over a hundred fatal stand-your-ground cases in Florida found that nearly half of those invoking self-defense had been arrested at least three times—many for violent offenses—before they killed someone. More than a third had previously threatened someone with a gun or illegally carried a weapon. So

far from having a deterrent effect on crime, the law is proving to be a great benefit to repeat criminals. . . . The cumulative effects of Stand Your Ground laws across the nation
have been similar to those in Florida. Studies have shown
that the laws have no deterrent effect on crime and encourage escalation in confrontations (Cheng and Hoekstra
2013). Other studies demonstrate that states experienced
a 7.1 percent increase in homicides after adopting Stand
Your Ground laws. (McClellan and Tekin 2012)

As for Lott's findings that the legalization of the carrying of
concealed weapons has a significant marginal effect on the deterrence of violent crime, his complex data set and arcane statistical analyses were far beyond the ken of most policymakers
and others interested in the issue of gun control when first published in 1997 and 1998. But of those scholars who understood
such complicated quantitative analysis, many soon poked holes
in his findings (see, e.g., Bartley and Cohen, 1998; Black and
Nagin, 1998; Dezhbakhas and Rubin, 1998; Duggan, 2001;
and Ludwig, 1998, 2000), and the coup de grace was struck in
2003 when a rigorous reassessment of Lott's data revealed that
he had committed fundamental errors in specifying his model
and conducting his analyses. When these errors were corrected,
Ayres and Donohue (2003) found no support for the "more
guns, less crime" thesis; instead, they actually found the data
were more in line with a "more guns, more crime" thesis (also
see Lambert, 2004, for an even more complete dismantling of
Lott's thesis; for Lott's rejoinder, see Lott, 2016).

The Magnification Hypothesis

Simple correlations do not take into consideration other variables that might be determinative of both gun prevalence and
violence (implying that the guns/violence correlation is spu-
rious). For example, rising immigration rates and subsequent
rises in violence based on cultural conflict could account for
the 1980s' rise in gun violence. Or, more likely, it might have

been the growing presence of violent youth gangs—springing from low to high levels of salience with the introduction of crack cocaine in many urban areas—that produced the surge in violent crime. In short, dealt with at a simplistic level of analysis, the data do not fit neatly either the pro–gun control or anti–gun control side of the debate. However, it is not unreasonable to hypothesize that the easy availability of guns, both legally and illegally, and their diffusion in urban areas during the 1980s greatly *magnified* the problems of violence associated with culture conflict and street gangs—even though some would argue that these forces would produce the same levels of violence even if guns were not on the scene.

The magnification hypothesis is supported when one considers that property crime (larceny, burglary, and auto theft) rates were flattening out in the United States during the late 1980s and early 1990s. Having ascertained that much of the rising crime rate in the 1960s and 1970s was due to the youthfulness of the population, demographers and criminologists had long ago predicted this flattening out. They predicted that as the post–World War II baby-boom generation aged, crime rates would fall (because crime is strongly correlated with youth: more than half of all street crime is committed by individuals under 25, with arrests peaking at age 18). If property crime was flattening out between 1984 and 1994, why wasn't violent crime (robbery, murder, aggravated assault) following a similar pattern? The diffusion of guns into urban areas—their availability, possession, and use—could account for the divergent trends in property crime and violent crime.

At the cross-national level, as noted earlier, one must also consider that the correlation between gun prevalence and violence can be accounted for by other factors, throwing suspicion on its causal nature. The two most important factors that must be taken into account are social homogeneity and economic inequality. Were the United States more socially and economically homogeneous, would its much greater prevalence of guns really matter that much? "A culture in which the citizens are very similar—sharing similar ethnicity, religious beliefs, income levels and values, such as Denmark—is more likely to have laws that represent the wishes and desires of a large majority of its people than is a culture where citizens come from diverse backgrounds and have widely disparate income levels and lifestyles, as in the United States" (Stephens, 1994, 23). For this reason, countries with a good deal of homogeneity normally have lower levels of law violation and violence than their heterogeneous counterparts. Kleck (1991, 393–394) presents data in support of the notion that culture and not gun availability is what best distinguishes the United States from other developed countries that have much lower rates of violent crime. For example, Great Britain and Canada—two countries with low gun availability and low homicide rates—are often contrasted with the United States. In those societies, guns were not restricted in the early part of the 20th century, yet their homicide rates were still extremely low (12–14 times lower than that of the United States).

It is difficult to rule out these alternative explanations for much greater levels of violence in the United States compared with other economically developed countries, though there is little doubt that heterogeneity plays a significant role in explaining the level of violence and crime in a nation. However, it is not unreasonable to hypothesize that the easy availability of guns greatly magnifies the problems of crime and violence encouraged by the high levels of social/cultural heterogeneity and economic inequality in the United States.

The magnification hypothesis is further supported when one considers the *lethality effect* that assault by guns produces. Numerous studies confirm that gunshot wounds are much more likely to result in death than wounds inflicted by a knife (the weapon generally assumed to be the next most lethal; see Cook and Ludwig, 2000, 34–36). In comparing U.S. violence rates to those of its peer nations, gun control advocates observe that assaults in the United States are more likely to involve guns and that "guns kill." There is support for this position. The

United Nations Office on Drugs and Crime (UNODC, 2015) tracks international violent crime rates using standardized definitions so that data are comparable across countries. UNODC (2016) data consistently show many of the United States' peer nations—that is, economically developed democracies—have violent assault rates that far exceed the U.S. rate. For example, in 2013 (the most recent year for which data are available), Sweden (839.8 assaults per 100,000 population), Finland (654.3), Belgium (621.0), Germany (612.4), the United Kingdom (564.3), the Netherlands (311.1), and France (299.6), all had rates of assault well above that of the United States (276.6). However, as noted earlier, the U.S. homicide rate is five times greater than its average peer nation (Carter, 2016; United Nations, 2016). The much greater homicide rate of the United States reflects the fact that when a violent assault involves a weapon, it is much more often a gun in the United States (as noted in Carter, 1997, 19, many of the United States' peer nations have historical assault-with-weapon rates on par with that of the United States, but the weapons rarely involved a gun). Such data support the argument that guns transform violent situations into lethal events. As epidemiologist David Hemenway phrases this notion, it is "the presence of a firearm [that] allows a petty argument to end tragically" (see Henigan, Nicholson, and Hemenway, 1995, 57). In short, compared with the rest of the economically developed world, what distinguishes the United States is not so much its overall violent crime rate, but its "extremely high rates of lethal violence," which is "a distinct social problem that is the real source of fear and anger in American life" (to quote criminologists Zimring and Hawkins in their book *Crime Is Not the Problem: Lethal Violence in America*, 1997, 3).

The complex data arguments regarding gun prevalence/violence have prompted some on the procontrol side to adopt a new view. They see the relevant data as not fitting either side neatly (e.g., in the face of a growing number of guns and of a relaxing gun control laws à la the growing number of states allowing the average citizen to carry a concealed firearm, violent and gun-related crime rates have fallen in the past two decades, but gun-related injury rates and mass shootings have risen—contrast Figures 1.7 and 1.9a with Figures 1.6 and 1.9b). Moreover, they believe that it will be a long time before the question of whether gun prevalence/ownership/possession foments or thwarts violent crime is convincingly answered. They know that the elimination of guns can and does reduce violence: put metal detectors in airports, and hijackings are reduced; put metal detectors in high schools, and shootings on school grounds disappear. However, with more than 350 million guns currently in private hands in the United States (Ingraham, 2015), the nation is not going to eliminate its guns—not soon, not ever. Neither, given its great levels of heterogeneity and inequality, is the United States going to eliminate crime. But, by keeping guns out of its streets as much as possible—that is, by strictly controlling them—the harm that they cause can be reduced. This view is becoming increasingly popular among those examining the medical and other costs of gun violence. Economists Philip J. Cook and Jens Ludwig (2000, 36) express this best when they observe that "guns don't kill people, but they make it real easy"; that is, controlling guns might not reduce violent crime but it can reduce the harm done in the commission of such crimes, as well as the harm created by gun-related suicides and accidents. Their analyses of the medical, job-related/productivity, criminal justice, school, and other expenses produced by gun violence in the year 2000 indicated that it cost the U.S. public "on the order of $100 billion per year, and affect[s] all of our lives in countless ways" (Cook and Ludwig, 2000, 117); by 2015, health economist Ted R. Miller estimated that the total cost of gun violence had risen to $229 billion annually (his findings are published in Follman et al., 2015). In the words of the editors of the *Annals of Internal Medicine*, from a public health perspective, "It does not matter whether we believe that guns kill people [the gun control stance] or that people kill people with guns [the gun

rights stance]—the result is the same: a public health crisis"
(see Taichman and Laine, 2015, 520).

The Second Amendment

A well regulated Militia, being necessary to the security of a free State, the right of the people to keep and bear Arms, shall not be infringed.
　　　　—Second Amendment to the U.S. Constitution

For many individuals involved in the debate over gun control in the United States—including scholars, lawyers, judges, journalists, politicians, and everyday citizens concerned about public policy and law—the Second Amendment, and how they interpret it, forms the foundation of their position. The proponents of "gun rights"—archetypically vocalized by the NRA—have long argued to the public, lawmakers, and judges that the amendment guarantees the *individual* the right to own and use arms for protection—protection of one's person, home, or property, as well as against a government that might descend from democracy into tyranny. On the other hand, the proponents of gun control—most strongly articulated by the Brady Campaign to Prevent Gun Violence—have long argued that the Second Amendment is a *collective* right that guaranteed *states*, not individuals, the right to form armed militias for protection in case the democracy of the fledgling nation failed. Some scholars believe that *both* the individual rights theory and the collective rights theory are off base—that is, both demonstrate a lack of "understanding [of] the eighteenth-century world in which the Second Amendment was drafted and adopted" (Cornell, 2004, 161). Until June 26, 2008, the weight of judicial opinions favored the gun control side of the debate—but since the momentous and controversial rulings of the U.S. Supreme Court in *District of Columbia v. Heller* (June 26, 2008) and *McDonald v. Chicago* (June 28, 2010), the most powerful court in the land has ruled that it is indeed an individual right—but not an unfettered one, that is, not one that prevents a variety of gun control regulations. The Supreme Court decisions, however, were both decided by the thinnest of majorities (5–4 votes) and have not ended the debate on the meaning of the Second Amendment. What is the average citizen to make of these differing points of view on the Second Amendment and how the amendment does or should influence the nature of gun control in the contemporary United States?

How the Proponents of Gun Control View the Second Amendment

The Brady Campaign and similarly minded organizations and individuals promoting gun control prominently advertise the fact that before the *Heller* and *McDonald* decisions no federal court had ever struck down a gun control law as unconstitutional based on the Second Amendment. The U.S. Supreme Court had given at least five prior judgments bearing on this amendment, and lower federal courts had made dozens more. In all but one of these decisions (*United States v. Emerson*), the courts had failed to rule that the Constitution guarantees the unfettered right of individuals to own or bear their own firearms. On the contrary, the courts had consistently decreed that both federal and state governments can restrict who may and may not own a gun, and can also regulate the sale, transfer, receipt, possession, and use of specific categories of firearms.

Advocates of gun control like to take the short view of history regarding the Second Amendment. Their favorite starting point is sometimes 1876 (*U.S. v. Cruikshank*) or 1886 (*Presser v. Illinois*), but they are on firmer and more morally comfortable ground when they begin with 1939 (*United States v. Miller*).

In *U.S. v. Cruikshank* (92 U.S. 542, 1876), Louisiana state officials—who happened to be members of the Ku Klux Klan— were challenged for conspiring to disarm a meeting of African Americans. Attorneys for the African Americans argued that the Second Amendment protected the right of all citizens to keep and bear arms. However, the Supreme Court held that the officials had the legal prerogative to disarm them in protection of the common good. More particularly, the Court held that "bearing arms for a lawful purpose . . . is not a right granted by the Constitution." More specifically, the Court ruled that the Second Amendment was not "incorporated," meaning that it only applied to the federal government, not to state governments. The states did not have to honor it, except that they could not prevent citizens belonging to the militia from possessing their own firearms—as long as the firearms were appropriate for use in the militia.

Although this ruling supports their contention that the Second Amendment should pose no barrier to the enactment of strict gun control laws, at least at the state level, many advocates of the gun control movement are not particularly eager to tout *U.S. v. Cruikshank*: the ruling was racist—providing a justification for keeping former slaves unarmed and in a position of vassalage in the South, thereby partly counteracting the effect of the Emancipation Proclamation. This fact is not lost on many African American and Jewish jurists, or on interest groups opposed to gun regulation such as the NRA. Even though African Americans and Jews generally tend to support strict gun control, some jurists have contended that regulations on gun possession are a means of suppressing a society's minorities and of allowing unjust rulers to hold sway because they control all weaponry (see Cottrol and Diamond, 1995).

There is no denying that totalitarian regimes in the modern era, from Fascist to Communist, have routinely denied ordinary citizens the right to keep and bear arms. Only the political elite could keep arms in Fascist Spain or in Communist East Germany and other countries behind the Iron Curtain. And closer to home, so-called Black Codes in the post–Civil War South routinely contained statutes such as Mississippi's code that "no freedman, free Negro, or mulatto not in the military service of the United States government, and not licensed so to do by the board of police of his or her county, shall keep or carry firearms of any kind, or ammunition, dirk, or Bowie knife" (as quoted in Cramer, 1994, Chapter 6). However, as democracy has entrenched itself in the political system and the culture of the United States over the course of two centuries, it is highly unlikely that the country will witness abuses of its citizens comparable to what occurred in the South after the Civil War and in totalitarian regimes elsewhere in the world. In the present-day United States, advocates of strict gun control emphasize there are authentic institutionalized means for changing the political system and getting one's concerns aired and remedied. Gun control advocates also argue that even if the fantastically improbable did occur—even if the United States went totalitarian—ordinary citizens armed with shotguns, deer rifles, .22s, pistols, and even semiautomatic military-style assault rifles could not do much in the face of a massive, well-trained, high-tech military. Indeed, making this point regarding the contention of some gun rights proponents that Jews in Nazi Germany could have averted or at least delayed their deportation to concentration (death) camps, historian Michael S. Bryant (2012, 413) has persuasively argued:

> Had the German Jews defended themselves with lethal force in November 1938 [Kristallnacht], the result would have been to hasten the Jews' demise, not avert it. . . . Armed Jewish resistance—particularly in the form of an organized Jewish militia, the only force that might have had some limited success repelling the attacks [of Kristallnacht]— may well have only confirmed Hitler's most fervid paranoid fantasies of Jewish treachery, and at the same time reduced Germans' aversion to pogrom violence. In short, far from preserving Jewish lives, armed confrontation might have triggered the onset of a Jewish Holocaust in November 1938.

Presser v. Illinois (116 U.S. 252, 1886) involved the case of Herman Presser, the leader of a German American labor

group called the *Lehr und Wehr Verein* (the Learning and Defense Club), who was arrested for parading the group through
downtown Chicago while carrying a sword. More specifically,
he was arrested for conducting an "armed military drill," which
could legally be done only with a license, under Illinois statutes in force at the time. Presser appealed, invoking the Second
Amendment in his defense. The Supreme Court judged against
him, citing the *U.S. v. Cruikshank* ruling discussed earlier. As
was the case with *Cruikshank*, the Supreme Court's decision
smacked of bigotry—in this instance, in the repression of ex-
ploited immigrant laborers trying to improve their collective
lot via unionization.

A more morally defensible starting point for gun control
advocates contending that there had been no constitutional
or other legal basis for disallowing the strict regulation of firearms prior to 2008 is *United States v. Miller* (307 U.S. 174,
1939). In that case, the Supreme Court ruled that the federal
government had the right, which it exercised in the 1934 National Firearms Act, to control the transfer of (and in effect,
to require the registration of) certain firearms. More particularly, the sawed-off shotgun, a favorite weapon of gangsters,
was deemed unprotected by the Second Amendment. The ruling reads, in part, "In the absence of any evidence tending to
show that possession or use of [a] 'shotgun having a barrel of
less than eighteen inches in length' at this time has some reasonable relationship to the preservation or efficiency of a well-
regulated militia, we cannot say that the Second Amendment
guarantees the right to keep and bear such an instrument."
Lower court decisions involving the National Firearms Act
and the kindred 1938 Federal Firearms Act used even more
direct language. In upholding the National Firearms Act, the
district court held in *United States v. Adams* that the Second
Amendment "refers to the Militia, a protective force of government; to the collective body and not individual rights."
Another district court decision in *United States v. Tot* referred
to this ruling in upholding the Federal Firearms Act. Both

court decisions made clear that no personal right to own arms existed under the federal Constitution.

However, in its *Miller* ruling, the Supreme Court noted that the writers of the Constitution clearly intended that the states had both the right and the duty to maintain militias and that a "militia comprised all males physically capable of acting in concert for the common defense. . . . And, further, that ordinarily when called for service, these men were expected to appear bearing arms supplied by themselves and of the kind in common use at the time. . . . This implied the general obligation of all adult male inhabitants to possess arms, and with certain exceptions, to cooperate in the work of defense. The possession of arms also implied the possession of ammunition, and authorities paid quite as much attention to the latter as to the former." Thus, the full text of the Supreme Court decision mitigates the impact of its decision on sawed-off shotguns. Such weapons had no place in a militia and were thus not protected, but the general principle of ordinary citizens owning arms and ammunition was clearly preserved.

Gun control advocates had been on their strongest ground with the more recent Supreme Court decision in *Lewis v. United States* (445 U.S. 95, 1980); here the Court ruled that the 1968 Gun Control Act's prohibition of felons owning firearms was constitutional. The Court held that "legislative restrictions on the use of firearms do not entrench upon any constitutionally protected liberties." Between 1980 and 2008, the Supreme Court had on six occasions made its interpretation of the Second Amendment known by letting stand lower court decisions regarding the regulation of firearms. One of these was *Farmer v. Higgens*, wherein the Eleventh Circuit Court of Appeals denied the plaintiff a license to manufacture a new machine gun, based on the 1986 Firearms Owners' Protection Act, which put an outright ban on new sales of machine guns and automatic weapons. Another was the Seventh Circuit Court of Appeals ruling that the Morton Grove (Illinois) ban on the possession and sale of handguns was within the legal bounds of the Second Amendment. More particularly, the Circuit Court affirmed that "possession of handguns by individuals is not part of the right to keep and bear arms." The Supreme Court refused to hear an appeal of this ruling.

Everything changed with the Supreme Court's 2008 *Heller* and 2010 *McDonald* decisions. In *Heller*, the Court held that the District of Columbia's ban on handgun possession in the home and its prohibition against rendering any lawful firearm in the home operable for the purposes of immediate self-defense did, indeed, violate the Second Amendment. The Court held that the Second Amendment protects an individual right to possess a firearm unconnected with service in a militia and to use that firearm for traditionally lawful purposes, such as self-defense within the home.

The 5–4 majority ruled the Constitution guarantees that "the right of the people, to keep and bear arms, shall not be infringed," and this mandate is independent of the "well regulated militia." Preserving the militia was the foremost reason that led the Founders to protect the right to keep and bear arms, but the right they guaranteed was not just for service in the militia.

In its follow-up 5–4 vote in June 2010, the sharply divided Court extended its ruling to include the 50 U.S. states and their municipalities in its *McDonald* ruling. The majority— Justices Alito, Roberts, Scalia, and Kennedy basing their decision on the due process clause of the Fourteenth Amendment, and Justice Thomas on the basis of the amendment's privileges or immunities clause—held that the Fourteenth Amendment makes the Second Amendment applicable to state and local governments, as it does most of the rest of the Bill of Rights.

Although both decisions were watershed victories for the gun rights movement, gun control activists noted that the Supreme Court acknowledged in both cases that the individual-right interpretation does not mean the right is unlimited. To quote from the *Heller* decision, "Like most rights, the Second Amendment right is not unlimited. It is not a right to keep and carry any weapon whatsoever in any manner whatsoever and for whatever purpose: for example, concealed weapons prohibitions have been upheld under the Amendment or state analogues. The Court's opinion should not be taken to cast doubt on longstanding prohibitions on the possession of firearms by felons and the mentally ill, or laws forbidding the carrying of firearms in sensitive places such as schools and government buildings, or laws imposing conditions and qualifications on the commercial sale of arms [nor on . . .] the historical tradition of prohibiting the carrying of dangerous and unusual weapons" (such as sawed-off shotguns or submachine guns). And in the *McDonald* case, the majority opinion included the statement that their ruling would allow for "[s]tate . . . and local experimentation with reasonable firearms regulations [to be] continue[d] under the Second Amendment."

Gun control advocates also took solace in Justice Breyer's dissenting observation that: "Since *Heller*, historians, scholars, and judges have continued to express the view that the Court's historical account was flawed" (Breyer's dissent is joined by Justices Ginsburg and Sotomayor). The separate dissent of Justice Stevens, his last opinion as a Supreme Court justice, is a paragon of the thinking of gun control activists and scholars regarding the limitations of the Second Amendment to contemporary American society. Among Stevens's observations these activists and scholars have extolled are: "The practical impact of various gun-control measures may be highly controversial, but this basic insight should not be. The idea that deadly weapons pose a distinctive threat to the social order—and that reasonable restrictions on their usage therefore impose an acceptable burden on one's personal liberty—is as old as the Republic. . . . The idea that States may place substantial restrictions on the right to keep and bear arms short of complete disarmament is, in fact, far more entrenched than the notion that the Federal Constitution protects any such right. Federalism is a far 'older and more deeply rooted tradition than is a right to carry,' or to own, 'any particular kind of weapon.'"

Thus, the strong dissent of Justices Breyer, Ginsburg, Sotomayor, and Stevens in the *McDonald* case leaves open the possibility that a change in the Court's composition might eventuate in a reversal of the *Heller* and *McDonald* decisions. Before any such reversal, however, both sides of the gun debate expected many lower-court cases in which the constitutionality of particular gun control laws would be challenged—and this expectation was indeed fully realized. The Supreme Court cases did not include a detailed standard against which to judge the reasonability of restrictions on the right to keep and bear firearms, thus opening up an onslaught of especially difficult litigation in the lower courts. Since the *Heller* decision, an average of about 130 cases challenging local, state, and federal gun laws have come before lower state and federal courts each year—cases in which the courts have been asked to rule on the legality of selected gun laws. The challenges have included critical components of the agenda of the pro–gun control movement (see Chapter 2), including banning possession of firearms by those convicted of felony; similarly banning possession by those convicted of a domestic violence crime, even if only a misdemeanor (per current federal law); granting law enforcement officials discretion in issuing concealed carry permits (as is currently the case in 9 states; in 40 states, law enforcement officials are required to issue such a permit to ordinary citizens, and in 5 others, including 4 of the 40, concealed carry is allowed even without a permit); prohibiting military-style assault weapons and large-capacity (greater than 10 rounds) ammunition magazines; requiring the registration of firearms; forbidding firearm possession to those involuntarily committed to a mental institution; and prohibiting the sale of firearms to those under the age of 21. Of these cases, over 90 percent have been upheld (see Law Center to Prevent Gun Violence, 2014; 2015b; cf. Tennant et al., 2015, 54–61.). Thus, even though challenges to gun control laws are expected to clog the courts for years to come, the language of the Supreme Court rulings in *Heller* and *McDonald*, as well as the overwhelming majority of lower court decisions that have followed, clearly support the notion that strong gun laws are constitutional (regardless of whether they can be determined as effective; see Figure 1.5, as well as Chapter 2).

The Gun Rights View of the Second Amendment

The NRA and other organizations similarly opposed to gun control prefer to take the long view of history with regard to the Second Amendment. As already noted, Supreme Court decisions between 1876 and 1938 contained language that supported the notion that the framers of the Constitution clearly intended ordinary citizens to possess arms and to be prepared to carry these arms into battle in defense of the state. However, the favorite starting point of gun control opponents is pre-Revolutionary America and even earlier—as far back as Saxon England in the seventh century. For then and thereafter, up through the ratification of the Second Amendment in 1791, various governments clearly intended that individual citizens have both the right *and the duty* to keep and bear firearms.

The Anglo-Saxon tradition of all free men having the right, and even the duty, to keep and bear arms was transferred to colonial America, where all the colonies individually passed militia laws that required universal gun ownership. Hunting was essential to many families, and in light of immediate threats from the French, Dutch, Spanish, and Native Americans, it is not surprising that colonial militia statutes required that all able-bodied males be armed and trained (see Hardy, 1986, 41; also see Halbrook, 1989). Intellectually, the colonial elite imbibed the writings of Whig political philosophers, who emphasized decentralized government, fear of a standing army, and the right of the common people to keep and bear arms in defense of themselves—against criminals, foreign powers, and especially the state itself (Colburn, 1965).

Critical in setting the stage for the beginning of the Revolutionary War were British attempts to disarm the local populations of Massachusetts. Indeed, the first battle at Lexington in

April 1776 was touched off when British soldiers approached a group of local militiamen in an attempt to enforce the new disarm-the-people policy. Colonialists bent on independence feared that the British would soon try to disarm not only the residents of Massachusetts, but also residents of the other 12 colonies. Indeed, their fears received confirmation when Britain's Colonial Undersecretary William Knox circulated to Crown officials the tract "What Is Fit to be Done with America?," which, among other things, advised that "The Militia Laws should be repealed and none suffered to be re-enacted, & the Arms of all the People should be taken away, . . . nor should any Foundery or manufactuary of Arms, Gunpowder, or Warlike Stores, be ever suffered in America, nor should any Gunpowder, Lead, Arms or Ordnance be imported into it without License" (as quoted in Peckman, 1978, 176). As the Revolutionary War got under way, the individual states began to adopt constitutions and bills of rights that were partly shaped by perceived and actual British attempts to disarm Americans (Halbrook, 1989, 17). Four states (Pennsylvania, North Carolina, Vermont, and Massachusetts) included the right to bear arms in their formal declaration of rights.

The core issues involved in constitutional debates on the right to bear arms in these four states resurfaced during the U.S. Constitutional Convention's deliberations in 1787 on the need for such a provision, as well as during the First U.S. Congress's debates that eventually led to the Second Amendment in 1789. These issues were fear of a standing army and federalism versus states' rights. States' rights advocates, such as Edmund Randolph, emphasized that citizens in new republics should fear standing armies at all costs; these advocates were quick to invoke the historical record in 1767–1776 Massachusetts, where the British army's presence inflamed and abused the local population—and where the standing army tried to weaken the people by disarming them. States' rights advocates were also quick to point to the sorry records of Charles I, Oliver Cromwell, and James II, who used their armies to disarm and tyrannize much of the English populace between 1639 and 1688. The states' rights advocates—also known as the Antifederalists—comprised the overwhelming majority of delegates, but their zeal was tempered by the ineffective governance that existed under the Articles of Confederation (1778–1789), which kept the federal government very weak and state governments very strong.

Federalists, such as Alexander Hamilton, were also fearful of standing armies, but believed the survival of the United States depended on a strong national government—a government that, among many other things, had its own army and navy. The great compromises between proponents and opponents of federalism were Article I, Section 8, of the Constitution and the Second Amendment of the Bill of Rights. In Article I, Section 8, Congress is granted the power to

- raise and support an army (8.12);
- provide and maintain a navy (8.13);
- call forth the militia to execute the laws of the Union, suppress insurrections, and repel invasions (8.15);
- provide for organizing, arming, and disciplining the militia, and for governing such part of them as may be employed in the Service of the United States (8.16).

Concessions to satisfy the Antifederalists included the right of the states to appoint officers to the militia and to train militiamen (according to standards set by Congress). State militias were seen as counteracting forces to the potential might of a standing federal army. Fears of a standing army were further assuaged by giving the civilian Congress control over the military's purse strings and by requiring that the secretary of war (defense) be a civilian (Heathcock, 1963, 81–83).

Nagging doubts over the power of the states to maintain and control militias were addressed in the First Congress and eventually alleviated with the passage of the Second Amendment. States' rights advocates wanted to be certain that federal power could not be used to annul state sovereignty. "The aim was to ensure the continued existence of state militias as a military and political counterbalance to the national army, and more broadly to national power" (the federalism question; see Spitzer, 1995, 36).

However, this was not the only intent of Congress regarding the Second Amendment—which in recent times is difficult to tell because the amendment is so sparsely worded. The spare language was doubtlessly due to the framers' shared understanding of the institutions and convictions behind it. But, in the long run, "these understandings have vanished as brevity and elegance have been achieved at the cost of clarity" (Malcolm, 1994, 161). Historian Joyce Malcolm's analysis of the First Congress's debate over the amendment resulted in her conclusion that its framers clearly intended the amendment to guarantee the *individual's* right to have arms for self-defense and self-preservation. For example, the First Congress, like its English predecessors, rejected language restricting the people's right only to "the common defence" (163).

How early Americans understood the Second Amendment is captured not only in the historical records of the First Congress, but also in how the amendment was announced and interpreted to the citizenry. The *Philadelphia Federal Gazette* and the *Philadelphia Evening Post* of June 18, 1789, in an article reprinted in New York and Boston, explained the Second Amendment as follows: "As civil rulers, not having their duty to the people duly before them, may attempt to tyrannize, and as the military forces which must be occasionally raised to defend our country, might pervert their power to the injury of their fellow-citizens, the people are confirmed . . . in their right to keep and bear their private arms" (as quoted in Malcolm, 1994, 164).

Finally, the meaning that the First Congress intended for the Second Amendment is revealed in its passage of the Militia Act of 1792. The act required all able-bodied men between the ages of 18 and 45 to own a firearm and ammunition and to be willing to put their weapons to use when called upon by the federal government. Each man within the specified age range was to

> provide himself with a good musket or firelock, a sufficient bayonet and belt, two spare flints, and a knapsack, a pouch with a box therein to contain not less than twenty-four cartridges, suited to the bore of his musket or firelock, each cartridge to contain a proper quantity of powder and ball: or with a good rifle, knapsack, shot-pouch and powder-horn, twenty balls suited to the bore of his rifle, and a quarter of a pound of powder, and shall appear, so armed, accoutred and provided, when called out to exercise, or into service, except, that when called out on company days to exercise only, he may appear without a knapsack. (*Militia Act*, Ch. 33, 1 Stat. 271–274, 1792; as quoted in Reynolds, 1995, 487)

A perusal of the deliberations of the First Congress on the Militia Act discloses no instance of any representative questioning whether individual citizens had the right to possess a firearm. Rather, the representatives agonized over how well citizens should be armed—fearing that the average citizen could not bear too much cost. One congressman asserted, "as far as the whole body of the people are necessary to the general defence, they ought to be armed; but the law ought not to require more than is necessary; for that would be a just cause of complaint." In response, other legislators argued that those Americans who did not possess arms should have them supplied by the states. Such discussions clearly indicated that the problem perceived by the representatives was how to get arms into the hands of the people, not how to restrict their possession (quotation excerpted from Shalhope, 1982, 610).

A Limited Individual Right

In sum, a dispassionate examination of history and of federal court decisions reveals that there is undeniable constitutional and historical support for the contention that the Second Amendment was meant to protect the right of *selected individuals* to keep and bear arms—those individuals being able-bodied men capable of serving in a government militia. This is a fundamental claim of the NRA and others who are opposed to the strict regulation of firearms; indeed, such groups and individuals have historically contended that, with the exception of convicted felons and those involuntarily institutionalized in a mental hospital, the right goes beyond selected individuals to include all individuals, including women, people of color, resident aliens, and many others that the Founding Fathers would have excluded from the keeping and bearing of arms. Recent history has proven them correct, as the individual rights interpretation of the Second Amendment was clearly supported in the U.S. Supreme Court decisions in *District of Columbia v. Heller* (2008) and *McDonald v. Chicago* (2010). However, the same examination also leads to the conclusion that this is a *limited right*—which is to say that both state and federal governments can "infringe" upon the possession ("keeping") and carrying ("bearing") of arms, and that many contemporary legislators and judges have not felt the need to be in lockstep with the full intentions of the framers of the Second Amendment.

More generally, these legislators and judges recognize the significant changes that have occurred in the United States since 1776, when an armed population was critical to the defense of the new nation. As pointed out by Spitzer (2015, 43–46) and Edel (1995, 28–36), in the past 240 years, the standing army has become entrenched in U.S. life, and notions that it is a threat to personal liberty have long ago been dispelled. The concept of defense being limited to fighting at the borders of one's homeland repelling foreign invaders has been greatly broadened to the point where the defense business of the United States includes sending soldiers to Europe, Asia, Central America, Africa, and the Middle East; in short, the place of the United States in world affairs has changed dramatically. In the 18th century, the protection of the home, the farm, the village, the town, and the city were left to the individual or to the militia; but by the middle of the 19th century, local police forces were the norm, and by the middle of the 20th century, national law enforcement agencies (the FBI, Secret Service, Customs Service, Drug Enforcement Administration, Immigration and Naturalization Service) were well established. In sum, 18th-century notions of the purpose and place of the militia in the community are out of step with the realities of the 21st century, and so too, consequently, is the need to ensure the keeping and bearing of arms in private hands.

More particularly, the states and the federal government can and do, before and after the momentous *Heller* and *McDonald* decisions, (1) outlaw the possession and transfer of certain categories of firearms (as they have done with machine guns, and as many gun control advocates would like to see done with handguns); (2) outlaw the right of certain categories of individuals to own firearms (most notably convicted felons and the mentally incompetent); (3) require shooters to be licensed and to have passed a firearms safety examination; and (4) require that the purchasers of certain classes of guns obtain special permits (most notably, handguns, as is now the case in 13 states and the District of Columbia). In short, "the Second Amendment poses no obstacle to gun control as it is debated in modern America"; and the Supreme Court decisions of *Heller* and *McDonald* included clear language that the individual right to possess a firearm is "limited," and "the Court has gone to great pains to say that most existing gun laws are presumptively constitutional" (Spitzer, 1995, 49; 2015, 46). Related to the aims of the modern gun control movement to strengthen U.S. gun laws, the amendment cannot account for the difficulties and defeats the movement has thus far encountered. With the biggest exceptions being the District of Columbia and Chicago laws involved in the *Heller* and *McDonald* cases, the courts have been consistently unwilling—before and after these cases—to strike down local, state, and federal gun control laws on the basis of the amendment. Finally, it should be noted that public opinion favors the limited individual-right interpretation of the Second Amendment—that is, it agrees with the Supreme Court's *Heller* and *McDonald* decisions that the amendment protects the right of individuals to possess firearms, but it also agrees that possession can be earnestly regulated by the government. Thus, for example, when the Gallup Organization interviewed a random sample of adult Americans immediately after the *Heller* decision, 73 percent agreed with the statement that "the Second Amendment to the Constitution guarantees the rights of Americans to own guns" (the individual-right interpretation), while just 20 percent agreed with the statement that "the amendment only guarantees the rights of state militia members" (the collective-right interpretation). However, in the same poll, 87 percent of the respondents agreed that either current gun regulations should remain (38%) or become even stricter (49%; see Jones 2008).

Public Opinion and Gun Control

Do Americans Want Strict Gun Control?

Overall, via local, state, regional, and national surveys, adult Americans are polled on their attitudes toward guns and gun control several dozen times per year. Variations in the wordings of questions concerning particular subissues can significantly affect the findings, as many researchers have demonstrated (see, e.g., Kleck, 1997, Chapter 10; Kopel, 2000). However, the overall pattern in the polling data is so consistent and so strong that the inescapable conclusion is that the U.S. public supports the strong control of firearms. However, Americans are opposed to restricting guns to the degree to which they are in many other industrialized countries—most importantly, they do not think handguns should be banned from private ownership, and they are increasingly comfortable with the liberalization of concealed carry laws.

Since 1972, the National Opinion Research Center (NORC) has polled a random sample of adult Americans on a variety of social issues (almost annually until 1994, with samples of approximately 1,600; and biannually since then, with samples of approximately 3,000). NORC's GSS provides one of the best data sources currently available on U.S. social structure, as well as on the attitudes and self-reported behaviors of the population. Because it asks the same question concerning gun control on all of its surveys, the GSS provides one of the most important overtime data sources available on this issue: *Would you favor or oppose a law which would require a person to obtain a police permit before he or she could buy a gun?* Over the past four decades, survey results reveal a strong and generally consistent tendency toward favoring police permits (see Figure 1.10). This implies support for the Brady Handgun Violence Prevention Act, which requires a background check for all firearm purchases from licensed gun dealers, manufacturers, or importers. The background check is conducted through information provided by the FBI's National Instant Criminal Background Check System, and it is intended to prevent

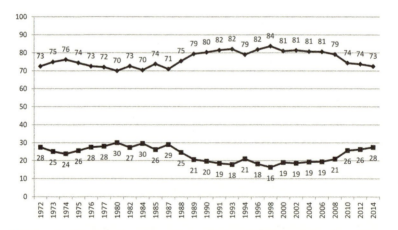

Figure 1.10 Trends in the Percentage of the U.S. Adult Population Supporting the Requirement of a Police Permit Before Being Able to Buy a Gun, 1972–2014.

Source: Raw data from General Social Survey (2014d): "Would you favor or oppose a law which would require a person to obtain a police permit before he or she could buy a gun?" (2014 data most recent available).

individuals convicted of a serious crime (carrying a sentence of at least a year), under a violence-based restraining order, having a drug-related arrest, classified as a fugitive from justice, deemed an illegal alien, or certified as mentally unstable from purchasing a firearm. Indeed, Gallup, Harris, and other national surveys consistently reveal strong support (80–90%) for the Brady law (more recently, the question asked is a variant of "Do you support a background check for everyone wanting to buy a firearm?"), even among gun owners (again, 80–90%). Enacted in November 1993, after overcoming strong opposition from the NRA, it is one of the most important national gun control laws in the United States today.

In their quest to reduce gun violence, proponents of strict gun control would like to see the enactment of *national* regulations on par with those in most other industrialized democracies. Among these regulations are banning handguns except for police and authorized security personnel; allowing concealed weapons to be carried only by law enforcement officers or a few select individuals who might have the need (e.g., those transporting large amounts of cash); limiting the size of ammunition magazines on semiautomatic handguns and long guns to 10 rounds or fewer; strengthening gun sale laws by requiring universal background check on all sales—no matter what the venue (from a retail gun store to a gun show to the Internet to a living room where two individuals are involved in a simple private sale); banning military-style, semiautomatic rifles and shotguns; registering all gun sales in a nationalized government database; requiring that all prospective gun buyers be licensed by local law enforcement to verify their identity and to ensure that they are not banned from possessing a firearm (e.g., as are convicted felons); requiring gun owners to store their weapons safely (e.g., in locked, heavy metal cabinets), so that children or the mentally distressed do not have easy access to them (often referred to as "child access protection" laws); banning and increasing the punishment for "straw purchases," whereby an individual who can pass a background check and buy a firearm legally does so but to make the purchase for an individual who would not be able to pass a background check (most probably because the individual is a convicted felon); barring convicted felons from possessing guns; barring those under 21 from possessing a handgun; and barring the mentally ill from buying guns. According to national surveys conducted over the past three decades, the general population strongly supports all but two of these regulations: the only strong gun control measure that the public routinely rejects is a ban on all handguns (with only about a quarter of the population supporting this, see, e.g., Gallup, 2016; note, however, that there is generally strong support for prohibiting those under 21 from possessing them), and the public is increasingly comfortable with concealed weapons permits being liberally given to ordinary, law-abiding citizens (not just to the police and related security personnel; e.g., a recent Gallup [2016] poll revealed that 56 percent of adults Americans believe that the United States is "safer" when law-abiding citizens are allowed to carry concealed weapons). As with the Brady legislation, the NRA and its allies strongly oppose all of these gun control measures—except for banning sales to felons (the NRA's views on these measures are available online at http://www.nraila.org/; also see Kopel's and Southwick's essays in Chapter 3 of the present volume; in general, gun rights groups support bans on firing weapons in heavily populated, urban areas, as well as bans on the possession of firearms by dangerous people—including convicted violent felons and those with well-established mental illnesses that can readily be expressed as violence; however, these groups also support "relief from disabilities"—that is, allowing convicted felons and those adjudicated as mentally ill to regain their gun-possession rights if they can show that they are no longer a danger to society).

Recent national public opinion survey findings on strong gun control regulations are presented in Figure 1.11 (for the generally similar historical findings, see Carter, 1997, Chapter 4; Gallup, 2016; Harris Poll, 2016; Kleck, 1997, Chapter 10; and *PollingReport.com*, 2016). Of great interest to those trying to predict the future of gun control efforts in the United States, public opinion polls reveal that gun owners are supportive of strong gun control measures—though, not surprisingly, generally not as strongly supportive as their non–gun-owning counterparts (see Figure 1.12).

Social and Economic Correlates of Support for Gun Control

Regardless of social or economic background, most U.S. adults *favor* the serious control of guns—as indicated, for example, in their responses to the GSS question concerning the strong requirement of having to obtain a police permit before being able to buy a gun. However, women, people of color, immigrants,

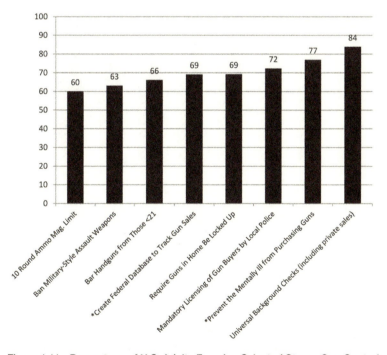

Figure 1.11   Percentage of U.S. Adults Favoring Selected Strong Gun Control Measures.
Source: Raw data from Barry et al. (2015) and *Pew Research Center (2015).

residents of metropolitan areas, Northeasterners, Democrats, political moderates and liberals, nonhunters, and non–gun owners are significantly more likely to favor gun control than their counterparts (men, non-Hispanic whites, native-born individuals, residents of nonmetropolitan areas, Midwesterners, Republicans, political conservatives, hunters, and gun owners; see Table 1.5).

None of these findings is particularly surprising—save perhaps for the fact that even Republicans express support for the GSS gun control item (as observed later in this chapter, the combination of a Republican president and a Republican Congress effectively eliminates the possibility for the passage of strong national gun control legislation). Hunters and gun

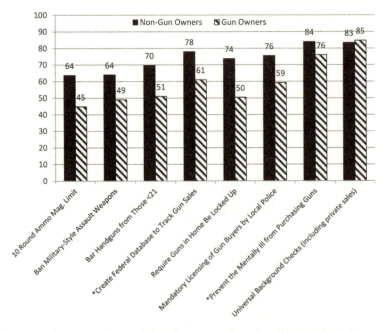

Figure 1.12 Percentage of Gun Owners vs. Non–Gun Owners Favoring Selected Strong Gun Control Measures.

Source: Raw data from Barry et al. (2015) and *Pew Research Center (2015).

Table 1.5   Social and Economic Correlates of Support for Gun Control

(*"Would you favor or oppose a law which would require a person to obtain a police permit before he or she could buy a gun?"*)

Attribute	Percentage in Favor	Attribute	Percentage in Favor
Gender		**Urbanization**	
Male	66.9	Metropolitan Area	75.7
Female	77.6	Nonmetropolitan Area	62.4
Race		**Region**	
White	69.0	Northeast	80.3
Black	82.3	Midwest	69.8
Other	83.4	South	70.2
Hispanic Origin		West	73.3
No	70.7	**Political Affiliation**	
Yes	82.2	Democrat/Leaning Dem.	84.0
Immigrant		Independent	69.8
No	70.0	Republican/Leaning Rep.	59.8
Yes	86.8	**Political Orientation**	
Years of Education		Liberal	79.6
Less than 12 years	71.2	Moderate	75.4
12 years	68.7	Conservative	63.9
13–15 years	72.6	**Hunter in Household**	
16+ years	76.7	No	76.5
Age		Yes	50.8
18–39	73.0	**Gun in the Household**	
40–64	72.3	No	81.1
65+	73.4	Yes	58.9

Note that the variables listed in this table are simple recodes of the following original GSS items: age, born, educ, hispanic, gunlaw, hunt, owngun, partyid, polviews, race, region, sex, and xnorcsiz.

Source: 2014 General Social Survey (*N* = 1,698, which is the total number of valid responses to the gunlaw item; see General Social Survey 2014d; all items have been weighted with the GSS weighting variable wtssnr).

owners are predictably less likely to favor restricting an essential part of their recreational lifestyles (whether hunting in the field or participating in gun club or range shooting) and personal philosophies (the right to use firearms in self-defense). In addition, hunters and gun owners are much more likely than their nonhunting/non–gun-owning counterparts to read gun magazines—such as *The American Rifleman*, *The American Hunter*, *Guns and Ammo*, and *Handguns*—where "gun rights" essays abound and which regularly contain articles arguing against existing or proposed gun control legislation.

Men are more likely to have a machismo attraction to weapons. In the words of psychologist Leonard Berkowitz, "for many, guns signify manliness" (as quoted in Gest, 1982, 38). Men are also much more likely to be hunters and gun owners (Smith and Son, 2015). The latter applies also to small town and rural dwellers. Those living in metropolitan areas, on the other hand, are less likely to be gun owners and hunters (Smith and Son, 2015); moreover, they are more likely to read about gun violence and to experience it personally, as well as to have heightened fears that guns can fall too easily into the wrong hands (e.g., those of gang members). Foreign-born individuals are more likely to have been raised in cultures where the notion of the individual right to bear arms is absent and where firearms are highly regulated and, in turn, are thus less likely to own guns.

While attitudes toward gun control tend to vary somewhat with the previously mentioned social background characteristics, they do *not* vary significantly with age and only modestly with education (with the most educated being slightly more likely than their less educated counterparts to favor gun control). The GSS finds essentially equal support for gun control among all ages and almost equal support among all educational levels. Sociologist Erich Goode (1984, 230) observes that "just about all aspects of our lives—from the newspapers we read to the ways we make love, from the food we eat to our political ideology and behavior—are either correlated or causally connected with socioeconomic statuses." But not here. Goode (1984, 321) also observes that "aging generates attitudes." But again not here. That support for gun control cuts across the lines of both social class (as indicated by level of education) and age bodes well for those wanting to strengthen gun control laws in the United States.

Is the Will of the People Being Thwarted?

Do U.S. adults want strict gun control? On balance, the answer is yes. As public opinion polls have repeatedly shown, most adults believe in limiting the size of ammunition magazines for semiautomatic weapons to a maximum of 10 rounds; banning military-style assault weapons; barring handguns from those under 21 years of age; registering firearms in a federal database; child access protection laws (requiring guns be locked away from children); a local police permit or license required before purchasing a gun; keeping guns out of the hands of felons, those under a domestic violence restraining order (or having even just a misdemeanor conviction for domestic abuse), and the mentally ill; and universal background checks—even when sales are between private individuals. Proponents of gun control see the nation's lack of strict gun control regulations as evidence that the will of the people is being thwarted.

The past few decades offer us many instances of the government being disconnected with popular sentiment. For example, the 1994 U.S. invasion of Haiti was preceded by a national opinion poll showing that only 18 percent of the population would support this action (Dickstein and Farley, 1994, 16). Similarly, the 1995–1996 deployment of U.S. troops in Bosnia-Herzegovina was preceded by a national poll showing only 29 percent of the adult population favoring the deployment (Taylor, 1995). And a third example, which could have been drawn from many others, almost half of U.S. adults sampled by the Gallup poll in the fall of 2004 agreed with the statement, "the Bush administration deliberately misled the American public about whether Iraq ha[d] weapons of mass destruction" (Gallup, 2005a).

What can explain the people's will not being acted upon with regard to gun control? This question is magnified by the preceding analysis of the Second Amendment, which revealed that the amendment should not pose a strong impediment to strict gun control legislation.

The Role of Politics

Ultimately, the informed citizen must make up his or her own mind about the issue of gun control on the basis of his or her fundamental values and view of human nature. For many, this choice will be manifested in their voting—as, politically speaking, certain features of U.S. society ensure that the gun debate will continue to be salient, and often heated, in the decades to come. First, the United States is awash in guns—with more than 350 million rifles, shotguns, and handguns as of 2016 in private hands, with 8 to 9 million new firearms—half of them handguns—being added to the total each year (Bureau of Alcohol, Tobacco, Firearms and Explosives, 2016; see, also, Brauer, 2013, 64; and Ingraham, 2015). Because guns don't wear out, the total number of firearms in the United States actually surpassed the size of its population in 2010 (something that was unthinkable a generation or two ago), and this gap, between the number of guns and the number of people, will only grow larger in the coming years. Easy availability of firearms—through both legal and illegal means—is a fact of life in contemporary U.S. society.

Second, crime rates in the United States have been falling for the past two decades (see, e.g., Figure 1.9a), partly in response to the baby-boom generation growing up (youth and crime are significantly correlated). However, while crime, in general, and gun crime, in particular, have dropped significantly, the same era has seen an escalation in the number of active-shooter, mass-murder incidents (see, e.g., Figure 1.9b). These two forces, an increased incidence of mass shootings and easy firearm availability, will

keep gun violence alive and well—in the poor neighborhoods it has traditionally plagued (see LaFraniere, Porat, and
Armendariz, 2016), as well as in middle-class settings it had
heretofore uncommonly been seen (the rise of mass shootings in churches, civic centers, concert halls, domestic settings, health care facilities, hotels, military properties, office
buildings, movie theaters, schools, and shopping centers; see
Everytown.org, 2015; FBI 2014b).

Such violence will undoubtedly continue to receive heavy
media coverage, which will very likely continue being slanted
toward the pro-control side of the gun debate (those in the
media tend to frame their reporting much more in support of
gun control than in support of gun rights; see, e.g., Wilson,
2006, Chapter 6; and 2015, 137). Sympathetic media coverage will keep the strict gun-control agenda of organizations like
the Brady Campaign to Prevent Gun Violence and Everytown
for Gun Safety in the limelight, and it should therefore be expected that their growing membership rolls and growing donations will continue for years to come. On the other side, the
NRA's—and allied gun rights organizations such as Gun Owners of America's and the National Shooting Sports Foundation's—large historical head start in membership and resources,
advantages that they have maintained year in and year out, will
allow the gun rights' agenda to continue its powerful presence
on Capitol Hill, no matter how much the Brady Campaign
and Everytown expand over the coming decade (e.g., in recent
years, gun rights groups have outspent gun control organizations in Washington, DC, lobbying efforts by a 7-to-1 dollar
ratio; see Gurciullo, 2015). Moreover, despite the media's generally negative depictions of the NRA (Wilson, 2006, Chapter 6;
and 2015, 172), this universally acknowledged powerhouse in
the gun control debate has been growing in popularity; for example, in 2000, 28 percent of U.S. adults characterized the
NRA as having about "the right amount of influence . . . over
gun control laws in this country," while 36 percent said so
in 2015 (Pew Research Center 2015, 4; in both years, about

40 percent said the NRA had "too much influence"); similarly, the Gallup poll reported 42 percent of Americans were "mostly" or "very" favorable toward the NRA in 1993, 52 percent had such opinions by 2000, and 58 percent by 2015(Gallup 2016, 10).

The trump card in this war over gun regulation will be the political makeup of Congress and the presidency. Each side of the debate makes its greatest gains when political opportunity favors it. History has demonstrated that a liberal president and a liberal majority in both Houses favor the gun control side. In contrast, conservative control of either House of Congress or of the presidency produces a standoff, with either minor legislation (some for the gun rights side; some for the gun control side) or no legislation on the control of firearms. Thus, the major gun control legislation of the past half century occurred in 1968 (Gun Control Act of 1968; President Lyndon Johnson), 1993 (Brady Act; President William Clinton), and 1994 (Federal Assault Weapons Ban; President Clinton)—all with liberal, Democratic presidents and with both houses of Congress controlled by the Democrats. In the past 20 years, only one brief two-year period witnessed both a liberal (Democratic) president *and* a liberal congress (with both houses controlled by the Democrats): 2009–2011; but during this period, President Barack Obama used the bulk of his political will and capital to get his national health care system passed (the Patient Protection and Affordable Care Act, or, colloquially, Obamacare). With Republicans controlling either the presidency or at least one House of the Congress, we can expect more of what occurred in September 2004, when the federal assault-weapons ban was allowed to expire (under the presidency of George W. Bush, whose Republican Party controlled both Houses of Congress); this occurred despite a Gallup poll revealing more adults supporting (50%) than opposing (46%) a complete ban on the manufacture, sale, or possession of assault rifles (Gallup, 2005b). Similarly, even though almost 90 percent of the public favored universal background checks at the time, the Manchin-Toomey proposal put before the Senate four months after the December 2012 massacre of 26 children and staff at Sandy Hook Elementary School in Newtown, Connecticut—that would have required universal background checks—failed to pass in the Senate; the proposal failed again in late 2015 after two shooters in San Bernardino, California, killed 14 people and injured 17 more who were attending a holiday party.

The 2016 election results indicate that the longtime federal drought regarding the passage of new and stricter gun control legislation will continue for the near future. President Donald Trump ran on a Republican platform that included strong support for gun rights. Recent history has taught us that until the Democrats control the presidency *and* both houses of Congress, success for those wanting stricter gun control measures will be defined by what they do not lose (e.g., more states approving laws allowing ordinary citizens to carry concealed firearms) rather than by what they gain. That said, given the growing presences of women, of immigrants, and of people of color in the voting booth, the chances of the Democrats taking control of the national government within the next decade are good. If and when this happens, then it would not be surprising to see a series of gun regulations enacted that would put the United States more in line with those of its peer nations in Western Europe. There would be a convergence of forces that has never occurred in U.S. history: a liberal Congress, a liberal president, public opinion favoring gun control, and a powerful and well-organized gun control movement, spearheaded by the Brady Campaign and its ally Everytown for Gun Safety, to counteract the NRA and other gun rights groups who have triumphed mightily in moving forward the gun rights agenda since 1997. The serious control measures that the gun control movement would like to see enacted on a national level are identified and assessed in detail in the next chapter.

References

Alba, Richard D., and Steven F. Messner. 1995. "'Point Blank' against Itself: Evidence and Inference about Guns, Crime, and Gun Control." *Journal of Quantitative Criminology* 11: 391–410.

Altheimer, Irshad. 2010. "An Exploratory Analysis of Guns and Violent Crime in a Cross-National Sample of Cities." *Southwest Journal of Criminal Justice* 6: 204–227.

Ayres, Ian, and John D. Donohue III. 2003. "Shooting Down the More Guns, Less Crime Hypothesis." *Stanford Law Review* 55: 1193–1312.

Azrael, Deborah. 2004. "Cook and Ludwig's *Principles for Effective Gun Policy*: An Extension to Suicide Prevention." *Fordham Law Review* 73: 615–621.

Barry, Colleen L., Emma E. McGinty, Jon S. Vernick, and Daniel W. Webster. 2015. "Two Years after Newtown—Public Opinion on Gun Policy Revisited." *Preventive Medicine* 79: 55–58.

Bartley, William Alan, and Mark A. Cohen. 1998. "The Effect of Concealed Weapons Laws: An Extreme Bound Analysis." *Economic Inquiry* 36: 258–265.

Bastian, Lisa D., and Bruce M. Taylor. 1994. "Young Black Male Victims." *Bureau of Justice Statistics Crime Data Brief, National Crime Victimization Survey, NCJ-147004.* Washington, DC: Bureau of Justice Statistics, U.S. Department of Justice. December.

Black, Dan A., and Daniel S. Nagin. 1998. "Do Right-to-Carry Laws Deter Violent Crime?" *Journal of Legal Studies* 27: 209–219.

Blumstein, Alfred. 1995. "Youth, Violence, Guns, and the Illicit-Drug Industry." *Journal of Criminal Law and Criminology* 86: 10–36.

Brady, Sarah. 2000. *Letter to the HCI Membership.* Washington, DC: Handgun Control Inc. November 7.

Brauer, Jurgen. 2013. *The U.S. Firearms Industry: Production and Supply*. Geneva, Switzerland: Small Arms Survey, Graduate Institute of International and Development Studies. http://www.smallarmssurvey.org/fileadmin/docs/F-Working-papers/SAS-WP14-US-Firearms-Industry.pdf (accessed June 2, 2016).

Bryant, Michael S. 2012. "Holocaust Imagery and Gun Control." In *Guns in American Society: An Encyclopedia of History, Politics, Culture, and the Law*, 2nd edition, Vol. 2, ed. Gregg Lee Carter, 411–415. Santa Barbara, CA: ABC-CLIO.

Bureau of Alcohol, Tobacco, Firearms and Explosives. 2016. *Annual Firearms Manufacturers and Export Report, 2014*. https://www.atf.gov/firearms/docs/afmer-2014-final-report-cover-revised-format-2–17–16/download (accessed May 24, 2016).

Bureau of Justice Statistics. 2010. *National Crime Victimization Survey, 2009*. http://www.bjs.gov/content/pub/pdf/cv09.pdf (accessed March 4, 2016).

Bureau of Justice Statistics. 2014. *National Crime Victimization Survey, 2013 (Revised)*. http://www.bjs.gov/content/pub/pdf/cv13.pdf (accessed March 3, 2016).

Bureau of Justice Statistics. 2016. *Data Collection: National Crime Victimization Survey (NCVS)*. http://www.bjs.gov/index.cfm?ty=dcdetail&iid=245 (accessed March 3, 2016).

Carter, Gregg Lee. 1997. *The Gun Control Movement*. New York: Twayne Publishers.

Carter, Gregg Lee. 2001. "Guns." In *Boyhood in America: An Encyclopedia*, ed. Priscilla Ferguson Clement and Jacqueline S. Reinier, 330–335. Santa Barbara, CA: ABC-CLIO.

Carter, Gregg Lee. 2006. *Gun Control in the United States: A Reference Handbook*. Santa Barbara, CA: ABC-CLIO.

Carter, Gregg Lee. 2016. "Gun Violence in the U.S.—The Empirical Narratives of Gun Control vs. Gun Rights Advocates." Paper presentation, American Studies Summer Institute, John F. Kennedy Presidential Library and

Museum, Boston, July 14. http://web.bryant.edu/~gcarter/ books/GunViolenceintheUS—andtheEmpiricalNarratives ofGunControlvsGunRightsAdvocates.pdf (accessed July 20, 2016).

CDC (Centers for Disease Control and Prevention). 2015. *Suicide: Facts at a Glance.* http://www.cdc.gov/violence prevention/pdf/suicide-datasheet-a.pdf (accessed January 9, 2016).

CDC. 2016a. *Web-based Injury Statistics Query and Reporting System (WISQARS).* Atlanta, GA: National Center for Injury Prevention and Control. http://www.cdc.gov/injury/ wisqars/ (accessed March 2, 2016).

CDC. 2016b. *10 Leading Causes of Death by Age Group, United States—2013.* National Center for Injury Prevention and Control. http://www.cdc.gov/injury/images/lc-charts/ leading_causes_of_death_by_age_group_2013-a.gif (accessed January 9, 2016).

CDC. 2016c. *Firearm Mortality by State*: 2013. http://www .cdc.gov/nchs/pressroom/sosmap/Firearm.htm (accessed January 9, 2016).

CDC. 2016d. *Behavioral Risk Factor Surveillance System* (BRFSS). National Center for Injury Prevention and Control. National Center for Injury Prevention and Control. http://www.cdc .gov/brfss/ (accessed January 13, 2016).

Cheng, Cheng, and Mark Hoekstra. 2013. "Does Strengthening Self-Defense Law Deter Crime or Escalate Violence? Evidence from Expansions to Castle Doctrine." *Journal of Human Resources* 48: 821–854.

Colburn, Treavor. 1965. *The Lamp of Experience: Whig History and the Intellectual Origins of the American Revolution.* Chapel Hill, NC: University of North Carolina Press.

Cook, Philip J., and Jens Ludwig. 1997. *Guns in America: National Survey on Private Ownership and Use of Firearms.* Research in Brief Report No. NCJ165476. Washington,

DC: National Institute of Justice, Office of Justice Programs, U.S. Department of Justice. May.

Cook, Philip J., and Jens Ludwig. 2000. *Gun Violence: The Real Cost.* New York: Oxford University Press.

Cook, Philip J., and Jens Ludwig. 2004. "Principles for Effective Gun Policy." *Fordham Law Review* 73: 589–613.

Cornell, Saul. 2004. "A New Paradigm for the Second Amendment." *Law and History Review* 22 (Spring): 161–167.

Cottrol, Robert J., and Raymond T. Diamond. 1995. "The Second Amendment: Toward an Afro-Americanist Reconsideration." *Guns: Who Should Have Them*, ed. David B. Kopel, 127–157. Amherst, NY: Prometheus.

Cramer, Clayton E. 1994. *For the Defense of Themselves and the State: The Original Intent and Judicial Interpretation of the Right to Keep and Bear Arms.* Westport, CT: Praeger.

DeFilippis, Evan, and Devin Hughes. 2015. "The Myth behind Defensive Gun Ownership: Guns Are More Likely to Do Harm Than Good." *Polico.com*: Jan. 14. http://www.politico.com/magazine/story/2015/01/defensive-gun-ownership-myth-114262_full.html (accessed March 18, 2016).

Dezhbakhas, Hashem, and Paul H. Rubin. 1998. "Lives Saved or Lives Lost? The Effects of Concealed-Handgun Laws on Crime." *American Economic Review Papers and Proceedings* 88: 468–474.

Dickstein, Leslie, and Christopher John Farley. 1994. "Vox Pop." *Time* May 10: 16.

Duggan, Mark. 2001. "More Guns More Crime." *Journal of Political Economy* 99: 1086–1114.

Edel, Wilbur. 1995. *Gun Control: Threat to Liberty or Defense against Anarchy.* Westport, CT: Praeger.

Everytown.org. 2015. *Analysis of Recent Mass Shootings.* http://everytownresearch.org/documents/2015/09/analysis-mass-shootings.pdf (accessed May 25, 2016).

FBI (Federal Bureau of Investigation). 2001. *Uniform Crime Reports: Crime in the United States, 2000.* https://www.fbi.gov/about-us/cjis/ucr/crime-in-the-u.s/2000/00sec2.pdf (accessed March 4, 2016).

FBI. 2014a. *Uniform Crime Reports: Crime in the United States, 2013.* https://www.fbi.gov/about-us/cjis/ucr/crime-in-the-u.s/2013/crime-in-the-u.s.-2013/ (accessed March 3, 2016).

FBI. 2014b. *A Study of Active Shooter Incidents in the United States Between 2000 and 2013.* https://www.fbi.gov/about-us/office-of-partner-engagement/active-shooter-incidents/a-study-of-active-shooter-incidents-in-the-u.s.-2000–2013 (accessed May 28, 2016).

FBI. 2015. *Uniform Crime Reports: Crime in the United States, 2014.* https://www.fbi.gov/about-us/cjis/ucr/crime-in-the-u.s/2014/crime-in-the-u.s.-2014/ (accessed March 7, 2016).

FBI. 2016. *Crime—National or State Level State-by-State and National Crime Estimates by Year(s).* http://www.ucrdatatool.gov/Search/Crime/State/StatebyState.cfm (accessed March 7, 2016).

Fleegler, Eric W., et al. 2013 "Firearm Legislation and Firearm-Related Fatalities in the United States." *JAMA Internal Medicine* 173: 732–740.

Follman, Mark, et al. 2015. "What Does Gun Violence Really Cost?" *Mother Jones*: May/June. http://www.motherjones.com/politics/2015/04/true-cost-of-gun-violence-in-america (accessed May 10, 2016).

Fox, James Alan. 2000. "Demographics and U.S. Homicide." In *The Crime Drop in America,* ed. Alfred Blumstein and Joel Wallman, 288–317. New York: Cambridge University Press.

Franks, Mary Ann. 2016. "Stand Your Ground Laws: Jeopardizing Public Safety in the Name of Public Safety."

Issues: Understanding Controversy and Society. ABC-CLIO. Web (forthcoming).

Gallup. 2005a. "Iraq." February. Princeton, NJ: The Gallup Organization. Available online for Gallup poll subscribers at http://www.gallup.com/poll/ (accessed January 28, 2016).

Gallup. 2005b. "Guns." January. Princeton, NJ: The Gallup Organization. Available online for Gallup poll subscribers at http://www.gallup.com/poll/ (accessed January 28, 2016).

Gallup. 2016. "Guns." Princeton, NJ: The Gallup Organization. http://www.gallup.com/poll/1645/guns.aspx?version=print (accessed January 7, 2016).

General Social Survey. 2014a. "Do You Happen to Have in Your Home (or Garage) Any Guns or Revolvers? If Yes, Is It a Pistol, Shotgun, Rifle, or What?" Chicago: National Opinion Research Center, Cross-Sectional Cumulative Data. http://gss.norc.org/get-the-data/spss (accessed January 6, 2016).

General Social Survey. 2014b. "Do You or Your (Husband/ Wife) Go Hunting?" Chicago: National Opinion Research Center, Cross-Sectional Cumulative Data. http://gss.norc .org/get-the-data/spss (accessed January 6, 2016).

General Social Survey. 2014c. "Do You Happen to Have in Your Home (or Garage) . . . a Pistol . . .?" Chicago: National Opinion Research Center, Cross-Sectional Cumulative Data. http://gss.norc.org/get-the-data/spss (accessed January 6, 2016).

General Social Survey. 2014d. "Would You Favor or Oppose a Law Which Would Require a Person to Obtain a Police Permit Before He or She Could Buy a Gun?" Chicago: National Opinion Research Center, Cross-Sectional Cumulative Data. http://gss.norc.org/get-the-data/spss (accessed May 12, 2016).

Gest, Ted. 1982. "Battle Over Gun Control Heats Up Across the *U.S." U.S. News and World Report* (May 31): 38.

Gius, Mark. 2014. "An Examination of the Effects of Concealed Weapons Laws and Assault Weapons Bans on State-Level Murder Rates." *Applied Economics Letters* 21: 265–267.

Goode, Erich. 1984. *Sociology.* Englewood Cliffs, NJ: Prentice Hall.

Gunpolicy.org. 2016. "Counting Privately Owned Guns." http://www.gunpolicy.org/documents/5360-global-civilian-small-arms-stockpiles (accessed January 5, 2016).

Gurciullo, Brianna. 2015. *Gun Rights vs. Gun Control.* Washington, DC: Center for Responsible Politics. https://www.opensecrets.org/news/issues/guns/ (accessed May 25, 2016).

Halbrook, Stephen P. 1989. *A Right to Bear Arms: State and Federal Bills of Rights and Constitutional Guarantees.* Westport, CT: Greenwood Press.

Hardy, David T. 1986. *Origins and Development of the Second Amendment.* Chino Valley, AZ: Blacksmith Publishers.

Harris Poll. 2016. "73% Favor Some Restrictions on Firearms Sales/Ownership; 16% Favor No Limitations." http://www.theharrispoll.com/politics/Gun-Rights.html (accessed May 14, 2016).

Harvard School of Public Health. 2016. *Firearm Access Is a Risk Factor for Suicide.* https://www.hsph.harvard.edu/means-matter/means-matter/risk/ (accessed June 3, 2016).

Heathcock, Claude L. 1963. *The United States Constitution in Perspective.* Boston: Allyn and Bacon.

Hemenway, David. 2002. "Accidents, Gun." In *Guns in American Society: An Encyclopedia of History, Politics, Culture, and the Law,* Vol. 1, ed. Gregg Lee Carter, 2–3. Santa Barbara, CA: ABC-CLIO.

Hemenway, David. 2004. *Private Guns, Public Health.* Ann Arbor: University of Michigan Press.

Hemenway, David, Deborah Azrael, and Matthew Miller. 2000. "Gun Use in the United States: Results from Two National Surveys." *Injury Prevention* 6: 263–267.

Hemenway, David, and Matthew Miller. 2000. "Firearm Availability and Homicide Rates Across 26 High-Income Countries." *Journal of Trauma* 49: 985–988.

Hemenway, David, and Sara J. Solnick. 2015. "The Epidemiology of Self-Defense Gun Use: Evidence from the National Crime Victimization Surveys 2007–2011." *Preventive Medicine* 79: 22–27.

Henigan, Dennis A., Nicholson, E. Bruce, and David Hemenway. 1995. *Guns and the Constitution: The Myth of Second Amendment Protection for Firearms in America.* Northampton, MA: Aletheia Press.

Ingraham, Christopher. 2015. "There Are Now More Guns Than People in the United States." *Washington Post*, Oct.

Johnson, Gregory R., Etienne G. Krug, and Lloyd B. Potter. 2000. "Suicides among Adolescents and Young Adults: A Cross-National Comparison of Thirty-Four Countries." *Suicide and Life Threatening Behavior* 20: 74–82.

Jones, Jeffrey M. 2008. "Americans in Agreement with Supreme Court on Gun Rights." Princeton, NJ: The Gallup Organization. http://www.gallup.com/poll/108394/americans-agreement-supreme-court-gun-rights.aspx (accessed May 12, 2016).

Kaleson, Bindu, et al. 2016. "Firearm Legislation and Firearm Mortality in the USA: A Cross-Sectional, State-Level Study." *The Lancet*: March 10 (online). http://dx.doi.org/10.1016/S0140-6736(15)01026-0 (accessed March 18, 2016).

Killias, Martin. 1993. "International Correlations between Gun Ownership and Rates of Homicide and Suicide." *Canadian Medical Association Journal* 148: 1721–1725.

Kleck, Gary. 1991. *Point Blank: Guns and Violence in America.* New York: Aldine de Gruyter.

Kleck, Gary. 1997. *Targeting Guns: Firearms and Their Control.* New York: Aldine de Gruyter.

Kleck, Gary, and Marc Gertz. 1995. "Armed Resistance to Crime: The Prevalence and Nature of Self-Defense with a Gun." *Journal of Criminal Law and Criminology* 86: 150–187.

Kopel, David. 2000. "Polls: Antigun Propaganda." Fairfax, VA: NRA Institute for Legislative Action. https://www.nraila.org/articles/20000913/polls-anti-gun-propaganda-by-david-ko (accessed May 28, 2016).

Kopel, David, and Stephen D'Andrilli. 1990. "What America Can Learn from Switzerland Is That the Best Way to Reduce Gun Misuse Is to Promote Responsible Gun Ownership." *American Rifleman* (February). http://www.guncite.com/swissgun-kopel.html (accessed January 7, 2016).

Krug, E. G., Powell, K. E., and L. L. Dahlberg. 1998. "Firearm-Related Deaths in the United States and 35 Other High- and Upper-Middle-Income Countries." *International Journal of Epidemiology* 27: 214–221.

LaFraniere, Sharon, Porat, Daniela, and Agustin Armendariz. 2016. "A Drumbeat of Multiple Shootings, but America Isn't Listening." *New York Times*: May 22. http://www.nytimes.com/2016/05/23/us/americas-overlooked-gun-violence.html (accessed May 25, 2016).

Lambert, Tim. 2004. *Do More Guns Cause Less Crime?* https://web.archive.org/web/20140528141856/http:/www.cse.unsw.edu.au/~lambert/guns/lott/lott.pdf (accessed May 10, 2016).

Law Center to Prevent Gun Violence. 2014. *The Second Amendment Battleground: Victories in Court and Why They Matter.* http://smartgunlaws.org/wp-content/uploads/2012/07/2014-for-web.pdf (accessed May 11, 2016).

Law Center to Prevent Gun Violence. 2015a. *2015 Gun Law State Scorecard.* http://gunlawscorecard.org/ (accessed January 14, 2016).

Law Center to Prevent Gun Violence. 2015b. *Post-*Heller *Litigation Summary.* http://smartgunlaws.org/wp-content/uploads/2014/11/Post-Heller-Litigation-Summary-March-2015-Final-Version.pdf (accessed May 11, 2016).

Lindgren, James, and Franklin E. Zimring. 1983. "Regulation of Guns." In *Encyclopedia of Crime and Justice,* ed. Sanford H. Kadish, 836–841. New York: Free Press.

Lott, John R., Jr. 1998. *More Guns, Less Crime: Understanding Crime and Gun-Control Laws.* Chicago: University of Chicago Press.

Lott, John R., Jr. 2000. *More Guns, Less Crime: Understanding Crime and Gun-Control Law,* 2nd edition. Chicago: University of Chicago Press.

Lott, John R., Jr. 2016. "Response to Tim Lambert." http://www.daviddfriedman.com/Lott_v_Teret/Response_to_Lambert.htm (accessed May 10, 2016).

Lott, John R., Jr., and David B. Mustard. 1997. "Crime, Deterrence, and Right-to-Carry Concealed Handguns." *Journal of Legal Studies* 261: 1–68.

Ludwig, Jens. 1998. "Concealed-Gun-Carrying Laws and Violent Crime: Evidence from State Panel Data." *International Review of Law and Economics* 18: 239–254.

Ludwig, Jens. 2000. "Gun Self-Defense and Deterrence." *Crime and Justice* 27: 363.

Mackellar, Landis F., and Machikio Yanagishita. 1995. *Homicide in the United States: Who's at Risk?* Washington, DC: Population Reference Bureau.

Malcolm, Joyce. 1994. *To Keep and Bear Arms: The Origins of an Anglo-American Right.* Cambridge, MA: Harvard University Press.

McClellan, Chandler, and Erdal Tekin. 2012. "Stand Your Ground Laws and Homicides." Institute for the Study of Labor. Discussion Paper Series 3–39. http://ftp.iza.org/dp6705.pdf (accessed May 9, 2016).

Merrill, Vincent C. 2002. *Gun-in-Home as a Risk Factor in Firearm-Related Mortality: A Historical Prospective Cohort Study of United States Deaths, 1993.* Ph.D. dissertation, Department of Environmental Health Science and Policy, University of California, Irvine.

Miller, Matthew. 2012. "Preventing Suicide by Preventing Lethal Injury: The Need to Act on What We Already Know." *American Journal of Public Health* 102 (Supplement 1): e1–e3.

Miller, Matthew, Deborah Azrael, and David Hemenway. 2001. "Firearm Availability and Unintentional Firearm Deaths." *Accident Analysis and Prevention* 33: 477–484.

Monuteaux, Michael C., et al. 2015. "Firearm Ownership and Violent Crime in the U.S.: An Ecologic Study." *American Journal of Preventive Medicine* 49: 207–214

National Research Council. 2005. *Firearms and Violence: A Critical Review,* Committee to Improve Research Information and Data on Firearms, ed. Charles F. Wellford, John V. Pepper, and Carol V. Petrie. Committee on Law and Justice, Division of Behavioral and Social Sciences and Education. Washington, DC: The National Academies Press.

Parker, Sarah. 2011. *Small Arms Survey 2011, States of Security—Balancing Act: Regulation of Civilian Firearm Possession.* Geneva, Switzerland: Small Arms Survey, Graduate Institute of International and Development Studies. http://www.smallarmssurvey.org/fileadmin/docs/A-Yearbook/2011/en/Small-Arms-Survey-2011-Chapter-09-EN.pdf (accessed June 10, 2016).

Peckman, Howard H., ed. 1978. *Sources of American Independence: Selected Manuscripts from the Collection of the*

William Clements Library, Vol. 1. Chicago: University of Chicago Press.

Pew Research Center. 2015. *Continued Bipartisan Support for Expanded Background Checks on Gun Sales*. http://www.people-press.org/files/2015/08/08-13-15-Guns-release.pdf (accessed May 14, 2016).

Phillips, Sandy. 2014. *Open Letter to the Friends of the Brady Campaign to Prevent Gun Violence: Official 2014 Brady Campaign National Survey on Guns and Gun Violence*. Washington, DC: Brady Campaign to Prevent Gun Violence.

Planty, Michael, and Jennifer L. Truman. 2013. *Firearm Violence, 1993–2011*. Washington, DC: Bureau of Justice Statistics. NCJ-241730. http://www.bjs.gov/content/pub/pdf/fv9311.pdf (accessed July 1, 2016).

PollingReport.com. 2016. *Guns*. http://www.pollingreport.com/guns.htm (accessed May 14, 2016).

Reynolds, Glenn Harlan. 1995. "Critical Guide to the Second Amendment." *Tennessee Law Review* 62: 461–512.

Richardson, Erin G., and David Hemenway. 2011. "Homicide, Suicide, and Unintentional Firearm Fatality: Comparing the United States with Other High-Income Countries, 2003." *Journal of Trauma* 70: 238–243.

Safavi, Arash, et al. 2014. "Children Are Safer in States with Strict Firearm Laws: A National Inpatient Sample Study." *Journal of Trauma and Acute Care Surgery* 76: 146–151.

Shalhope, Robert E. 1982. "The Ideological Origins of the Second Amendment." *Journal of American History* 69: 599–614.

Siegel, Michael, Ross, Craig S., and Charles King III, 2013. "The Relationship between Gun Ownership and Firearm Homicide Rates in the United States, 1981–2010." *American Journal of Public Health* 103: 2098–2105.

Siegel, Michael, et al. 2014. "The Relationship between Gun Ownership and Stranger and Nonstranger Firearm

Homicide Rates in the United States, 1981–2010." *American Journal of Public Health* 104: 1912–1919.

Smith, Tom, and Jaesok Son. 2015. *Trends in Gun Ownership in the United States, 1972–2014*. Chicago: National Opinion Research Center. http://www.norc.org/pdfs/GSS Reports/GSS_Trends in Gun Ownership_US_1972-2014 .pdf (accessed July 20, 2016).

Spitzer, Robert J. 1995. *The Politics of Gun Control*. New York: Chatham House.

Spitzer, Robert J. 2015. *The Politics of Gun Control,*. 6th ed. Boulder, CO: Paradigm Publishers.

Stanford Geospatial Center. 2016. *Mass Shootings in America*. https://library.stanford.edu/projects/mass-shootings-america (accessed March 7, 2016).

Stephens, Gene. 1994. "The Global Crime Wave." *The Futurist* 28: 22–28.

Stockburger, David W. 2013. *Introductory Statistics: Concepts, Models, and Applications*, 3rd ed. http://www.psychstat .missouristate.edu/IntroBook3/sbk.htm (accessed January 13, 2016).

Swift, Art. 2013. "Personal Safety Top Reason Why Americans Own Guns Today." Princeton, NJ: The Gallup Organization. http://www.gallup.com/poll/165605/ personal-safety-top-reason-americans-own-guns-today.aspx (accessed March 18, 2016).

Taichman, Darren B., and Christine Lane. 2015. "Reducing Firearm-Related Harms: Time for Us to Study and Speak Out." *Annals of Internal Medicine* 162: 520–521. https:// assets.documentcloud.org/documents/1699085/annals-of- internal-medicine-reducing-firearm.pdf (accessed May 10, 2016).

Taylor, Humphrey. 1995. "67%–29% Majority Opposes sending U.S. Troops to Bosnia." *The Harris Poll #74*: December 5. http://media.theharrispoll.com/documents/

Harris-Interactive-Poll-Research-67-pct-29-pct-
MAJORITY-OPPOSES-SENDING-US-TROOPS-TO-
BOSNIA-1995–12.pdf (accessed May 10, 2016).

Tennant, David H., et al. 2015. *Task Force on Gun Violence:
Draft Report*. Albany, NY: New York State Bar Association.
https://www.nysba.org/WorkArea/DownloadAsset.aspx?
id=54335 (accessed May 27, 2016).

United Nations. 1999. *United Nations International Study on
Firearm Regulation*. Vienna, Austria: Crime Prevention and
Criminal Justice Division, United Nations Office.

United Nations. 2016. *Global Study on Homicide: UNODC
Homicide Statistics 2013*. http://www.unodc.org/gsh/en/
data.html (accessed January 6, 2016).

UNODC (United Nations Office on Drugs and Crime).
2015. *International Classification of Crime for Statistical
Purposes*. http://www.unodc.org/documents/data-and-
analysis/statistics/crime/ICCS/ICCS_final-2015-March12_
FINAL.pdf (accessed April 2, 2016).

UNODC. 2016. *Statistics on Crime*. http://www.unodc.org/
unodc/en/data-and-analysis/statistics/crime.html (accessed
April 2, 2016).

U.S. Census Bureau. 2016a. *U.S. and World Population Clock*.
http://www.census.gov/popclock/ (accessed January 5,
2016).

U.S. Census Bureau. 2016b. *Quick Facts: United States*. http://
quickfacts.census.gov/qfd/states/00000.html (accessed
January 7, 2016).

Violence Policy Center. 2016. State Firearm Death Rates,
Ranked by Rate, 2014. http://www.vpc.org/fact-sheets/
state-firearm-death-rates-ranked-by-rate-2014/ (accessed
September 27, 2016).

WHO (World Health Organization). 2016. *Suicide Rates
by Country*. http://apps.who.int/gho/data/node.main
.MHSUICIDE?lang=en (accessed January 6, 2016).

Wiebe, Douglas J. 2003a. "Homicide and Suicide Risk Associated with Firearms in the Home: A National Case-Control Study." *Annals of Emergency Medicine* 41: 771–782.

Wiebe, Douglas J. 2003b. "Firearms in U.S. Homes as a Risk Factor for Unintentional Gunshot Fatality." *Accident Analysis and Prevention* 35: 711–716.

Wilson, Harry L. 2006. *Guns, Gun Control, and Elections: The Politics and Policy of Firearms*. Lanham, MD: Rowman & Littlefield.

Wilson, Harry L. 2015. *The Triumph of the Gun-Rights Argument: Why the Gun Control Debate Is Over*. Santa Barbara, CA: Praeger.

Zimring, Franklin E., and Gordon Hawkins. 1997. *Crime Is Not the Problem: Lethal Violence in America*. New York: Oxford University Press.

2 Problems, Controversies, and Solutions

Introduction

In this chapter, the most important measures to regulate guns are described and evaluated. The evaluations are incomplete because the majority of the measures are not in effect at the national level. Most action on gun control—public debate, passage of laws, and court decisions—occurs at the state and local levels, yet serious gun control, control that would be comparable to that in most other economically developed nations, must take place at the national level. As most policymakers and analysts realized long ago, local and state laws regulating access to firearms are easily evaded—for example, guns that might be difficult to buy in one state can be bought in another. Moreover, in 45 states, local governments are preempted by state authority from passing their own gun control laws if they are in conflict with state law. Everyone seriously involved in the gun control debate believes that some level of control over the possession and use of firearms is needed. Even the most ardent

---

Trevor Leis, exercising his open carry rights, stands armed in Public Square in Cleveland, Ohio, during the second day of the Republican convention on July 19, 2016. After a 25-year, highly successful struggle to legalize the right to carry a concealed weapon by ordinary citizens in every state, the gun rights movement turned its attention to the related right of gun owners to carry openly their firearms, even in urban areas where it had once been considered unthinkable. Some form of open carry is now allowed in 45 U.S. states. (AP Photo/John Minchillo)

proponent of "gun rights" agrees that violent felons should be barred access to firearms. At the other end of the spectrum, ardent proponents of "strict" gun control would like to see the total number of guns in circulation reduced; minors, felons, drug and alcohol abusers, the mentally incapacitated, and the perpetrators of domestic violence denied access to firearms; handgun possession and carrying severely restricted; a coherent national gun policy requiring all gun owners and users to be licensed and trained and all guns and ammunition to be registered; background checks for potential gun buyers to occur no matter where the sale occurs (a retail establishment, a flea market, a living room)—and no matter who the buyers or sellers are (licensed gun dealers or private individuals selling or trading their personal firearms); a coherent set of child access protection (CAP) laws requiring all gun owners to lock up their guns and ammunition—in separate places, whether at home or while in transport; a demand placed on gun manufacturers and distributors to monitor the retailers who sell their guns (ensuring that they are accountable for all guns sold and that guns sold are done so legally; relatedly, a return to the ability of municipalities and other groups to sue gun manufacturers if this monitoring is found to be deficit); a ban on military-style assault weapons, as well as on semi-automatic firearm ammunition magazines holding more than 10 rounds; a ban on extra-large-caliber firearms—most notably the .50 caliber handguns introduced to the market in the early 2000s; a restriction on concealed weapon permits to what they were in most states prior to 1987, that is, offering such permits only to law enforcement offices and to selected individuals with an obvious need (e.g., private security guards transporting large amounts of cash); a restriction on the number of guns that can be bought at any one time—to one or fewer per month; increased funding and reduced restrictions on the federal Centers for Disease Control and Prevention (CDC) to research gun violence and to create detailed databases on incidents of gun violence, and, relatedly, to allow the Bureau of Alcohol, Tobacco, Firearms and Explosives (ATF) to share more freely crime gun tracing data with public health researchers and criminologist; and, finally, the retooling of older guns and the redesigning of new guns with the latest in "smart-gun" technologies (e.g., a "gun-is-loaded" indicator light, trigger locks, guns only capable of firing in the owner's hands). Each of the measures proposed by those wanting stricter gun control would in itself likely reduce gun violence by only a small amount, but as the evidence in this chapter will demonstrate, the sum total of enacting many or all such measures would likely be significant and discernible.

It is important to note that there are many acts of gun violence for which no set of gun control laws would be preventative. There are so many guns in circulation in the United States today (over 350 million) that anyone with determination and a modicum of creativity can acquire one. And in a free society, anyone with determination and a modicum of creativity can shoot just about anyone they want. But that is no reason to conclude that gun control doesn't work. Rather, the evidence needed to show whether it works is at the aggregate level of analysis—do rates of gun-related injuries, deaths, and crimes fall or (as a few would hypothesize) rise in response to serious gun control? Demonstrating this correlation, between gun control and gun-related violence, is an extraordinarily difficult undertaking. To date, it has been only partially accomplished, but what part has been accomplished reveals that gun control can work in a manner that preserves the basic right of individuals to own selected kinds of firearms and use them in selected ways—including recreational target shooting, hunting, and defense of home and self.

The Public Health Approach

The most comprehensive and empirically grounded approach to gun control is that of *public health*. As detailed by Azrael et al. (2003), Gostin and Record (2011), Hemenway (2004,

Chapter 2; 2012), and Hemenway and Miller (2013), the public health approach sets aside the bifurcation of the social world that predominates in the modern gun control debate: instead of concentrating on *individuals* and looking at the world as divided into criminals and noncriminals, those who are mentally unstable and those who are not, those who mishandle firearms and those who do not, the public health approach looks at the *social and physical environments* and how these encourage or discourage gun-related harm. The ultimate goal is to change these environments in such ways as to reduce harm. The approach is proactive, not reactive. It has a long history of success, including the great reduction of communicable disease in the 19th and early 20th centuries, the noteworthy reduction of automobile-related injuries and deaths in the middle of the 20th century, and the significant decline in tobacco use and subsequent decline in tobacco-related diseases in the last third of the 20th century. In each case, the use of the public health approach began with the marshaling of huge amounts of data on the health problem at hand; these data pointed to the aspects of the physical and social environment that needed to be changed to solve the problem; the data also provided the evidence needed by the advocates for change as they argued for reform in the political and legal systems. In each case, focusing on environmental causes and large-scale, community-based, "public" solutions proved more effective than trying to change individuals. Not that the behavior of individuals is trivial or incapable of being transformed, but it has been found that this transformation is more readily accomplished after the environmental sources of the problem have been addressed.

Hemenway (2004, 9–10) offers the following description of how the public health approach has dramatically reduced the incidence of communicable disease and subsequently increased the overall health of humanity:

[T]he most important public health advance of the nineteenth century was the "great sanitary awakening," . . . which identified filth as both a cause of disease and a vehicle of transmission. Sanitation changed the way society thought about health. Illness came to be seen as an indicator not of poor moral or spiritual conditions but of poor environmental conditions. . . . [M]ost of the improvement in health of the American people (e.g., a rise in life expectancy from forty-seven years in 1900 to seventy-six years in 1990) has been accomplished through public health measures rather than direct medical advances.

National Violent Death Reporting Systems

As public health researcher Deborah Azrael and her colleagues observe, the critical building block of the public health approach to reducing injury and death is comprehensive, overtime data:

> The National Highway Traffic Safety Administration's Fatality Analysis Reporting System (FARS), which became operational in 1975, is the largest and most comprehensive national surveillance system for *injuries* in the United States. The system, which collects information on approximately 37,000 crashes and 40,000 fatalities annually, . . . [documents] more than one hundred variables . . . on each incident, including information on vehicles (for example, make model, safety features, inspection status), crash features (for example, points of impact, speed), environment (for example, type of roadway, weather conditions, visibility, time of day), [and] people (for example, seating, impairment, alcohol use, license status, previous infractions). . . . [FARS] research findings were instrumental in federal legislation that influenced states to establish 21 as the minimum age for [alcohol] purchase. This policy is in effect in all states and is credited with having saved more than 20,000 lives from 1975 through 2000. (Azrael et al., 2003, 416–417)

Indeed, Hemenway (2012) argues that the improvement in motor vehicle safety in the United States over the past 60 years provides an excellent model for reducing gun violence. Between

1952 and 1999, the death rate per motor vehicle mile dropped 80 percent, and by 2009, fewer people were dying on the roads than any year since 1950. This huge change in fatalities unfolded not because drivers got any better, but, rather, because comprehensive data collection and analysis revealed the many flaws in the design of cars (e.g., inflexible steering columns, unyielding dashboards, weak passenger compartments) and roadways (lack of shoulders, lack of guardrails) that were eventually corrected. He concludes "that in the firearm field the United States is currently where it was in motor vehicle safety in the 1950s" (592).

From the public health perspective, the potential for effective improvements in gun control policies has just begun to unfold in the United States: such policies should emerge from solid bases of evidence; but because we have lacked the comprehensive data to evaluate present and proposed gun control measures, as well as to develop new kinds of measures that might grow out of such data, thus far little can be concluded about the effectiveness of even the most basic of regulations—such as background checks and limitations on the size of ammunition magazines (e.g., a limit of 10 rounds). Thus, the first step in generating public support for serious gun control is the development of a national, ongoing, comprehensive data-collection surveillance system to monitor violence-related deaths and injuries. Such a system would be modeled on the National Highway Safety Administration's Fatality Analysis Reporting System (FARS).

As of 2016, this exact effort is well under way—and has an ultimate goal of equaling, or even surpassing, the comprehensiveness of FARS. The first steps began in 1999, when the Harvard Injury Control Research Center set up a violent reporting system in collaboration with the Medical College of Wisconsin and 10 other medical organizations (university medical centers and health departments) around the country. Labeled the National Violent Injury Statistics System (NVISS), it developed uniform standards for the collection and organization of data related to violent deaths. These standards were based on FARS, and they had the ultimate goal of doing what FARS had done for highway fatalities—that is, to reduce deaths by using multivariable analysis to ascertain the complex mix of causes that underlie incidents of firearms violence (though originally intended for firearm-related deaths, the system eventually expanded to include all types of violent deaths). Table 2.1 gives a sense of the comprehensiveness of the variables collected for each violent death incident in the NVISS system.

During its brief history, the NVISS data collection system was able to uncover some new findings regarding violent deaths. For example, NVISS data revealed that women are two and a half times more likely than men to commit suicide at home, and that suicides are twice as likely as homicides to occur at home (Hemenway, 2005).

The success of the NVISS led the federal CDC to develop a more comprehensive surveillance system in 2003 to monitor violence-related deaths and injuries, the National Violent Death Reporting System (NVDRS; see CDC 2016a, 2016b). The system collects data in the same systematic manner developed by NVISS (see Table 2.1), and makes the information publicly available through the CDC's user-friendly statistical analysis systems (see, e.g., CDC 2016c). It has grown from a pilot of program of 6 states in 2002, to 17 states by 2006, to 32 states by late 2016 (and by 2017, the number is expected to rise to 39, plus the District of Columbia; Alabama, Alaska, Arizona, California, Colorado, Connecticut, Georgia, Hawaii, Illinois, Indiana, Iowa, Kansas, Kentucky, Louisiana, Maine, Maryland, Massachusetts, Michigan, Minnesota, Nevada, New Hampshire, New Jersey, New Mexico, New York, North Carolina, Ohio, Oklahoma, Oregon, Pennsylvania, Rhode Island, South Carolina, Tennessee, Texas, Utah, Vermont, Virginia, Washington, West Virginia, and Wisconsin). The CDC's "goal is to include eventually all 50 states, all U.S. territories, and the District of Columbia in the system" (CDC, 2016d; see also, National Violence Prevention Network, 2016).

Although public health researchers readily admit that "the NVDRS is not currently a national system," which "limits its value [because] . . . the states included in the system . . . are not a representative or random sample of all fifty states" (Hemenway, Barber, and Miller, 2010, 1187), analyses of NVDRS data have yielded a number of new findings regarding the nature of gun violence that are likely to be confirmed when the NVDRS attains its full and desired comprehensiveness. Examples are: (1) 80 percent of homicide-suicides occur at home, where, for example, the December 2012 Sandy Hook Elementary School massacre actually began when Adam Lanza shot and killed his mother in her bed; almost all involve a gun, most often a handgun; key situation stressors immediately before the violence include mental illness, drug or alcohol abuse, and job-related, legal, financial, or serious physical health problems (Bossarte, Simon, and Barker, 2006); (2) among veterans under the age of 30, suicide rates decline significantly for those using Veterans Health Administration services and increase significantly for those not using these services—with nuanced analysis revealing that the differences between these two groups is due to the care received and not to a self-selection bias (that is, those less likely commit suicide seek out care; see Katz et al. 2012); (3) compared to NVDRS data, state-level vital statistics data undercount unintentional firearm deaths among youth, especially when the victim is shot by someone else (the case most often is by a brother or male friend; see Barber and Hemenway, 2011); and (4) before the NVDRS, there was no clear understanding of whether unintentional (accidental) shooting victims received their wounds from self-infliction or from others; however, using NVDRS data, Hemenway and colleagues (2010) found that about half were inflicted by others, and that the other-infliction rate increases sharply as the age of the victim, as well as of the perpetrator, drops further and further below 25. In each case, the study authors used the NVDRS analyses to make concrete recommendations for reducing the risks of the violence involved; respectively, (1) the victims of intimate partner violence need shelter and should be counseled on those stressors in their partners' lives that increase the risk of murder/suicide; (2) veterans, especially veterans recently on the frontlines of war (e.g., in Afghanistan or Iraq) should be directed early on to VA health care services; (3) NVDRS data should be used instead of state vital statistics data in assessing the severity of accidental youth shootings in any particular geographic area and in developing causal models to explain the differing levels of severity; and (4) given "that the danger to children and adolescents is largely from being shot by others—typically friends or siblings," the policy implications include "to improve gun storage, and to make it normative for parents to ask about the availability of guns in the homes visited by their children" (Hemenway et al., 2010, 1187; see next section).

Table 2.1 Selected Variables Collected by the Harvard Injury Control Research Center and Its Collaborators (Violent Death Statistics System)

Incident Information

Incident narrative

Investigating police agency

Death investigation source

Number of nonfatal victims

Person (victim and suspect) Information

Person ID

Person type

Age

Sex

Race

Ethnicity

Incident at person's residence?

Intoxication suspected?

Suspect Characteristics

Attempted suicide?

(Continued)

Table 2.1   (*Continued*)

Victim Information

Weapon type

Incident type

Medical examiner/coroner cause of death

Death certificate underlying cause of death

Victim-suspect relationship

Abuse

Date and time of injury

Date and time of death

Address of incident

Victim Circumstances

Violence circumstances

Accident/unintentional death circumstances

Suicide—mental health

Suicide intent

Suicide circumstances

Supplemental Homicide Report Variable

SHR homicide type and situation

SHR victim-offender relationship

SHR circumstance

SHR justifiable shooting circumstance

Victim Demographics

Residential address

Homeless status

Marital status

Veteran status

Birthplace

Pregnancy

Education

Employment status

Usual occupation

Usual industry

Victim Injury Information

Place of death

Number of wounds and location

Death certificate multiple condition codes

Autopsy performed

Alcohol presence

Blood alcohol level

Drug presence

Date and time body specimen collected

Firearm Information

Firearm ID

Type of firearm physical evidence

Firearm type

Firearm make

Firearm model

Firearm caliber/gauge

Firearm victim table

Stolen

Youth access to firearms

Source: Adapted from Azrael et al. (2003, 21); note that the NVDRS, which replaced the Harvard-based system, collects these variables, plus many more closely related ones (see CDC, 2015).

Controlling Guns in the Home: Child Access Protection Laws

The most sophisticated studies to date on whether a gun in the home is related to gun violence reveal a clear association between a gun in the home and an increased probability of accidental death, homicide, and suicide (e.g., see the literature review of Miller, Azrael, and Hemenway, 2013, 9–15, though contrast Merrill's [2002] finding regarding no increased risk of homicide). Along with protecting battered women, who are particularly vulnerable to dying in their homes if a firearm is present (Campbell et al., 2003), the public health approach is especially concerned with injuries and deaths associated with children obtaining guns in their own homes—most often guns that belong to their parents. These tragedies involve (1) youth suicide—with the most lethal means being by firearm and with several studies finding youths who have attempted or have actually committed suicide with a firearm having obtained the weapon in their own home (or the home of a relative; see, e.g., Grossman, Reay, and Baker, 1999; Miller and Hemenway, 1999); (2) youth mass shootings, with two-thirds of the cases of teenage boys committing such a shooting in a school setting obtaining their weapons at home (or, again, from the home of a relative; see Vossekuil et al., 2004, 27); and (3) accidental shootings. Regarding the last of these, in the 1980s, Garen J. Wintemute and his colleagues found that half of the incidents in which a child accidentally shot himself or herself or a play-mate involved loaded, unlocked firearms in the child's home (Wintemute, Teret, and Kraus, 1987). This study, as well as later related research confirming the Wintemute findings, eventually led to the passage of CAP laws in 27 states. CAP laws make parents and homeowners ultimately responsible for any firearm injury, including accidental shootings and suicides, occurring with guns stored on their property. The laws imply that guns should have trigger-lock devices or be secured in a cabinet or safe (and, ideally, that ammunition be locked in a separate place; this said, only 11 states formally require locking devices; for a summary of state CAP laws, which are generally complex regarding [a] storage measures, [b] what constitutes a violation, and [c] the nature and severity of penalties, see Law Center to Prevent Gun Violence, 2013a, 2015). The first CAP law was passed in Florida in 1989; the District of Columbia and 26 other states passed similar laws during the 1990s and early 2000s (California Colorado, Connecticut, Delaware, Georgia, Hawaii, Illinois, Indiana, Iowa, Kentucky, Maryland, Massachusetts, Minnesota, Mississippi, Missouri, Nevada, New Hampshire, New Jersey, North Carolina, Oklahoma, Rhode Island, Tennessee, Texas, Utah, Virginia, and Wisconsin).

Several studies have shown CAP laws to be moderately effective. For example, Peter Cummings and his colleagues found that there was a 41 percent reduction in accidental youth deaths in states with CAP laws (Cummings et al., 1997), while Daniel W. Webster and his colleagues found that CAP laws have significantly reduced adolescent suicide rates (preventing more than 300 suicides in youths 14–17 years old between 1989 and 2001; see Webster et al., 2004). Similarly, David C. Grossman and his colleagues found that youths under the age of 20 were significantly less likely to unintentionally shoot another person or to commit suicide with a gun in households where guns were locked up (Grossman et al., 2005). This particular study examined four CAP practices and found each one to have a "protective effect": keeping (1) guns locked, (2) guns unloaded, (3) ammunition locked, and (4) ammunition stored in a separate location. Such research led a major national police group, the Commission on Accreditation for Law Enforcement Agencies (CALEA), to adopt a relatively new guideline that off-duty police officers should store their weapons in locked boxes (CALEA Standard 1.3.9; for an example of how this standard is met at the local law enforcement level, see Providence Police Department [2015, 15]).

The fear of gun rights advocates is that CAP laws will reduce the ability of individuals to protect their homes from invasion by thieves and rapists. Indeed, Lott and Whitley (2002) found the introduction of CAP laws were associated with state-level increases in police-reported rapes (9%), robberies (8–10%), and burglaries (4–6%). However, Webster and Carroll (2012) argue that these are specious findings and are a result of the inadequacies of Lott and Whitley's statistical models (much the same way in that Ayres and Donohue [2003] refuted Lott's thesis that "more guns" leads to "less crime"; see Chapter 1).

Currently there is no national CAP law, which puts the United States out of step with its peer nations. By the 1990s, almost all of the economically developed democracies of Western Europe, plus Australia, Canada, Japan, and New Zealand, had national requirements for gun owners to store securely their firearms and ammunition (United Nations, 1999; also see Parker, 2011; note that U.S. law requires that licensed gun dealers selling a *handgun* must provide a secure lockbox unless the weapon has been equipped with a trigger lock or related device; however, because the law does not cover private sales, gun control activists consider it inadequate; see Law Center to Prevent Gun Violence, 2015). As noted in Chapter 1, these peer nations suffer a tiny fraction of the per capita gun violence experienced in the United States. And as indicated in the research reviewed immediately before, these two phenomena are likely connected. Indeed, in a review of 130 studies covering 10 countries on the effects of gun control laws on firearm deaths, public health researcher Julian Santaella-Tenorio and his colleagues found that "laws restricting the . . . access to (e.g., safer storage) firearms are . . . associated with lower rates of intimate partner homicides and firearm unintentional deaths in children, respectively" (Santaella-Tenorio et al., 2016, 140).

Trigger Locks, Internal Locks, and Personalized "Smart Gun" Technologies

Related to CAP laws are a set of gun control measures intended to reduce the unauthorized use of guns—for example, by children, thieves, or those not possessing a gun but wanting to use someone else's gun to commit a crime or suicide—by changing gun-firing technology. The simplest of these measures is encouraging the use of mechanical trigger locks, such as a combination or key lock that fits over the trigger area (the so called clamshell lock) or a cable lock that can be strung through the barrel or trigger guard. Since 1999, the U.S. Department of Justice, in conjunction with the National Shooting Sports Foundation, has funded the distribution of millions of cable and related trigger locks through its Project ChildSafe program (see Project ChildSafe 2016a, 2016b; note that over 37 million locks were given out free between 2003 and 2015, usually via a local law enforcement agency—with another 70 million free gun locks distributed by manufacturers between 1998 and 2015). The program credits itself as playing a key role in the reduction of fatal firearms accidents that has occurred in recent years (e.g., a 33 percent drop between 2002 and 2013; compare the total number of unintentional deaths in Table 1.3 in Chapter 1 [505 in the year 2013] with the total number reported in Carter [2006, 13; 762 deaths in 2002]).

At a more sophisticated level are internal locking systems involving an internal block preventing the firing pin from engaging. The most common version of this lock requires the use of a magnetic ring by the shooter; the ring unlocks a trigger bar so that the gun can be fired (see Smart Lock Technology, 2016; Tarnhelm Supply Company, 2016); DeBell (2012) reports that magnetic ring technologies are not in wide use because they are limited to a few selected firearms (e.g., the Colt 1911A1 pistol; the Ruger Security Six revolver), are not particularly convenient to use (requiring the user wear a ring to shoot), and suffer from the fear of potential buyers that their guns will not be reliable in a moment of crisis.

Other even more sophisticated versions requiring a radio frequency device on the user's clothing or person or a microchip that biologically identifies the gun's owner or authorized user have been in the research and development phase since the mid-1990s; however, despite significant government and private manufacturer funding, none have reached the marketplace in any significant way. The electronic technologies have thus far not been able to overcome the absolute and foremost obligation expected of all firearms—that the firearm discharge reliably without malfunction or error (see U.S. Department of Justice, 2016a, 5). One electronic technology that is actually promising for adoption in the near future involves the recovery of lost or stolen firearms, especially those that belong to law enforcement officers. "The technology is relatively straightforward"—a computer chip is embedded in a firearm "that transmits information about its location and use." Unlike electronic technologies intended to restrict the use of a particular firearm to a particular individual, "this type of real-time data collection does not affect the mechanical operation of the firearm" (U.S. Department of Justice, 2016a, 10).

Two simple technologies that gun control advocates would like to see mandatory on the manufacturing of all new semiautomatic handguns are a *loaded-chamber* indicator light or mechanism (usually a protruding metal tab), which alerts the user that the gun has a cartridge in its chamber, and a *magazine safety* (or "disconnect mechanism")—which prevents a gun from firing when its magazine has been removed even if a round is still in the chamber (many gun handlers seeing the ammunition magazine disconnected from a semiautomatic pistol erroneously assume that the gun is unloaded, ignoring the possibility of there still being a round in the chamber). A federal study of accidental firearm deaths in 10 cities revealed that nearly a quarter of them could have been prevented had the guns involved been equipped with either loaded-chamber indicators or magazine safeties (see U.S. General Accounting Office, 1991). A follow-up study on all accidental shootings in Maryland and Wisconsin between 1991 and 1998 revealed nearly identical findings: that 20 percent might have been avoided with a loaded-chamber indicator and another 4 percent with a magazine safety (Vernick et al., 2003). Despite such findings, both of these devices are not part of the basic manufacturing process for the majority of semiautomatic handguns, with estimates ranging from 10 percent to 20 percent coming equipped with one or both devices (Maddan, 2012; Vernick et al. 1999). Speaking on behalf of chamber-loaded indicators, public health researcher David Hemenway (2004, 33) laments that it is difficult to understand why a person with a firearm often cannot readily tell if it is loaded. It is important to note that current loaded-chamber indicators are not standardized in such a way that it would be common knowledge when they were activated—that is, they presently come in a variety of designs and shapes, and thus gun control advocates would like legislation that would require the gun-manufacturing industry to develop a uniform style.

Since 2007, California has required new semiautomatic handguns to have both a loaded-chamber indicator and a magazine safety—the only state to require both devices. Massachusetts, however, requires that such handguns have either one or the other device (Law Center to Prevent Gun Violence, 2013b). In a similar vein, in 2002, New Jersey passed a law requiring that all handguns sold in the state be "smart guns" within three years after a proven product is on the market; because no such gun has appeared, the law has had no effect— but it does lay down a fundamental principle about gun safety that may be put to use in the future. As of 2016, a total of seven states and the District of Columbia had high standards for handgun design to prevent accidental firings—including requiring at least one of the following: a loaded-chamber indicator, a magazine safety, being able to pass a strong threshold for not firing accidentally if dropped, or being on an approved roster of "safe guns" (such guns having passed drop tests, having strong safeties, and having high melting temperatures as an indicator of the quality of their construction): the states are California, Hawaii, Illinois, Maryland, Massachusetts, Minnesota, and New York (Law Center to Prevent Gun Violence, 2013b; for an example of an approved roster of "safe guns," see California Bureau of Firearms, 2016).

Gun rights advocates are generally opposed to personalized gun technologies. They contend that such technologies might lead to more gun violence for two key reasons: first, many gun owners will become complacent if they have a "smart gun" and leave it around unlocked and loaded; when the smart-gun technology fails, as do all mechanical and electronic devices, an accident will be waiting to happen. Second, a gun owner under attack, whether at home or on the street, will have a delayed reaction if he or she has to put on a magnetic ring, or might find another type of smart-gun technology failing just when it is needed most. In addition, some gun rights advocates are against magazine safeties, as they can lead someone handling a gun so equipped to think a gun is always safe because of a disconnected magazine instead of "actually checking the gun, opening the action, and making sure it is unloaded" (SAAMI, 2002, 4), and they oppose "safe gun rosters" because the firearms listed on them tend to be expensive and thus deny the poor access to inexpensive handguns—which the advocates contend deny them the ability to defend themselves (Southwick, 2012a, 730; also, see next section, "Cheap Handgun Control").

Cheap Handgun Control

Among its many provisions, the federal Gun Control Act of 1968 (GCA) sought to reduce the nation's stock of cheap handguns by banning the importation of these so-called Saturday night specials. The argument for trying to reduce this stock builds from three social facts: first, cheap handguns are most often bought by the poor and by the young, and there are strong correlations between poverty and violence and between youth and violence in the United States; second, to be priced so cheaply, these guns are often of poor quality and thus prone to malfunction; finally, these guns are often small and thus easily concealable. Unfortunately, from the perspective of those who favor stricter gun control, the banning of the importation of cheap handguns simply created a windfall for domestic manufacturers. Beginning in the 1970s, many of these manufacturers developed in southern California in an area that public health researcher Garen Wintemute (1994) once dubbed the "Ring of Fire." They included companies like Accu-Tek, Arcadia Machine & Tool (no longer in business), Bryco Arms (now Jimenez Arms of Henderson, Nevada), Davis Engineering (now Cobra Enterprises of Salt Lake City, Utah), Lorcin Industries (no longer in business), Phoenix Arms, and Sundance Industries (no longer in business). These manufacturers mainly produced—and those still in business continue to produce—small and medium-caliber handguns (e.g., .22s, .25s, and .380s) with retail prices hundreds of dollars cheaper than even the used versions of the better quality handguns manufactured by high-end companies like Smith & Wesson, Sturm Ruger, Glock, or Beretta (see Southwick, 2012a, 730). The production of these cheap handguns has been strongly correlated with street crime and the handgun murder rate, as so many of them end up in the hands of poor, inner-city youth (Law Center to Prevent Gun Violence, 2013b; Wintemute, 2002). It is important to note that four of the top 10 producers of semiautomatic pistols during the 1990s were Ring of Fire manufacturers (see Wintemute, 2002, 57); seven of the top 10 guns used by juveniles (aged 17 and under) in the commission of crime in 2000 were Ring of Fire semiautomatic pistols (with the Lorcin Engineering .380 at the top of the list), as were five of the top 10 crime guns used by those between the ages of 18 and 24, and three of the top 10 for those 25 and older. For all ages combined, Ring of Fire semiautomatics accounted for five of the top 10 guns used in crime (and for which successful trace requests were made; see Bureau of Alcohol, Tobacco, Firearms and Explosives, 2002, Table 5, 15–17).

Gun control proponents see two basic solutions to the cheap handgun problem: first, get their production outlawed; second, stop their trafficking into the hands of youths and criminals. The first strategy has been experimented with at the state level. For example, Maryland has had a law banning the manufacture and sale of cheap handguns since 1989; and at least one analysis revealed that the law has had an effect in reducing the number and use of these weapons (see Webster, Vernick, and Hepburn, 2002). The District of Columbia and six other states (California, Hawaii, Illinois, Massachusetts, Minnesota, and New York) currently have laws to discourage the purchase of cheap handguns (including, e.g., being able to pass a melting test of 800°F to 1,000°F.—as is the case in Hawaii, Illinois, Massachusetts, Minnesota, and New York). California's strengthening its laws in the early 2000s to discourage cheap handgun manufacturing and sales forced several Ring of Fire manufacturers out of business, while others opted to leave the state (fleeing to nearby Arizona, Nevada, and Utah). It is important to note that compared with its peer nations (other economically developed democracies), the United States stands out regarding its lax restrictions on the owning of handguns, as well as with regard to the percentage of households that have a handgun. Almost all of the peer nations of the United States put severe restrictions on handgun ownership (e.g., limiting them to the police, selected private security guards, and selected veterans of the military; see United Nations, 1999, Table 1.1). Indeed, as noted in Chapter 1, handguns are either outlawed or restricted so severely that ownership is extremely rare in most European countries, as well as in peer nations Australia, Canada, Japan, and New Zealand.

The second strategy focuses on reducing the trafficking of these guns from federally licensed firearms dealers into the wrong hands. Illegal gun buyers—including street gangs and drug cartels—are especially attracted to FFLs (federal firearms licensees—mainly gun retailers and pawnbrokers) because these dealers have access to so many firearms and to such a wide variety of them. This trafficking most commonly occurs via *straw* purchases. These are sometimes done on a small scale, such as when a noncriminal acquaintance of a criminal buys a gun for the criminal or when an older acquaintance buys a gun for a juvenile; but they also occur on much larger scales involving straw-purchasing rings. In the latter case, one or more street-level unlicensed dealers buy multiple guns from a licensed dealer and then sell them in the private market (e.g., person-to-person on the street, at flea markets or gun shows, on the Internet). Because of their low cost, Saturday night specials are among those types of guns with high attraction to straw-purchasing rings. Most juveniles and criminals get their guns through theft, back-street swaps (e.g., for drugs), unregulated private sales (e.g., at gun shows or on the Internet), or from the trafficking of guns from federally licensed dealers to the street through unscrupulous acquaintances or middlemen or corrupt dealers (Wintemute, 2002; also see Mayors against Illegal Guns, 2013; Pierce et al., 2004; Wright and Rayburn, 2012).

Tracing Crime Guns to Reduce Illegal FFL Trafficking

Glenn L. Pierce and his colleagues Anthony A. Braga, Raymond Hyatt Jr. and Christopher S. Koper were four of a small number of researchers who were once given access to the ATF gun-tracing data (Pierce et al., 2004). Their analyses revealed several facts about trafficking that could be used to reduce the supply of guns to the illegal market. The GCA allows for the gathering of data that trace any given firearm from its manufacturing or importation through its first retail sale. Manufacturers, importers, distributors, and FFLs must maintain records of all gun transactions, for example, sales and shipments. FFLs are also required to report multiple handgun sales and stolen weapons to the ATF. A particular trace begins when a law enforcement agency submits a request to the ATF's National Tracing Center to find all existing information on a firearm suspected of being used in the commission of a crime. Tracing is possible because every firearm is stamped with a unique serial number. Pierce and his colleagues found that three-quarters of all trace requests in 1999 involved handguns, especially semiautomatic pistols. Importantly, only one in 10 traced guns was possessed by the purchaser—strong evidence of illegal gun trafficking. Of similar importance, and a similarly strong indicator of trafficking, they found that nearly a third of all traced crime guns were sold less than four years prior to their recovery after a crime. That there are corrupt dealers involved in the trafficking was evidenced by the fact that only about 1 percent of the active FFLs at the time of the study were associated with more than half (55%) of the successfully traced crime guns. Kessler and Hill's (2004) analyses of ATF crime gun traces for the 1996–2000 period yielded similar findings to those of Pierce et al.'s. When such findings were first released, gun control activists assumed that the federal government would increase its inspections of FFLs, especially those linked to a high number of crime gun traces. However, since 2003, yearly congressional amendments to the Department of Justice's annual appropriations bill have significantly restricted law enforcement's ability to investigate gun crimes and to prosecute unscrupulous gun dealers. The amendments prohibit the ATF from releasing firearm trace data for use by cities, states, researchers, litigants, and members of the public (a few important exceptions were made after 2007; see Mayors against Illegal Guns, 2010, 36, note 4); they require that the Federal Bureau of Investigation (FBI) destroy all approved gun purchaser records within 24 hours; and they bar the ATF from mandating gun dealers to submit their inventories to law enforcement. In addition to firearm trace data, the amendments "prohibit the disclosure of data on multiple handgun sales reports as well as gun sales information a dealer is required to keep that may be required to be reported to the U.S. Attorney General for determining the disposition of one or more firearms in the course of a bona fide criminal investigation" (Law Center to Prevent Gun Violence, 2012). The amendments appeased the worries of gun rights activists that too much oversight from the ATF "could lead to a federal gun registry, which in turn could give the government a tool to confiscate firearms" (Mascia, 2015). But gun control advocates argue that requiring gun retailers to submit inventory records is the key to catching corrupt dealers and keeping them "from supplying the illegal market with guns they belatedly claim went missing" (Mascia, 2015). Moreover, restricted by the GCA from inspecting a gun dealer more than once a year, the ATF cannot even meet this very low standard because of underfunding—and in a typical year, less than 10 percent of FFL retailers are inspected (Mascia, 2015). Finally, because of the fear of creating a federal gun registration system, the ATF cannot enter gun dealer records into a computerized database unless the dealer has gone out of business. In sum, the prospects for reining in corrupt licensed gun dealers that the analyses of crime gun trace data revealed was possible and needed have never come to fruition at the federal level because of the yearly congressional amendments to the budget authorization for the Department of Justice (for a detailed discussion of these restrictions, called the Tiahrt amendments in recognition of their original sponsor, Kansas Republican Congressman Todd Tiahrt, see Law Center to Prevent Gun Violence, 2012). However, as observed in the next section, some states have closed the federal FFL inspection gap by creating their own monitoring systems—systems that have had discernible and positive effects.

Controlling the Trafficking of Cheap Handguns and Other Firearms—Monitoring FFLs and One-Gun-per-Month Laws

Two gun control measures that have at least a modest chance of success have been developed out of the analysis of crime gun trace data: first is the closer scrutiny of FFLs, and second is eliminating multiple gun purchases (and thus addressing the problem of large-scale straw purchases). The 1993 Federal Firearms Licensee Reform Act, the 1993 Brady Handgun Violence Prevent Act (the "Brady Law"), and the 1994 Violent Crime Control and Law Enforcement Act have combined to improve the background checking done on prospective FFLs to ensure that they are not criminals and are, instead, legitimate dealers in compliance with local and state gun laws. FFLs are now required to report multiple handgun sales and thefts to local and state law enforcement. The FFL fee was raised from $30 to $200 for the first three years, with $90 for renewals. In response, the number of FFLs fell from 286,531 in 1993 to 138,370 in 2016 (Bureau of Alcohol, Tobacco, Firearms and Explosives, 2000, 14; 2016, 2; note that only about half of FFLs are retailers, pawnbrokers, or home-based businesses who sell directly to the public—with 64,087 such FFLs in 2016; most other FFLs are collectors, manufacturers, and importers). Although still considered far too few by gun control advocates, the ATF has increased its inspections of

FFLs, and it now requires interviews for new applications and selected renewals. Given that the ATF is restricted to only one inspection of a gun dealer in a 12-month period, and given that underfunding means any one dealer can expect an inspection perhaps once in a 10-year period, 25 states have enacted their own dealer-monitoring laws (Alabama, California, Connecticut, Delaware, District of Columbia, Florida, Hawaii, Indiana, Maine, Maryland, Massachusetts, Michigan, Minnesota, Nebraska, New Hampshire, New Jersey, New York, North Carolina, Ohio, Rhode Island, Texas, Virginia, Washington, West Virginia, and Wisconsin). Two major studies to assess the effectiveness of state-level monitoring have revealed that it is indeed an important deterrent to problematic FFL gun sales: those states that do their own monitoring of FFLs have "significantly lower levels of intrastate gun trafficking" (Webster, Vernick, and Bulzacchelli, 2009, 525), as well as interstate trafficking (such states "export crime guns at a rate of 11.5 crime guns per 100,000 inhabitants, [while those] . . . states that do not allow or require state inspections export crime guns at a rate of 17.2 crime guns per 100,000 inhabitants, which is 50% greater than the rate of states that allow or require inspections of gun dealers" [Mayors against Illegal Guns, 2010, 27; note that the 10 greatest suppliers of interstate-trafficked crime guns come from the weak gun control law states of Mississippi, West Virginia, Kentucky, Alaska, Alabama, South Carolina, Virginia, Indiana, Nevada, and Georgia—seven of which lack state-level monitoring of FFLs]).

Eliminating multiple gun sales has been central to gun control efforts in several states. For example, Virginia enacted its famous "one-gun-per-month" law in 1993, after realizing that many of the guns sold in its state ended up as crime guns in New York, New Jersey, and several states in New England. In force through 2012, when gun rights activists won their battle in the state legislature to have it repealed, this law restricted individuals from buying more than a single gun in any 30-day period. Research on its effects revealed that it did indeed work as intended: the number of crime guns recovered in New York, New Jersey, and southern New England (Connecticut, Massachusetts, and Rhode Island) that originated in Virginia dropped from one in three between September 1989 and June 1993, to one in six between July 1993 and March 1995 (Weil and Knox, 1996). Gun control advocates would like similar laws enacted in other states—or, better yet, an all-encompassing national law—to shrink the trafficking of guns from other southern states to northern destinations. For example, guns bought in Mississippi routinely end up in Chicago—and are indicative of the so-called Iron Pipeline. This is the label law enforcement has given to guns purchased in weak gun control states of the south for transport to tough-control states in the Midwest and northeast, including Illinois, Connecticut, Massachusetts, New Jersey, New York, and Rhode Island. Chicago has strict laws controlling the sale of guns, requiring, for example, a firearm owner's identification card and a 72-hour waiting period. On the other hand, anyone with a state driver's license can buy as many guns as he or she likes from a Mississippi gun store without a waiting period (providing, of course, that they can pass the federal instant background check). Chicago gang members recruit family members and acquaintances in Mississippi to buy guns (Heinzmann, 2004; Quealy and Wallace, 2013). Mississippi authorities are well aware of this gun pipeline, but have addressed the problem only through a public education media campaign called "Don't Lie for the Other Guy." The cosponsored ATF–National Shooting Sports Foundation campaign provides educational materials to Mississippi gun dealers on identifying straw purchasers; it also involves a public awareness campaign to warn potential straw purchasers of the tragic consequences that their behavior can invite (the program has focused on Iron Pipeline southern states like Mississippi, plus U.S.-Mexico border states— which have been afflicted by straw purchasing rings buying semiautomatic firearms for Mexican drug gangs; see McDougal et al., 2013; National Shooting Sports Foundation, 2016a; U.S. Department of Justice, 2011; and Yakaitis, 2006). However, as gun violence researcher Daniel Webster observes: "Educational programs such as Don't Lie, while helpful, are not a substitute for vigilant law enforcement and regular compliance checks. . . . [Indeed,] an educational program is not likely to impact the most flagrant offenders. It's naive to think that a program like this is going to influence some corrupt gun dealers and straw purchasers. It's not a bad idea, but the public should not be fooled into thinking that programs like this are the answer" (as quoted in Yakaitis, 2006).

The success of Virginia's one-gun-per-month law has prompted the District of Columbia, California, Maryland, and New Jersey to pass similar legislation to curb trafficking. Although these laws are directed at handguns, Maryland's law also applies to military-style assault weapons. In a similar vein, New York City passed the Gun Industry Responsibility Act in early 2005, creating a "Code of Responsible Conduct" for gun dealers and manufacturers and a one-gun-per-every-90-days law.

Gun rights advocates see no real problem with cheap handguns. They contend that restricting such weapons only serves to disarm the poor from defending themselves and thus, ultimately, increases crime (as thieves will be less fearful about robbing the poor). Gun rights advocates also repeatedly lobby Congress to further restrict the already tight access of researchers to ATF crime gun trace data. A favorite tactic is to tack on amendments to spending bills, as has been common in recent years (see, e.g., as discussed above, the Tiahrt amendments tacked onto the budget authorization for the Department of Justice).

Moreover, gun rights advocates see no purpose to one-gun-per-month laws—calling them "ineffective" and "burdensome"—and won notable victories in South Carolina and Virginia when these states repealed their one-gun-per-month laws in

2004 and 2012, respectively (National Rifle Association, 2012a). The logic that some South Carolina lawmakers used in repealing the law demonstrates, at least to gun control activists, the importance and the need for national legislation. The law had originally been passed because gun traffickers were buying handguns in bulk and driving them to Washington, D.C., New York, and Chicago, where they were sold to gang members and street criminals. But as one lawmaker who voted for the repeal observed, "There's still a fairly high percentage of guns going to New York [City] from [other] southern states . . . [it is thus obvious that] there are ways to circumvent the South Carolina law that there [is] no way to prevent" (Markoe and Sheinin, 2004). As a final observation, it is important to note that gun rights proponents are against one-gun-per-month laws on philosophical grounds. As observed by Kopel (2012a, 662): "In practice, gun rationing is difficult to implement without *registration* [which many in the gun rights camp vehemently oppose—see forthcoming discussion; emphasis added]. Only if the state maintains a computerized list of gun buyers for at least 30 days after each purchase can the state tell if a person purchased more than one gun at retail; and only if private gun sales (e.g., buying a gun from a relative or a friend who is not a licensed gun dealer) are prohibited can the state be sure that the individual is not exceeding the rationing limit. Opponents to gun rationing therefore see rationing laws as a wedge to additional controls."

Transportation of Guns

As noted in Chapter 1, 45 states now have *preemption* laws that prohibit localities from enacting their own gun control laws. A key motivation for preemption is the possibility of providing uniform laws regulating the transportation of firearms. Municipalities across any particular state have a wide variety of restrictions regulating the transport of firearms, making it very difficult for otherwise law-abiding gun owners to conform to the variations in local ordinances. A state-level preemption law generally allows gun owners to transport their firearms anywhere in the state as long as they're unloaded and encased; in addition, these same states allow gun owners from other states to transport their guns through their states as long as the intent of the gun owner is a "peaceable journey." In this regard, the United States is similar to its peer nations. A United Nations (1999) study comparing cross-national gun laws reveals that the United States, like its peers (the economically developed democracies of Western Europe, plus Australia, Canada, Japan, and New Zealand), has strict laws governing the transporting of firearms.

The GCA allows the legal possessor of a gun to transport it in a vehicle across state lines as long as the gun is unloaded and neither the gun nor its ammunition is readily accessible to the driver or the passengers (in general, this would mean locking the gun in the trunk of a car). If there is no trunk or area that is apart from the driver and passengers, then the gun and its ammunition must be stored in a locked container other than the glove compartment (Section 926A; see Bureau of Alcohol, Tobacco, Firearms and Explosives, 2015, 28). Gun owners may transport their firearms and ammunition on commercial airlines as long as the guns are unloaded, locked securely in a hard-sided container, and not taken aboard as carry-on luggage but declared at the check-in counter; the same rules apply to ammunition (see Transportation Security Administration, 2016). Similar rules exist for the taking of guns and ammunition on Amtrak trains (Amtrak, 2016), but commercial bus and cruise lines generally prohibit them—whether as carry-ons or checked-in baggage (see, e.g., Carnival Cruise Line, 2016; Greyhound, 2016; note that federal law allows such carriers, if they so choose, to permit a legal gun owner to transport his or her weapon or ammunition on their line if he or she delivers "said firearm or ammunition into the custody of the pilot, captain, conductor or operator of such common or contract carrier for the duration of the trip"; see Section 922e in Bureau of Alcohol, Tobacco, Firearms and Explosives, 2015, 13).

Assault Weapons Control, Including High-Capacity Ammunition Magazines

In recent years, the U.S. public has become particularly fearful of military-style assault rifles, a key feature of which is their ability to handle quickly detachable, high-capacity, ammunition magazines. The public has grown similarly more fearful of selected semiautomatic handguns of the variety that can also handle these kinds of magazines. The fear has intensified since December 2012, when 20-year-old Adam Lanza slaughtered 20 elementary school children and six staff members at Sandy Hook Elementary School in Newtown, Connecticut, using a Bushmaster XM15-E2S carbine (one of many .223 caliber assault-style rifles produced by a multitude of gun manufacturers that are modeled on the AR-15 platform). This horrific shooting resulted in an outcry from gun control organizations, like the Brady Campaign, for a renewal of the federal assault weapons ban that had existed between 1994 and 2004. Moreover, public opinion was, and continues to be, behind such a renewal (see, e.g., Barry et al., 2015, 56, who report that 69% of a random probability sample of adult Americans supported such a ban when interviewed in January 2013, with 77% of non–gun owners, who constitute more than two-thirds of the adult population, in support; note that the percentages were almost identical for banning ammunition magazines of more than 10 rounds, a provision that was also part of the 1994 federal law). However, a Democratic proposal to renew the ban was defeated in the U.S. Senate in the spring of 2013.

Gun control organizations' pressure for banning assault weapons, both handguns and rifles (more technically, "carbines," as this is the label given to shorter-barreled rifles) and the large-capacity ammunition magazines that these guns use, continued to rise after the Newtown tragedy, as studies of subsequent active-shooter, mass-shootings (such as those ana-lyzed in Chapter 1, see Figure 1.9b) revealed an increasing use of these weapons and of their accompanying high-round, read-ily detachable magazines. For example, Follman and Aronsen (2013) and Follman, Aronsen, and Pan (2016) found that half of these shootings involve such ammunition magazines. Exam-ining all mass shootings involving four or more homicide vic-tims between 2009 and 2015 (and not just those restricted to active-shooter situations, per Figure 1.9b), Everytown for Gun Safety (2015) found that those incidents where high-capacity magazines were used resulted in a 155 percent increase in peo-ple shot compared to incidents not involving these magazines (13.2 people vs. 5.2), and a 147 percent increase in fatalities (7.5 vs. 5.1).

Since the Newtown tragedy, the majority of high-profile, active-shooter, mass-murders in the United States have involved large-capacity magazines attached to semiautomatic handguns and assault rifles. These include the Charleston, South Caro-lina Emanuel AME Church shootings (9 killed using a semi-automatic handgun with a 13-round magazine; 6/17/2015); the San Bernardino, California massacre (14 killed using two AR-15 style assault rifles, both with 30-round magazines; 12/2/2015); right up to the worst mass shooting in U.S. history—the Pulse nightclub massacre in Orlando, Florida (49 people killed with an AR-15 style assault rifle, with the shooter using multiple 30-round magazines, at one point firing 24 shots in nine seconds; 6/14/2016; for detailed, historical data sets on active-shooter, mass-shootings in the United States, see Follman, Aronsen, and Pan, 2016; Stanford Geospatial Center, 2016). After each of these mass shootings, Democratic con-gressional pleas for federal legislative efforts to enact a 1994-type of assault weapons ban have never even reached the floor of either the House or the Senate for a full vote (having been stalled in committees; for a recent typical example, see Congress.gov [2016]). Ironically, when such pleas are made, sales of semiautomatic weapons, including the AR-15 and related military-style assault rifles, surge. Buyers report either (1) that they fear a ban may actually be reinstalled, and they want to get their weapons while still readily available; or (2) that the mass shooting preceding the plea has frightened them into wanting to buy more weapons (as is almost always the case—that is, most of the buyers already own at least one firearm) or to buy their first one. Indeed, to the chagrin of those wanting fewer guns circulating in society, as well as tighter controls on the guns already in circulation, whenever a call for any stricter regulation is made, gun sales rise, usually dramatically (see, e.g., Creswell, 2016; Crockett, 2016; Ingraham, 2016; and Neate, 2016). Equally ironic is the impact of a major mass shooting on state gun laws: in Republican controlled state legislatures, gun laws are often actually weakened ("citizens need to have easier access to firearms to protect themselves from mass killers" is the basic logic), while in Democratic controlled legislatures, the opposite rarely happens—that is, gun laws are almost never strengthened (see Luca, Malhotra, and Poliquin, 2016).

Although assault weapons had been used in several infamous shootings during the mid-1980s, including in the San Ysidro, California, massacre at a local McDonald's (22 dead; 7/18/1984), and although they were increasingly implicated in a number of gang killings, it was Patrick Purdy's January 1989 use of an AK-47 assault rifle to gun down 34 children (killing 5 of them) in a Stockton, California, school playground that got under way the putting of legal limits on such weapons—as well as on the size of the ammunition magazines used by them. In the spring of 1989, California enacted the first law barring the sale of assault weapons (later amended to include ammunition magazines over 10 rounds), with the District of Columbia and six other states eventually following suit: Connecticut, Hawaii, Maryland, Massachusetts, New Jersey, and New York (each state with a slightly variant, e.g., Hawaii only bans assault pistols, while New Jersey's and Colorado's ammunition magazine maximum is set at 15 rounds; see Law Center to Prevent Gun Violence [2013c, 2013d]). At the federal level,

President George H.W. Bush responded with instructions to the ATF in March 1989 to put a temporary ban on the importation of AK-47 assault rifles and selected similar weapons. This sparked the introduction of several bills in Congress to outlaw or restrict assault pistols, rifles, and shotguns. President Bill Clinton eventually brokered one of the bills through Congress as part of the Violent Crime Control and Enforcement Act of 1994. The assault weapons provision banned 19 named guns and approximately 200 other guns that fit the generic definition of an "assault weapon" for a period of 10 years. This definition emphasized that selected pistols (e.g., the TEC-9 and the MAC-10), rifles (e.g., the AK-47), and shotguns (e.g., the SWD Street Sweeper, or Striker-12) were not appropriate for civilian use. Although gun rights groups complained that it was impossible to give a generic, operational definition of an "assault weapon," congressional researchers agreed with gun control groups that there were certain characteristics that differentiated military-style from civilian-style (for use in hunting and target shooting, as well as self-defense) weapons. Among the characteristics that define an assault weapon are "a more compact design, a barrel less than twenty inches in length, extensive use of stampings and plastics in its construction, lighter in weight (6–10 pounds), a pistol grip or thumbhole stock, a folding or telescoping grip, a barrel shroud, a threaded barrel for adding a silencer or flash suppressor, and the ability to receive a large [ammunition magazine] that holds twenty to thirty bullets" (Spitzer, 2012a, 53)—the last of which is their most functionally important feature (Koper, 2004, 1). Several foreign manufacturers tried to make minor alterations to their assault weapons to evade the law, but President Clinton used an executive order in April 1998 to ban the importation of 58 foreign-made substitutes. Nevertheless, a Violence Policy Center (2004) study found that U.S. manufacturers were generally successful in evading the ban using the same strategy of foreign manufacturers, the most famous example of which was the Bushmaster XM15-M4-A3 assault rifle used by John Allen

Muhammad and John Lee Malvo in October 2002 to murder 10 people and injure three others in the infamous Washington, D.C., sniper case.

The federal assault weapons ban was enacted by a Democrat-controlled Congress and a Democrat president. A decade after its passage, in September 2004, a Republican Congress and president (George W. Bush) allowed it to quietly die amid accusations that the ban was an ineffective crime-fighting tool and that it needlessly curbed the rights of gun owners (see, e.g., National Rifle Association, 2004a; note that many Republicans also protested, and still protest, the label "assault weapon," which traditionally has been reserved for fully automatic weapons; to the liking of gun manufacturers, they instead have preferred to call them "modern sporting rifles," "tactical rifles," or simply "black guns"). For gun control advocates, the death of the assault weapons ban was a setback. They were especially frustrated because there is at least a modest amount of empirical support for the ban's effectiveness—despite the continued yearly manufacture and sale of tens of thousands of assault weapons clones during the 10-year ban (weapons that evaded the 1994 ban by making minor, cosmetic changes to banned guns). In particular, a U.S. Department of Justice study reveals that the use of assault weapons in crime dropped significantly in the first two years after the ban, and that this drop could not be explained by other variables, including the overall drop in gun crime during the late 1990s (Roth and Koper, 1999). Indeed, in the first year after its passage, requests for ATF assault weapons traces declined 20 percent. Other studies revealed that the reduction of assault weapons used in crime continued throughout the 1990s (the Brady Center to Prevent Gun Violence, 2004; Koper, 2004). Assault weapons that were specifically named in the 1994 federal assault weapons act declined from 5.2 percent of all crime guns (according the ATF National Tracing Center data) to 1.1 percent between 1993 (the year before it took effect) and 2001; and when "copycat" assault weapons (similar to those specifically named in the 1994, but with minor, cosmetic modifications) are added in, the corresponding percentages are 6.2 (1993) and 2.6 (2001) (Koper, 2004, 42–43; note that the National Rifle Association (NRA) rejects the validity of crime gun trace research [National Rifle Association, 2004a]). After the assault weapons ban ended, one highly publicized study revealed a steady rise in crimes committed with high-capacity ammunition magazines: analyzing 1993–2010 crime gun trace data provided by the Virginia State Police, Fallis and Grimaldi (2011) found crime guns recovered by the police with magazines holding more than 10 rounds fell steadily after the ban began in 1994, from 17 percent of the crime guns recovered in 1997, down to 10 percent in 2004 (the last year of the ban), then rose steadily to 22 percent by 2010. However, it is likely the transformation of gun manufacturers from making largely revolvers until the 1980s and largely semiautomatics since then can also account for this upward trend in crime guns being high-capacity semiautomatic handguns (for selected data on this transformation, see Law Center to Prevent Gun Violence, 2013d). Indeed, this is the conclusion of Koper (2007, 5, 14) who analyzed changes in crime guns in Maryland between 1990 and 1999: "Semiautomatic pistols, which generally have larger ammunition capacities than other handguns . . . now account for the majority of handguns used in crime. . . . However, recent increases in criminal use of these weapons have largely followed manufacturing and sales trends in the general civilian hand gun market."

Beyond their greater use in crime, a central part of the rationale for the special regulation of assault weapons is that they facilitate "the rapid firing of high numbers of shots, which allows offenders to inflict more wounds on more persons in a short period of time, thereby increasing the expected number of injuries and deaths per criminal use" (Roth and Koper, 1999, 7; also see Koper, 2004, 81–83). This argument is supported by a comprehensive study of gun attacks in Jersey City, New Jersey, from 1992 through 1996. More particularly, Reedy and Koper (2003) found that attacks with semiautomatic pistols resulted in higher numbers of gunshot victims than attacks with revolvers (note: semiautomatics have ammunition magazine that hold a greater number of rounds than revolvers); their findings presaged those of the Everytown for Gun Safety (2015) study noted earlier (which found more injuries and more deaths in mass shootings involving high-capacity ammunition magazines). A glaring example of why gun control activists want to return to a national ban on large magazines was provided by the Jared Loughner mass shooting of Representative Gabrielle Giffords and 13 others in Tucson, Arizona, on January 8, 2011: Loughner was tackled as he was swapping out a 30-round magazine he had just emptied with rapid fire from his semiautomatic handgun with a second, fully loaded, 30-round magazine. Control activists contend, quite logically, that had he had to do the swap after firing 9–17 rounds, standard magazine sizes, there would have been less carnage and fewer casualties (note that the standard issue magazine for the Glock 19 that Loughner used is 15 rounds, 2 of which were in his possession; see Farago, 2011; and Isikoff, 2011).

Indeed, many gun control activists have come to contend that the real issue today is not the prohibiting of military-style assault weapons per the 1994 federal assault weapons ban—a ban that failed to the degree to which manufacturers made minor alterations to their assault weapons to evade the law (as the 2004 Violence Policy Center study noted earlier revealed). Rather, the real "target" should be high-capacity ammunition magazines. As Second Amendment expert Adam Winkler observed after the horrific Orlando nightclub massacre, the real culprit in explaining the devastation of mass shootings is large-capacity magazines—and that talking about "assault weapons," like the AR-15 semiautomatic rifle used in the shooting, represents nothing more than a "distraction" (as quoted in Beckett, 2016; see also Yablon, 2016). Although the FBI (2015) does not break down the firearms used in murders by whether they are semiautomatics, the most recent Uniform Crime Reports reveals that of the 8,124 individuals murdered with a gun in

2014, 5,562 were killed with a handgun to just 248 with a rifle (which the AR-15 would be categorized as); and the overwhelming majority of handguns on the market are semiautomatics (83% of those manufactured in the United States in 2014; see Bureau of Alcohol, Tobacco, Firearms and Explosives, 2016a; note that the FBI data on firearm type is seriously incomplete, as in 23% [1,959] of the gun homicide reports submitted to the FBI in 2014, no information was included on the kind of firearm used). Many of these handguns come standard with an ammunition magazine holding 11–17 rounds—numbers that would be considered "large capacity" according to the 1994 federal assault weapons law and to current definitions in the gun control laws of California, Connecticut, Hawaii, Maryland, Massachusetts, and New York. Thus, in short, the goal for many current gun control activists is to return to the 1994 federal assault weapons ban on high-capacity ammunition magazines, not on the weapons themselves (see, e.g., the discussions in Beckett, 2016; Isikoff, 2011; Law Center to Prevent Gun Violence, 2013d; and Yablon, 2015, 2016; note that strong gun control proponents cite Australia's 1996 ban on semiautomatic weapons and high-capacity magazines as proof that they work, as no mass shootings have occurred in the country since the ban—while 12 had occurred before it [see Hemenway and Vriniotis, 2011]; for the gun rights position, which opposes limits on magazine size, see National Rifle Association, 2016a; and National Shooting Sports Foundation. 2013a).

Ballistic Fingerprinting

A ballistic fingerprint is the unique set of markings left on a shell casing and bullet after firing. Law enforcement has used ballistic analysis in criminal investigations since the early 1930s, but advancements in computer image resolution technologies over the past few decades have brought ballistic fingerprinting into the forefront of crime analysis. In 1999, the FBI and ATF set up the National Integrated Ballistics Identification Network (NIBIN) to keep a national-level database of digitalized ballistic fingerprints of guns involved in crime incidents (Bureau of Alcohol, Tobacco, Firearms and Explosives, 2016b). Within a few years, many law enforcement agencies routinely began "to obtain ballistic fingerprints from firearms recovered from criminal suspects and crime scenes, and to attempt to match the ballistic fingerprints to those taken from other crime scenes" (Webster, 2002, 1; note, however, that a National Institute of Justice study found a significant number of local law enforcement agencies have not been using NIBIN to its full effectiveness [see King et al., 2013]).

The October 2002 Washington, D.C., sniper case, in which John Allen Muhammad and John Lee Malvo used an assault rifle over a three-week period to murder 10 people, brought into public discussion a key proposal of gun control advocates— that NIBIN should be expanded to hold ballistic fingerprints of *all* firearms, not just crime guns. Gun control advocates argue that had the NIBIN database existed for all firearms, the snipers could have been identified and consequently apprehended much more quickly. Sarah Brady of the Brady Campaign to Prevent Gun Violence told newspaper reporters, "if a nationwide ballistic fingerprinting system had existed (in the [D.C.] sniper case), police would have been able to trace the bullets to a specific gun" (as quoted in Baldwin, 2002). Selected NIBIN's successes support the claim of gun control advocates: for example, between March 2000 and July 2002, information in the database "resulted in 8,800 successful matches that linked 17,600 crimes" (Webster, 2002, 1). Braga and Pierce (2004, 2) report that the Boston Police Department realized a sixfold increase in the monthly number of ballistic matches after replacing traditional ballistics methods with NIBIN. Ballistic fingerprinting now plays a key role in connecting crime scenes "that occur within and across the different Boston Police districts," as well as "in the development of intelligence that better focuses Boston gun law enforcement operations" (for selected other success stories, see Bureau of Alcohol, Tobacco, Firearms and Explosives, 2016c).

Opponents of expanding NIBIN maintain that criminals will respond by altering their guns after initial ballistic fingerprints are made. This is not inconceivable, as such alternations can be readily accomplished by using a small file to alter the firing pin or barrel. Moreover, opponents claim that an expanded NIBIN would only further encourage criminals to steal the guns they want to use in crime or to use false identification when buying them at a gun show or retail detailer. Finally, opponents contend that it would be an infringement on Second Amendment rights to create a system of gun registration that would make government confiscation of ordinary citizens' firearms much easier. (Or, as phrased by gun rights advocate Chuck Baldwin [2002], "What Sarah Brady . . . [is] really promoting is federal firearms registration. . . . Ballistic fingerprinting is [thus] a bad idea. . . . Why? Because every time a national government has required its citizens to register their firearms, gun confiscation has always followed.") Indeed, in deference to this kind fear, NIBIN is not allowed to "capture or store ballistic information acquired at the point of manufacture, importation, or sale; nor purchaser or date of manufacture or sale information" (Bureau of Alcohol, Tobacco, Firearms and Explosives, 2016b). Thus it is constrained to collecting, analyzing, and storing information related to crime guns and criminal investigations.

Gun rights proponents observe that the two states requiring universal ballistic fingerprinting, New York and Maryland, saw little success during their existence. For example, a Maryland State Police (2004) study concluded that "there have been no crime investigations that have been enhanced or expedited through the use of [Maryland's Integrated Ballistics Identification System]"; and, indeed, the system was abandoned in 2008 (Maryland State Police, 2014). Similarly, a study of New York's ballistic fingerprinting database revealed that it had "not solved a single crime in the more than three years since its debut" (as reported by the National Rifle Association, 2004b); and it too was eventually abandoned in 2012. However, Webster (2002, 2) points out that Maryland and New York were limited by the lack of an equivalent national database. This was especially true for New York, as its highly restrictive state and local gun regulations have forced criminals to buy their guns from street dealers obtaining guns from states where there are few restrictions.

Bullet Serial Numbers and Microstamping

Two once popularly promoted—but eventually largely disappointing—gun control measures related to ballistic fingerprinting are bullet serialization and the microstamping of the firing pin and breech face of semiautomatic handguns (for a description of the technical components of a these guns, see Level 1 Firearms Safety and Training, 2016). The International Association of Chiefs of Police (2008, 6) once believed these technologies held great promise for the control of violent gun crime, but in recent years has lessened its expectation (though has not given up on them; see International Association of Chiefs of Police, 2013, 41–42).

Advances in computer imagery during the 1990s opened up the possibility of laser microstamping serial numbers on the base of every newly manufactured bullet (the expelled projectile that leaves the shell casing and then travels through and out barrel of the gun); the same microstamp serial numbers would also be put on the shell casing. This kind of coding system is prominent in other industries, including everything from soda cans to candy mints. Firing tests have revealed that a microstamp is capable of surviving the mangling that can occur after a bullet hits a solid object (though the validity of these tests are questioned by the NRA and the firearms industry; see National Rifle Association, 2008a, 2015a; and National Shooting Sports Foundation, 2013b). Proposals in several states to enact bullet-coding laws have all thus far failed, and firearms manufacturing associations claim that—if ever enacted—they could be the ruin of the ammunition industry, not to mention that they would have no effect on gun crime (see, e.g., National Shooting Sports Foundation, 2013b). A typical proposal would require all handgun ammunition packed in a particular box to carry the same code; the buyer's identity would be electronically recorded and linked with the ammunition by swiping his or her driver's license. Bullet serialization proposals have been defeated in Arizona, California, Connecticut, Hawaii, Illinois, Indiana, Kentucky, Maryland, Mississippi, Missouri, New York, Pennsylvania, Rhode Island, South Carolina, Tennessee, and Washington. And, as of 2016, no state legislatures had before them any such proposals.

Microstamping the firing pin of a semiautomatic handgun involves the laser engraving of unique identifying numbers. When fired, the pin imprints the numbers on the spent shell casing—the numbers identifying the make, model, and serial number of the gun. California has required this technology be employed on all new semiautomatic handgun sales since May 2013 (East, 2013). The District of Columbia enacted a similar provision effective January 1, 2018 (Law Center to Prevent Gun Violence, 2016a). However, to date, no manufacturers actually produce handguns that have microstamping technology, and two major gun manufacturers, Smith & Wesson and Ruger, have stopped selling new semiautomatic handguns in California because of the microstamping law (Mather, 2014). In support of the companies, two gun rights organizations, Calguns Foundation Inc. and the Second Amendment Foundation, sued the state—arguing that since no manufacturers could reasonably be expected to comply with the microstamping regulation, it amounted to a ban on guns and a violation of the Second Amendment. However, they lost in district federal court ("The law barring sales of handguns without the microstamping technology doesn't violate the Constitution's Second Amendment because gun owners don't have a right to buy specific types of firearms, U.S. District Judge Kimberly Mueller in Sacramento said in her ruling"; see Pettersson, 2015). The case has been appealed to the Ninth U.S. Circuit Court of Appeals in San Francisco, where it now awaits a ruling as of late 2016 (Palazzolo, 2016; for a clear statement of the unfairness of the microstamping law from the gun rights/gun industry point of view, see DeCarlo and Selfridge, 2015).

Registration

The National Rifle Association (2004b) contends that ballistic fingerprinting, bullet coding, and microstamping are backdoors to a national system of gun registration, which is far and away the worst form of gun control that gun rights advocates can imagine (aside from the actual confiscation of guns from law-abiding citizens). Gun registration means keeping a permanent record of any firearm sale or transfer in a central location. It is a critical component of the gun violence control efforts of peer nations—where it is believed to reduce the supply of guns to criminals, as well as help with criminal investigations involving a firearm. As noted earlier, many crime gun traces reveal that the possessor purchased the gun from a licensed retailer; and gun control advocates believe that a well-publicized national registration system would deter many would-be criminals from ever obtaining guns—in part because all legal owners, not just FFLs, would be discouraged to sell to criminals. Proponents of registration also argue that it would be an effective tool in removing guns from those under a domestic violence restraining order or who have been convicted of a domestic violence misdemeanor; as soon as either of these actions happened, local law enforcement could check to see if the batterer owned a gun (see, e.g., Zeoli and Frattaroli, 2013, 60). The same can be said for those involuntarily committed to a mental institution (and, indeed, suicide rates, overall and by firearm, are lower in states requiring the registration and licensing of handguns—implying "that such laws are associated with fewer suicide attempts overall, a tendency for those who attempt to use less lethal means, or both" [Anestis et al., 2015, 2059]).

Cross-nationally, the United States again stands out regarding the laxity of its gun regulations, as it is the only economically developed democracy that does not have an integrated system for registering firearms and keeping track of their owners (see United Nations, 1999, Table 2.5). If a U.S. citizen buys a gun from a federally licensed firearm retail dealer, his or her name and address, as well as the gun make, model, and serial number, are submitted to the ATF's National Tracing Center. If the gun is used in a crime, law enforcement officials may request this information from the Tracing Center, but if the gun has been resold in the private market, there is no national law that requires the new owner to register it, and the ATF loses track of the weapon.

Currently 11 states (California, Connecticut, Hawaii, Maryland, Massachusetts, Michigan, Nebraska, New Jersey, New York, Virginia, and Washington) and the District of Columbia have some form of mandated gun registration (with Hawaii and the District of Columbia having the strongest systems—see Table 5.1 in Chapter 5), but as noted earlier, the crime- and violence-prevention effect of these mandates are greatly mitigated because they are easily evaded by crossing a state line to purchase a gun where registration is not required. Gun rights advocates contend that even if the United States had a national registration system of all firearms—whether purchased from a federal licensed retailer or in the private resale market—there would be little impact on gun violence and crime because "criminals do not register their firearms. Tracing of crime guns through the use of registration leads law enforcement back to the last law-abiding person in the chain of possession" (Kopel and Caplan, 2012, 361; for similar arguments, see National Rifle Association 2016b, 2016c). Moreover, gun rights advocates contend that registration would violate the spirit of the Second Amendment: if the government has registration lists, it can use them to disarm the citizenry and thus prevent it from resisting a tyrannical government. Despite national opinion polls consistently revealing that the U.S. public supports the registration and licensing of all firearms (see references cited in Chapter 1, as well as Figures 1.11 and 1.12), the 1986 Firearm Ownership Protection Act was designed, in large part, with the goal of preventing the federal government from setting up national registries of firearms and their owners. A similar federal law prevents any government agency from using the National Instant Criminal Background Check System (NICS) to create a national registry of either guns or gun owners. The only guns and gun owners contained in a national registry are those covered by the National Firearms Act of 1934 (e.g., machine guns and sawed-off shotguns; see the discussion of key federal gun laws in Chapter 5; also see Kopel and Caplan [2012] for detailed discussions of federal laws prohibiting gun registration, as well as for the gun rights viewpoint on the dangers of doing so).

A 2001 study conducted by the Center for Gun Policy and Research at Johns Hopkins University touches on the potential effectiveness of mandatory registration. More particularly, Webster, Vernick, and Hepburn (2001) found that states with mandatory firearms registration and licensing have a third of their crime guns sold in-state compared with three-quarters of crime guns in states not requiring registration and licensing. The researchers conclude that "mandatory registration makes it easier to trace guns used in crime to their last known legal owner, and to investigate possible illegal transfers. In combination, these laws have the potential to significantly restrict gun acquisition by high risk individuals through stricter eligibility criteria, safeguards against falsified applications, and increased legal risk and costs associated with illegal gun transfers to proscribed individuals" (184).

Licensing

Closely related to the concept of gun registration is the licensing of gun owners to buy and/or possess a firearm. Obtaining a license (or permit) involves, depending on the state or jurisdiction, a combination of one or more of the following: (a) a "thorough" background check (well beyond the "instant" background check required by the Brady Law, in which the potential purchaser of a firearm is checked against computerized lists of prohibited persons [such as convicted felons]; e.g., "thorough" can involve interviewing family and coworkers, and verifying the nature of any institutional confinement for a mental or psychiatric condition—which requires the applicant to waive confidentiality); (b) safety training; (c) hands-on testing, including firing testing, to demonstrate safe use of firearms;. (d) written testing to demonstrate knowledge of applicable firearm laws; and (e) periodic renewal (most commonly, every five years) (for the complex state and local laws involving the licensing gun owners and purchasers, see Law Center to Prevent Gun Violence, 2016b). Gun control advocates defend licensing on several grounds: "It prevents certain categories of individuals, including criminals, children, and those considered mentally incompetent, from gaining easy access to guns; it ensures that those having guns demonstrate some degree of competency . . .; it facilitates criminal investigations and prosecutions, and it regulates the accessibility of an inherently dangerous commodity based, for example, on the needs of one's occupation" (Spitzer, 2012b, 514). The potential effectiveness of the licensing of individual gun buyers on gun violence and crime is indicated by the Johns Hopkins study noted earlier, where it was found that states requiring licenses had two and a half times fewer crime guns traceable back to an in-state dealer compared with states not requiring licenses (Webster, Vernick, and Hepburn, 2001). The potential effectiveness of requiring the strict licensing and monitoring of gun dealers is indicated by the finding that just 1 percent of gun dealers account for more than half of all traceable crime guns (see the section "Tracing Crime Guns to Reduce Illegal FFL Trafficking").

Here again, the United States stands out when compared with its peer nations (United Nations, 1999, Table 2.7.), which universally require a purchaser to obtain a license before buying a gun (often with a training requirement before a license is issued—see next section). Currently, the District of Columbia and 14 U.S. states require a prospective gun buyer to obtain a license for buying a handgun (California, Connecticut, Hawaii, Illinois, Iowa, Maryland, Massachusetts, Michigan,

Minnesota, Nebraska, New Jersey, New York, North Caro-lina, and Rhode Island), and the District of Columbia and six states add this requirement even for the purchase of a "long gun" (rifle or shotgun; California, Connecticut, Hawaii, Illi-nois, Massachusetts, and New Jersey); in addition, 24 states and the District of Columbia have licensing requirements for dealers that go beyond federal regulations (with the goal of deterring illegitimate dealers—those willing to sell to crimi-nals and minors—by requiring either periodic inspection of dealer transactions, or on-demand inspection by law enforce-ment agents; these states are Alabama, California, Connecticut, Delaware, Florida, Hawaii, Indiana, Maine, Maryland, Mas-sachusetts, Michigan, Minnesota, Nebraska, New Hampshire, New Jersey, New York, North Carolina, Ohio, Rhode Island, Texas, Virginia, Washington, West Virginia, and Wisconsin).

Gun rights advocates hold licensing in the same disdain as they do registration and for the same reasons: criminals don't get licenses, and law-abiding citizens are having their Second Amendment rights violated—ultimately risking the confis-cation of their firearms. Moreover, the NRA contends on its website that the "licensing of America's . . . gun owners and their . . . firearms would require creation of a huge bureau-cracy at tremendous taxpayer cost," with no "tangible" benefit (National Rifle Association, 2000).

Training

The District of Columbia and several of the states requiring an individual to obtain a license before obtaining a gun, especially a handgun, also require that successful applicants complete a safety course (California, Connecticut, Hawaii, Maryland, Massachusetts, and Rhode Island). No national training law exists. Somewhat surprisingly, this does not, unlike other seri-ous gun control measures, put the United States in a category of its own when compared with its peer nations (United Nations, 1999, Table 2.3; about half of these nations do not require safety training before acquiring a firearm). However, 28 states require gun safety training before issuing an individual a permit to carry a concealed firearm, and almost all states require a safety training course to acquire a hunting license (International Hunter Education Association, 2016).

Gun control activists consider Delaware as having the "model" for safety training that should be adopted nationally, if not by as many states as would be willing to do so. The Delaware requirements only apply to the application an individual makes to receive a license to carry a concealed weapon. The applicant must show proof of having taken a training course that has included (a) knowledge and safe handling of firearms and ammunition; (b) safe storage of firearms and ammunition and child safety; (c) safe firearms shooting fundamentals; (d) federal and state laws pertaining to the lawful purchase, ownership, transportation, use, and possession of firearms; (e) state laws pertaining to the use of deadly force for self-defense; (f) techniques for avoiding a criminal attack and how to manage a violent confrontation, including conflict resolution; (g) live fire shooting exercises on a range, including the expenditure of a minimum of 100 rounds of ammunition; and (h) identification of ways to develop and maintain firearm shooting skills (see Law Center to Prevent Gun Violence, 2016c).

At first wash, it would seem that gun safety training would be a key component of the legislative agenda of gun control advocates. Although training in the safe practice of handling and storing guns is indeed part of the agenda, and is related to the CAP laws discussed earlier, empirical studies have been unable to show the effect gun control advocates would expect or like to see. For example, one national survey of gun owners found that those who had received formal training "were more likely to store their guns in the least safe way"—that is, "loaded and unlocked"—even after controlling for more than a dozen factors, including whether the gun was kept for protection (Hemenway, 2004, 84; the study referred to was authored by Hemenway, Solnick, and Azrael, 1995; several other studies have yielded similar findings—see Hemenway,

2004, 84–87). Many public health researchers are especially wary of gun safety programs aimed at children, such as the NRA's "Eddie Eagle" youth gun safety course (see, e.g., Dolins and Christoffel, 1994; Hemenway, 2004; for details on the program, see National Rifle Association, 2016d). The problem, as they see it, is that such programs serve to increase children's curiosity and interest in guns, thus increasing their desire to handle them.

Gun rights advocates see safety courses as one of the twin pillars of effective gun control—the other is keeping dangerous individuals (especially criminals, terrorists, and the mentally deranged) from obtaining guns. The NRA contends, "voluntary firearms safety training, not government intrusion, has decreased firearms accidents." The NRA's safety programs are conducted throughout the nation by more than 125,000 certified instructors. "Youngsters learn firearm safety in NRA programs offered through civic groups such as the Boy Scouts, Jaycees, the American Legion, and schools. NRA's Eddie Eagle GunSafe program teaches children pre-K through [fourth] grade that if they see a firearm without supervision, they should 'STOP! Don't Touch. [Run Away]. [Tell a Grown-up].' Since 1988, the program has been used by more than [26,000] schools, civic groups, and law enforcement agencies to reach [28] million children" (National Rifle Association, 2008b; bracketed updates are from National Rifle Association, 2016d, 2016e). The NRA observes that accidental gun deaths have been on a downward trend for the past three decades (e.g., as noted early, between 2002 and 2013 alone, there was a 33% drop), and the drop has been even lower for those under the age of 10. The NRA attributes itself as one of the main reasons for these large declines: "fatal firearms accidents in the Eddie Eagle age group have been reduced by more than 80 percent since the program's nationwide launch, according to the National Center for Health Statistics. [The] NRA feels that gun accident prevention programs such as Eddie Eagle are a significant factor in that decline" (National Rifle Association, 2016d).

However, Hemenway (2004, 84) points out that even though "the NRA continuously touts Eddie Eagle, no evaluation study shows that it or any similar program reduces inappropriate gun use." Indeed, the evidence currently points the other way. For example, Himle et al. (2004a) compared the effects of 31 young children (ages 4–5) going through the Eddie Eagle study program versus a behavioral skills training program (being shown by an adult trainer what to do when a gun is found and then practicing the behavior) versus no treatment (no training). The researchers found that "the education-based approach of the Eddie Eagle program was successful for teaching children to verbally reproduce the target message (stop/don't touch/leave the area/tell an adult) when asked what they would do if they found a gun. However, the children were not significantly better than no-treatment controls at performing the skills when they found a gun during a role play or when they were assessed without their knowledge in a realistic situation." The children going through the behavioral skills program did better than the Eddie Eagle and no-treatment groups when role-playing in front of the researchers, but, unfortunately these same children "did not use the skills when placed in realistic situations in which they did not know they were being tested" (as quoted in Himle et al., 2004b, 2; compare the similar findings of Gatheridge et al. 2004).

More critical of safety training for the very young, Hardy (2002) found that 34 children ages four to seven who had done training on gun safety acted no more cautiously around guns than 36 children who had not received such training: in both sets of children, about half played with a semiautomatic pistol when given the opportunity. Hardy deemed the training a failure—guns are simply too tempting and too dangerous, and many children lack the mental maturity to appreciate the meaning of the gun safety training they receive, as well as the consequences of an accidental shooting (a fact lost on many parents, as Hardy's interviews with them revealed). Rather than relying on kids to handle guns safely, this aspect of the public health approach to gun control would place the burden on parents to keep their guns and ammunition locked up and out of the sight and minds of children (see the earlier section, "Controlling Guns in the Home: Child Access Protection Laws").

Point-of-Sale Controls

Background Checks

The 1993 Brady Act is one of the most important gun control measures existing on the national level in the United States. It amended the foundation of federal gun control regulations as codified in the GCA. Its main goal is to provide a means for background checking on a prospective gun buyer to make sure he or she is not prohibited from doing so according to the regulations of the GCA—as that act originally specified who was not allowed to have firearms or ammunition but did not give the government any means other than the voluntary admission of a person to confirm if he or she was not actually prohibited from receiving, transferring, or possessing them. As an interim policy, the Brady Act mandated a five-business-day waiting period before an individual could take possession of a handgun purchased from a licensed dealer—allowing for a background check on the buyer, as well as providing a "cooling off" period to deter the impulsive purchase of a handgun to commit suicide or a violent crime. The original five-day mandate only applied to handguns and was intended as a temporary measure to allow the federal government time to develop a computerized background checking system—which it had in place by December 1998. The original background check applied to all guns, and a long gun (rifle or shotgun) could be taken possession of before five days, as long as the background check had been completed. Starting December 1, 1998, federal regulations abandoned the five-day waiting period for handguns, and any gun could potentially be taken possession of as soon as the instant background check was completed (for most people, in a matter of minutes, even though the law mandates that the government has up to three days to complete the check; see FBI, 2016a).

A Brady background check is meant to ensure that an individual barred from buying a gun according to the GCA is actually denied the purchase—with both the seller (or provider) of the firearm or ammunition and the buyer (or recipient) of the firearm or ammunition being guilty of a serious felony (up to 10 years in prison as well as up to a $250,000 fine). The GCA applies to everyone (including private sellers) *but* the Brady check is only required of FFLs—mainly gun retailers, pawnbrokers, and home businesses. A prospective gun purchaser going through an FFL must complete ATF Form 4473 (see Bureau of Alcohol, Tobacco, Firearms and Explosives, 2016d), in which he or she attests *not* to:

(a)   be buying the firearm for another person;

(b)   be under indictment in any court for a felony, or any other crime, for which the judge could imprison him or her for more than one year;

(c)   ever having been convicted in any court of a felony, or any other crime, for which the judge could have imprisoned him or her for more than one year, even if he or she received a shorter sentence including probation;

(d)   be a fugitive from justice;

(e)   be an unlawful user of, or addicted to, marijuana or any depressant, stimulant, narcotic drug, or any other controlled substance;

(f)   ever having been adjudicated mentally defective (which includes a determination by a court, board, commission, or other lawful authority that he or she is a danger to himself or herself or to others or is incompetent to manage his or her own affairs) *or* ever having been committed to a mental institution;

(g)   having been discharged from the Armed Forces under dishonorable conditions;

(h)   be subject to a court order restraining him or her from harassing, stalking, or threatening his or her child or an intimate partner or child of such a partner;

(i)   ever having been convicted in any court of a misdemeanor crime of domestic violence;

(j)   having ever renounced his or her U.S. citizenship;

(k)   be an alien illegally in the United States;

(l)   be an alien admitted to the United States under a nonimmigrant visa;

(m)   be a minor (under 21 for handguns, under 18 for long guns).

In sum, this list originated with the GCA and barred the sale of guns to the categories of people noted on Form 4473, but the original GCA had no enforcement mechanisms (an individual could simply sign the form—attesting, in effect, that he or she was not in one of categories barred from possessing a firearm; but there was no investigative follow-up to confirm the attestation). In December 1998, the Brady Law's five-day waiting period was eliminated and replaced by an instant, computerized background check—via the NICS (for detailed information on the system, see FBI, 2016a, 2016b, 2016c, 2016d). However, the District of Columbia and 14 states have imposed their own waiting periods—ranging from 2 days in Nebraska (handguns only); to 3 days for Florida (handguns), Illinois (handguns), and Iowa (handguns); to 5 days in Washington (handguns); to 7 days for Maryland (assault weapons; handguns), Minnesota (assault weapons; handguns), New Jersey (handguns), and Rhode Island; to 10 days for California and the District of Columbia; to 14 days for Connecticut (handguns) and Hawaii (and, to acquire the needed license to purchase a gun in Massachusetts, a wait of 14–40 days is necessary; and for a handgun, it may take up to a whopping 180 days for New York for license approval; see Table 5.1 in Chapter 5).

The public health approach to controlling gun violence places central importance on the screening of prospective gun buyers. It points to the success of the Brady Act in preventing convicted felons—and other individuals at high risk for committing violence—from acquiring guns from federally licensed retail dealers. From March 1994—the first full month and year the Brady Act was implemented—through December 2014 (the most recent month and year for which denial data are available), 180.24 million background checks were conducted, and they yielded 2.82 million denials (a rejection rate of 1.6 percent; note that since 2013, well over 20 million background checks are now being conducted each year—and this number was holding strong through 2016; it is not expected to fall back below 20 million for years to come). A Brady background check involves a computerized search of an applicant for a firearm purchase against 85.9 million criminal records in the Interstate Identification Index; 5.6 million records maintained by the National Crime Information Center (NCIC)—which includes data on arrest warrants, restraining (protective) orders, and immigration violations; 13.8 million records in the NICS Index, which maintains data covering all of the prohibited categories (including, e.g., for involuntary commitment to a mental hospital); and a relatively small number of records in databases maintained by the U.S. Immigration and Customs Enforcement agency, which provide information on non-U.S. citizens who have attempted to receive a firearm in the United States. The most common reason for rejection is a felony conviction (37%), followed by having a domestic violence restraining order (20%) or conviction (18%). Three-quarters of rejections fall into these three categories. The remaining rejections involve small percentages for each category and all but a handful are distributed across the following: being an unlawful user of a controlled substance, being a fugitive from justice, being under indictment for a felony, having a mental disability; or being an unauthorized alien (see Bureau of Justice Statistics, 2014; FBI, 2016e, 2016f, 2016g; and Karberg et al., 2016, 4, 8; note that despite the massive number records an applicant is checked against for a potential gun purchase, there are also millions of records [no precise estimate is available] that are missing, especially involving mental health and drug abuse [see, e.g., National Shooting Sports Foundation, 2016b]).

Here is the FBI's recounting of an actual denial case and how the NICS system is ultimately intended to function from start to finish:

> On January 27, 2015, a NICS examiner processed a transaction for an FFL, a gun shop in Garland, Texas, for a long gun purchase. The NICS examiner identified a match based on descriptive data in the NCIC. The NICS examiner researched the transaction and determined that the NCIC entry contained a warrant issued on January 23 from a sheriff's office in Texas for aggravated assault with a weapon. The NICS examiner contacted the sheriff's office, which confirmed the active warrant. Based on the information received, the NICS examiner provided the FFL with the denial. Two hours later, the sheriff's office contacted the NICS examiner to request the subject's address. The sheriff's office had attempted to apprehend the individual at the FFL, but the individual had already left the store. The sheriff's office later advised the NICS Section that they had apprehended the subject. (FBI, 2016b, 9)

Many gun rights enthusiasts scoff at Brady background check data and point out that criminals typically don't go to retail dealers to buy their guns. This contention has considerable empirical support: in its review of the relevant scientific studies, the National Research Council (2005, Chapter 4) reports that the majority of criminals obtain their guns through sources other than retail dealers—for example, by theft, sales in the private (or so-called secondary) market (e.g., at gun shows, flea markets, online, or between private individuals), or via straw purchases (e.g., a friend or relative without a criminal record making the original retail purchase). Gun rights advocates also point to a 2001 U.S. General Accounting Office (GAO) finding that would-be criminals can easily thwart the Brady Law by using false IDs. GAO agents had no problem buying guns using fake identification cards that they constructed with simple computer software and an inexpensive laminator. They pulled off their scam at a variety of licensed gun retailers in every state in which they tried: Arizona, Montana, New Mexico, Virginia, and West Virginia. They ultimately concluded that "the instant background check does not positively identify purchasers of firearms," nor can it "ensure that the prospective purchaser is not a felon" (as quoted in Longley, 2001). Indeed, this is why the NRA, in its own words, "opposes expanding firearm background check systems, because background checks don't stop serious criminals from getting guns" (National Rifle Association, 2016f).

The Secondary Market

That a person prohibited from purchasing or possessing a firearm can easily do so by turning to the *secondary market* is the one of the hottest topics in the national debate over gun control—and one of the sorest points from the perspective of gun control advocates. The secondary market consists of the many forms of private sales transacted between individuals. Although many of these occur on the street or in the privacy of homes, a large number occur at gun shows, flea markets, swap meets, and on the Internet. The U.S. Department of Justice (2007, i) estimates that there are between 2,000 and 5,200 gun shows held annually in the United States. Though many of the dealers at these gun shows are federally licensed, as many as 70 percent are not (see Bureau of Alcohol, Tobacco, Firearms and Explosives, 1999, 4; City of New York, 2009, 9; Wintemute, 2007, 150). There are currently no federal enforcement mechanisms to govern the secondary market, although congressional legislation is regularly proposed to do so (e.g., during its 2015/2016 session, the 114th Congress had a proposal from Democratic House Representative Carolyn Maloney entitled "Gun Show Loophole Closing Act of 2015" [H.R. 2380], while in the Senate, Democrat Charles Schumer proposed "Fix Gun Checks Act of 2016" [S. 2934] to require a federal background check on all private sales—including those at gun shows). The end result is that a 1999 conclusion by the ATF is as relevant in 2016 as it was back then: "Under current law, large numbers of firearms at these public markets [gun shows; the Internet] are sold anonymously; the seller has no idea and is under no obligation to find out whether he or she is selling a firearm to a felon or other prohibited person. If any of these firearms are later recovered at a crime scene, there is virtually no way to trace them back to the purchaser" (Bureau of Alcohol, Tobacco, Firearms and Explosives, 1999, 1; see the similar conclusion expressed by Wintemute, 2007, 150). Note that the District of Columbia and 12 states have their own laws that require purchases between private parties to involve a background check of the purchaser from either a federally licensed dealer or law enforcement agency (California, Colorado, Connecticut, Delaware, Hawaii, Illinois, Massachusetts, New Jersey, New York, Oregon, Rhode Island, and Washington), while another 6 states have similar requirements but only for handguns (Iowa, Maryland, Michigan, Nebraska, North Carolina, and Pennsylvania). However, half of the top 10 states in which gun shows are conducted are not on either list: Texas, Florida, Ohio, Nevada, and Indiana (the remaining top 10 states are Pennsylvania, Illinois, California, and North Carolina; note that states are listed in rank order; see Bureau of Alcohol, Tobacco, Firearms and Explosives, 1999, 4).

In the spring of 2005, the *Buffalo News* ran a lengthy story exposing the kind of horrific consequences that the lack of regulations at gun shows can have. Street criminal James Nigel Bostic crossed from the strict gun control state of New York into the less restrictive state of Ohio in 2000, where he purchased 250 handguns at various gun shows. He then returned to New York and sold them on the streets of Buffalo to drug dealers, thieves, and gang members. During the next four years, 100 of Bostic's guns were recovered and linked to an array of violent crimes, including murder, kidnapping, assault, and robbery (*Buffalo News*, 2005). The Bostic case is similar to many ATF investigations, which together "paint a disturbing picture of gun shows as venues for criminal activity and a source of firearms used in crimes" (Bureau of Alcohol, Tobacco, Firearms and Explosives, 1999, 7).

However, there is reason to believe that universal background checks, including all transactions at gun shows, would reduce illegal gun trafficking: a study comparing 8 gun shows (60 vendors) in California—one of the 12 states noted above that requires background checks for all firearm sales (even at gun shows and even for private transactions between two individuals)—to 20 shows (212 vendors) in Arizona, Nevada, Texas, and Florida, where there is no secondary sales law, and where the majority of California's crime guns originate, found California vendors were much better behaved:

(1)   They obeyed state law, and thus there were no private party gun sales between attendees of the California shows. In the comparison states "private party sales appeared about equal in number to sales involving licensed retailers. They generally required less than 5 min to complete, and sometimes less than 1 min. In only one sale between attendees was identification or verification of in-state residence requested" (Wintemute, 2007, 153).

(2)   Those who were FFLs were less likely to allow "straw purchases" than their counterparts in the comparison states. This begs the question of why would any FFL, in California or any other state, risk a straw purchase (a clear violation of federal law for both the vendor and the buyer) when an anonymous purchase is easily accomplished? "These data suggest an answer: that licensed retailers have larger inventories and allow illegal buyers a wider selection. This proposition would be unconvincing if the risk of apprehension during a straw purchase was high. But only once, at a show attended while developing the

methodology for this study, did a retailer refuse to conduct an obvious straw purchase. Police action was never seen . . . [Indeed,] some illegal purchases took place with police officers in the immediate vicinity" (Wintemute, 2007, 154).

Reaching a similar conclusion regarding its study of gun shows across the country, a Mayors against Illegal Guns (2010, 14–15) research group found that states requiring background checks for all handgun sales had "an average export rate of 7.5 crime-guns per 100,000 inhabitants," while the "states that do not require background checks for all handgun sales at gun shows have an average export rate of 19.8 crime guns per 100,000 inhabitants, a rate more than two and a half times greater than the rate of states that do" (an exported crime gun is one that was bought in one state, but used in another state to commit a crime; see the Iron Pipeline discussion earlier in this chapter). Similarly, Pierce, Braga, and Wintemute (2015) found another key statistic related to crime guns, the time gap between when they are sold and when they are recovered (with crime guns having a short interval, implying that was the key reason for the gun's purchase in the first place), to be strongly positively related to the strength of state gun laws, including secondary sales background checks. Thus, in a strict gun-regulated state like California, the time-to-crime for a retail-purchased gun is very long, meaning, in part, that the gun was not bought by a legal purchaser and then quickly resold to a criminal in the secondary market. Relatedly, in one of the most comprehensive studies to date on the effects of various state gun laws on firearm-related deaths, Kaleson and his colleagues (2016) found that universal background checks, covering both FFL and private sales and transfers of firearms, is one of the most powerful predictors (reducers) of firearm mortality due to criminal homicide and suicide.

However, many gun rights advocates place no blame for street crime on unregulated gun shows. As the NRA states on its web page, if the gun show loopholes in federal law were closed, criminals would simply find another means to get their guns, for example, "through theft, on the black market, or from family members or friends" (National Rifle Association, 2016g).

In recent years, gun control advocates have become as fearful of firearm sales between private parties on the Internet as they are about such sales at gun shows. Major studies by the *New York Times* (Luo, McIntire, and Palmer, 2013) and the City of New York (2011) have revealed large numbers of private sales between individuals "with no questions asked." Indeed, the report of the City of New York (2011, 2) observes that firearms transactions are conducted every day on a multitude of websites among largely anonymous actors. "Criminal buyers who once had to purchase in person can now prowl hundreds of thousands of listings to find unscrupulous sellers. Negotiations can be conducted from the discreet remove of a phone call or an email exchange. . . . Importantly, the boom in online gun sales came long after the passage of federal laws that were designed with a physical marketplace in mind. In this and other respects, technology and e-commerce have far outpaced the law, creating new opportunities for abuse." And the *New York Times* study similarly observes that "gun shows have long been a source of concern for gun control advocates and law enforcement officials, because many allow unregulated sales without background checks. Web sites make such transactions far more widely available, with just a few clicks of a mouse . . . [and provide] 'a gun show that never ends'" (Luo et al., 2013, 3).

The City of New York study investigated 10 websites, finding more than 25,000 guns for sale. The websites chosen were not online storefronts for a particular retailer, in which the dealer offers guns for direct sale at a listed price; these kinds of websites are generally quite professional and represent licensed dealers—who "typically require users to confirm their identity by credit card before a purchase can be made, and ship firearms only to local licensed dealers, who are in turn responsible for conducting background checks on the buyers" (6). Rather, the

10 websites chosen were "sites that have relatively few rules requiring buyers and sellers to identify themselves, and may therefore be more attractive to prohibited or unscrupulous purchasers. The sites . . . typically permit potential buyers to view firearms ads that include the cell phone number and email address of the seller without registering with the site or otherwise revealing their identity" (9). Thus, a criminal or otherwise federally prohibited buyer can contact the seller directly and arrange for a private, face-to-face meeting to make a transaction. This allows the buyer and seller to sidestep, completely, doing a background check, and if the transaction happens in a state where both the buyer and seller are residents, no federal law is being broken by the seller (unless the seller knows for a fact that the buyer is on the federally prohibited list, as both FFLs and private individuals are barred from making such sales by the GCA; however, if the private seller takes a "don't-ask-don't-tell" approach, this law can easily be sidestepped; of course FFLs must "ask" via Form 4473 discussed earlier). The City of New York investigators wanted to see how far the private sellers on these 10 websites would be willing to go—that is, even if they knew the potential buyer was on the federally prohibited list, would the sellers still proceed? The investigators did this by first establishing that the seller was not a federally licensed firearms dealer (and thus not required to do a background check) by asking "You're not one of those licensed guys, are you?" Then the investigator would agree with the seller on a price, and as soon as this was done say "I probably couldn't pass a background check." Then the moment of truth came: after hearing this, would the seller agree to meet the investigator to complete the sale? Going through this protocol 125 times, the investigators found that 77 of the "online sellers agreed to sell a gun to someone who said he could not pass a background check—a 62% rate" (9–10).

Two key take-away conclusions for the City of New York (2011, 3) researchers were that (1) federal law should require a background check for *all* sales, including private sales—whether occurring in a parking lot, at a gun show, or online; and (2) the ATF should beef up its enforcement of existing laws (like no one being allowed to sell to a buyer they believe is on the prohibited list) via undercover investigations on a variety of websites, including those it and the *New York Times* studied (these websites have gained notoriety in recent years and are named in both studies).

The NRA maintains that fears about Internet gun sales are more or less unfounded. Rather, the "real purpose of legislative proposals to ban Internet sales is to ban the advertising of firearms on the Internet, which is a direct attack on both the First and Second Amendments. For much the same reason that anti-gun forces want to eliminate gun shows, they want to prohibit the free exchange of information about firearms on the Internet, and in doing so restrict the avenues law-abiding people have to find and obtain the firearms of their choice" (National Rifle Association, 2013; note that this statement was posted more than a year after the City of New York study was published—a study that was widely distributed to both the gun control and gun rights communities).

"Shall-Issue" (Right-to-Carry) Concealed Weapons Laws

Between 1987 and 2013, a revolution occurred in state-level concealed weapons laws, one bemoaned by the advocates of strong gun control. During the first third of the 20th century, the majority of U.S. states banned most private citizens from carrying concealed firearms (with special exceptions being made for occupational purposes, e.g., private security). These bans received little public resistance, even from gun enthusiasts. However, beginning with the state of Florida in 1987, and in the 25 years that followed, 33 states enacted "shall-issue" laws, allowing for the average citizen to acquire, relatively easily, a concealed weapons permit to carry a handgun. By 2016, a total of 41 states had either a shall-issue or no permit required to carry a concealed firearm. The usual requirements are not hard to meet: a Brady background check (revealing, e.g., no felony convictions or domestic violence abuse incidents) and a short course in gun safety. Concealed weapons permits are issued in every state, but are modestly to severely more difficult for the average citizen to obtain in the District of Columbia and the so-called may-issue states of California, Connecticut, Delaware, Hawaii, Maryland, Massachusetts, New Jersey, New York, and Rhode Island. "May-issue" implies that the final decision to issue a permit rests with local or state law enforcement agencies, who are reluctant to do so in some jurisdictions (see National Rifle Association, 2016h, which views these states as being in violation of the Second Amendment).

Gun control advocates feared that the enactment of such laws would bring with it a rise in handgun violence; they predicted, for example, a rise in (a) spur-of-the-moment shootings; (b) the number of criminals carrying guns (knowing that some of the public might now be armed); and (c) gun theft and thus the putting of more guns into the hands of criminals, as gun possession in the law-abiding population will increase the number of firearms available for stealing. But what gun control advocates feared has not yet come to pass. On the contrary, most crime categories, including gun-related crimes, have fallen since the mid-1990s; and as pointed out in Chapter 1, so have the percentage of households claiming to have a gun. Some gun control advocates, such as the Brady Campaign to Prevent Gun Violence (2014), credit the enactment of the 1993 Brady Law for the fall in the crime rate, while some gun rights advocates, such as the National Rifle Association (2012b), credit the sweeping liberalization of concealed weapons laws (claiming criminals become fearful when "potential victims are armed"). Neither claim is valid. Empirical studies of the effects of "shall-issue" laws have produced findings that are neither plain nor easy to interpret. As revealed in Figure 2.1, the differences in the average violent

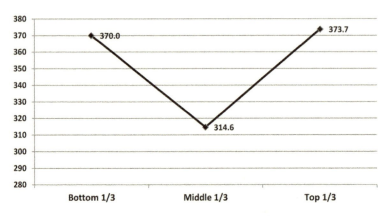

Notes: (a) In ten states, no concealed weapons permit is required by in-state residents, and thus these states are deleted; missing data for two states; in sum, 38 states are analyzed. The average percentage of adults having a concealed weapons permit for each third are given in parentheses (1.8, 5.9, and 9.9).

(b) Violent Crime Rate is the total number of murders, rapes, robberies, and aggravated assaults per 100,000 population.

Figure 2.1   State Average Violent Crime Rate by Percentage of Adults Having a Concealed Weapons Permit (2014–2015).
Source: Raw data from Lott, Whitley, and Riley (2015, 17–18) and FBI (2015, Table 5).

crime rate between those states with a high (top one-third) versus a low (bottom one-third) percentage of adults having a concealed weapon permit are almost identical and not statistically significant. More complex statistical analyses are no more revealing. For example, when controls for poverty, racial heterogeneity, region, and other significant correlates of crime are added, and when the dependent variable list is expanded to include other indicators of crime, as well as changes over time, researchers obtain the same relatively weak and insignificant differences among states with shall-issue versus may-issue laws. In one of the most comprehensive studies to date, Donohue (2003, 290) concludes that "shall-issue laws may not increase crime as much as many feared." Moreover, and quite notably, "the typical gun permit holder is a middle-aged Republican white male, which is a group at relatively low risk of violent criminal victimization with or without gun ownership." So it is not clear why there should be any "substantial crime reduction benefits . . . by arming this group further." If there is any significant effect, according to Donohue, it will be reflected in the creation of a greater level of social unease, because citizens are likely to become apprehensive when they realize that "greater numbers of individuals walking through shopping malls, schools, and churches and sitting in movie theatres are carrying lethal weapons." More forcefully, philosopher Firmin DeBrabander (2015, 203, 149) argues that "a society that is progressively more armed, exposing weapons in public and appealing to them with greater regularity, is one that erodes the rule of law. As more people are armed in public, it sends the message that rule of law is weak. . . . [And] if we do not address the underlying causes of crime [such as poverty and drugs], it not hard to see that a plethora of guns is a toxic ingredient added to the mixture." Most public health researchers would agree with Donohue's and Debrabander's assessments of current concealed weapons laws and find little benefit in their existence or growth and, indeed, would prefer their repeal (see, e.g., Hemenway, 2004, 244–251; Law Center to Prevent Gun Violence, 2016c).

Open Carry

In response to a 2012 federal appeals court ruling that it was unconstitutional for the state of Illinois to ban the concealed carry of a firearm, even with a license and safety training, the state became the last of the 50 states to allow concealed carry of a firearm. After achieving such an incredible record of accomplishment between 1987 (Florida's passing of concealed carry legislation that allowed the ordinary citizen to readily get a permit for a concealed handgun) and 2013 (when Illinois passed a concealed carry law, one that is almost as pleasing to gun rights activists as is the Florida law), the right-to-carry thrust of the gun rights movement began to ebb. But as this aspect of right-to-carry was ebbing, especially after 2006, when Nebraska became the 29th post-Florida state to legalize concealed carry for ordinary citizens, it began being replaced by a related aspect—increasing the rights of gun owners to carry openly their firearms, even in urban areas where it had once been considered unthinkable. Indeed, unthinkable even by gun rights enthusiasts: when a group of Texas open carry activists started entering coffee shops and restaurants openly displaying their semiautomatic weapons (including both rifles and shotguns) to make their point that the Second Amendment protected their right to do this, even the NRA reacted by calling such demonstrations counterproductive, posting on its website the following sharp criticism:

> Let's not mince words, not only is it rare, it's downright *weird* and certainly not a practical way to go normally about your business while being prepared to defend yourself. To those who are not acquainted with the dubious practice of using public displays of firearms as a means to draw attention to oneself or one's cause, it can be downright *scary*. . . . Using guns merely to draw attention to yourself in public not only defies common sense, it shows a lack of consideration and manners. That's not the Texas way. And that's certainly not the NRA way. (May, 30, 2014; as quoted in Domonoske, 2014)

Because the NRA generally opposes almost all proposed—and indeed most current—gun control legislation, the organization realized its May 2014 statement was a potential gaffe and soon retracted it. The original statement was taken down and the URL where it had been posted put up a replacement proclamation reading "Unequivocally, we support open carry. We've been the leader of open carry efforts across this country" (National Rifle Association, 2014). All of this noted, the gun rights movement has mixed feelings on open carry. Staunch gun rights proponent and founder of the Second Amendment Foundation Alan Gottlieb reacted to California open carry activists' entering coffee shops with their firearms in open display with the statement: "I just don't think it's politically intelligent . . . I would like to see gun owners think twice before they go to a rally like that with a firearm strapped on. It doesn't necessarily put our best face forward" (see Wilson, 2012, 664). Using a less political and more practical line of reasoning, other gun control proponents observe that it is of course easier to identify a person with a firearm who is carrying openly as opposed to one who is carrying concealed, which could encourage an attack by a criminal wanting to steal a gun.

This is actually one of the reasons gun control activists are so strongly opposed to open carry. Another key reason is that "open carrying poses particular challenges for law enforcement officers who must respond to a 911 call" (Law Center to Prevent Gun Violence, 2016d). As detailed by a California sheriff officer:

> Open carry advocates create a potentially very dangerous situation. When police are called to a "man with a gun" call they typically are responding to a situation about which they have few details other than that one or more people are present at a location and are armed. Officers may have no idea that these people are simply "exercising their rights." Consequently, the law enforcement response is one of "hypervigilant urgency" in order to protect the public from an armed threat. Should the gun carrying person fail to comply with a law enforcement instruction or move in a way that could be construed as threatening, the police are forced to respond in kind for their own protection. It's well and good in hindsight to say the gun carrier was simply "exercising their rights" but the result could be deadly. Simply put, it is not recommended to openly carry firearms. (Lunny, 2010)

More generally, gun control activists see the open carrying of firearms as intimidating the public, wasting law enforcement resources, and creating "opportunities for injury and death due to the accidental or intentional use of firearms" (Law Center to Prevent Gun Violence, 2016d). Regulations for open carry are complex and vary by state—with distinctions often made between long guns (the rifles and shotguns associated with hunting) and handguns, with 5 states currently banning open carry (California, Florida, Illinois, New York, and South Carolina) and another 14 requiring a special permit or license.

Gun Buyback Programs

A once popular but receding gun control measure falling under the public health approach is gun buyback programs that dozens of cities have developed over the past three decades. A typical program is Jersey City's "Operation Lifesaver." In one three-week stretch in 2005, the city collected 897 guns by offering amnesty to the individuals turning in the guns, as well as cash: $25 for a BB gun, $150 for a revolver, and $250 for a semiautomatic weapon. The guns ranged from cheap Saturday night specials to fully functioning machine guns (see George, 2005). Hemenway's (2004, 217–220) review of the evidence on the effectiveness of gun buyback programs leads him to conclude that they "*may* have . . . some beneficial effects, including reducing accidents and suicides, but [they do] not help rid the streets of the weapons most commonly used in fatal criminal shootings" (emphasis added). For example, a review of firearm fatality surveillance data for Milwaukee in the late 1990s revealed that five specific makes of handguns accounted for nearly half of the firearm deaths but only 6 percent of the guns collected in the city's buyback program. In short, "buyback campaigns more often than not end up with hunting rifles or old revolvers from someone's attic than with automatic weapons that criminals" more commonly use (Horn, 2013). A typical study finds what Marinelli et al. (2013) did when they examined the social characteristics of individuals participating in Connecticut's gun buyback program in comparison to the statistics of firearms sales and of violence in the state. Over the four-year period covered by the study (2009–2012), the buyback program collected 464 firearms, including 232 handguns—but in a single year of the study (2009), 91,602 firearms were sold. Given the inability of buybacks to deplete the overall stock of guns in circulation, as well as the lack of confirmatory positive findings in earlier research, Marinelli et al. were not surprised to discover that "the incidence of gun-related deaths was unchanged in the two years following the inception of the buy-back program." And they concluded that "a gun buy-back program alone is not likely to produce a measurable decrease in firearm injuries and deaths" (453). They found older white men and women were the most likely to be turning in guns, while young minority men were most likely to be the victims of firearm murders.

All of the above noted, some public health researchers still believe the buyback program have benefits: (1) "They raise awareness about a serious problem"; and (2) they "rally community groups to get more involved" (Horn, 2013). Moreover, these researchers believe that fine-tuning the programs to target the types of guns used in crimes may increase program effectiveness, for example, offering considerably more money for a semiautomatic handgun than for aged or nonworking revolver—as was done in December 2012 in Camden County, New Jersey, a buyback program that actually netted a small number of "automatic assault weapons" (see Wogan, 2013).

An interesting variant of the buyback program is the *toy* gun version. In this case, a community agency will offer to give a child another kind of toy in exchange for a toy gun. For example, during the summer of 2004, the city of Central Falls, Rhode Island, hosted a toy gun turn-in event, in which children threw their toy guns into a "bashomatic" (a trash compactor that crushed them). The Rhode Island State Attorney General's Office funded this and similar events in several Rhode Island cities in 2004 and 2005. Community activist Angel Garcia observes that the point of the program is "to get children and adults thinking about society's use of guns . . . It's not just about gun removal, it's about educating our families, enlightening kids about safe play. As a person that works with kids, I tend to want to err on the side of caution. Guns shouldn't be part of everyday development." Garcia's views were echoed by then Rhode Island attorney general Patrick Lynch: "Any chance we get to stop and talk to kids and engage them and try to explain the danger associated with guns is good" (Garcia and Lynch quotes excerpted from Pina, 2004).

Gun rights advocates view buyback programs as exercises in futility. The NRA contends the programs "are a waste of taxpayer money," and, even worse, they "can result in the disarming of future crime victims who could have used the guns defensively to prevent death, injury, or property loss" (National Rifle Association, 1999, 2015b). In support of its contention of the futility of buyback programs, the NRA cites the final report of the prestigious National Research Council's major study on firearm-related violence:

> The theory on which gun buy-back programs is based is flawed in three respects. First, the guns that are typically surrendered in gun buy-backs are those that are least likely to be used in criminal activities. Typically, the guns turned in tend to be of two types: (1) old, malfunctioning guns whose resale value is less than the reward offered in buy-back programs or (2) guns owned by individuals who derive little value from the possession of the guns (e.g., those who have inherited guns). . . .
>
> Second, because replacement guns are relatively easily obtained, the actual decline in the number of guns on the street may be smaller than the number of guns that are turned in.
>
> Third, the likelihood that any particular gun will be used in a crime in a given year is low. In 1999, approximately 6,500 homicides were committed with handguns. There are approximately 70 million handguns in the United States. Thus, if a different handgun were used in

each homicide, the likelihood that a particular handgun would be used to kill an individual in a particular year is 1 in 10,000. The typical gun buy-back program yields less than 1,000 guns. Even ignoring the first two points made above (the guns turned in are unlikely to be used by criminals and may be replaced by purchases of new guns), one would expect a reduction of less than one-tenth of one homicide per year in response to such a gun buy-back program. The program might be cost-effective if those were the correct parameters, but the small scale makes it highly unlikely that its effects would be detected.

In light of the weakness in the theory underlying gun buy-backs, it is not surprising that research evaluations of U.S. efforts have consistently failed to document any link between such programs and reductions in gun violence. (National Research Council, 2005, 95–96)

The Law Enforcement Approach

From our review of the key public health approaches to controlling gun violence, it is obvious that gun control and gun rights advocates have fundamental differences in values and worldviews. From the public health stance, too many guns with too few controls is a root cause of many contemporary social problems; from the gun rights stance, guns have become simply a scapegoat for many of the contemporary social problems. Nevertheless, both sides concur that the enforcement of current gun laws is critical to reducing gun violence and its costs to society. More specifically, both agree that violence-prone lawbreakers should be denied the right to buy and possess guns. When these individuals are caught, they should be taken off the streets with stiff prison sentences, especially if they are in possession of a firearm. Like the public health approach, the *law enforcement* approach is complex and multifaceted. Aspects of it that are particularly important to consider are the enforcement of current laws, gun-focused/place-oriented community policing, and gun courts.

Enforcement of Current Gun Control Laws

As gun-violence researcher Lawrence Southwick Jr. (2012b, 261) observes, often times the "issue of enforcement of gun laws is really a cover for opposing new gun laws. Those on one side of the issue argue that 'we need to make a law restricting guns,' while those on the other side say 'we don't need new laws—we need enforcement of existing gun laws.'" That said, both sides of the gun debate want aggressive enforcement of current laws regarding illegal possession, sale, transfer, or use of a firearm.

The most common weapons offense category is the possession of a firearm by a prohibited person (usually a convicted felon); the second most common category is the use of a firearm during the commission of a violent crime (e.g., bank robbery) or drug trafficking. These two categories account for nearly 85 percent of the annual average of about 8,000 federal weapons arrests that have occurred in recent years, as well as of the majority of the 160,000 or so weapons arrests made by state and local police (Saris et al., 2015; Southwick, 2012b; Snyder, 2012; United States Sentencing Commission, 2015). There are many other categories of weapons-related arrests, the most significant of which include the receipt or possession of an unregistered firearm; the unlawful importation, manufacture, distribution, shipment, or receipt of a firearm; and the possession of a stolen gun. Southwick (2012b, 264–265) observes that although both state/local versus federal arrests for weapons violations have similarly high conviction rates, about 80 percent, those convicted in the federal courts are much more likely to get a prison sentence (93% in the federal court system versus 44% in the state/local court system) and, moreover, are more likely to get a long sentence (84 months, on average, in the federal system versus 42 months, on average, in the state/local system). Finally, for violent crimes in which the weapons offense is not the most serious charge (e.g., being caught selling cocaine and also being found in possession of a gun), "the sentence for the more serious crime may be enhanced by a penalty for using or possessing a firearm in the offense." (Note that the sentence enhancements are not counted in the total numbers of weapons offenses just mentioned.) "The average enhancement [is] about six years, and about 40 percent of state courts and 56 percent of federal courts include sentence enhancements on criminals using firearms in their crime" (265). Southwick's take-away from all of these numbers is that criminal gun violence could be reduced if state and local judicial systems, which process far more firearms violations, substantially increased their penalties to levels on par with the federal system.

Gun-Focused/Place-Oriented Community Policing

In response to the rising gun violence of the 1980s, the U.S. Department of Justice, working in conjunction with state and local authorities and coordinating its key law enforcement groups (the ATF, FBI, and Drug Enforcement Administration [DEA]), developed Project Triggerlock in 1991. Over the years, Triggerlock has been expanded and reformulated—to accommodate the unique circumstances of various metropolitan areas—under dozens of guises in hundreds of local and regional jurisdictions (program titles include Project Exile, Operation Ceasefire, Project Felon, Project Safe Neighborhoods, Triggerlock II, and many others). Funding for most of these has come through the Violent Gang and Gun Crime Reduction Program (formerly known as Project Safe Neighborhoods), a centerpiece of the federal government's efforts to control gun violence since 2001. Other funding has been channeled through the Community Oriented Policing Services ("COPS"—created as part of the Violent Crime Control and Law Enforcement Act of 1994), and the Safe Streets Violent Crime Initiative (see, e.g., Center for Problem-Oriented Policing, 2003; FBI, 2016h; U.S. Department of Justice, 1999, 2016b). These programs use federal firearm statutes—for example, those barring the possession of firearms by high-risk individuals, including convicted felons, drug dealers, and domestic abusers—to prosecute gun-toting offenders in *federal* ("U.S. District") courts, where convictions rates are typically much higher and penalties much stiffer than in state and local courts. As just noted, although both the state/local and federal courts have about an 80 percent conviction rate for those brought up on firearms charges, 93 percent of those convicted in the federal system serve prison time, averaging 84 months; in contrast, only about 44 percent of processed through state or local systems end up in prison, averaging only 42 months (see Southwick, 2012b, Table 1; also see United States Sentencing Commission, 2015). The programs often contain media campaigns to increase public awareness of gun crime and its ramifications, including the death and maiming of innocent victims, the financial losses suffered by the community, and the stern penalties gun-carrying criminals will face when turned over to the federal judicial system (see, e.g., U.S. Department of Justice, 2016c, 2016d, 2016e). Sometimes the programs incorporate a "carrot" approach—for example, increasing funding for school and community development agencies, especially those that seek to take teens and young adults off the streets through recreational, educational, and job-placement programs.

Two highly publicized Triggerlock-type programs were Boston's Gun Project/Operation Ceasefire (GPOC) and Richmond's Project Exile. Gun rights advocates have extolled both as shining successes of the law enforcement approach to controlling gun violence. Begun in May 1996, Boston's GPOC aimed to reduce gun violence by disarming gang members. It created a task force composed of the office of the U.S. District Attorney, the Massachusetts State Probation Office, the ATF, the DEA, the FBI, the State Department of Youth Services, the country district attorney, area clergy, neighborhood street workers, and several community development organizations. GPOC strongly incorporated both "carrot" and "stick" approaches. For example, it sent gang-unit police, community-agency street workers, and clergy to schools and street corners gang members frequented to send a loud and clear message: use a gun, and you will suffer the maximum consequences; carry a gun, and law enforcement will find you, and the judicial system will make sure that you suffer the maximum consequences. When, for example, a gang member was stopped for a traffic violation, if a search of the vehicle turned up a gun, or even a single bullet, the results were immediate arrest and speedy disposition in federal court. In the months following GPOC's inception, there were dozens of federal weapons indictments and arrests. Recovered guns were subjected to ATF traces, and many were linked to multiple crimes, which in turn subjected the possessors to even harsher punishment. More extensive traces often turned up illegitimate gun dealers, who were rounded up and quickly prosecuted. Many of the 80 federally licensed firearms dealers in the Boston area were known to sell guns to street criminals. However, fearing prosecution, 65 of them decided to surrender their licenses or not to seek renewal.

On the "carrot" side, the Boston Jobs Project was created to help street youths get job training and eventual job placement through the Boston Private Industry Council. Employers were enticed into hiring these high-risk youth, because each youth came with a "voucher" from the recommending individual (usually a police or probation officer, a Department of Youth Services caseworker, or a minister). The voucher guaranteed the employer that the recommending individual would keep tabs on the new worker (e.g., checking in on the person to make sure he or she was going to work; making sure that the person had been assigned a case manager to assist in finding substance abuse services, transportation, housing, child care, and mental health counseling; see the Boston Strategy to Prevent Youth Violence, 2016).

In 2001, Harvard University and the City University of New York researchers concluded that GPOC was a huge success: the multifaceted program was credited with significant reductions in Boston area youth homicide (a 63% drop in the first two years following its inception), reports of "shots fired" called into the police (a 32% drop), and gun-assault incidents (a 25% drop; see Braga et al., 2001). Moreover, these reductions could not be accounted for by other factors, such as changes in the Boston job market or in the size and composition of the youth population.

A prototype of the "stick" emphasis of the law enforcement approach to controlling gun violence, Richmond's Project Exile sought to deter illegal gun use by diverting weapons-related offenses from the state to the federal court system—with the expected benefits of higher convictions rates and stiffer prison sentences. Begun in February 1997, the project provided training to law enforcement agents on federal gun laws and proper procedures for search and seizure, and it funded an advertising campaign telling would-be criminals that any gun offense would be dealt with swiftly and sternly by the judicial system. Gun rights enthusiasts extolled the program and credited it with reducing firearm-related murders by 40 percent during its first year alone. The state of Virginia was so impressed with the project that it developed its own statewide "Exile" program, passing a law mandating a minimum sentence of five years for those having a prior conviction for a violent felony and who are convicted of possessing a firearm (see Johnson, Smith, and Willard, 2001, 8). Similarly, a number of other cities have been similarly impressed with Exile's successes and since the early 2000s have begun instituting similar Exile-type programs (from Virginia communities such as Lynchburg, Petersburg, Portsmouth, Roanoke, and Suffolk, to communities in other states, include Baton Rouge [LA], Oakland [CA], Philadelphia [PA], Providence [RI], and Rochester [NY]). Nationally, Exile became part of the federal Project Safe Neighborhoods program and eventually expanded to dozens more communities (see Lansford, 2012; McGarrell et al., 2013).

Some scholars are not particularly impressed with GPOC or Project Exile. They point out that gun-violence rates were dropping throughout the country in the late 1990s, and many cities, without these kinds of community policing programs, experienced just as dramatic reductions (see, most notably, Winship, 2002; and Raphael and Ludwig, 2003). However, when the National Research Council (2005, 234) reviewed the effects of similar programs in Kansas City, Indianapolis, Pittsburgh, and New York, it concluded that the evidence was "compelling"—that they work, and that they can reduce violent crime in a community and not merely displace it from one neighborhood to another. Moreover, a 2013 complex statistical analysis of the effectiveness of Project Safe Neighborhoods programs (of the GPOC/Project Exile ilk) found that in a cross-city comparison of all U.S. cities with a population of more than 100,000, those 82 cities with a Project Safe Neighborhoods program had significantly greater reductions in violent crimes (homicide, aggravated assault, and robbery) compared to 170 cities without such a program (McGarrell et al., 2013, 7): "During the years 2000 to 2006, PSN [Project Safe Neighborhood] target cities . . . experienced statistically significant declines in violent crime compared to . . . non-PSN comparison cities. PSN target cities witnessed a nearly nine percent decline, whereas non-target cities were relatively unchanged." Impressively, this finding maintained itself after controlling for many of the major known predictors of violent crime—including poverty level, population density, police staffing levels, and incarceration trends.

Triggerlock-type programs suffered two setbacks during their first decade. First, in December 1995, the U.S. Supreme Court ruled in *Bailey v. United States* (516 U.S. 137, 116 S.Ct. 501) that persons in possession of a gun when arrested for a violent or drug-trafficking crime must have actually used it (e.g., firing or brandishing) if they were to be charged with a distinctive weapons offense apart from the actual crime. This immediately reduced the number of weapons charges made in federal district courts (see Scalia, 2000). Before *Bailey*, for example, if a drug dealer had a pistol under his or her car seat, federal prosecutors would charge the individual not only with drug dealing but also with using a weapon in the commission of a crime; the additional weapons charge added significant prison time if the individual was convicted on the drug charge. However, if the drug dealer is already a convicted felon, then an illegal firearm possession charge can of course still be made.

A second setback came at the end of 2004, when Congress cut $45 million that was directly earmarked to fund gun prosecutions from the proposed budget for Project Safe Neighborhoods. Another $106 million was cut from the budget that would have funded an ATF program meant to track and intercept illegal purchases of guns by youths. Many gun control advocates and law enforcement officials felt that these cutbacks sent "a troubling message about the federal commitment of fighting gun crime and trafficking" (Lichtblau, 2004, 32).

However, both setbacks were temporary. In the case of *Bailey v. United States*, federal prosecutors temporarily began channeling many of the weapons-possession cases for first-time drug and violent-crime offenders to state court systems (where many were prosecuted for violation of particular state-level firearms laws); and in 1998, Congress enacted the "Bailey Fix," amending federal legislation such that the "mere possession of a gun during a crime of violence or drug-trafficking would allow for an additional charge and for enhanced sentencing" (Maddan, 2012, 693–694). Moreover, even though the two years immediately following the Bailey decision (1996–1997) saw consecutive decreases in the number of federal firearms cases brought to U.S. District Courts (bottoming out at 3,162), by 1998 the number climbed back to pre-*Bailey* levels and has maintained healthy numbers ever since (with a current average of approximately 8,000 cases per year; see Maddan, 2012; Maguire and Pastore, 2004, Table 5.10, 405; United States Sentencing Commission, 2015). The resurgence in cases was due largely to the increasing number of urban areas adopting Project Triggerlock-type programs. As of 2016, it appears that improved cooperation among federal, state, and local officials is capable of overcoming losses of direct funding for gun prosecutions and gun trafficking control—as the general funding for the ATF and for the Violent Gang and Gun Crime Reduction Program (the new name for Project Safe Neighborhoods) has remained intact (U.S. Department of Justice, 2016f).

Gun Courts

A variant of Project Triggerlock-type programs are local area *gun courts.* The first to appear in the modern era was in Providence, Rhode Island, in September 1994. The court put gun-related prosecutions on the fast track. Before its creation, the average time for the disposition of a gun case—through a plea bargain or the start of a trial—was 518 days, with a conviction rate of 67 percent. After the special court was created, the maximum time for the disposition of a gun case fell to 126 days, while the conviction rate rose to 87 percent (see U.S. Department of Justice, 1999, Profile No. 37, 144). The speed of disposition and increased probability of conviction experienced in Providence encouraged many other jurisdictions to create gun courts, among the most notable are those in Birmingham, Detroit, Indianapolis, Minneapolis, New York City, Philadelphia, Seattle, and Washington, D.C. The motivating idea of courts specializing in gun cases is that "the judicial system can play an important role in reducing firearms offenses through speedier dispositions, mandatory sentences, and [in some cases] intensive service delivery" (Sheppard and Kelly, 2002). When gun cases get mixed into the mélange of cases that are part of everyday local area courts, overworked and "impatient judges frequently give defendants mild or probationary sentences in exchange for a waiver of their right to a lengthy jury trial. Channeling the cases to a gun court [ensures] that gun crimes are not ignored or reclassified at the demand of a public defender who threatens the judge with a jury trial" (Weyrich, 2000). Gun courts are the offspring of the drug court movement of the early 1990s, which were based on the same underlying reasoning regarding combating the illegal drug problem.

A variant within the gun court movement is the *juvenile* gun court. Because so much gun violence is perpetrated by young offenders, and because societal norms hold that we should try to save such offenders from a lifetime of crime and its consequences (injury, death, prison), gun courts specializing in juveniles began to appear in the mid-1990s. In contrast to their adult counterparts, juvenile gun courts typically use a carrot-and-a-stick approach. The best known is Jefferson County's Juvenile Gun Court in Birmingham, Alabama. Established in the spring of 1995, its core features were swift action (either a guilty plea or the start of a trial within 10 working days); a 28-day boot camp alternative for offenders considered at low risk for violence; a parent education program; a substance abuse program; community service; and a high level of supervision after release from boot camp or the state detention facility. According to the Alabama Department of Youth Services, the military-style boot camp aims "to develop and enhance positive behavior characteristics in delinquent youth through counseling, and includes self-concept development, academics, and physical fitness in a highly structured, intensive program" (as quoted in Sheppard and Kelly, 2002). The parent education program brings parents together with judicial officials, mental health counselors, and family specialists for 15 hours of class work spread over a period of 10 weeks. The emphases include the costs of gun violence to victims, offenders, and families, and instruction on improving parent-youth communication skills. The program is mandatory, and parents are threatened with jail time if they do not comply. Community service includes neighborhood cleanup and graffiti removal while under close supervision of the local police. Community service is part of an intensive post-release program that includes an 8:00 p.m. curfew (8:30 on weekends), home visits by the police and the juvenile's probation officer, intermittent drug testing, and the completion of a six-week substance abuse and anger management course.

Gun courts are clearly a success when measured by speed of disposition, conviction rates, and severity of sentences. On these measures, other gun courts have found success similar to Providence's. For example, within its first eight months New York City's Brooklyn gun court tripled its jail sentences from 14 to 44 percent, increased the average sentence from 90 days to one year, and eliminated probation-only sentences for felony offenders (the court eventually became overloaded with a backlog of cases and was suspended in 2009; however, in 2016, it was replaced by *two* new gun courts; see Ax, 2016). A similar success story unfolded in Philadelphia, where guilty pleas rose from 61–65 percent of gun law violators in the four years before the gun court started in 2005 to 78 percent after the gun court's first full year of operation (Kurtz et al., 2007, 3). Moreover, because this particular gun court was restricted to nonviolent firearms-related crime (mainly, illegal possession) and thus the expectation was that many of those convicted or pleading guilty would receive probation, it was given extra resources to handle those cases in which the convicted were actually given probation. These resources included a smaller caseload for each probation officer, allowing for increased contact with each probationer and increased drug testing. As a result, gun court probationers were better behaved: 12 percent of gun court probationers were arrested during their first year on probation versus 20 percent of those convicted of a gun crime before the creation of the special court; moreover, none of those rearrested that were part of the gun court program were arrested for a gun crime, while this did occur for the pre–gun court comparison group (Kurtz et al., 2007, 5).

Despite all of the above being taken into account, regarding the real aim of virtually all gun control measures, little systematic research has been done to see if gun courts actually reduce rates of violence in the wider community. As of 2016, the two best empirical studies on this issue were a time-series quantitative analysis of violent crime rates before and after the creation of the Philadelphia gun court and a focused case study on Birmingham's Jefferson County Youth Gun Court. In the quantitative study, Nobles (2008, 9–10) found that there were "no statistically significant declines in the aggregate rates of four gun-related crime categories in Philadelphia in the 24 months after the introduction of the court program." In the case study, University of Alabama researchers compared a group of Birmingham youth who had been processed through the Youth Gun Court with two other groups over a four-year period (1995–1999): a group of Birmingham youths who served time at the state detention center and were not processed through the gun court and its programs, but who received limited post-release supervision; and a group of youths who were processed through the juvenile court system of the nearby community of Bessemer, which did not include post-release supervision. On the positive side, the group that had gone through gun court had the lowest recidivism rate (17%), compared with 37 percent for the other Birmingham youths and 40 percent for the Bessemer youths. On the other hand, even though violent crime in Birmingham dropped dramatically during the four-year period, by 57 percent, it had a comparable drop in Bessemer (54%). The National Research Council (2005, 221) has concluded that there is too little research on gun courts to assess their crime-prevention effectiveness. The U.S. Department of Justice is more optimistic, however, and recommends that gun courts should be part of more comprehensive crime-fighting plans, which is how they are viewed by law enforcement and other public officials in all communities where they currently exist (see Sheppard and Kelly, 2002; U.S. Department of Justice, 2016g).

The Lawsuit Approach

Frustration with the lack of progress of the public health and law enforcement approaches to controlling gun violence once led many gun control advocates to place their hope with the judicial system—using it to sue manufacturers, wholesalers, retailers, and gun owners in civil courts. Five types of lawsuits were often filed before 2006: product liability suits against manufacturers for having produced and sold defective guns; suits against dealers for negligent sales to persons prohibited from possessing guns; suits against gun manufacturers for intentional shootings; suits against individuals when their guns have been used in either intentional or unintentional shootings; and litigation initiated by cities and states against manufacturers and distributors to recover costs associated with gun violence, including for health care and police services (see Coalition to Stop Gun Violence, 2016; Denning, 2002; Educational Fund to Stop Gun Violence, 2013; Legal Action Project, 2003, 2016; National Rifle Association, 2016i; and Seibel, 2005). The primary aim of all of these lawsuits has been—and though much fewer in number today, still is—to reduce gun-related crime, suicide, and accidents by reducing the overall number of firearms afloat in society; the number of firearms that fall into the hands of high-risk individuals (criminals; juveniles; the mentally ill, or incompetent); and the number of firearms that lack modern safety features (e.g., trigger locks; magazine disconnect safeties). A secondary aim has been to recover monetary compensation for the victims of gun violence, both at the individual and community levels. A cascade of these lawsuits began in the mid-1990s, and continued until 2005. Many received strong support from various gun control organizations, who provided both lawyers and funding. Two of the best-known groups were the Legal Action Project of the Brady Center to Prevent Gun Violence (Legal Action Project, 2016) and the Educational Fund to Stop Gun Violence (2013, 2016). Most of the lawsuits got caught up in multiple appeals of lower-court decisions, and most have taken, or are still taking, years to unfold to their final conclusions. The overall desired effects of the suits—at least from the viewpoint of gun control proponents—has been modest, at best, with many, but not all, lower court decisions eventually being overturned (Henigan, 2012a; National Rifle Association, 2016i). And beginning in 2006, filings of these suits reduced dramatically, as in the fall of 2005 Congress passed the Protection of Lawful Commerce in Arms Act. The act prohibits new "civil liability actions" against manufacturers, distributors, dealers, and importers of firearms or ammunition products, and their trade associations, for any harm caused by the criminal or unlawful misuse of firearms or ammunition. (Note, however, that the act does not exempt those in the gun industry breaking the law or selling defective weapons or ammunition, with a few successful lawsuits being made on these grounds; for details, see Henigan, 2012b; National Rifle Association, 2016i.)

Gun rights advocates contend that the use of civil lawsuits to control firearms and the violence associated with them is illegitimate and lacking in legal merit. Rather, they see the problems of firearms violence as resting with the criminals who misuse guns and with the carelessness of particular individuals who become involved in accidental shootings. Moreover, they believe that individuals, organizations, and communities that have filed these lawsuits ignore the "positive consequences" of guns, that is, their defensive use, which can prevent "many violent, predatory criminals from committing future crimes" (Izumi, 1999). Finally, they believe the relatively few lawsuits against the gun industry that have been won, and the even fewer that have been successful in the appeals process, supports their viewpoint. In sum, the "courts should not use the judiciary to effectuate gun control reform. This function is better served by Congress or state legislatures" (Bonney, 2000, 202). This particular line of reasoning ignores, however, that the most notable lawsuit victories, at least prior to 2006, have occurred as out-of-court agreements. Examples are the $2.5 million settlement against gun retailer Bulls Eye and gun manufacturer Bushmaster in 2004 for their responsibility in the 2002 Washington, D.C., sniper shootings; and the $1 million settlement against a West Virginia pawnbroker for selling 12 handguns to an obvious straw purchaser (one of the guns was eventually used to shoot two New Jersey police officers; see Butterfield, 2004; Henigan, 2012c).

Product Liability and Other Legal Theories Used in Gun Lawsuits

Observing the success of product liability suits in the 1980s and early 1990s against the tobacco industry, many victims of gun violence began similar actions against the gun industry. The initial success against tobacco was not winning the suits (even though the tobacco companies eventually lost; see Wilson, 1999). Indeed, early on the plaintiffs had generally lost or had positive judgments set aside. Instead, success was seen as the growing public awareness of the health problems associated with tobacco products. Similarly, the success of gun-related lawsuits has largely been in the area of increasing public awareness of the careless business practices of the gun industry that have allowed hundreds of thousands of firearms to find their way into the hands of felons and teenagers. Success has also been reflected in greater public awareness of the health-related and other costs of the gun violence to society. In a relatively small number of cases, the suits have actually motivated changes in the manufacture of guns to improve their safety, and the way in which gun dealers do business (e.g., training employees to recognize straw purchasers). They have also produced a handful of out-of-court financial settlements for the victims of gun violence.

As Kopel (2012b, 685) observes, "Lawsuits involving manufacturing defects are uncontroversial." For example, a gun is considered defective if it fires when dropped or when the safety is on. In 1979, the Alaskan Supreme Court upheld damages to a plaintiff who had sued gun manufacturer Sturm, Ruger &

Company for its defective .41 caliber revolver. Hundreds of accidental discharges of this gun had been reported since 1953, and the court held that the "manufacturer knew that its product was defectively designed and that injuries and deaths had resulted from the design defect, but continued to market the product in reckless disregard of the public's safety" (*Sturm, Ruger & Co., Inc. v. Day*, as quoted in Violence Policy Center, 2005). Many other "manufacturing-defect lawsuits have resulted in many victories by plaintiffs, leading manufacturers of substandard guns (particularly cheap European imports) to improve their guns" or pull them off the market (Kopel, 2012b, 688; note that when Congress created the Consumer Product Safety Commission in 1972, it specifically exempted domestically manufactured guns from any consumer safety standards).

The controversy between gun control and gun rights advocates arises when other legal theories are invoked. These include (a) *specific design-defects* suits going beyond shoddy safeties and firing pins, for example, the lack of indicators that let the handler know whether a gun is loaded, trigger locks, and magazine safeties (making the gun incapable of firing a bullet left in the chamber after the ammunition holder is removed); (b) *general design-defect* suits holding that a particular gun (usually a handgun) "is by its very nature defective" because it is ultra-hazardous—readily causing injury and death—and these hazards outweigh any sporting or other benefits the gun might have (Kopel, 2012b, 686); (c) *negligent marketing*, for example, wholesalers selling their weapons to gun show vendors instead of strictly to dealers doing business in the normal way, that is, from retail stores; and (d) *public nuisance* suits, which have been the basis for many of the actions that various cities have brought to court to recover losses associated with gun violence—for example, those related to their burdens on local health care and law enforcement systems; the usual contention is that manufacturers have created a public nuisance by flooding the community with guns and that local and state gun control does not work because dealers can readily cross into and then return from nearby states where gun laws are lax.

Immunity Legislation

In response to the large number of litigations and the possibilities of losing billions of dollars in settlements, the tobacco industry sought, unsuccessfully, to have Congress grant tobacco companies immunity from liability lawsuits. Similarly, in the late 1990s and early 2000s, major legislation was proposed and debated each year in Congress intended to provide the gun industry similar immunity. The legislation was regularly defeated until the fall of 2005, when the U.S. Congress passed the Protection of Lawful Commerce in Arms Act barring any future lawsuits against firearm and ammunition manufacturers and dealers for any harm caused by the criminal misuse of a gun.

Before the Protection of Lawful Commerce in Arms Act was passed, 34 U.S. states had already enacted legislation preventing counties and local communities from filing public nuisance and design-defect lawsuits against gun manufacturers and their distributors. As with the spate of "shall-issue" (right-to-carry) and preemption laws—preventing local communities from passing firearms laws stricter than those of the state—that were passed in 1990s, the firearm industry immunity laws have represented major victories for gun rights advocates. As a critical arm of the gun rights movement, the gun industry is now enjoying special protection, a protection that has greatly reduced, but not completely eliminated, lawsuits against it (notable exceptions include *Carter v. Forjas Taurus S.A.*, *Kunisch & Norberg v. Badger Guns*, *Miller v. Beemiller*, and *Shirley v. Glass*; see Brady Center to Prevent Gun Violence, 2016a, 2016b; National Rifle Association, 2016i).

Conclusion

Gun control laws cannot prevent many acts of firearm violence. Both sides of the contemporary gun debate agree with this observation. Both sides also agree that the strict enforcement of current gun laws can only help to reduce the violence. The two sides quickly part ways, however, when addressing whether increasing the strength of gun control regulations at the national level: (a) would reduce the overall level of firearm violence; and (b) could be done in such a way as to preserve the letter and the spirit of the Second Amendment. Gun rights advocates say "no" on both counts. They heavily root their response in the data presented in Figures 1.7 and 1.9a. That is, despite the huge increase in the number of firearms in the United States over the past three decades, and despite during the same time frame that most states enacted legislation allowing ordinary citizens to carry concealed handguns (with over 13 million have taken advantage of this legislation), criminal gun violence has dropped significantly; indeed, the strongest of these advocates would replace the word "despite" with the words "because of." Overall, gun rights advocates contend that new and stricter gun regulations would pose needless burdens on law-abiding gun owners, and, moreover, be fruitless in achieving the goal of reducing gun violence.

Gun control advocates retort with the data presented in Figure 1.3: even though the rate of gun homicide is down in recent decades, the rate of gun suicide is up and thus the total number of gun-related deaths has not gone down. Further, they point to Figure 1.9b, which shows the dramatic rise of active-shooter mass-shootings. They also point to Figure 1.5, as well as to many of the analyses in this chapter, showing that those states with the strongest gun control laws have the lowest rates of gun violence. Finally, they observe that strict gun control laws, both old and new, have overwhelmingly been upheld by the federal court systems both before and *since* the momentous 2008 *District of Columbia v. Heller* decision, in which the U.S. Supreme Court held that the Second Amendment guarantees law-abiding Americans the individual right to own firearms, including handguns.

References

Amtrak. 2016. *Firearms in Checked Baggage.* https://www .amtrak.com/firearms-in-checked-baggage (accessed June 19, 2016).

Anestis, Michael D., et al. 2015. "The Association between State Laws Regulating Handgun Ownership and Statewide Suicide Rates." *American Journal of Public Health* 10: 2059–2067.

Ax, Joseph. 2016. "New York Creates 'Gun Courts' in Hopes of Reducing Gun Violence." *Reuters*, January 12. http://www.reuters.com/article/new-york-guns-id USL2N14W1L220160112 (accessed June 30, 2016).

Ayres, Ian, and John D. Donohue III. 2003. "Shooting Down the More Guns, Less Crime Hypothesis." *Stanford Law Review* 55: 1193–1312.

Azrael, Deborah, et al. 2003. "Data on Violent Injury." In *Evaluating Gun Policy: Effects on Crime and Violence*, ed. Jens Ludwig and Philip J. Cook, 412–430. Washington, DC: Brookings Institution Press.

Baldwin, Chuck. 2002. "Ballistic Fingerprinting Is a Bad Idea." *Chuck Baldwin Live*, October 31. http:// chuckbaldwinlive.com/Articles/tabid/109/ID/895/ Ballistic-Fingerprinting-Is-A-Bad-Idea.aspx (accessed June 22, 2016).

Barber, Catherine, and David Hemenway. 2011. "Too Many or Too Few Unintentional Firearm Deaths in Official U.S. Mortality Data?" *Accident Analysis and Prevention* 43: 724–731.

Barry, Colleen L., et al. 2015. "Two Years after Newtown— Public Opinion on Gun Policy Revisited." *Preventive Medicine* 79: 55–58.

Beckett, Lois. 2016. "Pulse Nightclub Attack Renews AR-15 Rifle Debate: Would a Ban Make a Difference?"

The Guardian, June 13. https://www.theguardian.com/
us-news/2016/jun/13/ar-15-rifles-assault-weapons-ban-
orlando-shooting (accessed June 21, 2016).

Bonney, Shaun R. 2000. "Using the Courts to Target Firearm
Manufacturers." *Idaho Law Review* 378: 167–202.

Bossarte, R. M., T. R. Simon, and L. Barker. 2006.
"Characteristics of Homicide Followed by Suicide Incidents
in Multiple States, 2003–2004." *Injury Prevention*:
12(Supplement II): ii33–ii38. http://www.ncbi.nlm.nih
.gov/pmc/articles/PMC2563486/pdf/ii33.pdf (accessed
June 3, 2016).

Boston Strategy to Prevent Youth Violence. 2016. *The Boston
Strategy to Prevent Youth Violence: The Programs.* http://
www.sasnet.com/bostonstrategy/programs/03_BPIC.html
(accessed June 30, 2016).

Brady Campaign to Prevent Gun Violence. 2014. "Brady
Campaign Releases a Report Analyzing 20 years of
Effective Background Checks." http://www.bradycam
paign.org/inthenews/brady-campaign-releases-a-report-
analyzing-20-years-of-effective-background-checks
(accessed June 27, 2016).

Brady Center to Prevent Gun Violence. 2004. On *Target:
The Impact of the 1994 Federal Assault Weapons Act.*
Washington, DC: Brady Center to Prevent Gun Violence.
http://www.bradycampaign.org/sites/default/files/on_
target.pdf (accessed June 21, 2016).

Brady Center to Prevent Gun Violence. 2016a. *Shirley v. Glass.*
http://www.bradycampaign.org/content/shirley-v-glass
(accessed July 1, 2016).

Brady Center to Prevent Gun Violence. 2016b. *Williams v.
Beemiller.* http://www.bradycampaign.org/content/
williams-v-beemiller (accessed July 1, 2016).

Braga, Anthony A., et al. 2001. "Problem-Oriented Policing,
Deterrence, and Youth Violence: An Evaluation of Boston's

Operation Ceasefire." *Journal of Research in Crime and Delinquency* 38: 195–225.

Braga, Anthony A., and Glenn L. Pierce. 2004. "Linking Crime Guns: The Impact of Ballistics Imaging Technology on the Productivity of the Boston Police Department's Ballistics Unit." *Journal of Forensic Sciences* 49: 1–6.

Buffalo News. 2005. *Gun by Gun: Five Years of Damage Done by Weapons James Nigel Bostic Bought from Ohio Gun Dealers*. June 12. http://www.buffalonews.com/gun_by_gun__five_years_of_damage_done_by_weapons_james_nigel_bostic_bought_from_ohio_gun_dealers.html (accessed June 26, 2016).

Bureau of Alcohol, Tobacco, Firearms and Explosives. 1999. *Gun Shows: Brady Checks and Crime Traces*. https://www.atf.gov/file/57506/download (accessed June 25, 2016).

Bureau of Alcohol, Tobacco, Firearms and Explosives. 2000. *Commerce in Firearms in the United States*. http://permanent.access.gpo.gov/lps4006/020400report.pdf (accessed June 17, 2016).

Bureau of Alcohol, Tobacco, Firearms and Explosives. 2002. *Crime Gun Trace Reports (2000) National Report*. Washington, DC: Bureau of Alcohol, Tobacco and Firearms, Department of the Treasury.

Bureau of Alcohol, Tobacco, Firearms and Explosives. 2015. *Federal Firearms Regulations Reference Guide*. https://www.atf.gov/file/11241/download (accessed June 19, 2016).

Bureau of Alcohol, Tobacco, Firearms and Explosives. 2016a. *Annual Firearms Manufacturers and Export Report, 2014*. https://www.atf.gov/firearms/docs/afmer-2014-final-report-cover-revised-format-2-17-16/download (accessed June 21, 2016).

Bureau of Alcohol, Tobacco, Firearms and Explosives. 2016b. *Fact Sheet—National Integrated Ballistic Information*

Network. https://www.atf.gov/resource-center/fact-sheet/fact-sheet-national-integrated-ballistic-information-network (accessed June 23, 2016).

Bureau of Alcohol, Tobacco, Firearms and Explosives. 2016c. *NIBIN Success Stories.* https://www.atf.gov/firearms/success-stories (accessed June 22, 2016).

Bureau of Alcohol, Tobacco, Firearms and Explosives. 2016d. *Firearms Transaction Record Part I—Over the Counter: ATF Form 4473 (5300.9).* https://www.atf.gov/firearms/docs/4473-part-1-firearms-transaction-record-over-counter-atf-form-53009/download (accessed June 24, 2016).

Bureau of Justice Statistics. 2014. *Background Checks for Firearm Transfers, 2012—Statistical Tables.* http://www.bjs.gov/content/pub/pdf/bcft12st.pdf (accessed June 25, 2016).

Butterfield, Fox. 2004. "Gun Dealer Settles Case over Sale to Straw Buyer." *New York Times,* June 23. http://www.nytimes.com/2004/06/23/us/gun-dealer-settles-case-over-sale-to-straw-buyer.html?_r=0 (accessed June 30, 2016).

California Bureau of Firearms. 2016. *Roster of Handguns Certified for Sale.* http://certguns.doj.ca.gov/ (accessed June 16, 2016).

Campbell, Jacquelyn. C., et al. 2003. "Risk Factors for Femicide in Abusive Relationships: Results from a Multisite Case Control Study." *American Journal of Public Health* 93: 1089–1097.

Carnival Cruise Line. 2016. *Restricted Items List.* https://help.carnival.com/app/answers/detail/a_id/2261/~/restricted-items-list (accessed June 19, 2016).

Carter, Gregg Lee. 2006. *Gun Control in the United States: A Reference Handbook.* Santa Barbara, CA: ABC-CLIO.

CDC (Centers for Disease Control and Prevention). 2015. *National Violent Death Reporting System Web Coding Manual (Version 5.1).* Atlanta: National Center for Injury Prevention and Control. https://www.cdc.gov/

violenceprevention/pdf/nvdrs_web_codingmanual.pdf (accessed June 2, 2016).

CDC. 2016a. *The National Violent Death Reporting System (NVDRS): A Powerful Tool for Prevention.* Atlanta: National Center for Injury Prevention and Control. http://www.cdc .gov/violenceprevention/pdf/nvdrs_overview-a.pdf (accessed June 2, 2016).

CDC. 2016b. *National Violent Death Report System (NVDRS): Fact Sheet.* Atlanta: National Center for Injury Prevention and Control. http://www.cdc.gov/violenceprevention/pdf/ nvdrs_factsheet-a.pdf (accessed June 2, 2016).

CDC. 2016c. *Web-based Injury Statistics Query and Reporting System (WISQARS): National Violent Death Reporting System.* Atlanta: National Center for Injury Prevention and Control. https://wisqars.cdc.gov:8443/nvdrs/nvdrsDisplay.jsp (accessed June 6, 2016).

CDC. 2016d. *National Violent Death Reporting System: State Profiles.* Atlanta: National Center for Injury Prevention and Control. http://www.cdc.gov/violenceprevention/nvdrs/ stateprofiles.html (accessed June 2, 2016).

Center for Problem-Oriented Policing. 2003. *Gun Violence among Serious Young Offenders.* http://www.popcenter .org/problems/pdfs/GunViolenceFinal.pdf (accessed June 29, 2016).

City of New York. 2009. *Gun Show Undercover: Report on Illegal Sales at Gun Shows.* http://everytownresearch.org/ documents/2015/04/gun-show-undercover.pdf (accessed June 25, 2016).

City of New York. 2011. *Point, Click, Fire: An Investigation of Illegal Online Gun Sales.* http://everytownresearch .org/documents/2015/04/point-click-fire.pdf (accessed June 26, 2016).

Coalition to Stop Gun Violence. 2016. *Special Protection for the Gun Industry.* http://csgv.org/issues/special- protection-for-the-gun-industry/ (accessed June 30, 2016).

Congress.gov. 2016. *H.R.4269-Assault Weapons Ban of 2015.*
https://www.congress.gov/bill/114th-congress/house-
bill/4269/all-actions?overview=closed#tabs (accessed
June 20, 2016).

Creswell, Julie. 2016. "After Mass Shootings, Some on Wall
St. See Gold in Gun Makers." *New York Times*, January 6.
http://www.nytimes.com/2016/01/07/business/after-mass-
shootings-some-on-wall-st-cash-in-on-gun-shares.html?_
r=0 (accessed June 20, 2016).

Crockett, Zachary. 2016. "What Happens after a Mass
Shooting? Americans Buy More Guns." *Vox Media*,
June 15. http://www.vox.com/2016/6/15/11936494/
after-mass-shooting-americans-buy-more-guns (accessed
June 20, 2016).

Cummings, Peter, et al. 1997. "State Gun Safe Storage Laws
and Child Mortality due to Firearms." *Journal of
the American Medical Association* 278: 1084–1086.

DeBell, Matthew. 2012. "Magna-Trigger." In *Guns in
American Society: An Encyclopedia of History, Politics,
Culture, and the Law*, 2nd ed., Vol. 2, ed. Gregg Lee Carter,
531. Santa Barbara, CA: ABC-CLIO.

DeBrabander, Firmin. 2015. *Do Guns Make Us Free?
Democracy and the Armed Society*. New Haven, CT: Yale
University Press.

DeCarlo, Daniel C., and Lance A. Selfridge. 2015. *Brief of
Amici Curiae the National Shooting Sports Foundation,
Inc. and the Sporting Arms and Ammunition Manufacturers'
Institute, Inc. in Support of Reversal of the Judgment Below
[United States District Court for the Eastern District Of
California . . . Case No. 2:09-CV-01185]*. http://nssf.org/
share/pdf/NSSF_SAAMI_Amicus_Brief_07–27–15_11–2
.pdf (accessed June 23, 2016).

Denning, Brandon. 2002. "Firearms Litigation Clearing
House." In *Guns in American Society: An Encyclopedia of*

History, Politics, Culture, and the Law, Vol. 1, ed. Gregg Lee Carter, 209. Santa Barbara, CA: ABC-CLIO.

Dolins, Judith C., and Katherine K. Christoffel. 1994. "Reducing Violent Injuries: Priorities for Pediatrician Advocacy." *Pediatrics* 94: 638–651.

Domonoske, Camila. 2014. "NRA Retracts Statement Calling Open Carry Rallies 'Downright Weird'." NPR, June 4. http://www.npr.org/sections/thetwo-way/2014/06/04/318763239/nra-retracts-statement-calling-open-carry-rallies-downright-weird (accessed June 28, 2016).

Donohue, John J. 2003. "The Impact of Concealed-Carry Laws." In *Evaluating Gun Policy: Effects on Crime and Violence*, ed. Jens Ludwig and Philip J. Cook, 287–324. Washington, DC: Brookings Institution Press.

East, Rochelle C. 2013. *Information Bulletin: Certification of Microstamping Technology Bureau of Firearms Pursuant to Penal Code Section 31910, Subdivision (b)(7)(A)*. May 17. http://oag.ca.gov/sites/all/files/agweb/pdfs/firearms/infobuls/2013-BOF-03.pdf (accessed June 22, 2016).

Educational Fund to Stop Gun Violence. 2013. *Justice Denied: The Case against Gun Industry Immunity*. http://www.efsgv.org/wp-content/uploads/2013/11/Justice-Denied-Report-PDF.pdf (accessed June 30, 2016).

Educational Fund to Stop Gun Violence. 2016. *The Educational Fund to Stop Gun Violence*. http://efsgv.org/ (accessed June 30, 2016).

Everytown for Gun Safety. 2015. *Analysis of Recent Mass Shootings*. http://everytownresearch.org/documents/2015/09/analysis-mass-shootings.pdf (accessed June 20, 2016).

Fallis, David S., and James V. Grimaldi. 2011. "VA Data Show Drop in Criminal Firepower during Assault Gun Ban." *Washington Post*, January 23. http://www.washingtonpost.com/wp-dyn/content/article/2011/

01/22/AR2011012203452.html?sid=ST2010121406431
(accessed June 21, 2016).

Farago, Robert. 2011. "Giffords' Shooter Jared Loughner
Used a Glock 19." *The Truth about Guns*, January 8. http://
www.thetruthaboutguns.com/2011/01/robert-farago/
giffords-shooter-jared-loughner-used-a-glock-with-
extended-clip/ (accessed June 22, 2016).

FBI (Federal Bureau of Investigation). 2015. *Uniform Crime
Reports: Crime in the United States, 2014 (Expanded
Homicide Data—Table 8)*. https://www.fbi.gov/about-us/
cjis/ucr/crime-in-the-u.s/2014/crime-in-the-u.s.-2014/
tables/expanded-homicide-data/expanded_homicide_
data_table_8_murder_victims_by_weapon_2010–2014
.xls (accessed June 21, 2016).

FBI. 2016a. *National Instant Criminal Background Check
System: Fact Sheet*. https://www.fbi.gov/about-us/cjis/nics/
general-information/fact-sheet (accessed June 25, 2016).

FBI. 2016b. *CJIS Annual Report 2015*. https://www.fbi.gov/
about-us/cjis/annual-report-2015/2015_cjis_annual_
report.pdf/view (accessed June 25, 2016).

FBI. 2016c. *National Instant Criminal Background Check
System*. https://www.fbi.gov/about-us/cjis/nics/nics
(accessed June 25, 2016).

FBI. 2016d. *National Instant Criminal Background Check
System: Participation Map*. https://www.fbi.gov/about-us/
cjis/nics/general-information/participation-map (accessed
June 25, 2016).

FBI. 2016e. *NICS Firearm Background Checks: November 30,
1998–May 31, 2016*. https://www.fbi.gov/about-us/cjis/
nics/reports/nics_firearm_checks_-_month_year.pdf
(accessed June 25, 2016).

FBI. 2016f. *National Instant Criminal Background Check
System (NICS) Operations 2014*. https://www.fbi.gov/

about-us/cjis/nics/reports/2014-operations-report (accessed June 25, 2016).

FBI. 2016g. *Federal Denials: Reasons Why the NICS Section Denies (November 30, 1998–May 31, 2016).* https://www .fbi.gov/about-us/cjis/nics/reports/federal_denials.pdf (accessed June 25, 2016).

FBI. 2016h. *Violent Gang Task Forces (Safe Streets Violent Crime Initiative).* https://www.fbi.gov/about-us/investi gate/vc_majorthefts/gangs/violent-gangs-task-forces (access June 29, 2016).

Follman, Mark, and Gavin Aronsen. 2013. "'A Killing Machine': Half of All Mass Shooters Used High-Capacity Magazines." *Mother Jones*, January 30. http:// www.motherjones.com/politics/2013/01/high-capacity-magazines-mass-shootings (accessed June 20, 2016).

Follman, Mark, Gavin Aronsen, and Deanna Pan. 2016. "The Full Data Set from Our In-Depth Investigation into Mass Shootings, Plus Additional Cases form 2013–2016." *Mother Jones*, June 12. http://www.motherjones.com/ politics/2012/12/mass-shootings-mother-jones-full-data (accessed June 20, 2016).

Gatheridge, Brian J., et al. 2004. "Comparison of Two Programs to Teach Firearm Injury Prevention Skills to 6- and 7-Year-Old Children." *Pediatrics* 114: e294–e299.

George, Jason. 2005. "Buyback Nets 897 Firearms in Jersey City." *New York Times*, February 10: B-5.

Gostin, Lawrence O., and Katherine L. Record. 2011. "Dangerous People or Dangerous Weapons: Access to Firearms for Person with Mental Illness." *New England Journal of Medicine* 305: 2108–2109.

Greyhound. 2016. *Prohibited and Permitted Items on Board Greyhound Lines, Inc. Coaches.* https://www.greyhound.com/~/ media/greyhound/pdf/helpandinfo/110307policy prohibiteditemsupdated43015.pdf?la=en (accessed June 19, 2016).

Grossman, David C., Donald T. Reay, and Stephanie A. Baker. 1999. "Self-Inflicted and Unintentional Firearm Injuries among Children and Adolescents: The Source of the Firearm." *Archives of Pediatrics and Adolescent Medicine* 153: 875–878.

Grossman, David C., et al. 2005. "Gun Storage Practices and Risk of Youth Suicide and Unintentional Firearm Injuries." *Journal of the American Medical Association* 293: 707–714.

Hardy, Marjorie S. 2002. "Teaching Firearm Safety to Children: Failure of a Program." *Journal of Developmental and Behavioral Pediatrics* 23: 71–76.

Heinzmann, David. 2004. "Gangs Run Pipeline from Delta to Chicago." *Chicago Tribune*, April 2. http://www .chicagotribune.com/news/chi-0402050318feb05-story .html (accessed June 18, 2016).

Hemenway, David. 2004. *Private Guns, Public Health*. Ann Arbor: University of Michigan Press.

Hemenway, David. 2005. "Examples of New Insights Gained from 2001 NVISS Data from Connecticut, Maine, Utah, Wisconsin, Allegheny County, and San Francisco County." Personal communication, April 21.

Hemenway, David. 2012. "Motor Vehicle Laws as a Model for Gun Laws." In *Guns in American Society: An Encyclopedia of History, Politics, Culture, and the Law*, 2nd ed., Vol. 2, ed. Gregg Lee Carter, 591–593. Santa Barbara, CA: ABC-CLIO.

Hemenway, David, Catherine Barber, and Mathew Miller, 2010. "Unintentional Firearm Deaths: A Comparison of Other-Inflicted and Self-Inflicted Shootings." *Accident Analysis and Prevention*: 42: 1184–1188.

Hemenway, David, and Matthew Miller. 2013. "Public Health Approach to the Prevention of Gun Violence." *New England Journal of Medicine* 368: 2033–2035.

Hemenway, David, S. J. Solnick, and Deborah Azrael. 1995. "Firearm Training and Storage." *Journal of the American Medical Association* 272: 46–50.

Hemenway, David, and Mary Vriniotis. 2011. "The Australian Gun Buyback." *Bulletins* 4: 1–4. https://cdn1.sph.harvard .edu/wp-content/uploads/sites/1264/2013/01/bulletins_ australia_spring_2011.pdf (accessed June 22, 2016).

Henigan, Dennis A. 2012a. "Lawsuits against Gun Manufacturers." In *Guns in American Society: An Encyclopedia of History, Politics, Culture, and the Law*, 2nd ed., Vol. 2, ed. Gregg Lee Carter, 496–500. Santa Barbara, CA: ABC-CLIO.

Henigan, Dennis A. 2012b. "Protection of Lawful Commerce in Arms Act of 2005." In *Guns in American Society: An Encyclopedia of History, Politics, Culture, and the Law*, 2nd ed., Vol. 2, ed. Gregg Lee Carter, 694–696. Santa Barbara, CA: ABC-CLIO.

Henigan, Dennis A. 2012c. "Legal Action Project (LAP)." In *Guns in American Society: An Encyclopedia of History, Politics, Culture, and the Law*, 2nd ed., Vol. 2, ed. Gregg Lee Carter, 501–504. Santa Barbara, CA: ABC-CLIO.

Himle, Michael B., et al. 2004a. "An Evaluation of Two Procedures for Training Skills to Prevent Gun Play in Children." *Pediatrics* 113: 70–77.

Himle, Michael B., et al. 2004b. "Teaching Safety Skills to Children to Prevent Gun Play." *Journal of Applied Behavior Analysis* 37: 1–9.

Horn, Dan. 2013. "Gun Buybacks Popular But Ineffective, Experts Say." *USA Today*, January 13. http://www.usato day.com/story/news/nation/2013/01/12/gun-buybacks- popular-but-ineffective/1829165/ (accessed June 29, 2016).

Ingraham, Christopher. 2016. "Gun Sales Hit New Record Ahead of New Obama Gun Restrictions." *Washington Post*, January 5. https://www.washingtonpost.com/news/wonk/wp/2016/01/05/gun-sales-hit-new-record-ahead-of-new-obama-gun-restrictions/ (accessed June 20, 2016).

International Association of Chiefs of Police. 2008. *2008 Resolutions.* http://www.theiacp.org/Portals/0/documents/pdfs/Resolutions/2008Resolutions.pdf (accessed June 23, 2016).

International Association of Chiefs of Police. 2013. *Report of the 120th Annual IACP Conference.* http://www.policechiefmagazine.org/magazine/issues/122013/pdfs/Report_of_the_120th_Annual_IACP_Conference_Philadelphia.pdf (accessed June 23, 2016).

International Hunter Education Association. 2016. *Hunter Education Requirements: United States.* http://www.ihea.com/hunting-and-shooting/requirements/hunter-education-requirements (accessed June 24, 2016).

Isikoff, Michael. 2011. "Tucson Shooting with High-Capacity Magazines Reignites Gun Debate." *NBC News*, January 9. http://investigations.nbcnews.com/_news/2011/01/09/5801374-tucson-shooting-with-high-capacity-magazines-reignites-gun-debate (accessed June 21, 2016).

Izumi, Lance T. 1999. "Gun Lawsuits: Misfired Public Policy." *Capital Ideas* 4: 1–2. http://www.pacificresearch.org/article/gun-lawsuits-misfired-public-policy/ (accessed July 1, 2016).

Johnson, Sherri, Tracey Smith, and Trina Bogle Willard. 2001. *Evaluation of the Virginia Exile Program: Interim Report.* Richmond, VA: Criminal Justice Research Center, Department of Criminal Justice Services. https://www.dcjs.virginia.gov/research/documents/exileEvaluation2001.pdf (accessed July 1, 2016).

Kaleson, Bindu, et al. 2016. "Firearm Legislation and Firearm Mortality in the USA: A Cross-Sectional, State-Level Study." *The Lancet*: March 10 (online). http://dx.doi.org/10.1016/S0140–6736(15)01026–0 (accessed March 18, 2016).

Karberg, Jennifer C., et al. 2016. *Background Checks for Firearm Transfers, 2013–14, Statistical Tables.* Washington, DC: Bureau of Justice Statistics. http://www.bjs.gov/content/pub/pdf/bcft1314st.pdf (accessed July 14, 2016).

Katz, Ira A. et al. 2012. "Suicide among Veterans in 16 States, 2005 to 2008: Comparisons between Utilizers and Nonutilizers of Veterans Health Administration (VHA) Services Based on Data from the National Death Index, the National Violent Death Reporting System, and VHA Administrative Records." *American Journal of Public Health* 102: S105–S110. http://www.ncbi.nlm.nih.gov/pmc/articles/PMC3496455/pdf/AJPH.2011.300503.pdf (accessed June 3, 2016).

Kessler, Jim, and Ed Hill. 2004. *Selling Crime: A Handful of Gun Stores Fuel Criminals—A Study of Gun Stores with Over 200 Crime Gun Traces (1996–2000).* Washington, DC: Americans for Gun Safety Foundation. http://content.thirdway.org/publications/11/AGS_Report_-_Selling_Crime_-_High_Crime_Gun_Stores_Fuel_Criminals.pdf (accessed June 17, 2016).

King, William, et al. 2013. *Opening the Black Box of NIBIN: A Descriptive Process and Outcome Evaluation of the Use of NIBIN and Its Effects on Criminal Investigations, Final Report.* Washington, DC: U.S. Department of Justice. https://www.ncjrs.gov/pdffiles1/nij/grants/243875.pdf (accessed June 22, 2016).

Kopel, David B. 2012a. "One-Gun-per-Month Laws." In *Guns in American Society: An Encyclopedia of History,*

Politics, Culture, and the Law, Vol. 2, ed. Gregg Lee Carter, 659–663. Santa Barbara, CA: ABC-CLIO.

Kopel, David B. 2012b. "Product Liability Lawsuits." In *Guns in American Society: An Encyclopedia of History, Politics, Culture, and the Law,* Vol. 2, ed. Gregg Lee Carter, 684–689. Santa Barbara, CA: ABC-CLIO.

Kopel, David B., and David I. Caplan. 2012. "Gun Registration." In *Guns in American Society: An Encyclopedia of History, Politics, Culture, and the Law,* 2nd ed., Vol. 2, ed. Gregg Lee Carter, 359–363. Santa Barbara, CA: ABC-CLIO.

Koper, Christopher S. 2004. *Updated Assessment of the Federal Assault Weapons Ban: Impacts on Gun Markets and Gun Violence, 1994–2003.* Philadelphia: Jerry Lee Center of Criminology, University of Pennsylvania.

Koper, Christopher S. 2007. *Crime Gun Risk Factors: Buyer, Seller, Firearm, and Transaction Characteristics Associated with Gun Trafficking and Criminal Gun Use.* Philadelphia: Jerry Lee Center of Criminology, University of Pennsylvania. https://www.ncjrs.gov/pdffiles1/nij/grants/221074.pdf (accessed June 21, 2016).

Kurtz, Ellen, et al. 2007. *Philadelphia's Gun Court: Process and Outcome Evaluation Executive Summary.* https://www.courts.phila.gov/pdf/criminal-reports/Gun-Court-Evaluation-report-executive-summary.pdf (accessed June 30, 2016).

Lansford, Tom. 2012. "Project Exile." In *Guns in American Society: An Encyclopedia of History, Politics, Culture, and the Law,* 2nd ed., Vol. 2, ed. Gregg Lee Carter, 689–690. Santa Barbara, CA: ABC-CLIO.

Law Center to Prevent Gun Violence. 2012. *Federal Law on Tiahrt Amendments.* http://smartgunlaws.org/federal-law-on-tiahrt-amendments/ (accessed June 16, 2016).

Law Center to Prevent Gun Violence. 2013a. *Child Access Prevention Policy Summary*. http://smartgunlaws.org/child-access-prevention-policy-summary/ (accessed June 7, 2016).

Law Center to Prevent Gun Violence. 2013b. *Design Safety Standards Policy Summary*. http://smartgun laws.org/gun-design-safety-standards-policy-summary /#footnote_23_5929 (accessed June 16, 2016).

Law Center to Prevent Gun Violence. 2013c. *Assault Weapons Policy Summary*. http://smartgunlaws.org/assault-weapons-policy-summary/#footnote_34_5773 (accessed June 21, 2016).

Law Center to Prevent Gun Violence. 2013d. *Large Capacity Ammunition Magazines Policy Summary*. http:// smartgunlaws.org/large-capacity-ammunition-magazines-policy-summary/ (accessed June 21, 2016).

Law Center to Prevent Gun Violence. 2015. *Safe Storage and Gun Locks Policy Summary*. http://smartgunlaws.org/safe-storage-gun-locks-policy-summary/ (accessed June 7, 2016).

Law Center to Prevent Gun Violence. 2016a. *Microstamping and Ballistic Identification in the District of Columbia*. http://smartgunlaws.org/microstampingballistic-identification-in-washington-d-c/ (accessed June 23, 2016).

Law Center to Prevent Gun Violence. 2016b. *Licensing of Owners and Purchasers*. http://smartgunlaws.org/gun-laws/policy-areas/gun-owner-responsibilities/licensing-of-owners-purchasers/ (accessed June 23, 2016).

Law Center to Prevent Gun Violence. 2016c. *Concealed Weapons Permitting*. http://smartgunlaws.org/gun-laws/policy-areas/firearms-in-public-places/concealed-weapons-permitting/ (accessed June 24, 2016).

Law Center to Prevent Gun Violence. 2016d. *Open Carrying.*
http://smartgunlaws.org/gun-laws/policy-areas/firearms-in-
public-places/open-carrying/ (accessed June 28, 2016).

Legal Action Project. 2003. *Smoking Guns: Exposing the Gun
Industry's Complicity in the Illegal Gun Market.* http://www
.bradycampaign.org/sites/default/files/smokingguns.pdf
(accessed June 30, 2016).

Legal Action Project. 2016. "The Legal Action Project:
Working to Reduce Gun Violence Victims through the
Courts." http://www.bradycampaign.org/legal-action-
project (accessed June 30, 2016).

Level 1 Firearms Safety and Training. 2016.
Semi-Automatic Pistol Components and Operations.
http://www.level1firearms.com/Education/Semi-
Automatic_Pistol_Components_and_Operations
.html (accessed June 23, 2016).

Lichtblau, Eric. 2004. "Key Antigun Program Loses
Direct Financing." *New York Times*, December 2. http://
www.nytimes.com/2004/12/02/politics/key-antigun-
program-loses-direct-financing.html?_r=0 (accessed
July 1, 2016).

Longley, Robert. 2001. "Fake IDs Foil Brady Check—
GAO." http://usgovinfo.about.com/library/weekly/
aa032801a.htm (accessed June 26, 2016).

Lott, John R., Jr., and John E. Whitley. 2002. "Safe Storage
Gun Laws: Accidental Deaths, Suicides, and Crime."
Journal of Law and Economics 44: 659–689.

Lott, John R., Jr., John E. Whitley, and Rebekah C. Riley.
2015. *Concealed Carry Permit Holders across the United
States.* http://papers.ssrn.com/sol3/papers.cfm?abstract_
id=2629704 (accessed July 15, 2016).

Luca, Michael, Deepak Malhotra, and Christopher Poliquin.
2016. *The Impact of Mass Shootings on Gun Policy.*

Cambridge, MA: Harvard Business School. Working Paper 16–126. http://www.hbs.edu/faculty/Publi cation%20Files/16–126_2f0bfe60-e0c7–4008–8783– 9a3853f94e68.pdf (accessed July 1, 2016).

Lunny, Lt. Ray. 2010. "Unloaded Open Carry." San Mateo, CA: San Mateo Sheriff's Office, January 14. http://www .calgunlaws.com/wp-content/uploads/2012/09/San- Mateo-County-Sheriffs-Office_Unloaded-Open-Carry .pdf (accessed June 28, 2016).

Luo, Michael, Mike McIntire, and Griff Palmer. 2013. "Seeking Gun or Selling One, Web Is a Land of Few Rules." *New York Times*, April 17. http://www.nytimes .com/2013/04/17/us/seeking-gun-or-selling-one-web-is- a-land-of-few-rules.html?pagewanted=all&_r=0 (accessed June 26, 2016).

Maddan, Sean. 2012. "Project Triggerlock." In *Guns in American Society: An Encyclopedia of History, Politics, Culture, and the Law*, 2nd ed., Vol. 1, ed. Gregg Lee Carter, 693–694. Santa Barbara, CA: ABC-CLIO.

Maguire, Kathleen, and Ann L. Pastore, eds. 2004. *Sourcebook of Criminal Justice Statistics 2002*. Washington, DC: U.S. Department of Justice.

Marinelli, Laura W., et al. 2013. "Hartford's Gun Buy-Back Program: Are We on Target?" *Connecticut Medicine* 77: 453–459.

Markoe, Lauren, and Aaron Gould Sheinin. 2004. "Ban on Buying More Than One Gun a Month Passes, Awaits Governor's OK." http://www.freerepublic.com/focus/ f-news/1136103/posts (accessed June 18, 2016).

Maryland State Police. 2004. *MD-IBIS Progress Report #2: Integrated Ballistics Identification System*. Pikesville, MD: Forensic Sciences Division, Maryland State Police.

Maryland State Police. 2014. *Maryland Shell-Casing Reference Database*. Pikesville, MD: Forensic Sciences Division, Maryland State Police. http://dlslibrary.state.md.us/publications/JCR/2014/2014_154.pdf (accessed June 22, 2016).

Mascia, Jennifer. 2015. "Only 7 Percent of Licensed Gun Dealers Were Inspected Last Year." *The Trace*, October 29. https://www.thetrace.org/2015/10/gun-store-atf-inspection/ (accessed July 14, 2016).

Mather, Kate. 2014. "Smith & Wesson Says It Won't Follow California 'Microstamping' Law." *Los Angeles Times*, January 23. http://www.latimes.com/local/lanow/la-me-ln-smith-wesson-microstamping-law-20140123-story.html#axzz2rLgnuhU8 (accessed July 15, 2016).

Mayors against Illegal Guns. 2010. *Trace the Guns: The Link between Gun Laws and Interstate Gun Trafficking*. http://tracetheguns.org/report.pdf (accessed June 17, 2016).

Mayors against Illegal Guns. 2013. *Felon Seeks Firearm, No Strings Attached*. http://www.nyc.gov/html/om/pdf/2013/felon_seeks_firearm.pdf (accessed June 17, 2016).

McDougal, Topher, et al. 2013. "Made in the U.S.A.: The Role of American Guns in Mexican Violence." *The Atlantic*, March 18. http://www.theatlantic.com/international/archive/2013/03/made-in-the-usa-the-role-of-american-guns-in-mexican-violence/274103/ (accessed June 18, 2016).

McGarrell, Edmund F., et al. 2013. *Promising Strategies for Violence Reduction: Lessons from Two Decades of Innovation: Project Safe Neighborhoods Case Study Report #13*. https://www.bja.gov/Publications/MSU_PromisingViolenceReductionInitiatives.pdf (accessed June 30, 2016).

Merrill, Vincent. C. 2002. *Gun-in-Home as a Risk Factor in Firearm-Related Mortality: A Historical Prospective Cohort*

Study of United States Deaths, 1993. PhD dissertation, University of California, Irvine.

Miller, Matthew, Deborah Azrael, and David Hemenway. 2013. "Firearms and Violent Death in the United States." In *Reducing Gun Violence in America: Informing Policy with Evidence and Analysis*, ed. Daniel W. Webster and Jon S. Vernick, 3–20. Baltimore: Johns Hopkins University Press.

Miller, Matthew, and David Hemenway. 1999. "The Relationship between Firearms and Suicide: A Review of the Literature." *Aggression and Violent Behavior* 4: 59–75.

National Research Council. 2005. *Firearms and Violence: A Critical Review.* Washington, DC: National Academies Press.

National Rifle Association. 1999. *The False Hope of Gun Turn-In Programs.* https://www.nraila.org/articles/19990909/the-false-hope-of-gun-turn-in-programs# (accessed June 29, 2016).

National Rifle Association. 2000. *Licensing and Registration and Licensing.* https://www.nraila.org/articles/20001007/licensing-and-registration (accessed June 23, 2016).

National Rifle Association. 2004a. *Good Riddance to the Clinton Gun Ban.* https://www.nraila.org/articles/20040522/good-riddance-to-the-clinton-gun-ban (accessed June 21, 2016).

National Rifle Association. 2004b. *Ballistic Fingerprinting Not Effective.* https://www.nraila.org/articles/20040604/ballistic-fingerprinting-not-effective (accessed June 22, 2016).

National Rifle Association. 2008a. *Why Microstamping and Bullet Serialization Won't Work.* https://www.nraila.org/articles/20080801/why-microstamping-and-bullet-serializat (June 23, 2016).

National Rifle Association. 2008b. *Firearm Safety Summary.* https://www.nraila.org/articles/20080923/firearm-safety-summary (accessed June 24, 2016).

National Rifle Association. 2012a. "Legislation to Repeal One-Gun-a-Month Signed into Law by Governor Bob McDonnell." https://www.nraila.org/articles/20120228/legislation-to-repeal-one-gun-a-month-signed (accessed June 18, 2016).

National Rifle Association. 2012b. *Right-to-Carry 2012.* https://www.nraila.org/articles/20120228/right-to-carry-2012 (accessed June 27, 2016).

National Rifle Association. 2013. *The Truth about "Internet" Gun Sales.* https://www.nraila.org/articles/20130111/the-truth-about-internet-gun-sales# (accessed June 26, 2016).

National Rifle Association. 2014. *Good Citizens and Good Neighbors: The Gun Owners' Role.* https://www.nraila.org/articles/20140530/good-citizens-and-good-neighbors-the-gun-owners-role (accessed June 28, 2016).

National Rifle Association. 2015a. *Microstamping and Ballistic Fingerprinting.* https://www.nraila.org/issues/micro-stamping-and-ballistic-fingerprinting/ (accessed June 23, 2016).

National Rifle Association. 2015b. *Mississippi Gun Turn-In Scrapped due to New NRA-Backed Law.* https://www.nraila.org/articles/20150612/mississippi-gun-turn-in-scrapped-due-to-new-nra-backed-law (accessed June 29, 2016).

National Rifle Association. 2016a. *"Assault Weapons' and "Large" Magazines.* https://www.nraila.org/issues/assault-weapons-and-semi-automatic-firearms/ (accessed June 21, 2016).

National Rifle Association. 2016b. *Registration and Licensing.* https://www.nraila.org/issues/registration-licensing/# (accessed June 23, 2016).

National Rifle Association. 2016c. *What "Strong Case" for Registration?* https://www.nraila.org/articles/20160603/what-strong-case-for-gun-registration (accessed June 23, 2016).

National Rifle Association. 2016d. *Eddie Eagle GunSafe® Program.* https://eddieeagle.nra.org/ (accessed June 24, 2016).

National Rifle Association. 2016e. *Firearms Training.* https://explore.nra.org/interests/firearms-training/ (accessed June 24, 2016.

National Rifle Association. 2016f. *Background Checks/NICS.* https://www.nraila.org/issues/background-checksnics/ (accessed June 25, 2016).

National Rifle Association. 2016g. *Gun Shows.* https://www.nraila.org/issues/gun-shows/ (accessed June 26, 2016).

National Rifle Association. 2016h. *Right-to-Carry Laws.* https://www.nraila.org/gun-laws/ (accessed June 27, 2016).

National Rifle Association. 2016i. *The Protection of Lawful Commerce in Arms Act: Facts and Policy.* https://www.nraila.org/articles/20160525/the-protection-of-lawful-commerce-in-arms-act-facts-and-policy-1 (accessed June 30, 2016).

National Shooting Sports Foundation. 2013a. *Another Ban on "High-Capacity" Magazines? The Evidence Shows It Would Not Reduce Crime Rates.* http://www.nssf.org/factsheets/PDF/HighCapMag.pdf (accessed June 21, 2016).

National Shooting Sports Foundation. 2013b. *Bullet Serialization.* https://www.nssf.org/factsheets/PDF/BulletSerialization.pdf (accessed June 22, 2016).

National Shooting Sports Foundation. 2016a. *"Don't Lie for the Other Guy": A National Campaign to Prevent the Illegal "Straw Purchase" of Firearms.* http://www.dontlie.org/ (accessed June 18, 2016).

National Shooting Sports Foundation. 2016b. *FixNICS.* http://www.fixnics.org/about.cfm (accessed July 14, 2016).

National Violence Prevention Network. 2016. *State by State.* http://www.preventviolence.net/statebystate/statebystate .html (accessed June 2, 2016).

Neate, Rupert. 2016. "US Gunmaker Shares Soar after Pulse Nightclub Massacre." *The Guardian,* June 13. https://www .theguardian.com/us-news/2016/jun/13/gun-company-stocks-rise-orlando-pulse-attack (accessed June 21, 2016).

Nobles, Matthew Robin. 2008. *Evaluating Philadelphia's Gun Court: Implications for Crime Reduction and Specialized Jurisprudence.* PhD dissertation, University of Florida. http://etd.fcla.edu/UF/UFE0022084/nobles_m.pdf (accessed July 15, 2016).

Palazzolo, Joe. 2016. "California Ruling Could Pave the Way for Smart-Gun Mandates." *Wall Street Journal,* May 12. http://www.wsj.com/articles/california-ruling-may-sup press-smart-gun-technology-1463096189 (June 23, 2016).

Parker, Sarah. 2011. *Small Arms Survey 2011, States of Security—Balancing Act: Regulation of Civilian Firearm Possession.* Geneva: Small Arms Survey, Graduate Institute of International and Development Studies. http://www .smallarmssurvey.org/fileadmin/docs/A-Yearbook/2011/en/ Small-Arms-Survey-2011-Chapter-09-EN.pdf (accessed June 10, 2016).

Pettersson, Edvard. 2015. "California Cartridge-Microstamp Law Upheld in Gun Group Loss." *Bloomberg,* Feb. 27. http://www.bloomberg.com/news/articles/2015–02–27/ california-gun-microstamping-law-is-upheld-by-federal-judge (accessed June 23, 2016).

Pierce, Glenn L., et al. 2004. "Characteristics and Dynamics of Illegal Firearms Markets: Implications for a Supply-Side Enforcement Strategy." *Justice Quarterly* 21: 391–422.

Pierce, Glenn L., Anthony A. Braga, and Garen J. Wintemute. 2015. "Impact of California Firearms Sales

Laws and Dealer Regulations on the Illegal Diversion of Guns." *Injury Prevention* 21: 179–184.

Pina, Tatina. 2004. "Toy Guns Target of 'Bashing' Event's Anti-Violence Message." *Providence Journal* (Blackstone Valley Edition), August 20: C-1.

Project ChildSafe. 2016a. *About Project ChildSafe*. http:// www.projectchildsafe.org/about (accessed June 10, 2016).

Project ChildSafe. 2016b. *Fact Sheet*. http://www .projectchildsafe.org/sites/default/files/Fact%20Sheet .pdf (accessed June 10, 2016).

Providence Police Department. 2015. *Department-Issued/ Authorized Weapons. Providence: Department of Public Safety*. http://www.providenceri.com/sites/default/files/ ppd-directives/310.01%20-%20Department-Issued%20 Authorized%20Weapons.pdf (accessed June 15, 2016).

Quealy, Kevin, and Tim Wallace. 2013. "Where 50,000 Guns Recovered in Chicago Came from . . . Close Ties to Mississippi." *New York Times*, January 29. http://www .nytimes.com/interactive/2013/01/29/us/where-50000- guns-in-chicago-came-from.html (accessed June 18, 2016).

Raphael, Steven, and Jens Ludwig. 2003. "Prison Enhancements: The Case of Project Exile." In *Evaluating Gun Policy: Effects on Crime and Violence*, ed. Jens Ludwig and Philip J. Cook, 251–286. Washington, DC: Brookings Institution Press.

Reedy, Darin C., and Christopher S. Koper. 2003. "Impact of Handgun Types on Gun Assault Outcomes: A Comparison of Gun Assaults Involving Semiautomatic Pistols and Revolvers." *Injury Prevention* 9: 151–155.

Roth, Jeffrey A., and Christopher S. Koper. 1999. *Impacts of the 1994 Assault Weapons Ban: 1994–96*. Washington,

DC: National Institute of Justice, U.S. Department of Justice. NCJ 173405 (March). https://www.ncjrs.gov/pdffiles1/173405.pdf (accessed June 21, 2016).

SAAMI (Sporting Arms and Ammunition Manufacturers' Institute). 2002. *Loaded Chamber Indicators, Magazine Disconnect Features: Background Paper #9.* Newtown, CT: SAAMI. http://www.saami.org/specifications_and_information/publications/download/SAAMI_ITEM_229-Owner_Recognition_Technology.pdf (accessed June 15, 2016).

Santaella-Tenorio, Julian, et al. 2016. "What Do We Know about the Association between Firearm Legislation and Firearm-Related Injuries." *Epidemiologic Reviews* 38: 140–157.

Saris, Patti B., et al. 2015. *Overview of Federal Criminal Cases Fiscal Year 2014.* http://www.ussc.gov/sites/default/files/pdf/research-and-publications/research-publications/2015/FY14_Overview_Federal_Criminal_Cases.pdf (accessed June 29, 2016).

Scalia, John. 2000. *Federal Firearm Offenders, 1992–1998.* Washington, DC: U.S. Department of Justice. NCJ 180795 (June).

Seibel, Brian. J. 2005. "Gun Industry Immunity: Why the Gun Industry's 'Dirty Little Secret' Does Not Deserve Congressional Protection." *University of Missouri—Kansas City Law Review* 73: 1–35. http://www.bradycampaign.org/sites/default/files/umkc-article.pdf (accessed June 30, 2016).

Sheppard, David, and Patricia Kelly. 2002. *Juvenile Gun Courts: Promoting Accountability and Providing Treatment.* Washington, DC: Office of Juvenile Justice and Delinquency Prevention, Office of Justice Programs, U.S. Department of Justice. https://www.ncjrs.gov/pdffiles1/ojjdp/187078.pdf (accessed July 1, 2016).

Smart Lock Technology. 2016. *Magloc® Smartgun System*: FAQ. http://www.smartlock.com/faq.htm (accessed June 15, 2016).

Snyder, Howard N. 2012. *Arrest in the United States, 1990–2010*. NCJ239423. Washington, DC: Bureau of Justice Statistics. http://www.bjs.gov/content/pub/pdf/aus9010.pdf (accessed June 29, 2016).

Southwick, Lawrence, Jr. 2012a. "Saturday Night Specials." In *Guns in American Society: An Encyclopedia of History, Politics, Culture, and the Law*, 2nd ed., Vol. 3, ed. Gregg Lee Carter, 727–731. Santa Barbara, CA: ABC-CLIO.

Southwick, Lawrence, Jr. 2012b. "Enforcement of Gun Control Laws." In *Guns in American Society: An Encyclopedia of History, Politics, Culture, and the Law*, 2nd ed., Vol. 1, ed. Gregg Lee Carter, 261–266. Santa Barbara, CA: ABC-CLIO.

Spitzer, Robert J. 2012a. "Assault Weapons." In *Guns in American Society: An Encyclopedia of History, Politics, Culture, and the Law*, 2nd ed., Vol. 1, ed. Gregg Lee Carter, 53–54. Santa Barbara, CA: ABC-CLIO.

Spitzer, Robert J. 2012b. "Licensing." In *Guns in American Society: An Encyclopedia of History, Politics, Culture, and the Law*, 2nd ed., Vol. 2, ed. Gregg Lee Carter, 514–515. Santa Barbara, CA: ABC-CLIO.

Stanford Geospatial Center. 2016. *Mass Shootings in America*. https://library.stanford.edu/projects/mass-shootings-america (accessed June 20, 2016).

Tarnhelm Supply Company. 2016. *The Magna-Trigger Conversion*. http://www.tarnhelm.com/magna-trigger/gun/safety/magna1.html (accessed June 15, 2016).

Transportation Security Administration. *Transporting Firearms and Ammunition*. https://www.tsa.gov/travel/

transporting-firearms-and-ammunition (accessed June 19, 2016).

United Nations. 1999. *United Nations International Study on Firearm Regulation.* Vienna, Austria: Crime Prevention and Criminal Justice Division, United Nations Office.

U.S. Department of Justice. 1999. *Promising Strategies to Reduce Gun Violence.* Washington, DC: U.S. Department of Justice, NCJ 173950. http://www.ojjdp.gov/pubs/gun_violence/173950.pdf (accessed June 29, 2016).

U.S. Department of Justice. 2007. *The Bureau of Alcohol, Tobacco, Firearms and Explosives' Investigative Operations at Gun Shows.* https://oig.justice.gov/reports/ATF/e0707/final.pdf (accessed June 25, 2016).

U.S. Department of Justice. 2011. *Review of ATF's Project Gunrunner.* Washington, DC: Office of the Inspector General, Evaluation and Inspections Division, U.S. Department of Justice. https://oig.justice.gov/reports/ATF/e1101.pdf (accessed June 18, 2016).

U.S. Department of Justice. 2016a. *Report to the President Outlining a Strategy to Expedite Deployment of Gun Safety Technology.* Washington, DC: Departments of Justice, Homeland Security, and Defense. https://www.whitehouse.gov/sites/default/files/docs/final_report-smart_gun_report.pdf (accessed June 15, 2016).

U.S. Department of Justice. 2016b. *Project Safe Neighborhoods (PSN): Overview.* Washington, DC: Bureau of Justice Assistance. https://www.bja.gov/programdetails.aspx?program_id=74 (accessed June 29, 2016).

U.S. Department of Justice. 2016c. *Project Safe Neighborhoods (PSN): Public Service Announcements—Print.* Washington, DC: Bureau of Justice Assistance. https://www.bja.gov/Programs/PSN/psa/national/print.html (accessed June 30, 2016).

U.S. Department of Justice. 2016d. *Project Safe Neighborhoods (PSN): Public Service Announcements— Television*. Washington, DC: Bureau of Justice Assistance. https://www.bja.gov/Programs/PSN/psa/national/tv.html (accessed June 30, 2016).

U.S. Department of Justice. 2016e. *Project Safe Neighborhoods (PSN): Public Service Announcements—Radio*. Washington, DC: Bureau of Justice Assistance. https://www.bja.gov/ Programs/PSN/psa/national/radio.html (accessed June 30, 2016).

U.S. Department of Justice. 2016f. *Violent Gang and Gun Crime Reduction Program (Formerly Project Safe Neighborhood "PSN" Initiatives)*. http://ojp.gov/about/ pdfs/BJA_Violent%20Gang%20&%20Gun%20Crime% 20(Formerly%20PSN)%20Prog%20Summary_For% 20FY%2017%20PresBud.pdf (accessed June 30, 2016).

U.S. Department of Justice. 2016g. *OJJDP Model Programs Guide: Gun Courts*. http://www.ojjdp.gov/mpg/Resource/ LitReviews (accessed June 30, 2016).

U.S. General Accounting Office. 1991. *Accidental Shootings: Many Deaths and Injuries by Firearms Cause by Firearms Could Be Prevented*. Washington, DC: U.S. General Accounting Office. http://www.gao.gov/assets/160/150 353.pdf (accessed July 1, 2016).

United States Sentencing Commission. 2015. *U.S. Sentencing Commission's 2015 Sourcebook of Federal Sentencing Statistics*. http://www.ussc.gov/research/sourcebook-2015 (accessed June 29, 2016).

Vernick, Jon S., et al. 1999. "'I Didn't Know the Gun Was Loaded': An Examination of Two Safety Devices That Can Reduce the Risk of Unintentional Firearm Injuries." *Journal of Public Health Policy* 20: 427–440.

Vernick J. S., et al. 2003. "Unintentional and Undetermined Firearm Related Deaths: A Preventable Death Analysis for Three Safety Devices." *Injury Prevention* 9: 307–311. http://injuryprevention.bmj.com/content/9/4/307.full .pdf+html (accessed June 15, 2016).

Violence Policy Center. 2004. *United States of Assault Weapons: Gunmakers Evading the Federal Assault Weapons Ban.* http://www.vpc.org/graphics/USofAW.pdf (accessed June 21, 2016).

Violence Policy Center. 2005. *The Endgame: Any Settlement of Firearms Litigation Must Address Three Specific Areas of Gun Industry Conduct and Include a Strict Enforcement Mechanism.* http://www.vpc.org/studies/endprod.htm (accessed June 30, 2016).

Vossekuil, Bryan, et al. 2004. *The Final Report & Findings of the Safe School Initiative—Implications for the Prevention of School Attacks in the United States.* Washington, DC: U.S. Department of Education. https://www2.ed.gov/admins/ lead/safety/preventingattacksreport.pdf (accessed June 8, 2016).

Webster, Daniel W. 2002. *Comprehensive Ballistic Fingerprinting of New Guns: A Tool for Solving and Preventing Violent Crime.* Baltimore, MD: Center for Gun Policy and Research, Bloomberg School of Public Health, Johns Hopkins University.

Webster, Daniel W., and Walter F. Carroll. 2012. "Child Access Prevention (CAP) Laws." In *Guns in American Society: An Encyclopedia of History, Politics, Culture, and the Law*, 2nd ed., Vol. 1, ed. Gregg Lee Carter, 150–511. Santa Barbara, CA: ABC-CLIO.

Webster, Daniel W., Jon S. Vernick, and Maria T. Bulzacchelli. 2009. "Effects of State-Level Firearm Seller Accountability Policies on Firearm Trafficking." *Journal of Urban Health* 86: 525–537.

Webster, Daniel W., Jon S. Vernick, and L. M. Hepburn. 2001. "Relationship between Licensing, Registration, and Other Gun Sales Laws and the Source State of Crime Guns." *Injury Prevention* 7: 184–189.

Webster, Daniel W., Jon S. Vernick, and L. M. Hepburn. 2002. "Effects of Maryland's Law Banning Saturday Night Special Handguns on Homicides." *American Journal of Epidemiology* 155: 406–412.

Webster, Daniel W., et al. 2004. "Association between Youth-Focused Firearm Laws and Youth Suicides." *Journal of the American Medical Association* 292: 594–601.

Weil, Douglas S., and Rebecca C. Knox. 1996. "Effects of Limiting Handgun Purchase on Interstate Transfer of Firearms." *Journal of the American Medical Association* 275: 1759–1761.

Weyrich, Noel. 2000. "The Orphaned Gun Fix." *Philadelphia City Paper*, July 13–20. http://mycitypaper.com/articles/071300/cb.citybeat.gun.shtml (accessed July 1, 2016).

Wilson, Harry L. 2012. "Open Carry Laws." In *Guns in American Society: An Encyclopedia of History, Politics, Culture, and the Law*, 2nd ed., Vol. 2, ed. Gregg Lee Carter, 663–664. Santa Barbara, CA: ABC-CLIO.

Wilson, Joy Johnson. 1999. *Summary of the Attorneys General Master Tobacco Settlement Agreement*. http://academic .udayton.edu/health/syllabi/tobacco/summary.htm (accessed June 30, 2016).

Winship, Christopher. 2002. *End of a Miracle? Crime, Faith, and Partnership in Boston in the 1990's*. March. Cambridge, MA: Department of Sociology, Harvard University. http://scholar.harvard.edu/files/cwinship/files/end_of_a_miracle_0_0.pdf (accessed July 1, 2016.

Wintemute, Garen J. 1994. *Ring of Fire: The Handgun Makers of Southern California*. Sacramento, CA: The Violence Prevention Research Program.

Wintemute, Garen J. 2002. "Where the Guns Come From: The Gun Industry and Gun Commerce." *Children,*

Youth, and Gun Violence 12 (2): 55–71. https://sfadebate
.wikispaces.com/file/view/Where+Guns+come+from+02
.pdf (accessed June 16, 2016).

Wintemute, Garen J. 2007. "Gun Shows Across a Multistate
American Gun Market: Observational Evidence of the
Effects of Regulatory Policies." *Injury Prevention* 13: 150–55.

Wintemute, Garen J., Stephen P. Teret, and J. F. Kraus.
1987. "When Children Shoot Children: Eighty-Eight
Unintended Deaths in California." *Journal of the American
Medical Association* 257: 3107–3109.

Wogan, J. B. 2013. "Cities Rethinking Gun Buyback
Programs." *Governing*, March. http://www.governing.com/
topics/public-justice-safety/gov-cities-rethink-gun-buyback-
programs.html (accessed June 29, 2016).

Wright, James D., and Rachel L. Rayburn. 2012. "Felons
and Gun Control." In *Guns in American Society: An
Encyclopedia of History, Politics, Culture, and the Law*,
2nd ed., Vol. 1, ed. Gregg Lee Carter, 278–280. Santa
Barbara, CA: ABC-CLIO.

Yablon, Alex. 2015. "High-Capacity Gun Magazine Bans:
The Numbers, the Opposing Arguments, the Unexpected
Origin Story." *The Trace*, July 29. https://www.thetrace
.org/2015/07/magazine-capacity-limit-explainer/ (access
June 22, 2016).

Yablon, Alex. 2016. "Bans on High-Capacity Magazines,
Not Assault Rifles, Most Likely to Limit Mass Shooting
Carnage: The Orlando Shooting Shows It's Not What the
Gun Looks Like That Matters—It's How Many Rounds It
Can Fire without Reloading." *The Trace*, June 21. https://
www.thetrace.org/2016/06/high-capacity-magazines-
orlando-shooting/ (accessed June 21, 2016).

Yakaitis, Chris. 2006. "National Awareness Program Public,
Licensed Dealers Includes TV Ads, Mobile Classrooms."
Baltimore Sun, June 14. http://articles.baltimoresun

.com/2006-06-14/news/0606140346_1_gun-dealers-
straw-purchases-licensed-gun (accessed June 18, 2016).

Zeoli, April M., and Shannon Frattaroli. 2013. "Evidence for
Optimism: Policies to Limit Batterers' Access to Guns." In
*Reducing Gun Violence in America: Informing Policy with
Evidence and Analysis*, ed. Daniel W. Webster and Jon S.
Vernick, 53–63. Baltimore: Johns Hopkins University
Press.

Introduction

Chapters 1 and 2 have given the reader a sense of the complexity of the contemporary debate over gun control in the United States. Although there is an underlying theme in these chapters that the strict regulation of firearms can and does work to reduce the human tragedies and costs that gun violence can incur (involving homicide, suicide, accidental death, and injury), there is also a serious taking into account and presentation of the gun rights side of the debate. In the essays that follow, three well-known and highly respected intellectuals on the debate give their bottom line views on it.

Robert J. Spitzer agrees with the underlying theme of this book—that thoughtful, evidence-based, and enforced regulations on guns should be the path the United States takes as a nation in the future. On the other side of the debate, Lawrence Southwick sees the regulation of guns having the unintended consequence of actually making them a greater problem for society; as such, the country should move forward without new

---

Rob Gotham calls in a background check for a customer at Great Lakes Outdoor Supply in Middlefield, Ohio, in January of 2013. Although federal law requires a background check on a potential gun purchaser who goes through a federally licensed firearms dealer, such as a gun store or a pawn shop, it does not require a check if the purchase is made from a private individual. Gun control advocates contend that this "loophole" allows criminals to readily buy firearms at gun shows, flea markets, and online. (AP Photo/ Mark Duncan)

gun control laws, enforcing the ones that are currently on the books, and, indeed, considering eliminating those that have "backfired." In the final essay, David B. Kopel makes an argument closer to Southwick's than to Spitzer's, but still contends that society can be made safer with selected controls on firearms—and, importantly, the controls he finds most appealing are ones that do not infringe upon the Second Amendment rights of the citizenry.

Stricter Gun Laws Are Reasonable and Sensible
Robert J. Spitzer

Should a convicted felon be allowed to buy a gun? How about a person determined to be mentally incompetent? Should a civilian be allowed to discharge a firearm within the confines of a city? Should school children be allowed to bring guns to school? Should a person be allowed to buy a gun if the person knows nothing about how to load, operate, or store a gun? If your answer to any of these questions is "no," then you support gun control.

In the fierce debate over gun policy in America, the public is often conveniently divided up into those who favor gun control and those who oppose it. In fact, this is a false division, because nearly everyone—even including gun owners and those who believe most strongly in gun rights—favors at least some gun controls, as the questions above illustrate. The real question for us is not, "Should there be gun controls?" but rather, "What kind of gun controls should there be, and to whom should they be applied?" When hyperbole is left behind, the actual arguments on behalf of stricter gun regulation are obvious, straightforward, simple, and supported by most Americans.

We Regulate That Which Is Dangerous
The first purpose of government is to protect the lives, health, and safety of its people. So, for example, automobiles are

required to have an array of safety features including air bags, seat belts, collapsible steering columns, padded dashboards—all to protect passengers—and catalytic converters to clean automobile exhaust. Lead has been removed from paint, asbestos has been removed from building materials, and cigarette advertisements have been removed from television and radio, all in the name of protecting citizens. In fact, thousands of consumer products are tested annually for safety and reliability. Products deemed defective or unsafe are subject to regulation or recall.

Guns are consumer products, no less than refrigerators or baby strollers, except that, unlike other consumer products, guns have only one purpose: to cause injury or death. The uniquely great ability of guns to cause more injury than any other weapon is called the "instrumentality effect," meaning that guns are more likely to cause harm and death than any other weapon. In the case of gun suicide, for example, a gun is more likely to cause death than any other method. No one understands the uniquely dangerous nature of guns more than gun owners. Any responsible gun owner knows that guns should be treated with caution, knowledge, and respect. For this reason alone, guns should be subject to sensible regulations.

This does not mean banning guns customarily owned by civilians, although it does and should include restricting access to weapons that are unusually dangerous or destructive. Not only are bans of conventional firearms not feasible, but the Supreme Court has ruled against the outright banning of guns normally used by civilians, including handguns, rifles, and shotguns. To regulate is not to ban, any more than automobiles and automobile driving run the risk of being banned because cars and drivers are regulated. On the other hand, some weapons, like some motor vehicles, do not belong in the hands of civilians. A civilian cannot own and operate an M1 Abrams battle tank like a motor vehicle; a special license and extra training are required before a person can legally operate an 18-wheel tractor trailer. One may similarly argue that civilians have no business owning and using bazookas, or shoulder-fired stinger missiles, for example.

To cite a different example of an unusually dangerous gun that most agree should be restricted but is not, consider the .50 caliber sniper rifle. First developed or "purpose-designed" by the Barrett Company in the 1980s for military use, the weapon can hit a target from over a mile away to devastating effect if aimed at fuel storage tanks, helicopters, personnel carriers, parked airplanes, or a person. These features make this weapon useful for the military, but a hazard in the hands of terrorists and criminals. It has no justifiable civilian purpose like hunting, as it would obliterate any animal hit by a round. Yet Barrett began selling the weapon commercially to civilians. Such weapons have occasionally been used in crime (Violence Policy Center, 2010). For example, in 2004, a shooter in Kansas City used such a weapon against police and emergency personnel. Even more disturbing, antiterrorist experts have repeatedly cited the weapon as posing a significant security threat to such targets as American airports. Yet even now, federal efforts to restrict access to such weapons have failed, and only the District of Columbia and California bar .50 caliber rifles—and no state bans .50 caliber handguns—to civilians. Today, such rifles are easier to purchase than a handgun in most places. There is simply no justifiable reason for allowing civilians to purchase such a weapon.

Some firearms already in wide circulation in society probably should be subject to greater regulation. Gun control supporters have focused much attention on handguns, because they are uniquely appealing to criminals seeking guns. While Americans own twice as many long guns (rifles and shotguns) as handguns, and long guns are easier to obtain in most places, about 80 percent of all gun crimes are committed with handguns. In addition, handguns are rarely used for hunting and sporting purposes. Instead, the main reason people cite for owning handguns is personal self-protection (an activity protected by law). Yet there are many ways to enhance personal safety in addition to guns, and guns kept for personal self-protection can result in bad consequences, including gun accidents, gun thefts, and gun suicides (in fact, of the 30,000–33,000 Americans killed by guns yearly, gun suicides outnumber gun homicides and gun accidents every year). All these suggest that handguns should be subject to stricter regulation than long guns, as is already true in some places. In New York State, for example, a civilian who wishes to own a handgun must first undergo a background check, submit the names of four character references, be fingerprinted and photographed, and explain to a judge the reason for wanting to own a handgun. It's a more complicated process than that found in most states, but it also keeps handguns out of the hands of those who shouldn't have them (in New York, 90% of guns used in crimes come from out of state).

And one more thing about gun laws: gun control opponents often argue that gun laws are useless because criminals still get guns and commit crimes regardless of the law. But the very reason we have law is to separate acceptable from unacceptable behavior. Do we repeal laws against murder because people still commit murders? Hardly. And when gun control foes say that all we have to do is enforce the laws on the books, they fail to mention that they do everything possible to keep existing gun laws weak and unenforced.

Most Gun Regulations Are Perfectly Legal

Gun ownership is as old as America, but so are gun laws. Even before America became an independent nation, the colonies enacted laws to bar gun ownership to Native Americans, blacks, Catholics, the poor, and those who would not swear loyalty to the government. Laws were also enacted to regulate gun storage, hunting practices, gun carrying, and even the brandishing of guns (that is, displaying them in a menacing way). In fact, laws barring gun carrying in towns, states, and territories were common throughout the country in the 19th century, even in the country's so-called Wild West frontier areas.

The idea that the Second Amendment's "right to bear arms" protects personal gun rights is, ironically, a recent idea. In 2008 and 2010, the Supreme Court carved out for the first time a new, individual right for citizens to own handguns for personal self-protection in the home (up to this time, the federal courts had interpreted the Second Amendment as pertaining only to gun ownership in connection with citizen service in a "well-regulated militia" as referenced in the first half of the amendment; see Cornell, 2006). Yet this new right was carefully limited by the court. In its 2008 ruling in *District of Columbia v. Heller*, the U.S. Supreme Court struck down a ban on handgun ownership in the District of Columbia, but it also said that "nothing in our opinion should be taken to cast doubt on long-standing prohibitions on the possession of firearms by felons or the mentally ill, or laws forbidding the carrying of firearms in sensitive places such as schools and government buildings, or laws imposing conditions and qualifications on the commercial sale of arms." (In its 2010 ruling, *McDonald v. Chicago*, the Supreme Court applied the same standards to the states. The *Heller* ruling applied only to the federal government.) In addition to lending support for long-standing gun regulations, such as laws barring the concealed carrying of firearms, the Court also suggested that certain types of especially powerful weapons might also be subject to regulation and that laws regarding the safe storage of firearms would also be allowable. Thus, the dark fear of gun confiscation so often invoked by gun control foes was expressly rejected by the Court.

Gun Laws Are Effective If We Want Them to Be

Among developed nations, the United States has the highest rate of gun ownership, amounting to more than 300 million guns in a nation of 325 million people. Even so, gun ownership is gradually declining: in the 1960s, about one home in two had at least one gun; by the end of the first decade of the 21st century, it was less than a third of all homes (about a quarter of all adults report owning at least one gun). Still, with tens of millions of Americans owning guns, there is no chance that guns are going away. But that doesn't mean that the government should do nothing. Two different examples illustrate the beneficial effects of sensible regulation.

In 1934, Congress enacted the first comprehensive national gun control law, the National Firearms Act. Passed at a time of highly publicized gangster violence (the notorious criminal John Dillinger was gunned down in the summer of 1934), the law regulated through taxation the manufacture, sale, and transfer of weapons and materials associated with gangster violence, including machine guns—that is, fully automatic weapons, meaning those that fire a continuous stream of bullets when the trigger is depressed. Citizens can own fully automatic weapons only if such weapons are registered in a central registry kept by the federal Bureau of Alcohol, Tobacco, Firearms and Explosives (ATF). Prospective purchasers of these weapons undergo a background investigation by the Federal Bureau of Investigation (FBI), and must submit a written application that requires, among other things, fingerprints and a photograph, and the weapon itself must be registered. The result? Not only did this law stem the flow of machine guns like the notorious "Tommy gun," but it has kept the lid on the circulation of such weapons in society. According to the ATF's National Firearms Act Inventory, as of the late 1990s, about 250,000 machine guns were in civilian hands nationwide (primarily licensed gun collectors). The criminal use of fully automatic weapons is extremely rare, as is their prevalence in society. In other words, this 1934 law succeeded in keeping such destructive weapons out of circulation—from the hands of civilians and criminals.

To take a different example, in 1994 Congress enacted a ban on civilian sale and possession of 19 types of semiautomatic assault weapons. The ban had been spurred by a spate of shootings involving such weapons, and because control advocates (and most Americans; see Figure 1.11 in Chapter 1) saw (and still see) no reason for civilians to possess such weapons. While opponents of the ban argued that there was no difference between assault weapons and traditional hunting rifles that also fired semiautomatically (that is, firing a bullet with each pull of the trigger), assault weapons were, in fact, designed for military use, and possess a series of specific military characteristics, including extensive use of lightweight stampings and plastics (making them lighter weight—about 6–10 pounds), flash suppressors, bayonet fittings, shorter barrels or collapsible stocks, the ability to receive high-capacity bullet magazines, pistol or thumb-hole grips, and similar features that allow the shooter to lay down "spray fire" across a wide area. Their greater concealability added to these weapons' criminal appeal.

Before the ban's enactment, about 1.5 million such guns were privately owned, and they accounted for somewhere between 2 and 8 percent of gun crimes. During the ban, studies of assault weapon crimes in cities showed declines in their use, ranging from 17 percent to 72 percent. Little noticed, but arguably more important, was the law's provision to stem the sale of large-capacity ammunition magazines, defined as those holding more than 10 bullets. These have been very attractive to criminals because they mean less reloading, whereas they have no legitimate hunting or sporting purpose. According to a study by the ATF, criminals prefer assault weapons compared to honest citizens by a ratio of 8:1. A study of high-capacity gun magazine use in Virginia found a steady decline in the criminal use of assault weapons during the 10-year period when the assault weapons ban was in place, but then a steady increase in their criminal use from 2005 to 2010.

Yet fierce gun lobby opposition to the ban resulted in narrowing the law's scope and insertion of large loopholes, which limited its effectiveness. Assault guns manufactured before 1994 were grandfathered in, leaving pre-1994 weapons in circulation, as was true of pre-1994 large-capacity magazines. In addition, the federal government allowed manufacturers to rebuild worn pre-1994 guns using new parts, including new serial numbers and the replacement of the firing mechanism (called receivers). Many gun manufacturers skirted the law by making minor changes in banned weapons to make them legal. For example, the banned Colt AR-15 was modified to become the legal Bushmaster AR-15 (the gun used in the 2002

Washington, D.C. area sniper killings). And finally, the law was limited to 10 years, and could only continue if Congress acted to renew it. The law could have been modified to account for these limitations, but was not because of political pressure from the gun lobby. Predictably, the bill lapsed and was not renewed, and police in large cities reported an increase in assault weapons crime since 2004.

Finally, nowhere is the gun lobby's desire to keep gun regulation weak and ineffective more evident than in its relentless attacks against the ATF, particularly regarding its efforts to regulate gun dealers. A government study revealed that a few corrupt gun dealers are the largest source of guns illegally trafficked. Nearly 60 percent of guns used in crimes come from about 1 percent of gun dealers; yet the ATF's ability to monitor and shut down these rogue dealers has been crippled, thanks to the gun lobby. Since the enactment of a National Rifle Association (NRA)–backed federal law in 1986, the ATF was limited to conducting only one random inspection of gun dealers per year—even for dealers who've previously violated the law. That same law also reduced gun dealer violations from felonies to misdemeanors. The legal standard for dealer prosecutions was raised so that gun dealers must be found to have violated the law "willfully." Virtually no other criminal conduct must meet such a high standard. In 2005, gun dealers were also granted special immunity from lawsuits—a protection unique to this one industry. Gun lobby pressure has kept the ATF chronically understaffed, underfunded, and not computerized. Thanks to NRA pressure, the ATF's gun-tracing process has not been computerized, meaning that all gun tracing still has to be done by hand. The result: most gun dealers are rarely or never inspected (including the nearly 10,000 dealers that border Mexico and that supply Mexican drug gangs with guns), and corrupt dealers are rarely prosecuted.

Gun control is no single cure-all for gun crime, accidents, suicides, and related mayhem, but guns' unique danger means that they should be regulated at least as much as (rather than less than) other consumer products. History has shown that this can be down without infringing on legitimate gun owner-ship, activities, and rights.

References

Cornell, Saul. 2006. *A Well Regulated Militia: The Founding Fathers and the Origins of Gun Control in America*. New York: Oxford University Press.

Violence Policy Center. 2010. *Criminal Use of the 50 Caliber Sniper Rifle*. http://www.vpc.org/regulating-the-gun-industry/criminal-use-of-50-caliber/ (accessed July 3, 2016).

Robert J. Spitzer (PhD Cornell) is Distinguished Service Professor of Political Science at the State University of New York at Cortland. He is the author of 15 books, including The Politics of Gun Control *(6th ed., 2015),* Guns across America: Reconciling Gun Rules and Rights *(2015), and three others on gun control, as well as over 600 articles, essays, and papers. He served as a member of the New York State Commission on the Bicentennial of the U.S. Constitution, is a former president of the Presidency Research Group of the American Political Science Association, and has testified before Congress on several occasions. He is often interviewed and quoted in national and international news outlets, and also writes for the* Huffington Post.

The United States Doesn't Need More Gun Laws—Indeed Fewer
Lawrence Southwick

Should the United States enact stricter gun control laws? The first step is to ask what is meant by this. Does it mean that states should be more restrictive of who is allowed to own or carry guns? Does it mean the U.S. government should enact such restrictions? Does it mean in either case that particular weapons should be more restricted? An alternative meaning could be to make the laws less restrictive. In this essay, I will ex-amine selected state and federal restrictions. Since the emphasis is more often on making laws more restrictive, that will be our major focus.

An initial suggestion could be from the Hippocratic Oath to "do no harm." Any new laws should fit that criterion. In the context of gun laws, this would imply that there should be a net benefit to the citizens affected by the law. Any law that is opposed by somebody indicates that the opponent believes he will be made worse off by the law; similarly, any law favored by somebody must have that person believing he or she will be made better off. For example, drug smugglers would prob-ably not want legalization of recreational drugs because of the probable increase in competition. Do we really care about their wants in this regard? For guns, in similar fashion, we want to know about the wants of noncriminals. Criminals would prob-ably desire more restrictions on their potential victims, but we should not care about their wants in this regard.

Laws restricting the ownership of guns will make some peo-ple feel less safe. They will make others feel more safe. The issue is not whether they are empirically less or more safe; it is about their feelings. Can we explore empirically what their feelings are? That would usually be by a survey. Can we also explore whether such laws actually make people more or less safe? To do the latter, we could look at the crime rates in the states with stricter gun laws as compared with states with less-restrictive gun laws. Of course, feelings make a big difference in regard to the passage of laws.

On the feelings side, Hemenway, Solnick, and Azrael (1995, 124) performed a telephone survey that found that "85% of non-gun owners would feel less safe if more people in their community acquired guns" and "for gun owners, acquisition of firearms by others in the community would leave about equal numbers feeling less safe as feeling more safe." They also found that those gun owners whose primary reason for gun owner-ship was self-defense overwhelmingly felt safer due to their gun ownership. Since gun ownership is by a minority (depending on the survey, between 31 and 41 percent of U.S. households contain a gun—see Smith and Son [2015] vs. Gallup [2016]), the less safe feeling is likely to carry the greater weight in deciding on passing laws.

What about actual crime rates? John Lott (1998) looked at the actual crime rates using 1992 data. He found that crime rates were substantially lower in those states that allowed all law-abiding adults to carry concealed handguns than in those states that did not. For example, states with the most liberal (least restrictive) laws had an average murder rate of 5.1 per 100,000 people while somewhat less liberal states had an average murder rate of 7.3 per 100,000 people and the least liberal states had an average murder rate of 11.6 per 100,000 people. (Robbery rates were 108.8, 220.9, and 224.1, respectively; note that Lott's statistical regression analyses have been challenged as insufficiently robust as to data selection—see Chapter 1 of the present book; however, I am unaware of any challenges to the categorization used here.) Keep in mind, however, that correlation is not causation; maybe the lack of liberality was due to the crime rate rather than the reverse.

It would certainly seem that feelings should not be credited with a better understanding than actual crime data. However, voters are what matters to the elected officials, so we may see such laws passed.

Another way of looking at how feelings matter is to see whether guns cause or are caused by crime. My own quantitative research reveals that if crime rates fall/rise, the incentive to buy guns is likely to fall/rise as well; however, there does not appear to be support there for the idea/belief that guns cause crime (Southwick, 1997).

It is important to keep in mind that some researchers may have the results desired in mind when they design their research. Such biased researchers' conclusions should be viewed with caution. I would suggest that a better reason for doing research in this area is that, if a study is done carefully and results in some conclusion, that conclusion will upset somebody and thus will be quoted widely. No matter what conclusion is reached, attacks on that by one side or the other will thus occur, which will induce the researcher to be cautious and to generally try to do good work.

Much of the controversy involved in this field is because gun control is essentially a religion. The antigun people will believe in antigun research while the pro-gun people will believe in research that supports their position. Like any religion, individual positions are strongly held; it will take extraordinary research to convince very many people to change.

Now let's get to the issue of passing some new law. What will this new law accomplish? (That is, an accomplishment other than allowing some legislators to claim they have done something about some real or imagined problem without actually doing so.) Will it result in reduced crime? Or will it result in increased crime? Will it result in lowered suicide rates? Or will it increase them? What about accidents; will there be an increase or a decrease?

For accidental deaths involving firearms, the numbers have fallen from 1,667 in 1980, to 1,115 in 1990, to 776 in 2000, to 505 in 2013 (see Table 146 in *Statistical Abstract of the United States* [1999, Table 146; 2003, Table 116]; and Table 1.3 in Chapter 1 of this book). Both population and the number of guns have increased over that period, so whatever accident problem there was has been decreasing rapidly. Is it possible that safety training works?

Without going into detail, there does seem to be an effect of the number of guns on the number of gun suicides but the overall suicide rate does not seem to vary much. Total suicide rates rose somewhat from 12.2 per 100,000 population in 1980 to 12.5 per 100,000 in 1990, fell to 10.4 per 100,000 in 2000, and rose again to 12.6 in 2013 (see CDC, 2015; and *Statistical Abstract of the United States* [2008, Table 110]). Guns per capita have risen over that time period, so it is doubtful that there is much effect of guns. If guns are made less available, other methods of suicide will still remain available.

In order to help answer the crime question, let us divide the population into two groups, criminals and potential victims. Of course, these may overlap; a drug dealer could be robbed by another criminal. Now, let us suppose that a new law restricting gun possession or carrying is passed. Who will obey this law?

First, look at the criminal. Suppose he is a dealer in illegal drugs. For him, occasional arrest and imprisonment are occupational hazards, a cost of doing business. However, suppose a supplier or a customer tries to cheat him on a transaction. There is no recourse to the courts as there would be with a legal transaction. Thus, he may feel the need to be able to engage in contract enforcement himself. Further, as noted earlier, some person may decide to rob the dealer; will the court system penalize the robber? While this occasionally does happen, the dealer will not be able to recover his property. Again, he will feel the need to protect himself. His decision to have a gun, even if illegal, is not likely to be much affected by the law.

Second, look at the law-abiding citizen. The direct penalty imposed by the restrictive law will be only a part of the full cost to him of being arrested for violating that law. In addition to those penalties, he will pay a price in reputation that may well affect his employment opportunities in the future. A conviction may also have effects on his family that are not present in the career criminal's situation.

Finally, the career criminal is more likely to encounter situations where a gun is useful than is the potential victim who has to be chosen by the criminal for victimization. Thus the expected benefits are lower to the noncriminal. A new law that raises the costs to both will, as a consequence of the above, create more inducements to the potential victim not to carry a gun than it will to the criminal. This implies that new restrictive laws will be far more likely to be obeyed by the potential victims than by the criminals. See Kates and Michel (2007) for analysis of this effect. That reduction in self-protection will make criminals more confident of their success in committing violent crimes and thereby induce them to commit more such crimes. This, in turn, will induce citizens to avoid certain activities and locations so as to avoid being victimized by such crime. They will be less able to perform active self-protection and therefore will resort to this passive method of crime avoidance. As law-abiding people avoid the more crime-ridden areas, this will make those areas less viable economically. In fact, people may well avoid cities that outlaw self-defense and those cities may experience economic decline as a consequence.

How about self-defense? If people have guns, will they be able to protect themselves? Will they shoot the wrong people? Will criminals be more likely to harm the victims? I have used data on criminal victimization and guns to answer these questions (Southwick, 2000). Victims of crime who had guns and were able to use them suffered both lower losses and lesser injury rates. Further, it was found that having more potential victims be armed would reduce both losses and injuries from crime and further would reduce criminals' incentive to be armed. If additional laws prevent victims from being armed to a greater extent than they prevent criminals from being armed, they will result in a net harm to victims as opposed to not having such laws.

Now, it should be obvious that even people who have guns will not necessarily be able to use them in a situation where self-defense is needed. However, it should be even more obvious that people who have been disarmed will not ever be able to use guns in self-defense. Kates and Mauser (2007) found that countries with fewer guns had greater crime rates.

The problem is how to deprive criminals of guns at the same time as permitting noncriminals to have guns for self-defense. Many jurisdictions have imposed additional punishments for those criminals who use deadly weapons in committing their crimes. To the extent that criminals expect such penalties to apply, that may give appropriate incentives. Of course, prosecutors often deal out reduced penalties in order to induce plea bargaining, so these penalties may not actually be applied. The result of the plea bargain, however, may still be a larger expected net penalty for the actual crime and may still induce better behavior—less crime.

Now, just possibly, some consideration should be given to making it easier for the law-abiding citizen to own and to carry a gun for self-defense. In recent years, the majority of U.S. states have enacted laws requiring that all legal adult citizens who have not been convicted of major crimes and have not been adjudicated incompetent be issued permits to own and carry guns. In addition, many of these states have allowed similar citizens of other states with the same rules reciprocally equal status.

While a number of hysterics forecasted bloodbaths, these have not occurred. The National Research Council (2005), even though having social scientists predisposed to more gun control, concluded from its compilation of findings that there is neither significantly more nor significantly less crime when such concealed carry permissions were given.

In 1993, the Brady Act was passed. Among other regulations, it imposed a waiting period for the purchase of a handgun, effective March 1994 through November 1998. However, it didn't apply to all of the states. For those states that already had a longer waiting period than the Brady Act imposed, it had no effect (these would supposedly be "strong" gun control states). However, for those states that had a lower or no waiting period, a five-day period was imposed (states that some might label as "weak" gun control states). There were 32 states that had this imposed and 19 (including the District of Columbia) that did not. The result is a quasi-experimental design.

In the 26 months prior to the waiting period being imposed, the crime rates per 100,000 population in the Brady and non-Brady states averaged the numbers in Table 3.1. (The monthly data were obtained from the FBI; the organization makes the monthly data available for a nominal fee.)

Table 3.1   Average Violent Crime Rates for the 26 Months Prior to the
Brady Act Taking Effect (per 100,000 Population)

Crime	State Having to Use the 1993 Brady 5-Day Waiting Period (32)	States Not Having to Use the Brady Waiting Period (19)	Significance
Murder	6.9	11.0	0.000
Rape	42.3	40.1	0.037
Robbery	122.6	285.4	0.000
Aggravated assault	322.7	438.3	0.000

Except in the case of rape where guns seldom play any role, the violent crimes where guns are more useful in both offense and defense were more prevalent in the states that did not have to adopt the new Brady waiting period of five days (because their gun control laws were already "stronger" and required at least a 5-day wait, e.g., California has a 10-day waiting period). These are highly significant results with a probability that they are wrong of less than one chance in 1,000. This raises the question of why the states with a lesser crime problem appeared to be those most affected by the Brady Act. One might logically think that the government would seek to apply whatever was apparently working in the lower crime states to the higher crime states.

Of importance to the Brady Act would seem to be how it impacted crime rates in the states to which it applied. It should not be expected to impact crime in the states to which it did not apply, of course, unless as a lesser secondary effect. A way to do this is to take the monthly crime rates for a state prior to the Brady Act and see how the rates changed four years later. (This keeps the seasonality the same across the pre-Brady and post-Brady comparisons.) The results are given in Table 3.2.

These results show that, while there was a general downward trend in crime over the period in question, the states where the Brady Act imposed a greater waiting period had significantly smaller reductions in crime than the non-Brady states did. This

Table 3.2   Changes in Violent Crime Rates Four Years before and after the Brady Act Took Effect

Crime	State Having to Use the 1993 Brady 5-Day Waiting Period (32)	States Not Having to Use the Brady Waiting Period (19)	Significance
Murder	−0.6	−1.9	0.000
Rape	−4.0	−5.3	0.000
Robbery	−9.4	−53.4	0.000
Aggravated assault	−17.2	−28.8	0.003

would appear to indicate that the Brady Act actually resulted in more crime in the states to which it applied than would have been the case absent the Brady Act. It doesn't really look as though the Brady Act was a treatment "that does no harm," does it? That was where we started this essay.

Before any new laws are passed restricting gun ownership, let us ask for competent research demonstrating that such laws would make citizens better off. Particularly on the national level, such restraint is to be preferred. For individual states, so long as the laws do not violate the Constitution, either of the United States or of the state involved, the ability to experiment does not need to be as circumscribed. Still, the passage of laws should not be driven by hysteria but by reason. Much of what passes for debate in regard to gun laws is not reasoned but is driven by what amounts to religious fervor.

I would find it difficult to conclude other than Wright, Rossi, and Daly (1983) concluded, that banning or substantially reducing gun availability would not have the beneficial effects on crime that are simplistically believed.

References

CDC (Centers for Disease Control and Prevention). 2015. *Suicide: Facts at a Glance.* http://www.cdc.gov/violenceprevention/pdf/suicide-datasheet-a.pdf (accessed July 3, 2016).

Gallup. 2016. *Guns*. Princeton, NJ: The Gallup Organization. http://www.gallup.com/poll/1645/guns.aspx?version=print (accessed January 7, 2016).

Hemenway, David, Sara J. Solnick, and Deborah R. Azrael. 1995. "Firearms and Community Feelings of Safety." *Journal of Criminal Law & Criminology* 86: 121–132.

Kates, Don B., and C. D. Michel. 2007. "Local Gun Bans in California: A Futile Exercise." *University of San Francisco Law Review* 41: 1–27. http://michellawyers.com/wp-content/uploads/2010/06/Local-Gun-Bans-in-California_-a-Futile-Exercise1.pdf (accessed July 3, 2016).

Kates, Don B., and Gary Mauser. 2007. "Would Banning Firearms Reduce Murder and Suicide? A Review of International and Some Domestic Evidence." *Harvard Journal of Law & Public Policy* 30: 650–694. http://www.law.harvard.edu/students/orgs/jlpp/Vol30_No2_KatesMauseronline.pdf (accessed July 3, 2016).

Lott, John R., Jr. 1998. *More Guns, Less Crime: Understanding Crime and Gun-Control Laws*. Chicago: University of Chicago Press.

National Research Council. 2005. *Firearms and Violence: A Critical Review*. Washington, DC: National Academies Press.

Smith, Tom, and Jaesok Son. 2015. *Trends in Gun Ownership in the United States, 1972–2014*. Chicago: National Opinion Research Center. http://www.norc.org/PDFs/GSS%20Reports/GSS_Trends%20in%20Gun%20Ownership_US_1972–2014.pdf (accessed July 3, 2016).

Southwick, Lawrence. 1997. "Do Guns Cause Crime? Does Crime Cause Guns? A Granger Test." *Atlantic Economic Journal* 25: 256–73.

Southwick, Lawrence. 2000. "Self-Defense with Guns: The Consequences." *Journal of Criminal Justice* 28: 351–370.

Statistical Abstract of the United States. 1999. Washington, DC: U.S. Census Bureau. http://www.census.gov/library/

publications/1993/compendia/statab/113ed.html (accessed
July 3, 2016).

Statistical Abstract of the United States. 2003. Washington,
DC: U.S. Census Bureau. http://www.census.gov/library/
publications/2003/compendia/statab/123ed.html (accessed
July 3, 2016).

Statistical Abstract of the United States. 2008. Washington,
DC: U.S. Census Bureau. http://www.census.gov/library/
publications/2007/compendia/statab/127ed.html

Wright, James. D., Peter H. Rossi, and Kathleen Daly. 1983.
Under the Gun: Weapons, Crime and Violence in America.
New York: Aldine de Gruyter.

Lawrence Southwick has a PhD in economics from Carnegie Mellon University and taught in the School of Management at the State University of New York at Buffalo for almost four decades. He has published many peer-reviewed papers in economics and management, as well as several scholarly articles and encyclopedia entries on gun rights and gun violence. His work has appeared in such publications as Managerial and Decision Economics, Journal of Criminal Justice, American Economic Review, Journal of Economic and Social Measurement, *and* Applied Economics.

Whether Gun Laws Should Be Strict Depends on the Type of Law
David B. Kopel

First of all, the question of whether "the United States should enact strict gun control laws" assumes that "gun control" is simply one thing, and that there can be "more" or "less" of it. Thus the question, "Should there be stricter gun laws?" is akin to "Should people eat more ice cream or less ice cream?" Yet in fact, gun laws do not all fit onto a one-dimensional line for which the only measurement is "more" or "less." There are many types of gun laws, and a person can rationally support more gun laws of one particular type, while at the same time favoring fewer or less restrictive gun laws of another type.

Second, the "more" versus "less" question frame misses the fact that for many gun control laws, there may be a moderate and optimal level. So instead of asking "more or less?" we should be asking whether a proposed law moves us closer to the optimal level for laws of this particular type.

Third, in our constitutional republic, the laws that control all other laws are those of the federal and state constitutions. The Second Amendment and its analogues in 44 state constitutions represent the public's conclusive determination about the right to possess, use, and carry firearms. Because constitutions control the enactment of all lesser laws, legislative statutes or administrative regulations about firearms must strictly comply with the constitutional right to arms. Conscientious adherence to the federal and state constitutions does not prohibit all gun laws, but it does channel those laws away from limitations on legitimate gun owners, and toward the strict application of laws against gun abusers.

For decades, opinion pollsters have been asking questions about whether gun control laws should be made more strict, less strict, or stay about the same. The long-term trend of the polls shows continuing decline in support for the "more strict" position. These findings are consistent with other questions showing a long-term decline in support for banning handguns (which has not been supported by a majority of Americans in the last 57 years); the number of people who say that protecting gun rights is more important than gun control used to be the minority, but now predominate (see Newport, 2015; Pew Research Center, 2014).

The long-term trend is negative for organizations such as the Brady Campaign (formerly called Handgun Control, Inc., and before that the National Council to Control Handguns) and similar lobbies that have a long record of supporting any type of antigun laws, which appears to be politically viable (Kleck, 2001). However, in-depth research into gun control attitudes has shown that much of the American public has almost no idea what contemporary gun laws really require, and how strict those laws already are (Wright, Rossi, and Daly, 1983). For example, except for gun owners, few people know that ever since the federal Gun Control Act of 1968, there has been a dealer-based registration system for retail firearms purchases. When you buy a gun at a store, you must fill out a registration form (federal Form 4473), which records your name, address, race, and so on, as well as the make, model, and serial number of the gun. The registration form must be retained for at least 20 years by the dealer, and can be inspected by agents of the federal Bureau of Alcohol, Tobacco, Firearms and Explosives (ATF) whenever they wish, in the course of a bona fide criminal investigation. The forms can also be inspected by ATF during annual compliance inspections of the licensed firearms dealer.

Public ignorance about the strictness of existing gun laws is sometimes exacerbated by public officials such as former New York City mayor Michael Bloomberg, who created a gun control organization known as "Everytown for Gun Safety." For example, Mayor Bloomberg has told national television audiences that gun shows are special places where "unlicensed dealers" are allowed to sell firearms without the restrictions (such as the federal registration Form 4473) that apply when guns are sold elsewhere. Bloomberg is referring to states where private sellers can buy and sell guns at gun shows without performing background checks, but these practices are legal precisely because they are not licensed dealers. Bloomberg's charge tars the reputation of legitimate dealers. In fact, the laws for selling guns at gun shows are exactly the same as for selling guns anywhere else. Nor is there any such thing as an "unlicensed dealer." Since 1968, federal law has required that anyone who is "engaged in the business" of selling firearms may only do so if the person has been issued a Federal Firearms License. A person who deals in guns (making repetitive transactions for profit) without a federal license is committing a felony every time he sells a gun (18 U.S. Code sect. 921(a)(21)). Private individuals who are not licensed may make gun sales because it is not a business for them.

Accordingly, many people who tell pollsters that they believe that gun laws should be "more strict" may simply be expressing their position in favor of laws that, unbeknownst to them, already exist, such as requiring licenses for all gun dealers, registering all sales by those dealers, and strictly applying those same rules when the dealer sells at a gun show, as well as at the dealer's storefront or home-based business.

Pro-gun groups, such as the National Rifle Association, have long touted their support for "strict" laws against gun possession by convicted criminals. Generally speaking, such laws are presumptively constitutional under the Supreme Court's 2008 decision in *District of Columbia v. Heller*.

As a matter of common sense, almost everyone would agree that a person who has just walked out of prison after serving a ten-year sentence for armed robbery should not be able to possess a firearm immediately after release. However, the cumulative effect of these "strict" laws has gone farther than people may realize.

For example, the strict federal laws are retroactive. So if someone cheated on his taxes in 1961, was convicted, and paid an appropriate fine, the Gun Control Act of 1968 retroactively banned him from possessing a gun for the rest of his life. Similarly, the 1994 federal crime bill retroactively expanded the list of federal "prohibited persons" to include domestic violence misdemeanants. Thus, if the police were called to the scene of a loud argument in 1975, either the husband or wife might have actually been innocent of any crime, but might have pleaded guilty anyway to a misdemeanor, and paid a $50 fine, rather than be faced with the heavy expense of paying an attorney to take the case to trial. These people too are retroactively banned from gun possession for the rest of their lives. Most states have similar laws.

Under the federal system, the Gun Control Act has a "relief from disabilities" provision. This provision allows someone to ask for administrative relief from the gun ban; that is, the person asking for relief must show that she has been completely rehabilitated, and has lived a crime-free life for years. However, congressional appropriations riders prevent ATF from considering petitions for relief from disability. So there is no practical method for restoring an important right to persons who made a mistake years ago, and who can prove themselves to be law-abiding and peaceable. Similar problems exist in many states.

So at some point, "strict" laws can become unreasonable and arbitrary, with no safety valve to mitigate their effects. Unfortunately, prospects for fixing the problem seem slim, since the "antigun" groups generally support existing gun restrictions, while the "pro-gun" groups are reluctant to spend any of their finite political capital on behalf of convicted criminals.

One type of strict gun law that makes sense is the regulation of the discharge of firearms. In a densely populated urban area, the risk that a stray shot could injure an innocent person is significant. Accordingly, many urban areas have enacted bans on the discharge of firearms. These bans are both strict and sensible, provided that they include appropriate exceptions such as self-defense, gun use at a range where the bullets will be contained, use of BB or pellet guns with appropriate backstops, and so on.

American history shows that some forms of strict gun control are not inconsistent with respect for the right to keep and bear arms. For example, during the early Republic, some large cities had laws regulating the discharge of firearms. Similarly, during the American Revolution, the "Loyalists" who took up arms in order to participate in King George III's military campaign might have their guns taken away, if they were captured. Today, the disarmament of violent jihadists would likewise not be inconsistent with respect for the right to keep and bear arms.

Other gun control laws, while sometimes upheld by the courts, spring from the worst side of American history, and have no place the 21st century. Before the Civil War, many states prohibited slaves from possessing firearms without permission from their masters. Some states also banned free blacks from owning guns, or required free blacks to obtain a special license. After the Civil War, many of the ex-slave states attempted to keep blacks in de facto slavery by, among other things, forbidding gun possession, or requiring special licenses.

Congress attempted to put a stop to these abuses by enacting the Second Freedmen's Bureau Bill and the Civil Rights Acts of 1866 and 1870, and the Fourteenth Amendment was added to forbid state and local governments from violating the Bill of Rights. Unfortunately, many states, especially in the South, evaded the Constitution by enacting laws that were formally racially neutral, but which were aimed at blacks. These included laws that outlawed inexpensive handguns (which blacks could afford) while still allowing the expensive, large "Army and Navy model" handguns owned by the ex-Confederate soldiers. A few states today still have bans on smaller or less-expensive handguns; these laws have the selective effect of disarming the poor. During the Jim Crow period, many states also enacted laws requiring a permit to carry a handgun for self-defense, and the permits were often refused to all blacks, while being granted to political favorites.

Today, eight states still retain highly discretionary systems for the licensing of handgun carrying, with permits sometimes issued on the basis of favoritism.

Thus, one especially sensible form of strict gun control is strict control on the issuance of licenses and permits, according to objective conditions. In most states, state law specifies that carry permits "shall" be issued to persons who meet certain objective criteria. These criteria typically include having a clean record (as verified by a 10-point FBI fingerprint records check), being an adult, and passing a safety training class. The permit cannot be denied simply because a local sheriff is hostile to a particular individual, or to the general right to carry.

The licensing system can still leave some room for discretion, but in a carefully controlled manner. Many state systems for the licensing of handgun carry have a provision, which is informally called "the naked man rule." Under this rule, an applicant can be denied a permit, even if he has a clean record, if the sheriff provides specific evidence that the applicant could be a danger to himself or others. The paradigmatic example of the "naked man" rule is an applicant who has no criminal convictions and no record of being committed to a mental facility, but who is well-known for sitting naked on his front lawn and shouting loud and bizarre rants. Under the naked man rule, a permit denial can be reviewed by a court, with the sheriff or other licensing official having the burden of proving the facts at issue.

Many other gun control laws also are based on objective criteria. The federal laws about who can be issued a federal firearms license to sell guns and the federal laws about who cannot possess guns use objective, factual standards. Thus, the risks of abuse of discretion, or discriminatory enforcement, are greatly reduced. Most state firearms laws also use objective criteria. However, a few states, such as New Jersey and Massachusetts, grant almost limitless discretion to local authorities for permitting the carrying and even for the purchase of firearms. As one might predict, some local officials misuse their discretion and greatly infringe the right to keep and bear arms.

In the American population, a minority believe that people should not be allowed to own guns, even for self-defense. The First Amendment rights of such people should be strictly protected, even in places where such views are anathema. At the same time, antigun advocates should recognize the rest of the Constitution. On some policy matters (whether the United States should have a king, whether Congress should be allowed to establish post offices, whether the government can establish an official religion), the federal and state constitutions conclusively settle the matter. Forty-four state constitutions guarantee a right to keep and bear arms. So, of course, does the U.S. Constitution, and, as the Supreme Court ruled in the 2010 case *McDonald v. Chicago*, the Fourteenth Amendment means that state and local governments have to obey the Second Amendment.

Gun control advocates must recognize that the Second Amendment–based right affirmed in *Heller* and *McDonald*, even if they don't like it: that citizens have a constitutional right to own guns for personal self-protection. Antigun advocates should not infringe the right to arms by imposing laws that seriously limit the practical ability to defend oneself. For example, some people want to outlaw magazines (detachable boxes that hold the ammunition for most types of handguns, and for some types of rifles) that hold more than 10 rounds. This presumes that people never need more than 10 rounds for self-defense. Anyone who has even been attacked by a gang or who has been the victim of a group of gay-bashing assailants could explain the falsity of this assumption. Again, strict respect for constitutional rights is not necessarily inconsistent with strict laws against gun misuse. The key question is whether a proposed law narrowly targets misuse, or instead would impose a burden on law-abiding users. Does the law aim to perfect the exercise of the right or to infringe it?

Finally, an often-overlooked source of authority for strict gun laws is the federal and state militia powers. Article I, Section 8, Clauses 15–16, of the U.S. Constitution grants Congress broad authority over arming and training the militia. The Second Amendment tells us that a "well-regulated militia" is so important that it is "necessary to a free State" (that is, to a free, non-enslaved, political order). Most state constitutions spell out state powers over the militia, and explain that the militia comprises all able-bodied adult males in a certain age range (with a few exceptions, such as clergy). Thus, the state and federal governments can, as they did in earlier times, require that all persons in the militia possess a certain type or types of firearm, and prove to the government that they have such a gun in good working order. Likewise, governments can require that all militiamen meet at specified times and places for training.

More broadly, some states in colonial America mandated gun ownership by all households (not just the militia), and required gun carrying by all adults in certain circumstances, such as when going outside of a settled town. Today, a few municipalities, such as Kennesaw, Georgia, have similar mandates for household gun ownership, with exceptions for pacifists and for persons who are not allowed to legally own firearms. Such laws might improve public safety, since the enactment of the Kennesaw ordinance was followed by a sharp decline in home invasion burglaries (Kopel, 2001).

On the other hand, some persons who reluctantly complied with an ownership mandate might feel oppressed or endangered, and might not take the time to learn the rules of safe and responsible ownership and storage of firearms. Laws that attempt to control personal behavior (such as the prohibition of alcohol or marijuana) and that are not supported by almost all of the public often cause more harm than good. The same is true of laws that ban guns, and might also be true of broad mandates for gun ownership.

The federal and state constitutions do not tell us that we must mandate gun ownership, that we must enact firearms discharge restrictions in urban areas, or that we must prohibit gun ownership by certain groups of particularly dangerous people. Rather, the constitutions guarantee the right to own and carry firearms, especially for lawful self-defense, while allowing legislatures and the public significant room for judgment about many details of gun laws.

Common sense tells us that many of these laws can and should be strict, but not unreasonably or unfairly so.

References

Kleck, Gary. 2001. "Absolutist Politics in a Moderate Package: Prohibitionist Intentions of the Gun Control Movement." In *Armed: New Perspectives on Gun Control*, ed. Gary Kleck and Don B. Kates, 129–172. Amherst, NY: Prometheus Books.

Kopel, David B. "Lawyers, Guns, and Burglars." 2001. *Arizona Law Review* 43: 345–367.

Newport, Frank. 2015. "American Public Opinion and
Guns." *Gallup*, December 4. http://www.gallup.com/
opinion/polling-matters/187511/american-public-opinion-
guns.aspx (accessed July 3, 2016).

Pew Research Center. 2014. "Growing Support for Gun
Rights." (December). http://www.people-press.org/2014/
12/10/growing-public-support-for-gun-rights/ (accessed
July 3, 2016).

Wright, James, Peter H. Rossi, and Kathleen Daly. 1983.
Under the Gun: Weapons, Crime, and Violence in America.
Hawthorne, NY: Aldine de Gruyter.

*David B. Kopel is Research Director of the Independence Institute,
a think tank in Denver, Colorado. He is also adjunct professor of
Constitutional Law at Denver University, Sturm College of Law;
and an Associate Policy Analyst at the Cato Institute, in Washington, D.C. He is the author of 17 books and over 100 scholarly
articles, many of them on firearms law and policy. He is coauthor
of the first law school textbook on the subject,* Firearms Regulation and the Second Amendment *(2012), and a columnist for
the* Washington Post *on the paper's Volokh Conspiracy law blog.*

MOMS=
DEMAN
ACTION
FOR GUN SENSE IN A
www.momsdemandac

This chapter presents brief biographies of many of the key politicians, researchers, and activists involved in the gun control debate as it has evolved in the United States over the past four decades. A few have retired, but most are still very much involved in their gun-related activities.

They are roughly equally divided among being researchers, politicians, and activists. Although no deliberate attempt was made to present a balance based on which side of the gun debate they fall—those favoring the rights of gun owners versus those favoring greater gun control—there is, indeed, a fairly even balance: 54 percent are on the gun rights side, and 46 percent are on the gun control side. Thus, even though many of those on the gun rights side often complain that the media and the faculty of major universities are biased against guns, in fact the likes of George W. Bush, Wayne LaPierre, John Lott Jr., and other strong gun rights proponents get (or have gotten) strong media coverage, as do the National Rifle Association (NRA) and many of the academicians and intellectuals who question the effectiveness and constitutionality of gun control legislation.

Liz Banach, of Maryland Moms Demand Action for Gun Sense in America, talks to reporters in Annapolis, Maryland, on October 14, 2014. The strong gun control advocacy groups Moms Demand Action for Gun Sense in America and Mayors Against Illegal Guns merged in 2013 to form Everytown for Gun Safety. (AP Photo/Brian Witte)

The number of organizations involved with the gun debate is immense. The groups described in this chapter represent the better-known and more influential of them. All can be readily classified as being on one side or the other of the gun debate. Thus, to maintain a logical structure, like the individuals detailed in this chapter, the organizations are divided according to which side of the debate they fall. Although more gun control than gun rights groups are described, far and away the organization given the longest profile—more than twice the length of any other—is the NRA.

For those wanting to involve themselves directly in the political debate over gun control and to try to bring about stronger regulations, the two most important organizations to contact, at least initially, are the Brady Campaign (http://www.bradycampaign.org/) and Everytown for Gun Safety (http://everytown.org/); and for those wanting to work toward protecting the rights of gun owners, the premier groups to contact first are the NRA (https://home.nra.org/) and Gun Owners of America (https://gunowners.org/). Also, there are many state and local organizations that allow for more personal, face-to-face involvement—and their websites are generally available from these four national organizations.

The Gun Control Side: Key Individuals and Organizations

Individuals

Joseph Biden Jr. (1942–)

Joseph Biden Jr. made significant contributions to gun control policy as a Democratic U.S. senator from Delaware, the most notable being his cosponsoring of the Crime Control Act of 1990, which, among other increased penalties toward gun-related crimes, allowed the federal government to crack down on the transfer of firearms across state lines by extending Congress's power to regulate interstate commerce. Biden also spearheaded the Violent Crime Control and Law Enforcement

Act of 1994, which is well-known for the controversial Public Safety and Recreational Firearms Use Protection Provision—which included the Federal Assault Weapons Ban.

Most recently, Biden has served as vice president to President Barack Obama. Following the 2013 Sandy Hook Elementary School mass shooting in Newtown, Connecticut, his efforts toward getting more federal gun control legislation enacted, as well as his encouraging President Obama in the creating of executive orders to move forward selected, minor gun control measures, resulted in the NRA assigning him an "F" rating for his failure to protect gun rights. Ultimately, however, the legislation he fought to get enacted, which included universal background checks for all those wanting to buy or receive a firearm, failed (the blocking of proposals by Senators Machin and Toomey, in 2013, following the Sandy Hook tragedy; and again in 2015, following the San Bernardino mass shooting).

Michael Bloomberg (1942–)

Michael Bloomberg is an entrepreneur and philanthropist who served as the mayor of the city of New York from 2002 to 2013. Bloomberg's tenure in New York City was marked with an economic and social revitalization of the city. He spearheaded numerous efforts to increase economic growth and small business development as well as strengthening public schools and public health initiatives. An adherent of strong crime control, he increased the mandatory minimum sentence for illegal possession of a loaded handgun in the city of New York in hopes to dissuade the flow of illegal weapons into the city.

Bloomberg's stance on illegal guns led him to cofound Mayors against Illegal Guns with Boston mayor Thomas Menino in 2006. The coalition now includes over 1,000 mayors from across the country. In 2013, Mayors against Illegal Guns merged with Moms Demand Action for Gun Sense in America to form Everytown for Gun Safety. Bloomberg currently serves as the cochair of the organization.

Hillary Diane Rodham Clinton (1947–)

Hillary Diane Rodham Clinton is a former New York senator. She served as the First Lady of Arkansas for 12 years, as well as the First Lady of the United States for 8 years under the administration of her husband, William J. Clinton. Hillary Clinton learned firsthand the challenges of passing federal gun legislation, as she was by her husband side when he arduously brokered through the Brady Act (1993) and the Federal Assault Weapons Ban (1994) during his administration.

During her 2016 campaign for the presidency, Ms. Clinton vowed to "strengthen background checks and close dangerous loopholes in the current system . . . hold irresponsible dealers and manufacturers accountable . . . [and] keep guns out of the hands of terrorists, domestic abusers, other violent criminals and the severely mentally ill." Her plan to achieve these goals included increasing the number of gun sales subject to background checks, repealing immunity protection legislation for the gun industry, upgrading straw purchases to a federal crime offense, and closing loopholes to keep severely mentally ill patients from acquiring guns. Her loss to Donald Trump has put her gun control agenda, which is tantamount to that of the Democratic Party, on hold until at least 2020.

William J. Clinton (1946–)

William "Bill" Jefferson Clinton is the former governor of Arkansas as well as the 42nd president of the United States. Clinton served two terms in the White House and is considered the first elected president to take a public stance against the NRA. He sought to enact gun control legislation even after the Democratic Party lost control of Congress. In 1993, Clinton signed the Brady Act into law, which mandated background checks of individuals buying firearms from federal licensed firearms dealers, along with an interim requirement that the purchaser of a handgun had to wait five business days before taking possession (this provision lapsed in 1998, after the establishment of the National Instant Criminal Background Check System). He also pushed through and signed a series of strong gun control measures after the Brady Act, the most important of which where the Federal Assault Weapons Ban, the Gun-Free Schools Act, and the Violence against Women Act (which, along with the Lautenberg Amendment, barred those under a domestic violence restraining order or who were convicted of even a misdemeanor crime of domestic violence from possessing a firearm or ammunition).

Philip J. Cook (1946–)

Philip Jackson Cook is a leading public policy researcher who had made significant contributions toward gun violence policy with his work as a faculty member of Duke University. Cook's research initially focused on the regulation of unhealthy and unsafe behavior and it evolved into the costs of gun availability and violence. His research within the gun field includes studies on gun markets, defensive uses of handguns against criminal attacks, tracing guns used in crimes, and economic impacts of gun violence. Much of his work appears in articles and books that he has coauthored or coedited with Jens Ludwig (director of the University of Chicago Crime Lab), most importantly including *Guns in America: Results of a Comprehensive National Survey on Firearms Ownership and Use* (Washington, D.C.: U.S. Department of Justice, 1997); *Gun Violence: The Real Costs* (New York: Oxford University Press, 2002); and *Evaluating Gun Policy: Effects on Crime and Violence* (Washington, D.C.: Brookings Institution Press, 2003). More recently, his research and thinking on gun violence and gun control has appeared in his coauthored book with Kristin A. Goss, *The Gun Debate: What Everyone Needs to Know* (New York: Oxford University Press, 2014). Among their most cited analyses are those used to calculate the total cost of gun violence (taking into account everything from medical care of victims to their lost wages), which they calculated was an astounding $100 billion in 2000 (a figure that has since risen to $229 billion as of 2016; see "The Magnification Hypothesis" section in Chapter 1).

Dianne Feinstein (1933–)

The oldest serving senator as of 2016, Dianne Feinstein has been representing the state of California since 1992. She is a member of the Senate's Judiciary Committee and uses her credentials to strengthen federal legislation that combats crime and promotes gun control. Feinstein played prominent roles in the passing of several gun control measures, including the Gun-Free Schools Act and Assault Weapons Ban of 1994, while suffering defeats trying to extend the ban in 2004 and closing what has become known as the "gun show loophole" (that is, in trying to enact legislation requiring universal background checks for the purchase and transfer of firearms).

In 1978, Feinstein was sworn in as the mayor of San Francisco following the assassination of Mayor George Moscone and Board of Supervisors member Harvey Milk—who were shockingly gunned down in their city hall offices by a disgruntled former city supervisor with a revolver. She subsequently issued a municipal ordinance banning handguns in the city, which prompted death threats and an attempted bombing of her home. Nevertheless, Feinstein's persistence won her the mayoral recall election and an eventual seat in the Senate.

Feinstein was a strong proponent of renewing the Federal Assault Weapons Ban in 2004. After failing, over the next decade she tried several more times to get it reinstated, including in January of 2013—a month after the horrific mass killing of 20 elementary school children and 6 staff members at Sandy

Hook Elementary School in Newtown, Connecticut—but in every case the U.S. Senate handed her defeat. Likewise, she unsuccessfully fought the 2005 Protection of Lawful Commerce in Arms Act (PLCAA), which extended immunity to the gun manufacturers and dealers from lawsuits resulting from the mishandling or criminal use of the firearms they had manufactured or sold.

Feinstein continues to fight for gun control measures in the Senate, most recently in supporting legislation proposed after the June 2016 mass shooting in Orlando, Florida. The legislation, involving denying gun sales to those on the FBI's Terrorist Watchlist and requiring a background check on all gun transfers or sales (including between private parties), has thus far failed passage (as of 2017).

Gabrielle Giffords (1970–)

Gabrielle Giffords is a former member of the U.S. House of Representatives. Giffords served in the Arizona State House and Senate from 2000 to 2005 prior to winning the eighth Congressional District seat in the U.S. House of Representatives in 2006.

On January 8, 2011, Jared Lee Loughner shot and seriously wounded Giffords in a Tucson store at a meet-and-greet political rally. Loughner also gunned down 18 others, killing 6 of them. Although she survived the assassination attempt, she eventually had to resign from Congress due to the mental and physical disabilities she suffered. In response to the December 2012 Sandy Hook Elementary School mass shooting, Giffords and her husband, retired navy captain and astronaut Mark Kelly, formed Americans for Responsible Solutions (ARS) to elect politicians with gun control-focused platforms. Since its inception, the group has recruited over 810,000 members. ARS has also taken credit for lobbying for mandatory background checks in five states: Colorado, Connecticut, Delaware, Maryland, and Washington.

David Hemenway (1945–)

David Hemenway is a professor of Health Policy at Harvard University's T.H. Chan School of Public Health. He directs the Harvard Injury Control Research Center (HICRC) and served as the president of the National Association of Injury Control Research Centers as well as the head of the Injury Council of the National Association of Public Health Policy. He was principal investigator for the pilot of the National Violent Death Reporting System, now a Centers for Disease Control and Prevention (CDC) data collection and analysis system that is building a standardized and detailed data set on circumstances surrounding violence-related deaths (homicides, suicides, and accidents), including those involving firearms.

Hemenway's research is wide ranging, and key themes and analyses involving gun violence and gun policy are summarized in his highly praised book *Private Guns, Public Health* (Ann Arbor: University of Michigan Press, 2006). He makes summaries of his and his colleagues' research on gun violence publicly available on the website of the Harvard School of Public Health (https://www.hsph.harvard.edu/hicrc/firearms-research/).

Hemenway is a leader in promoting the public health approach to reducing gun violence. This approach focuses less on the individual and more on the social and physical environments that can encourage or discourage gun violence. The ultimate goal is to change these environments—which can be accomplished by socially beneficial changes in the activities of gun manufacturers and gun retailers, as well as many other groups, including foundations, the faith community, and criminal justice. In 2012, he was recognized by the CDC as one of the 20 "most influential injury and violence professionals over the past 20 years."

Arthur L. Kellermann (1955–)

Arthur L. Kellermann is the dean of the F. Edward Hébert School of Medicine at the Uniformed Services University of the Health Sciences, the only federal medical school in the country. Prior to taking this position, Kellermann served as the director of the Center for Injury Control at Emory University's Rollins School of Public Health. He is best known for his controversial research on firearm-related injuries and deaths, in measuring whether the benefits of keeping a firearm in the home are worth the risks.

In a 1986 *New England Journal of Medicine* (*NEJM*) article, Kellermann and his colleagues studied firearms-related homicides and suicides that occurred in the home in King County (Seattle), Washington, and in 1993 published a second study in the *NEJM* focusing only homicides, but expanding the data base to include Shelby County, Tennessee, and Cuyahoga County, Ohio. The fundamental conclusion of both articles was that "rather than confer protection, guns kept in the home are associated with an increase in the risk of homicide by a family member or intimate acquaintance" (*NEJM*, vol. 329, 1091).

Although this conclusion is respected and often cited by public health researchers, other analysts, those most often cited by gun rights advocates, have been critical of Kellermann's research. Among other criticism, these analysts point out that his research did not take into account the defensive uses of firearms in the home (e.g., fending off would-be robbers and assailants), and it did not distinguish households at high risk for violence (e.g., those with drug addicts or felons) from ordinary households. Criticisms of Kellermann's research, which received some financing from the federal CDC, partly underlay the 1996 "Dickey Amendment" in which Congress removed the appropriations for the CDC's gun violence research and, in effect, barred the CDC from spending any funds that would "advocate or promote gun control." Although President Obama authorized the CDC to produce a report on gun violence in the wake of the December 2012 Sandy Hook Elementary School massacre in Newtown, Connecticut (http://www.nap.edu/read/18319/chapter/1), the Dickey Amendment has not been rescinded as of 2016.

Barack H. Obama (1961–)

Barack Hussein Obama is a former Democratic Illinois State senator who also served a short time in the U.S. Senate prior to becoming the nation's 44th president, defeating John McCain in 2008 and Mitt Romney in 2012. The first African American president in U.S. history, Obama is a Harvard Law School graduate who supported stricter regulations on purchasing and possessing guns while serving in the Illinois and U.S. senates. However, gun control was overshadowed by the financial crisis during the 2008 presidential campaign, prompting Obama to list his support for gun control reforms but not actively campaign for them.

During his first term, Obama did little to move forward gun control legislation and spent much of his political capital getting his national health care package passed in 2010 (the Patient Protection and Affordable Care Act). Gun control proponents had had high expectations for him to pick up where his Democratic predecessor Bill Clinton had left off in 2000. Clinton's deft and hard-fought battles for gun control yielded great success during the 1990s, especially with the passage of the 1993 Brady Act and the 1994 Federal Assault Weapons Ban. The Brady Campaign to Prevent Gun Violence gave Obama a failing grade for gun control and, overall, gun control advocates felt betrayed.

However, soon after his election to a second term in 2012, Obama's lack of effort in trying to move forward gun control measures, either their legislation or by executive action, underwent a dramatic change after the massacre at Sandy Hook Elementary School in Newtown, Connecticut, on December 14, 2012. He put his support behind federal bills that would have revived the 1994 Federal Assault Weapons Ban, put in place universal background checks for all gun sales and transfers, and stiffen penalties for illegal gun trafficking. Congress passed no new gun legislation, but Obama issued 23 executive orders aimed at increasing the control of firearms, including authorizing the CDC to study gun violence and to produce a report on our current knowledge on the topic (http://www.nap.edu/read/18319/chapter/1).

Throughout his second term, Obama pressed Congress to move on gun control legislation after every high-profile mass shootings, including Roseburg, Oregon (October 1, 2015); San Bernardino, California (December 2, 2015); and Orlando, Florida (June 12, 2016)—all to no avail, as no major legislation was enacted.

Charles E. Schumer (1950–)

Representing his home state of New York, Charles Ellis "Chuck" Schumer served in the U.S. House of Representatives until being elected to the Senate in 1998, where he has maintained a high profile ever since. Throughout his career, he has been a strong advocate of strong gun control legislation and was key in getting the 1993 Brady Act and the 1994 Federal Assault Weapons Ban passed through Congress and signed into law. Such efforts led the NRA to publicly label him "the criminal's best friend in Congress" (see *New York Times*, April 13, 1994, B9).

As of 2016, Schumer was still pushing forward strong gun control legislation and was the sponsor of the Fix Gun Checks Act (S.2934), a proposed amendment to the Gun Control Act of 1968 that would require universal background checks for all firearm sales and improve the comprehensiveness and efficiency of the National Instant Criminal Background Check System (NICS).

Robert J. Spitzer (1953–)

Robert James Spitzer is a Distinguished Service Professor of Political Science at the State University of New York, College at Cortland. Holding a PhD from Cornell University, he is the author of 15 books, including *The Politics of Gun Control*, 6th edition (Boulder, CO: Paradigm Publishers, 2015) and *Guns across America: Reconciling Gun Rules and Rights* (New York: Oxford University Press, 2015). He served as a member of the New York State Commission on the Bicentennial of the U.S. Constitution, is a former president of the Presidency Research Group of the American Political Science Association, and has testified before Congress on several occasions.

In his writings and public commentary, Spitzer argues that gun control measures can be effective, including more extensive background checks for prospective gun buyers (including, e.g., requiring letters of reference and sending local law enforcement officials to interview coworkers, neighbors, and acquaintances, if necessary); universal background checks (whether the purchase or transfer of a firearm is through a federally licensed retailer or between private parties—whether negotiated in a living room or on the Internet); and restrictions on high-capacity, detachable ammunition magazines. He believes that research on topics like the Iron Pipeline (whereby firearms purchased in lax gun control states are transported and then sold in the private market in strong control states) lead to the conclusion that gun laws are more effective if they are national. He sees no conflict between strong gun control measures and the Second Amendment, and indeed agrees that the amendment is more about guaranteeing the collective right of the people to arm a militia for self-defense than about guaranteeing the right of an individual "to keep and bear arms." His writings also explain how a well-organized, single-issue group like the NRA can yield huge influence over the American political system, at both the state and national levels.

Franklin E. Zimring (1942–)

Franklin Zimring is a leading researcher on the relationship between guns and violence. He is currently the William G. Simon Professor of Law, Wolfen Distinguished Scholar, and chair of the Criminal Justice Research Program, Institute for Legal Research, at Boalt Hall School of Law at the University of California at Berkeley. Zimring has written on a variety of gun topics, but is most famous for his and Gordon Hawkins's *Crime Is Not the Problem: Lethal Violence in America* (New York: Oxford University Press, 1999). Zimring and Hawkins empirically show that the United States has many categories of crime, including assault, that are well below the rates of its peer nations (other industrialized democracies, e.g., Australia, Canada, New Zealand, and those of Western and Northern Europe); what distinguishes the United States is its crime-related death rate—which is many times higher and is so, primarily, because of the far greater use of guns in the United States in assault and robbery, producing much higher death rates.

The influential thesis in *Crime Is Not the Problem* grew out of Zimring's early work on the instrumentality effect of weapons. The key question is whether the weapon used in a crime affects the seriousness of injuries incurred. After a careful study of Chicago police records on assault, Zimring concluded that "fatality seemed to be an almost accidental outcome of a large number of assaults committed with guns or knives" rather than from the attacker's intent. This strengthened evidence that the lethality of the weapon determines the outcome of the attack rather than the attacker; this promoted more responsibility being placed on a firearm in an attack than the attacker. Zimring's research and reasoning is concisely and well summarized in his 2004 *Journal of Medicine & Ethics* article "Firearms, Violence, and the Potential Impact of Firearms Control" (vol. 34, 34–37).

National Organizations

Americans for Responsible Solutions/Law Center to Prevent Gun Violence

Led by former Arizona Representative Gabrielle Giffords and her husband, retired astronaut and Navy Captain Mark Kelly,

Americans for Responsible Solutions (ARS) is a 501(c)(4) advocacy group and political action committee that seeks increased legislative action for gun control. Giffords and Kelly founded ARS after Giffords survived a 2011 assassination attempt at a Tucson, Arizona, meet-and-greet that left six others dead and forced her to resign from Congress. Further spurred by the 2012 Sandy Hook Elementary School massacre, ARS has recruited over 810,000 members in its efforts to match support by gun lobbyists. The primary goal of ARS is to expand background checks in order to restrict firearm access to the mentally ill. This request is to make background checks "universal" and mandatory for public and private sales and transfers.

Formerly known as the Legal Community against Violence, the Law Center to Prevent Gun Violence (LCPGV) was formed after the infamous mass shooting at 101 California Street in July 1993 in San Francisco. Its founding members were San Francisco area lawyers initially focused on strengthening local and state gun control measures in California. By 2000, the group had a national strategy to extend assistance to states where preemption laws would allow for some form of local regulation (most states "preempt" local governments from enacting their own firearms laws, especially those laws that would be stricter than an equivalent state law). In 2001, LCPGV started a website that has become a premier source of expert information on gun control laws and legal cases, at both the state and national levels. The website is often consulted and cited by academics, government officials, gun control advocates, journalists, and lawyers (http://smartgunlaws .org/). In 2016, LCPGV merged with Americans for Responsible Solutions.

LCPGV closely monitors state and federal legislation and assists lawmakers and gun control advocates in crafting and promoting gun regulations. Their work is pro bono (free) and includes pro bono educational seminars, assistance in recruiting local area attorney volunteers, and filings of "friend of the court" (amicus) briefs in important court cases where Second Amendment claims are at stake.

Brady Campaign to Prevent Gun Violence/Brady Center to Prevent Gun Violence

The Brady Campaign to Prevent Gun Violence and, its affiliate group, the Brady Center to Prevent Gun Violence comprise the nation's oldest and best-known gun control organization. In 1974, University of Chicago graduate student Mark Borinsky founded the National Council to Control Handguns after being robbed at gunpoint. In 1981, the organization was renamed Handgun Control, Inc. (HCI), focusing on lobbying for gun control legislation and electing appropriate officials into Washington, D.C.

HCI was instrumental in helping to write and pass the Brady Act in 1993. Named in honor of James Brady, who was seriously wounded in the 1981 assassination attempt on President Ronald Reagan, the legislation put teeth into trying to ensure that the categories of persons prohibited from buying or receiving a firearm noted in the Gun Control Act of 1968 were actually barred from doing so—by requiring that a buyer going to a licensed firearms dealer to undergo a background check before taking actual possession of a purchased gun. Through 2014, the law had successfully blocked 2.6 million gun purchase attempts by those in prohibited categories; the most common reason for rejection has been a felony conviction, followed by having a domestic violence conviction or restraining order.

In 2001, HCI officially changed its name to the Brady Campaign to Prevent Gun Violence. Under its new brand, the organization continues to speak out and lobby on behalf of increased gun control. Following the 2007 Virginia Tech massacre, the campaign successfully helped pass the NICS Improvement Act to further close any loopholes allowing convicted felons and mentally unstable to legally obtain firearms. The Brady Campaign publicly voiced a call for action following the 2011

Tucson, Arizona, shooting that wounded Congresswoman Gabrielle Giffords; the 2012 Aurora, Colorado, movie theater shooting; and the 2013 Sandy Hook Elementary School massacre. In fact, following Sandy Hook, the Brady Campaign gained nearly 100,000 new members.

Founded in 1983 as the Center to Prevent Handgun Violence, the Brady Center to Prevent Gun Violence is an affiliate of the Brady Campaign to Prevent Gun Violence. The center argues that, although gun control legislation can decrease gun violence, education and pro bono legal representation can also be part of a more comprehensive solution—and these are the services it provides.

The Brady Center provides legal representation through its Legal Action Project (LAP) division, which also files "friend of the court" briefs to voice out in courtroom proceedings. Starting in 1998, LAP assisted more than two dozen city governments, as well as the state of New York, to file suits to recover the costs of gun violence incurred by the general public (e.g., the costs of arrests, prosecutions, and emergency medical care). The lawsuits claimed that gun manufacturers had not taken advantage of safe-gun technologies, and that their distribution systems encouraged straw purchases and the flow of firearms into the black market. The strategy, however, was brought to a near halt with the passage of the PLCAA—which now shields the gun industry from civil liability suits based on the criminal misuse of their products. Although LAP's activities have been curbed, it still moves forward each year with new cases that are provided for by certain allowances in the PLCAA (e.g., defective manufacturing or the criminal misconduct of a dealer knowingly selling a firearm to a person in a prohibited category, such as a convicted felon; see http://www.bradycampaign.org/legal-action-project).

The Brady Center has published a number of high-profile reports on gun violence over the years, including: *Brady Background Checks: 15 Years of Saving Lives*; *No Check. No Gun. Why Brady Background Checks Should Be Required for All Gun Sales*;

and *Guns and Hate: A Lethal Combination* (these and many other reports can be found at http://www.bradycampaign.org/search/Reports).

Coalition to Stop Gun Violence/Educational
Fund to Stop Gun Violence

The Coalition to Stop Gun Violence (CSGV) is a national 501(c)(4) nonprofit formed in 1974 by the United Methodist General Board of Church and Society as the National Coalition to Ban Handguns. The group of 48 national religious and labor organizations originally sought to reduce gun-related violence by banning handguns—the number one weapon implicated in murders and suicides. In 1989, the organization dropped its original goal—still considering it highly desirable but also realizing that it had no chance of success because it lacked fundamental public support—and changed its name to the Coalition to Stop Gun Violence. It began supporting a variety of gun control measure that receive greater favor in public opinion polls and thus have a greater chance of enactment. Key among these measures are universal background checks, banning assault weapons, banning open carry in public places and urban areas, repealing or ramping down the legal allowances given to gun owners to "stand their ground" in the face of an apparent criminal attack (which CSGV sees as replacing the common law approach of reacting to an attack with proportional force with a "shoot first, ask questions later" attitude), requiring microstamping technologies to become standard for semiautomatic handguns (see the section "Bullet Serial Numbers and Microstamping" in Chapter 2), and repealing the 2005 PLCAA (that now shields gun manufacturers and dealers from lawsuit seeking damages for the criminal misuse of the firearms they have sold).

A sister organization of the CSGV, the Educational Fund to Stop Gun Violence (EFSGV) is a 501(c)(3) organization that engages the public in policy development, technical assistance, policy advocacy, and community and stakeholder engagement. The EFSGV influences policymaking decisions by drafting policy, educating policymakers, lobbying for the passage of gun control measures in Congress, and spreading the message of needed gun legislation through media outreach. Examples of the fund's activities include its having helped launch a public education campaign in California, having helped launch a nationwide campaign to change the public perception on the issue of gun control, having provided technical assistance to the District of Columbia following the *Heller* (2008) Supreme Court decision, and having organized a consortium of the nation's leading researchers and advocates in public safety and mental health.

Everytown for Gun Safety

Everytown for Gun Safety was founded in 2014, when Mayors against Illegal Guns merged with Moms Demand Action for Gun Sense in America. Everytown supports all of the high-profile measures that the wider gun control movement would like to see adopted on a national level, especially universal background checks for gun sales and transfers (including stopping the growth of firearms transactions conducted on the Internet, where private sales go unchecked and largely unmonitored); stronger laws to keep guns out of the hands of domestic abusers (including granting the authority of local law enforcement agents to remove guns from the possession of stalkers); stronger child access protection laws, such that all guns are kept in safe storage (e.g., in locked boxes or safes) and that ammunition is also kept in safe storage but in a different location than firearms; and the cracking down on gun trafficking, especially by closing down the Iron Pipelines by which guns are purchased in large quantities in weak gun law states (many of which are in the south) and then transported and sold in the backstreet black markets of strong gun law states (such as Connecticut, Massachusetts, Illinois, New Jersy, and New York).

In 2016, the organization claimed on its website to have over 3 million members (everytown.org). And even though very young, Everytown maintains that its founding groups had major gun control victories just prior to their merger: in 2013, Mayors against Illegal Guns successfully led a Colorado campaign to adopt a law requiring background checks for all gun sales, becoming just one of 18 states to have such as requirement. And in 2014, Mayors against Illegal Guns and Moms Demand Action for Gun Sense cooperated in convincing the online social network Facebook to take privacy and security steps to limit illegal gun sales.

Taking a page from the success story of the NRA, Everytown sends regular newsletters and e-mail notifications informing its members about state-led grassroots efforts toward gun control.

Harvard T.H. Chan School of Public Health: Harvard Injury Control Research Center

The Harvard T.H. Chan School of Public Health's Injury Control (HICRC) seeks to reduce the societal burden of injury and violence through research, intervention, and outreach. HICRC has conducted extensive research on firearms topics ranging from accidents to child access, guns at college, and policy evaluation. It receives funding from the Joyce Foundation, with a special mandate not only to conduct research on firearm-related violence, but then to disseminate findings through press releases, a special (play-on-words) newsletter entitled "Bullet-ins" (https://www.hsph.harvard.edu/hicrc/bullet-ins/), and its own Harvard website (https://www.hsph.harvard.edu/hicrc/firearms-research/). HICRC also provides technical assistance to the CDC's National Violent Death Report System (see the section "National Violent Death Report Systems" in Chapter 2 of this volume). Finally, HICRC provides significant technical and financial assistance to the Means Matters Campaign, which promotes the idea that the intent to commit suicide is most likely to end up as a completed act if the attempter uses a firearm. The campaign's main mission is to encourage suicide prevention groups to promote activities that reduce a suicidal person's access to a gun—for example, by having the gun kept in locked storage or even removed from the home (https:// www.hsph.harvard.edu/means-matter/).

States United to Prevent Gun Violence

The States United to Prevent Gun Violence (SUPGV) is a non-profit organization focused on reducing gun deaths and injuries. SUPGV operates via state-level organizations, all of which share similar policy goals as the Brady Campaign to Prevent Gun Violence. SUPGV works to extend background checks for all firearms purchases; provide more information regarding the dangers of guns; and enact more comprehensive regulations limiting the carrying of firearms in public.

In 2011, after the mass shooting of Representative Gabrielle Giffords (D-AZ) and 18 others, in which she was severely wounded and 6 were killed, SUPGV pledged its support to the Fix Gun Checks Act—a bill that has been before the U.S. Congress for a decade and that would require universal background checks for all firearm purchases and transfers. Later in 2011, in response to the international terrorist group Al Qaeda encouraging its American members to exploit the country's weak gun control laws, SUPGV and three other major gun control groups urged President Obama to strengthen federal gun laws. In recent years, SUPGV has focused on growing its membership by distributing information through e-mail newsletters and has made affiliations with 31 state gun violence prevention organizations.

United States Conference of Mayors

The United States Conference of Mayors was an early member of the National Coalition to Ban Handguns, which eventually became the Coalition to Stop Gun Violence. The coalition gave strong support to passage of both the 1993 Brady Act and the 1994 Assault Weapons Ban. Virtually all strong gun control legislation since then has been supported by the conference, as well as by its much more focused affiliate Mayors against Illegal Handguns (now part of Everytown for Gun Safety).

Most recently, the conference passed a set of strong resolutions at its June 2016 annual meeting. They included (1) strong support and appreciation for President Barack Obama's recent executive actions aimed at reducing gun violence; (2) encouraging all mayors to ensure that every domestic violence and drug abuse prohibiting record is entered into the NICS background check system (accomplished, in part, by issuing guidance to their law enforcement officers to investigate and prosecute cases in which prohibited individuals attempt to purchase guns from licensed dealers and fail a background check); (3) encouraging all local agencies to share crime gun trace data with their colleagues; (4) encouraging mayors to work with their local and state legislatures to ban replica handguns that are made to look and feel like real handguns; (5) encouraging engagement with legal gun owners to ensure that they know the rules and regulations regarding lost and stolen firearms and that they take appropriate steps to ensure safe and secure storage of all firearms in their possession; and (6) encouraging mayors to work with governors, attorneys general, and other executives at the state and county levels to take action in reducing the flow of illegal guns from jurisdictions with lax gun laws to jurisdictions with strong gun laws.

Violence Policy Center

The Violence Policy Center (VPC) is a 501(c)(3) nonprofit that strives to move beyond the narrow view of firearms violence being largely a crime issue and to demonstrate that gun violence is better understood as a broad-based public health issue of which crime is just the most recognized aspect. Founded in 1988 by John Sugarmann, it has produced a long list of research reports investigating how firearm-related homicides, suicides, and accidents are related to lax gun control laws and the lack of product and health regulations enjoyed by the gun industry. Regarding the latter, the VPC observes that "guns are the only consumer products manufactured in the United States that are not subject to federal health and safety regulation." All other consumer products are regulated by a federal health and safety agency. For example, the Consumer Product Safety Commission "regulates household and recreational products such as toasters, lawn mowers, and toys," while the Food and Drug Administration "oversees the safety of food and prescription drugs," and the National Highway Traffic Safety Administration regulates motor vehicles. However, because of its strong political clout, the gun lobby was able to ensure that "firearms escaped safety regulation in the 1970s when the U.S. Congress created the major product safety agencies" (http://www.vpc .org/regulating-the-gun-industry/regulate-htm/).

Violence Prevention Research Program

The Violence Prevention Research Program (VPRP) is a research center at the University of California, Davis, that investigates the causes and prevention of violence. VPRP has focused heavily on evaluating the effectiveness of gun control measures, such as waiting periods and background checks. VPRP researchers, most notably Garen J. Wintemute, have published studies on the links of alcohol and drug abuse with gun violence; the use of background checks—including by regulating secondary sales at gun shows—and of safe storage practices to keep firearms out of the hands of individuals at high risk for violent crime, suicide, and accident; the beneficial effects of strong regulations on firearms dealers and their selling of firearms regarding the preventing of the diversion of guns into illegal markets; the benefits of taking away firearms from those having domestic violence restraining orders—and, relatedly, the increased risk of intimate-partner homicide among women who purchase handguns; refining the protocols of gun buyback programs to improve their effectiveness; and the importance of physicians advising patients about the dangers of having a gun in a home having an individual at risk for suicide.

The Gun Rights Side: Key Individuals and Organizations

Individuals

George W. Bush (1946–)

George Walker Bush was elected the 43rd president of the United States in November 2000 and served two terms. As the foremost ambassador of the Republican platform, he enthusiastically expressed the need to "[a] defend the constitutional right to bear arms [and] . . . [b] oppose federal licensing of law-abiding gun owners and national gun registration as a violation of the Second Amendment and an invasion of privacy of honest citizens" (http://www.ontheissues.org/Archive/2000_RNC_Platform_Gun_Control.htm). He thus received strong support from the NRA and other gun rights organizations during his elections bids and while serving as president. During his tenure, Bush did nothing to stop the expiration of the Federal Assault Weapons Ban in 2004. He also signed into law major federal legislation to shield gun manufacturers and sellers from civil lawsuits (the PLCAA in 2005), as well the equally major NICS Improvement Act of 2007 (a response to the 2007 Virginia Tech mass shooting and a rare piece of gun legislation that received support from both Democrats and Republicans, as it had provisions in it that satisfied both gun control and gun rights advocates). The single exception to Bush's strong support of gun rights was his view, as expressed in the U.S. solicitor general's brief filed in the landmark U.S. Supreme Court Case of *District of Columbia v. Heller* (2008), that the Supreme Court should acknowledge that the Second Amendment guaranteed an *individual* right (not just the collective right of a state) to bear and possess arms, but abstain from a judgment and instead return the case to the lower court from which it came—as that court's ruling was so broad as to possibly void federal gun laws, including the Federal Firearms Act of 1934 that put regulations on automatic weapons and saw-off shotguns.

Paul D. Clement (1966–)

Paul D. Clement is a partner at Bancroft PLLC and served as the 43rd solicitor general of the United States from 2005 to 2008. While in this position, Clement represented the federal government's views during the U.S. Supreme Court hearing of the landmark case *District of Columbia v. Heller* (2008). The Court ruled for the defendant, Dick Heller, and determined that handguns are "arms" protected by the Second Amendment— and, most importantly, the amendment was intended to guarantee this right to *individuals* (not just to the individual states so that they could form militias).

In representing the Bush administration, Clement agreed with the individual-right interpretation, claiming the phrase "to bear arms" should not be exclusively held within a military context and that lawful acts involving firearms, such as hunting and self-defense, were protected by the Second Amendment. However, he also contended that the lower court ruling in favor of Heller could be misinterpreted as allowing for the repeal of long-standing federal gun laws—such as restrictions on owning machine guns. Clement's position stunned many gun rights advocates, and conservative columnist Robert Novak even accused Clement of betraying President Bush's actual position. This position not only strongly supported the individual-right interpretation of the Second Amendment but also strongly supported the lower court decision affirming this right (and what was being challenged by the District of Columbia).

Not long after his presentation to the Supreme Court, and well before its final decision on June 26, 2008, Clement resigned from the solicitor general position (effective June 2, 2008) and eventually rejoined his former law firm of King and Spalding. As a partner in this firm, he returned to the gun debate by arguing on behalf of the NRA in a second landmark gun rights case, *McDonald v. City of Chicago* (2010). The *McDonald* case was similar to the *Heller* case, but more wide reaching. *Heller* applied only to federal jurisdictions like the District of Columbia, while in the *McDonald* case Clement and the other lawyers involved for the plaintiff (three cases were actually combined into one, so there were multiple attorneys involved) argued that the right of the individual to possess a firearm, including a handgun and for self-defense (not just recreation or hunting), should not be rescindable by local or state laws (Chicago had a ban on handgun ownership by an average person, such as its resident Otis McDonald).

Both the District of Columbia and the city of Chicago lost their cases and the outcome was a huge victory for those on the gun rights side of the gun debate. However, in both decisions, the Supreme Court ruled that the Second Amendment right is not "unlimited." For example, in the *Heller* decision, the Court ruled that its decision "should not be taken to cast doubt on longstanding prohibitions on the possession of firearms by felons and the mentally ill, or laws forbidding the carrying of firearms in sensitive places such as schools and government buildings, or laws imposing conditions and qualifications on the commercial sale of arms [nor on . . .] the historical tradition of prohibiting the carrying of dangerous and unusual weapons" (such as sawed-off shotguns or submachine guns). And in the *McDonald* case, the majority opinion included the statement that their ruling would allow for "[s]tate . . . and local experimentation with reasonable firearms regulations [to be] continue[d] under the Second Amendment."

Nevertheless, since the *Heller* decision, an average of about 130 cases challenging local, state, and federal gun laws have come before lower state and federal courts each year—cases in which the courts have been asked to rule on the legality of selected gun laws. The challenges, however, have been largely unsuccessful—with over 90 percent of the gun laws under review having been ruled as not being in violation of Second Amendment or associated state constitutional protections for gun ownership.

Chris W. Cox (1978–)

Having served as the executive director of the NRA's Institute for Legislative Action (ILA) since 2002, Chris W. Cox has been responsible for the NRA's annual political and lobbying budget of over $30 million, granting him substantial power in lobbying efforts of the gun rights movement. Cox received his start in politics as a senior legislative aide in Congress, with a focus on criminal justice reform and firearms freedom. He joined the NRA in 1995, and quickly climbed the ranks of the ILA division to his current position.

Cox is also the chairman of the NRA's political action committee (PAC): the Political Victory Fund. As chairman, he has directed NRA electoral efforts, from local races to presidential campaigns, with an abundance of success. For example, in 2014 over 90 percent of NRA-backed congressional candidates won their respective elections.

Cox has a strong presence in the public media, appearing frequently on major news networks like CNN and Fox News, as well as often being quoted in national newspapers such as the *USA Today* and the *New York Times*. He tenaciously defends the gun rights negative take on proposed firearms-related legislation and its similar guns-are-not-the-problem take on tragic mass shootings—such as those occurring in Orlando, Florida (June 12, 2016), and San Bernardino, California (December 2, 2015).

Jay W. Dickey Jr. (1939–)

Jay Woodson Dickey Jr. is a former member of the U.S. Congress, having served in the House as a Republican from Arkansas's Fourth District from 1993 to 2001. During his tenure, he maintained a strong relationship with the NRA. His claim to fame in the contemporary gun debate is the 1996 "Dickey Amendment," a provision in the annual federal bill authorizing funding for the CDC. The amendment barred the organization from using any of its funds "to advocate or promote gun control." It was in response to the CDC-funded research of Arthur Kellermann (see his profile earlier in this chapter), who coauthored two studies linking a gun in the home to an increased probability of being the victim of a homicide or suicide. Since 1996, the CDC has eliminated any major research in which the central focus is gun violence and how it might be reduced.

Despite protestations by a number of major medical and public health professional organizations—including the American Medical Association and the American Psychological Association—the amendment has become a regular part of the federal spending bill authorizing appropriations for the CDC (and still is as of 2016). President Barack Obama defied the amendment in 2013, when in response to the December 2012 Sandy Hook Elementary School massacre, he directed the CDC to produce a comprehensive report on the current state of our understanding of gun violence (http://www.nap .edu/read/18319/chapter/1).

Ironically, after the July 2012 mass shooting in an Aurora, Colorado, theater, Dickey coauthored an editorial in the *Washington Post* admitting that he had been the "NRA's point person in Congress" in 1996, and he expressed regret that his amendment had deterred the CDC's research on the problem of gun violence. He has since repeated this expression in a letter to Congress, and after the October 2015 Roseburg, Oregon, mass shooting at a community college, in an interview with the *Huffington Post*. In this interview, he admitted to carrying a sense of responsibility for progress not made since his amendment went into effect in 1996, telling the interviewer "I wish we had started the proper research and kept it going all this time . . . I have regrets" (http://www.huffingtonpost.com/entry/jay-dickey-gun-vio lence-research-amendment_us_561333d7e4b022a4ce5f45bf).

John D. Dingell (1926–)

John David Dingell (D-MI) served the longest tenure in U.S. congressional history, being succeeded by his wife, Debbie, in 2015 after 59 years of representing Michigan's Twelfth District. He served many years on the NRA board of directors, and it was therefore not surprising that he was a staunch opponent of gun control. He was especially well known for using "killer amendments" that would radicalize a portion of a gun control bill to keep it from passing in the House of Representatives. His colleague Carolyn McCarthy (D-NY) dubbed him "Mr. NRA," and Dingell referred to the government organization the NRA considered most threatening to gun rights, the Bureau of Alcohol, Tobacco, Firearms and Explosives, as being "as large a danger to American society as I could pick today" (http://www.motherjones.com/politics/2013/01/atf-obama-gun-reform-control-alcohol-tobacco-firearms).

Dingell gained even more power through being the chair of the House Committee on Energy and Commerce, where he was often able to keep gun control legislation from reaching the House floor from the early 1980s to the mid-1990s (though obviously not the two biggest gun control bills of the era, the Brady Act and the Federal Assault Weapons Ban). Nevertheless, three watershed events eventually softened Dingell's abhorrence to gun control legislation. First, even though he protested the federal assault weapons ban section of the Violent Crime Control and Law Enforcement Act of 1994, an act strongly opposed by the NRA, he voted for it and in doing so felt he must resign from the association's board of directors—which he did in August of 1994. Second, when a 1995 NRA fund-raising letter to its membership included a characterization of agents of the Bureau of Alcohol, Tobacco, Firearms and Explosives being "jack-booted government thugs," he publicly responded that this was a "ludicrous and offensive implication" (the notion that federal agents are encouraged by the government to commit acts of violence against ordinary people). Third, after the horrific mass shooting at Virginia Tech, he cosponsored and helped push through both houses of Congress the NICS Improvement Act of 2007—legislation supported by the Brady Campaign to Prevent Gun Violence and that is intended to improve the computerized records that licensed firearms dealers consult before selling a firearm to ensure that the buyer is not on the prohibited list.

In 2014, President Barack Obama presented John Dingell with the Presidential Medal of Freedom. Dingell was credited with being "a lifelong public servant, the longest serving Member of Congress in American history, and one of the most influential legislators in history." The award acknowledged his work for "landmark pieces of legislation," including "civil rights legislation in the 1960s, to legislation protecting our environment in the 1970s, to his persistent fight for health care, from Medicare to the Affordable Care Act" (https://www.whitehouse.gov/campaign/medal-of-freedom).

Alan Merril Gottlieb (1947–)

Alan Merril Gottlieb is the founder of two well-known gun rights organizations—the Citizens Committee for the Right to Keep and Bear Arms and the Second Amendment Foundation (SAF). His company, Merril Associates, distributes his organizations' messages via several radio stations in the Pacific Northwest and his publishing house, Merril Press. He has authored and coauthored numerous tracts on gun rights through this press, prominent among them are *Gun Rights Affirmed: U.S. v. Emerson* (2010), *Gun Rights: Fact Book* (2010), and *Politically Correct Guns* (2010). Merril Press's list of authors encompasses several well-known gun rights proponents, including David B. Kopel (author of the classic *The Samurai, the Mountie and the Cowboy: Should America Adopt the Gun Controls of Other*

Democracies?), John R. Lott Jr. (of *More Guns, Less Crime* fame), and Timothy Wheeler (the founder of the gun rights organization Doctors for Responsible Gun Ownership [a project of the SAF]).

Alan Gura (1971–)

Alan Gura is an Adjunct Professor of Law at Georgetown University as well as a founding partner of Gura & Possessky, PLLC in Washington, D.C. His practice focuses on "appellate litigation and constitutional law." Gura has also worked with the SAF, a prominent gun rights group that specializes in gun rights litigation. In 2009, he made the *Legal Times'* list of Washington's top 40 lawyers under the age of 40, and in 2013, he was named one of the 100 Most Influential Lawyers in America by the *National Law Journal*.

Gura's most notable cases were his successes in the 5–4 U.S. Supreme Court decisions of *District of Columbia v. Heller* (2008) and *McDonald v. Chicago* (2010). These cases transformed the legal interpretation of the Second Amendment from that of it guaranteeing the *collective* right of the individual states to field an armed militia to that of an *individual's* right to keep and bear arms—for all legal purposes, including self-defense.

In the years before the *Heller* case, many observers following the gun debate thought that the NRA was reluctant to pursue a gun rights case all the way to the Supreme Court—fearing the Court would rule against the individual-right interpretation of the Second Amendment. Setting this fear aside, Robert Levy, director of the libertarian think tank Cato Institute, and Clark Neily, an attorney at the Institute for Justice, recruited Gura to serve with them as cocounsels in *Heller* (with Gura actually be asked to serve as lead counsel). After their astonishing win, the NRA did join in the litigation of the *McDonald* case (see the profile of Paul D. Clement earlier in chapter).

More recently, Gura has been working with the SAF to challenge a number of state-level laws, including, for example, the New York's may-issue concealed carry law.

Stephen P. Halbrook (1947–)

Stephen Halbrook is a practicing attorney (based in Fairfax, Virginia), scholarly writer, and strong gun rights advocate, with expert knowledge on U.S. firearms law, the gun cultures of Switzerland and Germany, and historical and contemporary interpretations of the intent of the Second Amendment. He has argued and won dozens of cases involving challenges to firearms laws, including three in front of the U.S. Supreme Court. The most famous of these was *Printz v. United States* (1997), in which he successfully argued that the 1993 Brady Act could not be used to compel local law enforcement authorities (in this particular case, Sheriff Jay Printz of Ravillia Country, Montana) to do background checks on the prospective purchasers of handguns because it would constitute a violation of the Tenth Amendment ("The powers not delegated to the United States by the Constitution, nor prohibited by it to the States, are reserved to the States respectively, or to the people"). Most local law enforcement agencies were complying with the law at the time; moreover, the June 1997 decision had only a short time of salience, as the mandatory background check was an interim provision set to expire in November of 1998. Thus, the immediate impact of the *Printz* decision was minimal. However, some legal scholars, including David B. Kopel, view its long-term impact as enormous: "First of all, the case foreclosed the proposed 'Brady II' congressional gun control legislation, which would have ordered state governments to set up handgun licensing and registration systems according to a federal scheme. Even more significant, *Printz* was one of a series of Supreme Court cases, beginning with *New York v. United States* in 1991, in which the Court began paying renewed attention to federalism and states' rights and enforcing constitutional limits on congressional power."

Halbrook's lengthy list of academic and legal publication include major books on the Second Amendment (*That Every Man Be Armed: The Evolution of a Constitutional Right*, revised and updated edition, 2013), firearm laws (*Firearms Law Deskbook: Federal and State Criminal Practice*, 2015–2016 edition, updated annually), and the use of gun control laws for those in power to abusively maintain their power (*Gun Control in the Third Reich: Disarming the Jews and "Enemies of the State*," 2013). He also makes many of his journal articles available online at http://stephenhalbrook.com/.

Marion Hammer (1938–)

Marion Hammer has been a high profile member of the NRA and strong advocate of gun rights for the past four decades. She was elected to the NRA's board of directors in 1982, serving as its vice president in 1992, and then as its first female president during 1995–1998. She currently serves on its board and its executive committee and was elected for life to its executive council.

In 1975, Hammer founded Unified Sportsmen of Florida (USF), an NRA affiliate, and has been a lobbyist for the USF and the NRA in Florida since 1978. She explains that she founded USF "because Florida was seeing what I would call a burst of gun control measures being filed by northerners who had moved to South Florida and had brought the stuff that they had moved away from with them" (http://nraontherecord .org/marion-hammer/).

Among her most notable and successful lobbying efforts was the enactment of Florida's 1987 "shall-issue" concealed carry law. This opened up the floodgates for similar laws, with 32 states subsequently enacting "shall-issue" laws—allowing for the average citizen to readily acquire a concealed weapons permit to carry a handgun, as long as he or she can pass a federal background check. Hammer was similarly involved with the enactment of a 2005 stand-your-ground law in Florida, a law, like the state's shall-issue concealed carry law, that many states modeled similar statues on in the years that followed (a stand-your-ground statue denotes an individual is not obligated to retreat in the face of a violent threat). She became infamous in the public health and family medicine fields for arguing for a 2011 Florida law that prohibits physicians and other licensed health care practitioners from asking questions of patients about firearms being in the home.

Hammer's most recent quest is to allow for the open carry of handguns in Florida. She sees this, as she does all of her past fights for gun rights, as fulfilling her (and the NRA's) goal of restoring the "Second Amendment to the full intent of the founding fathers and to protect freedom at all costs."

Don B. Kates Jr. (1941–)

A graduate of Reed College and Yale Law School, Don B. Kates developed a personal and—what turned out to be a lifelong—scholarly interest in the Second Amendment and gun rights when he spent a summer during law school as a civil rights worker. He learned from fellow workers that it was a good idea to carry a handgun for protection from white supremacists. When he explored the history and meaning of the Second Amendment, it became clear to him that it was not only meant as protection against a potentially tyrannical government (and also was meant as a deterrent for one ever to unfold), but also as a guarantee for the right of self-defense against individual villains. Indeed, he argued that the Founding Fathers "saw no distinction between resistance to a lone criminal and resistance to a large army controlled by a criminal government. The difference was only quantitative (more criminals to resist) rather than qualitative; good people had a right to use arms against criminal violence" (Kates details his argument in his 1992 *Constitutional Commentary* article "The Second Amendment and the Ideology of Self-Protection,"

87–104). Moreover, he found little credibility in the public health research, sharply criticizing it over the years (see, e.g., his coauthored 1994 article in the *Tennessee Law Review*, "Guns and Public Health: Epidemic of Violence or Pandemic of Propaganda?" 513–596).

Although Kates generally does not receive a lot of media attention, in part because he eschews social media and the Internet, he and well-known gun rights advocate Professor Gary Mauser generated considerable media attention when they published an article critical of gun control in the *Harvard Journal of Law & Public Policy* ("Would Banning Firearms Reduce Murder and Suicide? A Review of International and Some Domestic Evidence," 2007, 649–694). After their review of the evidence, Kates and Mauser conclude that the "burden of proof rests on the proponents of the more guns equal more death and fewer guns equal less death mantra, especially since they argue public policy ought to be based on that mantra. To bear that burden would at the very least require showing that a large number of nations with more guns have more death and that nations that have imposed stringent gun controls have achieved substantial reductions in criminal violence (or suicide). But those correlations are not observed when a large number of nations are compared" (693). The public health community involved in gun violence, the standard bearer for which is the HICRC, felt compelled to respond. After reviewing a host of scientific research that contradicts the Kates/Mauser article, the director of the center, David Hemenway, concludes "the article is simply a one-sided polemic, usually misleading, and does not deserve much attention" (https://cdn1.sph.harvard.edu/wp-content/uploads/sites/1264/2013/06/Kates-Mauser.pdf).

Despite such criticism, one of Kates's profilers, David B. Kopel, holds that Kates's "greatest significance . . . has been in his tireless work as a behind-the-scenes advocate of the Second Amendment. Working with Academics for the Second Amendment, the National Rifle Association, and the Second

Amendment Foundation, Kates has presented many weekend-long courses on an introduction to firearms law and policy. These courses are invitation-only events for scholars, journalists, or other writers interested in learning more about the Second Amendment. The seminars have been an important cause of the increased scholarly attention paid to firearms issues" (Kopel, op. cit., 469).

Gary Kleck (1951–)

Gary Kleck is the David J. Bordua Professor of Criminology at Florida State University. His studies are often cited by gun rights advocates. These advocates are especially impressed by Kleck's research on defensive gun use (DGU). In a highly controversial 1995 *Journal of Criminal Law and Criminology*, he and Marc Gertz reported the results of their National Self-Defense Survey, which they argue is more accurate than the Bureau of Justice Statistics' National Criminal Victimization Survey (NCVS). The NCVS is generally preferred by public health researchers when discussing the topic of how often a gun is used to fend off a criminal attack (such as an attempted assault, armed robbery, or burglary), usually by simply saying "I have a gun" or by showing or brandishing the weapon. NCVS data indicate perhaps 100,000 DGUs occur in a typical year in the United States, and this number is fairly stable. In contrast, Kleck and Gertz estimated "that each year in the U.S. there are about 2.2–2.5 million DGUs of all types by civilians against humans, with about 1.5–1.9 million of the incidents involving use of handguns" ("Armed Resistance to Crime: The Prevalence and Nature of Self-Defense with a Gun," 164).

Many gun violence researchers do not believe the Kleck/Gertz DGU estimate. These researchers contend that it is just too far out of line with the annually consistent findings of the NCVS, which is based on huge sample sizes (almost 160,000 individuals per year in recent years, compared to 4,977 in the

Kleck/Gertz survey). Moreover, these researchers note that there is a severe "false-positive" problem (people misreporting what actually occurred) because the question being asked encourages a "social desirability" response. Thus, for example, "an individual who acquires a gun for protection and then uses it successfully to ward off a criminal is displaying the wisdom of his precautions and his capacity to protect himself. His action is to be commended and admired." And, finally, even though social desirability bias is not uncommon in survey research and can often have minimal effects, this is not the case regarding the particular research problem at hand because defensive gun use is such a rare event. When a survey is attempting to estimate the incidence of a rare event, a small percentage bias can lead to extreme overestimation. In the Kleck/Gertz "self-defense gun survey, if as few as 1.3 percent of respondents were randomly misclassified, the 2.5 million figure would be thirty-three times higher than the true figure. [In short,] using surveys to estimate rare occurrences with some positive social-desirability bias, will lead to large overestimates" (quoted material from David Hemenway, *Private Guns, Public Health*, Ann Arbor: University of Michigan Press, 2004, 239–240).

Kleck's research in the area of gun violence is wide ranging, and Florida State University makes many of his journal articles readily available online. In 1993, his book *Point Blank: Guns and Violence in America* (1991, 2005) won from the prestigious American Society of Criminology's annual Michael J. Hindelang Award as the most outstanding contribution to research in criminology published within the preceding three years.

David B. Kopel (1960–)

David B. Kopel has been research director of the libertarian think tank Independence Institute since 1992. He is also adjunct professor of Constitutional Law at Denver University, Sturm College of Law; and an Associate Policy Analyst at the Cato Institute, in Washington, D.C. He is a prolific writer, whose works range from op-eds. to blogs, to law review and academic journal articles, to scholarly books and more polemical tracts. He is an expert on the Second Amendment, and his intellectual work combines legal analysis with historical and social science research.

His first major contribution to the literature on gun control and gun violence was *The Samurai, the Mountie, and the Cowboy* (1992). Although coming out from a small publishing house with little fanfare, it eventually made its way into the libraries of many serious students of the gun debate. His major thesis is that America's high rate of gun violence when compared to its peer nations (industrialized democracies) should not be blamed on its relatively weak control laws. Rather, fundamental cultural and historical differences can account for varying cross-national crime rates, not gun prevalence and not gun regulations.

A key cultural distinction that Kopel has emphasized throughout his career is that in the United States, thanks to the Second Amendment (and the English ideological traditions emphasized in the Bill of Rights and Constitution in general), gun ownership is a right, not a privilege. He thus concurs with the philosophical underpinnings of right-to-carry laws, once a major controversy in the gun debate; the controversy has receded in recent years because all but a handful of U.S. states now grant the right of concealed handgun carry to ordinary citizens (given, of course, that they can pass a federal background check). Moreover, he sees no methodological reason to discount the findings of those contending that the huge increase in concealed carry permits has not created more violence and crime, and, if anything, has reduced their rates. As argued in a vast array of writings covering all major topics in the gun debate (from concealed carry to restrictions on assault weapons to gun registration to universal background checks) that he makes available on his website (davekopel.org), Kopel contends the Second Amendment guarantees individuals the right to keep and bear arms and that this right ultimately makes

American society safer, freer, and more stable. His longtime contention that this amendment guarantees an individual right (and not just a *collective* right) for gun ownership received the ultimate confirmation in the landmark decisions by the U.S. Supreme Court in *District of Columbia v. Heller* (2008) and *McDonald v. Chicago* (2010). Indeed, he wrote extensive amicus briefs for both of these cases, briefs that were cited by multiple justices in their opinions (by Justice Breyer in *Heller*, see http://www.davekopel.org/Briefs/07-290bsacreprintIntlLaw EnforcementEduc&Trainers.pdf; and by Justices Alito and Stevens in *McDonald*, see http://papers.ssrn.com/sol3/papers .cfm?abstract_id=1511425).

Wayne R. LaPierre Jr. (1950–)

Wayne R. LaPierre Jr. has been the executive vice president and chief executive officer of the NRA since 1991. Along with the NRA's board, he is responsible for overseeing and implementing the NRA's national policies and operations. He has provided much of the public face of the association for the past two and a half decades and is frequently quoted on its homepage and in the press—and has appeared on many national news and information radio and television programs.

He is a staunch, uncompromising defender of the Second Amendment and the rights of gun owners. He has led the NRA in its hugely successful efforts to keep gun control legislation at a minimum at both the state and national levels ever since its major losses to the gun control movement in the mid-1990s (including the 1993 Brady Act and the 1994 Federal Assault Weapons Ban). At the same time, under his leadership the organization has helped to move forward significant increases in the number and breadth of the rights of gun owners—most significantly in extending liberal right-to-carry laws in the majority of states; ensuring preemption statutes (or equivalent judicial rulings) in all but a handful of states (such that a local or county government cannot enact a gun law stricter than an equivalent law at the state level, if allowed to enact any gun law at all); and in getting national legislation passed that shields the gun industry from most kinds of civil lawsuits (the PLCAA of 2005).

In 1991, the NRA was estimated to have about 2.5 million members. Over the course of LaPierre's tenure, it had doubled in size by 2016. Moreover, the association has grown more respected, as indicated by national public opinion polls. For example, the Gallup poll reported 42 percent of Americans were "mostly" or "very" favorable toward the NRA in 1993, 52 percent had such opinions by 2000, and 58 percent by 2015 (http://www.gallup.com/poll/1645/guns.aspx). Under LaPierre's leadership, the organization has continued to be a role model of how a well-organized, well-led, single-issue advocacy group can wield huge political power. Not only has the NRA successfully lobbied in state legislatures and the U.S. Congress for the promotion of gun rights measures (and the defeat of gun control measures), but it has also seen great success in seeing the candidates it supports getting elected. For example, in the 2014 midterm elections alone, 95 percent of NRA-backed congressional candidates were victorious (http://www.commoncause.org/research-reports/ whose-government-whose-voice/whose-government-whose-voice.pdf).

John R. Lott Jr. (1958–)

John R. Lott Jr. became one of the leading and most controversial figures in the contemporary gun debate with the 1998 publication of *More Guns, Less Crime: Understanding Crime and Gun Control Laws* from the prestigious University of Chicago Press. The book's thesis is in its title, as it argues states that enact liberal concealed carry laws reduce their violent crime rate. Lott is thus critical of that small handful of states having resisted the "shall-issue" approach to an ordinary citizen obtaining a permit to carry a concealed handgun. A "shall-issue" law dictates that an adult who can pass a federal background check, and in some states take a short course on gun safety, must be granted a license to carry a concealed weapon. Lott's research has been praised by gun rights advocates and strongly criticized by scholars in the public health community. His research uses arcane statistical techniques that are beyond the understanding of the average policymaker or average advocate (on either side) of the gun debate. However, his interpretation is straightforward and intuitively appealing: criminals are rational beings and are thus less likely to try a robbery or assault if they think the potential victim might be armed. A classic illustration Lott offers is that in Canada and the United Kingdom there are highly restrictive gun laws; thus, not surprisingly to Lott, near half of all burglaries are "hot burglaries," that is, where a resident is at home when a criminal strikes. In contrast, the United States, with less restrictive gun laws, the "hot burglary" rate is only 13 percent. "Criminals are not just behaving differently by accident. . . . The fear of potentially armed victims causes American burglars to spend more time than their foreign counterparts 'casing' a house to ensure that nobody is home" (Lott, 1998, 5).

Because of the huge criticism his book received from a variety of scholars with training in the complex statistical analysis techniques Lott employed in it, he came out with successive editions of his book in 2000 and 2010—in which he provided detailed responses. After reviewing the relevant academic literature and doing its own original analysis, the highly regarded National Research Council concluded that "it is impossible to draw strong conclusions . . . on the causal impact of these laws . . . the results are sensitive to the inclusion of controls. That is, whether one concludes that right-to-carry laws increase or decrease crime based on models of this sort depends on which control variables are included. Such laws have no obvious effect in the model without controls (and therefore no clear level effect in the raw data). Moreover, as demonstrated above, seemingly minor changes to the set of control variables substantially alter the estimated effects. Given that researchers might reasonably argue about which controls belong in the model and that the results are sensitive to [these controls . . .], the committee is not sanguine about the prospects for measuring the effect of right-to-carry laws on crime" (*Firearms and Violence: A Critical Review,* Washington, DC: National Academies Press, 2005, 121, 149).

Lott has published extensively in the area of gun violence and gun control, with the bulk of his research being critical of most gun control measures. He makes many of his commentaries, articles, and reports available on his website: http://johnrlott .blogspot.com/. He is also the founder of the 501(c)3 Crime Prevention Research Center—"a research and education organization dedicated to conducting academic quality research on the relationship between laws regulating the ownership or use of guns, crime, and public safety; educating the public on the results of such research; and supporting other organizations, projects, and initiatives that are organized and operated for similar purposes" (http://crimeresearch.org/), where a number of his studies are made available, including those on the impact of concealed weapons permits on crime.

Larry Pratt (1942–)

Larry Pratt is the executive director of Gun Owners of America (GOA), a position he has held since its founding in 1975. He is well known to both sides of the gun debate, and he and the GOA are well known for contending that the NRA is too concessionary on gun control. Indeed, conservative senator John McCain (R-AZ), whom the NRA has given a grade of "B+" for his stands on gun rights is deemed "a liberal gun grabber" on the GOA website (https://gunowners.org/mcgungrab.htm). In 2013, four U.S. senators whom the NRA graded "A" for their voting records on gun rights were graded "F" by GOA (https://www.washingtonpost.com/news/the-fix/wp/2012/

12/17/where-the-senate-stands-on-guns-in-one-chart/). Conservative, libertarian congressman Ron Paul (R-TX) has called the GOA "the only no-compromise gun lobby in Washington" (as the organization emblazes atop its homepage: https://gun owners.org/).

In an extended analysis of Guatemala's decision to combat domestic terrorism by arming everyday civilians, Pratt concluded that the approach worked; and in a similar examination of the Philippines, he came to a similar conclusion (see his *Armed People Victorious*, Nashville, TN: Legacy Publishing, 1991). In 1995, he published an extensive collection of his essays and editorials that extol gun rights and gun ownership in his *Safeguarding Liberty* (Nashville, TN: Legacy Publishing), and in 2001, he published a sequel, *On the Firing Line* (Nashville, TN: Legacy Publishing). For a sample of his strident and well-composed essays, see his "We Don't Need No Stinkin' Background Checks" in the March 2016 issue the GOA's monthly newsletter, *The Gun Owners* (https://gunowners.org/images/pdf/n20160310.pdf).

National Organizations
Citizens Committee for the Right to Keep and Bear Arms/Second Amendment Foundation

The Citizens Committee for the Rights to Keep and Bear Arms (CCRKBA) and the SAF are key components of a network of gun rights enterprises overseen by Alan Gottlieb (see earlier).

CCRKBA is a nonprofit organization whose mission "is dedicated to protecting your firearms rights [and] . . . to educat[ing] grass root activists, the public, legislators and the media. Our programs are designed to help all Americans understand the importance of the Second Amendment and its role in keeping Americans free" (http://www.ccrkba .org/?page_id=2518). It has an estimated 650,000 members, a political action committee, and more than 100 affiliated state organizations (groups like the California Rifle and Pistol

Association and the Colorado State Shooting Association). While the CCRKBA aggressively promotes political activities in support of gun rights, its companion organization, the SAF, focuses more on education and legal action (see the Alan Gura and Don B. Kates Jr. profiles). Like GOA, the CCRKBA sees itself as an even stronger force for gun rights than the NRA, but both it and the GOA rank well behind the NRA regarding size and influence.

The CCRKBA and SAF share ownership of several talk radio stations in the Pacific Northwest. They also cosponsor an annual Gun Rights Policy Conference. The conference advertises itself as chance for gun rights advocates "to network, get an insider look, and plan pro-gun rights strategies for the coming year." The seminars and presentations examine "critical issues," including "city gun bans, 'smart' guns, concealed carry, federal legislation, legal actions, gun show regulation, and state and local activity" (https://www .saf.org/grpc/).

Gun Owners of America

GOA regards itself as a generally more aggressive advocacy group for gun rights than its much larger big brother, the NRA. Indeed, when in June 2016 Senate Minority Leader Harry Reid (D-NV) decried "the NRA is bad, really bad, but Gun Owners of America is even worse than bad," GOA proudly posted the comment on its social media and YouTube accounts.

Former California state senator Bill Richardson founded the GOA in October 1975 when he started a direct mail campaign to defeat a proposed bill in the state legislature to ban handguns. He saw this bill as part of the "inroads the radical left [was] making in politics, most specifically their consistent attempts to disarm Americans" (https://gunowners.org/ hlrichardson.htm). He became a life member of the NRA and subsequently served on its board of directors for more than a decade.

While Richardson is the lifelong chair of GOA, Larry Pratt (see the profile provided earlier) has been the day-to-day operations manager—serving as executive director since the association's founding in 1975. Under Pratt's administration, the GOA hosts a weekly radio news hour, regularly updates its YouTube channel and a variety of social media (Twitter, Facebook, and Instagram), and publishes *The Gun Owners*, which is a monthly newsletter largely dedicated to gun legislation and national politics. A typical article has a catchy title like its March 2016 lead essay by Tim Macy, "Gun Rights Would Not Survive an Obama Appointment to the Supreme Court" (https://gunowners.org/images/pdf/n20160310.pdf). GOA was a trailblazer in first using fax and then e-mail alerts to mobilize its membership to rally for or against gun-related legislation at both the state and national levels—and it has been this kind of quick grassroots mobilization that has been a key reason why the gun rights movement has won so many more political battles in the past two decades compared to the gun control movement.

National Rifle Association

The NRA is the nation's largest, oldest, and most politically powerful interest group that opposes gun laws and favors gun rights. It publishes several magazines (*American Rifleman, American Hunter, America's 1st Freedom, Shooting Illustrated, Shooting Sports USA,* and *NRA Insights*) and consists of several divisions, the largest and most powerful of which is its political arm, the ILA. Other activities include gun safety, education, public service, and youth programs, and a variety of shooting, hunting, and collecting programs and information. The NRA also includes a 501(c) nonprofit corporation, the NRA Foundation, spanning activities that include the Firearms Civil Rights Legal Defense Fund, the International Shooter Development Fund, the NRA Junior Programs Fund, the National Firearms Museum Fund, the NRA Range

Development Fund, and the NRA Special Contribution Fund. The NRA also offers various estate-planning and will services, hoping to encourage gifts and donations to it from life insurance, securities or real estate gifts, and charitable remainder trusts. The NRA has maintained long and close ties to the firearm manufacturing industry, serving as its political front until the 1990s, when the industry assumed a more visible and active political role.

The NRA's enduring political clout rests on three factors. First, it is one of the nation's oldest and most experienced political lobby groups, and its resources and experience dwarf those of other gun-related organizations. Second, it maintains a grassroots membership base that cares deeply about the single issue of guns and that can be effectively mobilized to vote, write letters, attend meetings, contribute money, and otherwise make its political voice heard. The members' single-issue devotion to guns and gun issues makes them a potent political force, even though most Americans favor stronger gun laws, because gun control foes maintain much stronger feelings for their cause than their opponents. NRA members' intensity of feeling often carries the day over majority wishes on gun issues precisely because that majority is not similarly intense in its political beliefs on behalf of gun control. Third, the organization is consistently successful at raising and spending large amounts of money for political purposes through the ILA and the NRA's political action committee, the Political Victory Fund. In the 2008 elections, for example, the NRA spent $40 million to support political allies and oppose its foes. After the landmark U.S. Supreme Court decision in *Citizens United v. Federal Election Commission*, which has ultimately allowed corporations, labor unions, and associations like the NRA to make indirect donations channeled to candidates through independent political groups, the organization's political contributions jump dramatically. The decision partly underlay the ability of the NRA to triple its midterm election contributions between 2010 and 2014—from approximately

$10 million to $31.4 million (http://www.commoncause
.org/research-reports/whose-government-whose-voice/gun-
control.html).

When Congress turned its attention to gun control in the
1960s, so did the NRA. From that point on, the NRA devoted
increasing time and resources to its political agenda. The NRA
opposed enactment of what became the Gun Control Act of
1968. Despite its failure to block enactment of the bill, the
NRA and its allies did succeed in weakening the original bill,
which had included provisions for nationwide firearm registration and gun licensing.

By the mid-1970s, membership reached a million. It hit
2 million by the early 1980s, rose to 2.5 million around 1990,
and then climbed to over 5 million by 2016.

Although the NRA opposed gun controls for decades, the
NRA leadership had maintained the organization's primary
focus on sporting, hunting, and other recreational gun uses
through the 1960s. The "old-guard moderates" in control of
the organization sought to turn the organization away from
politics and back toward hunting and conservation. Symp-
tomatic of this effort were plans promoted by the old guard
to create a national shooting center in New Mexico and move
the NRA's headquarters to Colorado Springs. Meanwhile,
the NRA's recently formed ILA, headed by hard-liner Harlon
Carter (see his profile), complained bitterly at the devotion
of organizational resources to these nonpolitical efforts. The
response of the old guard was to fire 74 employees, most of
whom were hard-liners. The simmering dispute surfaced at
the NRA's 1977 national convention in Cincinnati. Rallying
a faction called the Federation for NRA, Carter won organizational changes giving the convention members greater control over decision making. He and his allies then used those
rules to depose the old guard at the convention in what was
dubbed the "Revolt at Cincinnati." From this point forward,
the ILA became the primary power center of the NRA and
politics became the NRA's primary focus.

Since that time, the hard-liners have pushed the organization toward total, complete, and unwavering opposition to all forms of gun regulation. For example, up until the mid-1970s, the NRA supported waiting periods for handgun purchases. Since that time, however, it has opposed waiting periods, and it fought vehemently against the ultimately successful enactment of a five-business-day waiting period for handgun purchases, enacted in 1993 as part of the Brady Bill. This emphasis on 100 percent purity has helped the organization mobilize and activate its faithful, but it has also alienated former and potential allies and tarnished the organization's national reputation. The NRA's right-wing turn reached its furthest point in the early 1990s, when it refused to support conservatives with long records of backing the organization, including President George H. W. Bush in 1992 and Republican presidential nominee Robert Dole in 1996, despite the fact that both of these candidates were opposed by gun control supporter Bill Clinton.

A key to the effort to improve the NRA's image, and to beat back efforts by an even more extreme element to win control of the organization, was the elevation of actor Charlton Heston to the presidency of the organization in 1998. Heston's well-known face became the embodiment of the NRA's new image, which it advanced aggressively, and successfully, to blunt new national gun control initiatives advanced in the wake of the 1999 Columbine High School shooting. Heston was reelected president every year until 2003, when he stepped down after having been diagnosed with Alzheimer's disease.

The NRA reached new heights of political influence during the presidency of George W. Bush, the most gun-friendly president in history. Bush's first attorney general, John Ashcroft, had been the NRA's staunched ally during his years in the U.S. Senate, and he embraced NRA positions on a host of legal matters related to guns. Most significantly, he reversed decades of Justice Department policy that had long interpreted the Second Amendment's right to bear arms as a militia-based right. Under Ashcroft, the government embraced the individualist view, meaning that the amendment was seen as granting a personal right to guns. This change helped precipitate the Supreme Court's about-face in Second Amendment interpretation when the high court embraced the individualist view in the 2008 case of *District of Columbia v. Heller*. Ironically, NRA legal strategists initially opposed the suit that led to the *Heller* ruling, feeling that the Court was not ready to take the step it ultimately did. Two years later, the Supreme Court applied or "incorporated" the Second Amendment to the states in the case of *McDonald v. City of Chicago*.

In the first decade of the 21st century, the NRA also logged legislative successes, including enactment of the PLCAA of 2005, which provided legal immunity for the gun industry, the right to carry guns in national parks, and the destruction of gun background check data after 24 hours. A former NRA president offered this advice to those trying to understand the NRA's single-minded zeal: "You'd get a far better understanding if you just approach us as if [we were] one of the world's great religions" (as quoted in Michael Powell, "Call to Arms," *Washington Post*, Aug. 6, 2000, W8).

National Shooting Sports Foundation

Founded in 1961, the National Shooting Sports Foundation (NSSF) promotes recreational hunting and sport shooting. It is the largest trade association for the shooting, hunting, and firearms industry—whose members include manufacturers, distributors, and retailers of firearms, ammunition, and shooting accessory equipment. More than 5,500 companies and organizations belong to the NSSF. It also represents the hunting and shooting sports industry through one of its major divisions, the National Association of Firearms Retailers. Since 1979, most funding for the NSSF's programs and activities comes from the NSSF-owned industry trade show, the SHOT Show (http://www.shotshow.org/).

The NSSF is actively engaged in lobbying and informing its membership and the wider public about legal, regulatory, and legislative issues involving the rights of gun owners. For example, the organization sponsored a national media campaign designed to correct what the organization believed were misperceptions about Colt AR-15 and related rifles. Some gun control groups have held up the AR-15 as an example of a military-style "assault weapon," but the NSSF campaign emphasized that most AR-15s have been and are used in sport shooting competitions (http://www.nssf.org/factsheets/semi-auto.cfm).

The NSSF also cooperates with law enforcement agencies. For example, the organization partners with the Bureau of Alcohol, Tobacco, Firearms and Explosives and the Office of Justice Programs to assist law enforcement in educating firearms retailers to better identify and thus deter illegal "straw purchases"—and to raise public awareness that straw purchasing is a serious crime. The "Don't Lie for the Other Guy" program and retailer kits are designed to halt individuals with no criminal records from procuring firearms for convicted felons and others barred by federal law from buying or possessing guns. In a related cooperative effort, the NSSF works with the U.S. Department of Justice to fund the distribution of millions of cable and related trigger locks through Project ChildSafe.

Introduction

This chapter begins with succinct summaries of key federal and state gun laws as of 2016. Many of these laws are discussed in detail in Chapter 2.

The gun laws sections are followed by the 27-word Second Amendment, which has been at the center of much of the gun debate for the last half century. Depending on which part of the amendment one places focus—the first part emphasizing the intent of the amendment to protect the collective right of each individual state to field a well-regulated militia; or the latter part, which emphasizes the right of the people to keep and bear arms—very different implications are set in place regarding the depth and breadth of gun regulations. Those favoring strong gun control laws emphasize the first part of the amendment, leading to an interpretation of the entire amendment as ensuring a collective *right of the people of a state (say, Rhode Islanders); while those favoring strong rights for gun owners emphasize the latter part of the amendment— leading to an interpretation of the entire amendment as protecting*

Jonathan Mossberg, whose iGun Technology Corp. is working to develop a "smart gun," poses with the firearm, in Daytona Beach, Florida, in April of 2016. Mossberg is among a group of pioneers looking to build a safer gun. Mossberg is working to develop a firearm that cannot be fired by the wrong person, but works without fail in the hands of its owner. Despite significant government and private manufacturer funding, no smart gun has reached the marketplace in any significant way. (AP Photo/Lisa Marie Pane)

the individual *right of each ordinary citizen to arm him- or her-self for defense of the state, as well as for self-defense. The final section of this chapter provides the "syllabus" (legal summary) for the landmark decision of the U.S. Supreme Court in* District of Columbia v. Heller, *in which the law of the land was firmly established that* individuals *do indeed have right to own guns, especially those that would be considered valuable for self-defense—including handguns.*

Summaries of Key Federal Gun Laws

This section reviews major U.S. federal gun laws as of 2016. The provisions of these laws are often difficult for the average person, even if well educated, to decipher. The descriptions given here are written in plain English, which means that some aspects of particular laws may get lost in translation. Thus, the legislation as described below should not be used for legal purposes.

Mailing of Firearms Act (Miller Act) (1927)

Officially entitled "An Act Declaring Pistols, Revolvers, and Other Firearms Capable of Being Concealed on the Person Nonmailable and Providing Penalties," this act was the first federal legislation aimed at controlling guns. Also known as the Miller Act, it sought to prohibit the interstate shipment of handguns. Still in effect today, the act prohibits the sending through the U.S. Post Office of pistols and other firearms that could be considered concealable weapons.

In actuality, the law was easy to skirt because mailers could legally send guns via private delivery companies such as UPS.

National Firearms Act (1934)

The National Firearms Act (NFA) of 1934 mandated all persons who were engaged in the business of selling "gangster-type" weapons—such as machine guns, short-barreled shotguns, and silencers—and all owners of these to register with the

Collector of Internal Revenue and pay applicable taxes for the firearm transfer.

The NFA was enacted under the taxing power granted to Congress in Article I, Section 8, of the U.S. Constitution. It is administered by the Bureau of Alcohol, Tobacco, Firearms and Explosives (ATF). Among its central provisions, the NFA instituted a unique system of registration whereby NFA-related firearms are registered to their owners in a central registry maintained by the ATF. In addition, the NFA prohibits the transfer or manufacture of NFA-related firearms without the prior approval of the ATF. The written application forms require, among other things, that the person submit a photograph and fingerprint card.

It should be noted that approximately one-half century later (in 1986), Congress banned the sale of new machine guns altogether—except to the government. Section 922(o) of the Firearms Owners' Protection Act (FOPA) of 1986 now prohibits a private citizen from possessing or transferring a machine gun that was not made and registered before May 19, 1986, unless such transfer or possession is under the authority of federal or state governments or their departments or agencies. Since the enactment of FOPA, the ATF will not approve nongovernment NFA applications to acquire any machine gun made after May 19, 1986.

Federal Firearms Act (1938)

The Federal Firearms Act imposed the first federal limitations on the sale of ordinary firearms. It was aimed at those involved in selling and shipping firearms through interstate or foreign commerce. The law required the manufacturers, dealers, and importers of guns and handgun ammunition to obtain a federal firearms license (FFL; at an original annual cost of one dollar) from the Internal Revenue Service. Dealers had to maintain records of the names and addresses of persons to whom firearms are sold. Gun sales to persons convicted of violent felonies were prohibited.

Federal Aviation Act (1958)

As part of the Federal Aviation Act, individuals flying on passenger aircraft are barred from bringing on board any firearm, ammunition, or firearm part, except as part of their check-in luggage. The Transportation Security Administration summarizes the law and its related amendments in its 2016 circular *Transporting Firearms and Ammunition* (https://www.tsa.gov/travel/transporting-firearms-and-ammunition). Firearms and ammunition declared to the air carrier during the ticket counter check-in process must meet the regulations detailed in this circular—including the firearm must be unloaded, and carried in a locked, hard-sided container.

Gun Control Act of 1968

Those statutes which are now called the Gun Control Act of 1968 (GCA) were actually combined from two different bills: the Gun Control Act and the Omnibus Safe Streets and Crime Control Act. Most of the statutes are found at 18 U.S. Code sections 921–929. New federal guns laws (e.g., the Brady Act, the 1994 Assault Weapons Ban) are usually codified as amendments to the GCA statutes—and, indeed, the GCA represents the foundation of federal gun control regulation.

The GCA's most important provisions include restrictions on sales of guns and ammunition across state lines, restrictions on the import of firearms, creating the "prohibited persons" list of classes of persons who are barred from possessing guns (e.g., convicted felons), and creating a point-of-sale system of gun owner registration.

Interstate pistol sales were banned. Interstate long-gun sales were banned, except when contiguous states enacted laws to authorize such sales. Mail-order and package delivery service (e.g., UPS) gun sales were shut down. Interstate ammunition sales were prohibited. All of these bans applied only to purchases by consumers. FFL holders—including gun manufacturers and wholesalers—were still allowed to sell across state lines to each other, and to use the mails. A new class of FFL was created for gun collectors, allowing them to engage in interstate and mail-order transactions for "curios and relics," but requiring them to submit to various registration and paperwork rules. In addition, the secretary of the Treasury was given authority to ban the import of any gun not "particularly suitable for" sporting purposes. Under this authority, the secretary of the Treasury prohibited imports of foreign military surplus firearms.

Finally, the GCA led to the creation of ATF—upgraded from its previous status as a division—within the Department of the Treasury. Effective from January 2003, the Homeland Security Act transferred the ATF to the Department of Justice and added "Explosives" to the name. Although ATF's law enforcement functions were included in the transfer, its tax and trade functions remained in the Treasury Department with the new Alcohol and Tobacco Tax and Trade Bureau.

Armed Career Criminal Act (1984)

The Armed Career Criminal Act of 1984 (18 U.S.C. § 924[e]) increased the penalties for firearm possession by convicted felons as specified in the GCA. The 1984 act was amended in 1986 and 1988, and its guidelines have received several updates over the years. These amendments and updates represent an effort to meet the true spirit of the legislation, which is aimed at incapacitating hardened criminals—those with three or more previous violent felony or serious drug offense convictions—by putting them in prison for a minimum of 15 years if they are found in possession of a firearm.

Firearms Owners' Protection Act (McClure-Volkmer) (1986)

Enacted as Public Law 99–308, 100 Stat. 449, the Firearms Owners' Protection Act (FOPA)—known also as the McClure-Volkmer Act—made technical changes to the GCA. FOPA prohibited forfeitures of personal firearms on charges for which a defendant had been acquitted; prohibited punishment of unintentional violations by the GCA (by requiring that the government prove that the violation was willful or knowing); clarified what was meant by the GCA requirement that an FFL was necessary for persons "engaged in the business"; allowed an FFL holder to sell guns away from their principal place of business as long as the sales complied with all relevant laws (thus allowing FFL holders to sell their guns at their regular place of business, plus at gun shows and online); reclassified certain paperwork violations as misdemeanors; limited ATF compliance inspections of gun dealers to one per dealer per year (while still allowing unlimited inspections in case of a criminal investigation); required the ATF to process FFL applications in a timely manner and not to deny the application without good cause; imposed controls on ATF license revocations; provided for the award of attorney's fees against the ATF if the court found that that case was abusive; prohibited the ATF from creating a national gun registry; removed federal restrictions on interstate ammunition sales; relegalized interstate long-gun sales (if the seller is an FFL and the sale is legal in the buyer's home state as well as in the seller's state); and broadened the scope of firearms allowed to be imported. FOPA left intact the GCA banning of consumers being able to purchase handguns across state lines.

Law Enforcement Officers Protection Act (1986)

Enacted as Public Law 99–308, the Law Enforcement Officers Protection Act bans so-called cop killer handgun bullets—or more accurately, bullets with very dense cores made from certain metals—that are capable of piercing bullet-resistant vests and other body armor. Amended in 1994, the statute defines "armor piercing ammunition" as a handgun bullet "constructed entirely" from "tungsten alloys, steel, iron, brass, bronze, beryllium copper, or depleted uranium," or with a jacket having a weight greater than one-quarter of the projectile's total weight.

Undetectable Firearms Act (Terrorist Firearms Detection) (1988, Reauthorized 1998, 2003, 2013)

Codified at 18 U.S.C. section 922(p), the Undetectable Firearms Act, also known as the Terrorist Firearms Detection Act, arose in response to the development of plastic guns that combined the use of plastic polymers with metallic firearm components. For a period of 10 years, the act banned the manufacture, importation, possession, receipt, and transfer of guns with less than 3.7 ounces of metal, as well as required all handguns to include enough metal to show a gun profile when passed through a metal detector.

The act was due to expire in November 1998, but was renewed for five years in October 1998. In November 2003, the law was once again renewed—this time for a 10-year period. At the end of 2013, the law was once again renewed for a 10-year period. The renewal took on special meaning this time around, as selected and newly refined 3-D printing devices were now capable of producing working, plastic firearms.

Crime Control Act (1990)

Enacted as Public Law 101–647, the Crime Control Act bans the importing or domestic manufacturing from foreign parts of certain semiautomatic firearms designated as "assault weapons"; other types of semiautomatic rifles, shotguns, and pistols were still allowed to be imported. The act also created gun-free school zones, making it a federal crime to carry a firearm within 1,000 feet of a school; however, this portion of the act was overturned in a circuit court ruling in 1993—that was subsequently upheld by the ruling of the Supreme Court in *United States v. Lopez* (1995).

Brady Handgun Violence Prevention Act (1993)

Enacted by Congress as Public Law 103–159 (107 U.S. Statute at Large 1536), the Brady Act required a five-government-business-day waiting period for a purchase of a handgun, for

the purpose of conducting a background check on the prospective buyer, and to provide a cooling-off period in order to
minimize impulse purchases that might lead to violence. Five
years after the enactment of the law, the five-day waiting period
was eliminated, and replaced by an instant background check
system for all retail firearms sales.

Handgun (and to impart the full impact of the GCA) and
other firearm purchases are to be rejected if the applicant was
in a "prohibited" category of persons (see the list of these categories in the description of the 1968 GCA).

The Brady law required that local law enforcement must
make a "reasonable effort" to check the backgrounds of gun
buyers. In addition, it provided for ending the five-day wait
after five years, to be replaced with an instant background
check, which began in December 1998. Such checks are conducted through the FBI's National Instant Criminal Background Check System (NICS) or state equivalent.

Public Safety and Recreational Firearms Use Protection Act (Assault Weapons Ban) (1994)

Enacted under Title XI as part of the Violent Crime Control
and Law Enforcement Act (PL 103–322; 108 Stat. 1796), the
federal "Assault Weapons Ban" prohibited, for 10 years, the
future manufacture and transfer of 19 named assault weapons, and approximately 200 firearms covered by the law's generic definition of "assault weapon." Under the terms of the
law, semiautomatic assault weapons were defined under three
categories: rifles, pistols, and shotguns. Semiautomatic rifles
and pistols fell under the law if they had the ability to accept
a detachable magazine and possessed at least two other characteristics of such weapons; shotguns were considered assault
weapons if they possessed at least two of the assault weapon
features. The law also specifically exempted 661 named weapons. In addition, it banned large-capacity ammunition-feeding
devices (those that could hold more than 10 rounds). The ban
did not apply to assault weapons already in circulation. Guns
neither banned nor protected by the law were exempted from

its regulations. In 2004, the Assault Weapons Ban, originally enacted to last for 10 years, was allowed to expire.

Gun-Free Schools Act (1994)

The Gun-Free Schools Act requires that any state receiving federal education funds "shall have in effect a State law requiring local educational agencies to expel from school for a period of not less than one year a student who is determined to have brought a weapon to a school."

Lautenberg Amendment (Domestic Violence Offender Gun Ban) (1996)

The Lautenberg Amendment to the GCA, also called the Domestic Violence Offender Gun Ban, expanded the prohibition of gun purchase or possession to include any person subject to a domestic violence protection order or convicted of a domestic violence misdemeanor offense. It also made it unlawful to knowingly transfer or sell a gun or ammunition to such a person. Finally, under the original law, police and military personnel were exempted from domestic offender firearm prohibitions, but this exemption was eliminated.

GCA Firearms Safety Updates (1998)

As part of the Omnibus Consolidated and Emergency Appropriations Act (PL 105–277), the GCA was modified to require federal firearms licensees to offer for sale safe gun-storage boxes and safety devices (the law being intended for retail gun dealers). Other changes include banning firearm sale, transfer, or possession by most of those holding nonimmigrant visas, including those who have overstayed the limits of their temporary visas.

The "Bailey Fix" (1998)

The U.S. Department of Justice, working in conjunction with state and local authorities, and coordinating key law enforcement groups (the ATF, FBI, and Drug Enforcement Administration), developed Project Triggerlock in 1991. Over the years, Triggerlock was expanded and reformulated. These programs use federal firearm statutes—for example, those barring the possession of firearms by high-risk individuals, including convicted felons, drug dealers, and domestic abusers—to prosecute gun-carrying offenders in *federal* ("U.S. District") courts, where convictions rates are typically much higher and penalties much stiffer than in state and local courts. Triggerlock-type programs suffered a serious setback 1995, when the U.S. Supreme Court ruled in *Bailey v. United States* (516 U.S. 137, 116 S.Ct. 501) that persons in possession of a gun when arrested for a violent or drug-trafficking crime must have actually used it (e.g., firing or brandishing) if they are to be charged with the separate offense of having used a gun in the crime. This immediately reduced the number of weapons charges filed in federal district courts. In response, 1998 federal legislation commonly referred to as the "Bailey Fix" dictated that the mere possession of a firearm during a crime of violence or drug-trafficking crime allows for an additional charge and for enhanced sentencing if the possession was in furtherance of the crime.

Nonimmigrant Aliens Firearms and Ammunition Amendments (2002)

In 2002, the U.S. Customs Service and the ATF announced that they would begin enforcement of the Nonimmigrant Aliens Firearms and Ammunition Amendments to the GCA (as enacted by Congress in 1998 as Public Law 105–277). These amendments require nonimmigrant aliens wanting to bring firearms or ammunition into the United States for hunting or sporting purposes to obtain an import permit from ATF prior to entering the country.

Arming Pilots against Terrorism Act (2002)

The Nonimmigrant Aliens Firearms and Ammunition Amendments noted earlier were in response to the 9/11 terrorist attacks. A similar response was the Arming Pilots against Terrorism Act, which allows airline pilots to carry firearms on passenger flights (if they so desire, and after having gone through a Transportation Security Administration training program). The law was later amended to also allow carrying by cargo pilots.

Background Check Restriction
("Tiahrt Amendments") (2004)

In January, as part of the fiscal year 2004 Consolidated Appropriations Bill (PL 108–199), Congress approved provisions reducing the length of time the Department of Justice can maintain background-check records on firearm sales, from 90 days to 24 hours. Records are kept on file to ensure that if an individual prohibited from buying guns (e.g., a convicted felon or individual under a domestic violence restraining order) is inadvertently allowed to make such a purchase, the mistake can be corrected. Sponsored by Todd Tiahrt (R-KS), the so called Tiahrt Amendments have been included every year since 2004 in the Consolidated Appropriations Bill. Gun control advocates have complained that requiring these records to be destroyed within 24 hours has resulted in the Justice Department being unable to correct most errors, and their expectation is that more guns will end up in the hands of those prohibited from possessing them. However, gun rights proponents note that if a background check produces a rejection, then all information related to that potential sale is kept indefinitely. They also contended that retaining the background check records of lawful gun purchasers amounts to a partial registry of gun owners, which was prohibited by FOPA in 1986.

Law Enforcement Officers Safety Act
(2004, Amended 2010)

The Law Enforcement Officers Safety Act (LEOSA) allows current and retired qualified law enforcement officers to carry concealed firearms throughout the country without a concealed carry permit, with a few restrictions (e.g., they may not carry into state government buildings in contravention of state law; they cannot carry their firearms into federal courtrooms, buildings, and lands where firearms are banned). The LEOSA was amended in 2010, refining the definition of "qualified" and extending it to include Amtrak police and selected other federal agents.

Protection of Lawful Commerce in Arms Act (2005)

During the late 1990s and early 2000s, Handgun Control, Inc. (now the Brady Campaign) greatly developed its Legal Action Project, which used lawsuits to push firearms manufacturers and dealers to develop products and practices aimed at reducing gun violence. Starting in 1998, the Legal Action Project assisted more than two dozen city governments, as well as the state of New York, to file suits to recover the costs of gun violence to the general public—including those associated with the police and courts, and with emergency medical care. The governments claimed that gun manufacturers had failed to take advantage of safe-gun technologies, and that their distribution systems encouraged straw purchases and the flow of firearms into the black market. The strategy, however, was brought to a near halt with the passage of the Protection of Lawful Commerce in Arms Act—which now shields gun and ammunition dealers and manufacturers from civil liability suits based on the criminal misuse of their products.

Child Safety Lock Act (2005)

The Child Safety Lock Act (CSLA) was adopted as part of the Protection of Lawful Commerce in Arms Act and makes it unlawful for a federal firearms licensee to sell or transfer a handgun without providing a secure gun storage or safety device. The CSLA also shields an individual in possession or control of a handgun from civil liability suits if he or she has used a secure gun storage or safety device. Thus if a gun owner has safely stored his or her handgun (or has used a trigger-lock) and another party breaks into the storage box or disables the trigger-lock, and a tragedy results (e.g., a crime is committed with the gun, or an accidental shooting occurs), then the gun owner cannot be held civilly liable.

NICS Improvement Act (2008)

The final passage of which was motivated by the Virginia Tech massacre, the NICS Improvement Act encourages states to improve their recordkeeping and transmittal to the FBI's NICS, especially for mental health adjudications. The central provisions provide federal dollars in support of states' efforts to maintain and submit the appropriate data—and at the same time, threaten the states with the loss of funding for other programs for noncompliance. The act also includes a series of processes and requirements allowing opportunities for gun buyers previously deemed ineligible to restore their rights.

Protecting the Right of Individuals to Bear Arms in the National Park and National Wildlife Refuge Systems (2009)

Enacted as part of the Credit Card Accountability Responsibility and Disclosure Act, this law dictates that the "Secretary of the Interior shall not promulgate or enforce any regulation that prohibits an individual from possessing a firearm . . . in any unit of the National Park System or the National Wildlife Refuge System" if the individual is not otherwise prohibited by state or federal law from possessing a firearm in a state park of the host state. In other words, an individual can carry a firearm in a national park or wildlife refuge under the same conditions in which he or she can carry a firearm in a state park in the relevant state.

Amtrak Checked-Baggage Firearms Program (2010)

As part of the Consolidated Appropriations Act of 2010 (PL 111–117), there was a reversal of the post-9/11 ban on the transporting of firearms in locked luggage on Amtrak trains (section 159). Amtrak was directed to develop a program similar to that used by the airlines to allow for secure firearms transport. As implemented, the locked luggage must be "checked"—meaning that it is accessible only to Amtrak employees. However, because not all routes have checked baggage service, there are some trains on which firearms cannot be transported—including, for example, Amtrak's very popular Acela line, which does not offer checked baggage service.

Sources: A comprehensive account of federal gun laws can be found in Stephen Halbrook's *Firearms Law Deskbook: Federal and State Criminal Practice*, 2015–2016 edition (Eagan, MN: West, 2014), which is revised annually. The Law Center to Prevent Gun Violence provides online descriptions of federal firearms regulations, which it frequently updates (http://smart gunlaws.org/). A final, excellent source to consult is the actual published federal regulations! The ATF provides them free in a readily downloadable pdf document—which includes a helpful appendix of "frequently asked questions" (see *Federal Firearms Regulations Reference Guide*; https://www.atf.gov/file/11241/ download). The bureau also frequently publishes online updates to this document and federal gun laws (https://www.atf .gov/rules-and-regulations).

Key State Gun Laws

Two gun-related organizational websites provide comprehensive presentations of state firearm regulations: the Law Center to Prevent Gun Violence (http://www.smartgunlaws.org) and the National Rifle Association's Institute for Legislative Action (http:// www.nraila.org/gun-laws/state-gun-laws/). The best print resource is Stephen P. Halbrook's Firearms Law Deskbook, *2015–2016 edition (St. Paul, MN: West, 2014, updated annually).*

Table 5.1 briefly summarizes major state gun laws as of September 2016. Please note that these laws are generally quite consistent from year to year, but that significant changes do occasionally occur—so be sure to check the relevant state attorney general's office for possible updates to any particular regulation that might be relevant to your situation.

Table 5.1 does not contain information on every possible gun-related law, but instead focuses on those that are at the center of the national debate over gun control. As presented in Chapter 2, gun control advocates believe that all of the following should be regulated at the national level, as state-level laws are often easily evaded by simply crossing the border between a strict and lax gun control state: waiting periods; registration; licensing (permits to purchase); juvenile possession and sales; records of sale; secondary sales regulations; restrictions on assault weapons and high-capacity ammunition magazines; ballistic fingerprinting; limiting gun purchases to one per month; having child access protection regulations ("safe storage" of firearms and ammunition, e.g., in locked cabinets or safes); a "may-issue" application process for a permit or license to carry a concealed handgun (such that local law enforcement has some discretion in granting such a permit, e.g., by requiring letters of reference or a more extensive checking of the applicant's background via interviewing coworkers or neighbors and the like); and the abolishing of "preemption" laws that put severe restrictions on local jurisdictions—towns, cities, counties— enacting their own gun control regulations.

The last column in Table 5.1 lists the letter "grade" each state receives for the strictness of its gun control laws according to one of the most fervent organizations advocating gun control—the Law Center to Prevent Gun Violence. Of course, whether one views a law center "A" (denoting that the state has very strong gun control laws) as good or bad depends on whether one is a "gun control" versus a "gun rights" advocate. Federal gun control laws do not preempt those at the state level. Rather, federal laws set the minimum standard for all states. For example, federal law does not allow private individuals to sell handguns to individuals under the age of 18, but California, Connecticut, Delaware, Hawaii, Illinois, Iowa, Maryland, Massachusetts, New Jersey, New York, Ohio, and Rhode Island have set a higher age minimum (21), which trumps the federal requirement. On the other hand, as noted in Chapters 1 and 2, most states now have preemption laws or judicial rulings that highly restrict localities from enacting their own gun control measures. Only a handful of states do not have strong preemption: California, Connecticut, Hawaii, Massachusetts, Nebraska, New Jersey, and New York (note that firearm preemption laws are complex; for a lucid introduction to them, see: http://smartgunlaws .org/gun-laws/policy-areas/other-laws/local-authority/).

Table 5.1 Key State Gun Laws

STATE	(A) NICS Background Check	(B) State Waiting Period[B]	(C) Registration Laws[C]	(D) Permit to Purchase Required	(E) Juvenile Possession Laws[E]	(F) Juvenile Sales Laws[F]	(G) Record of Sale[G]	(H) Secondary Sales Law[H]
Alabama	Y[A1]	N	N	N	N	N	Y[G1]	N
Alaska	Y[A1]	N	N	N	Y[E1]	Y[F1]	N	N
Arizona	Y[A1]	N	N	N	N	Y[F1]	N	N
Arkansas	Y[A1]	N	N	N	N	Y[F1]	N	N
California	Y[A2]	Y[B1]	Y[C1]	Y[D1]	Y[E11]	Y[F2]	Y[G2]	Y[H1]
Colorado	Y[A2]	N	N	N	N	N	Y[G3]	Y[H1]
Connecticut	Y[A2]	Y[B2]	Y[C2]	Y[D2]	Y[E2]	Y[F2]	Y[G4]	Y[H1]
Delaware	Y[A1]	N	N	N	N	Y[F2]	Y[G3]	Y[H2]
Florida	Y[A4]	Y[B3]	N	N	Y[E3]	Y[F1]	Y[G3]	N
Georgia	Y[A1]	N	N	N	N	N	Y[G5]	N
Hawaii	Y[A2]	Y[B4]	Y[C3]	Y[D3]	Y[E4]	Y[F3]	N	Y[H3]
Idaho	Y[A1]	N	N	N	Y[E3]	Y[F1]	N	N
Illinois	Y[A2]	Y[B5]	N[C4]	Y[D4]	Y[E5]	Y[F3]	Y[G6]	Y[H3, H4]
Indiana	Y[A1]	N	N	N	Y[E3]	N	N	N
Iowa	Y[A3]	Y[B6]	N	Y[D5]	Y[E4]	Y[F2]	N	Y[H5]

State	A	B	C	D	E	F	G	H
Kansas	Y^{A1}	N	N	N	N	N	N	N
Kentucky	Y^{A1}	N	N	N	N	N	N	N
Louisiana	Y^{A1}	N	N	N	N	Y^{F1}	N	N
Maine	Y^{A1}	N	N	N	N	Y^{F4}	Y^{G7}	Y^{H6}
Maryland	Y^{A5}	Y^{B7}	Y^{C5}	Y^{D6}	Y^{E2}	Y^{F2}	Y^{G8}	$Y^{H3, H7}$
Massachusetts	Y^{A1}	Y^{B8}	Y^{C6}	Y^{D7}	Y^{E2}	Y^{F2a}	Y^{G9}	Y^{H5}
Michigan	Y^{A3}	Y^{B9}	Y^{C7}	Y^{D8}	Y^{E3}	N	Y^{G10}	N
Minnesota	Y^{A1}	Y^{B10}	N	Y^{D9}	Y^{E6}	Y^{F5}	N	N
Mississippi	Y^{A1}	N	N	N	N	Y^{F1}	N	N
Missouri	Y^{A1}	N	N	N	N	N	N	N
Montana	Y^{A1}	N	N	N	Y^{E7}	N	N	N
Nebraska	Y^{A3}	Y^{B11}	Y^{C8}	Y^{D10}	Y^{E3}	Y^{F5}	N	$Y^{H5, H7}$
Nevada	Y^{A2}	N	N	N	N	N	N	Y^{H8}
New Hampshire	Y^{A7}	N	N	N	N	N	N	Y^{H3}
New Jersey	Y^{A2}	Y^{B12}	Y^{C9}	Y^{D11}	Y^{E4}	Y^{F2}	Y^{G11}	Y^{H3}
New Mexico	Y^{A1}	N	N	N	Y^{E8}	N	N	N
New York	Y^{A1}	Y^{B13}	Y^{C10}	Y^{D12}	Y^{E9}	Y^{F6}	Y^{G12}	Y^{H9}
North Carolina	Y^{A3}	Y^{B14}	N^{C11}	Y^{D13}	N	N	Y^{G3}	Y^{H5}
North Dakota	Y^{A1}	N	N	N	N	Y^{F5}	N	N
Ohio	Y^{A1}	N	N	N	N	Y^{F2}	N	N

(continued)

Table 5.1 (continued)

STATE	(A) NICS Background Check	(B) State Waiting Period[B]	(C) Registration Laws[C]	(D) Permit to Purchase Required	(E) Juvenile Possession Laws[E]	(F) Juvenile Sales Laws[F]	(G) Record of Sale[G]	(H) Secondary Sales Law[H]
Oklahoma	Y[A1]	N	N	N	Y[E3]	Y[F1]	N	N
Oregon	Y[A2]	N	N	N	Y[E3]	Y[F1]	Y[G5]	Y[H9]
Pennsylvania	Y[A2]	N[B15]	N	N[D14]	Y[E10]	Y[F1]	Y[G13]	Y[H10]
Rhode Island	Y[A1]	Y[B16]	N	Y[D15]	Y[E3]	Y[F2]	Y[G14]	Y[H11]
South Carolina	Y[A1]	N	N	N	Y[E11]	Y[F5]	N	N
South Dakota	Y[A1]	N	N	N	N	N	N	N
Tennessee	Y[A2]	N	N	N	N	N	N	N
Texas	Y[A1]	N	N	N	N	Y[F1]	N	N
Utah	Y[A2]	N	N	N	Y[E3]	N	N	N
Vermont	Y[A1]	N	N	N	N	Y[F7]	Y[G15]	N
Virginia	Y[A2]	N	Y[C12]	N	N	N	N	N
Washington	Y[A6]	Y[B17]	Y[C13]	N	Y[E3]	N	Y[G16]	Y[H9]
West Virginia	Y[A1]	N	N	N	N	N	N	N
Wisconsin	Y[A3]	N	N	N	Y[E3]	Y[F1]	N	N
Wyoming	Y[A1]	N	N	N	N	N	N	N

STATE	(I) Restrictions on Assault Weapons	(Ia) Restrictions on High-Capacity Magazines	(J) Ballistic Fingerprinting[J]	(K) One Gun Per Month Law[K]	(L) CAP Law[L]	(M) "May-Issue" Concealed Carry Law	(N) Preemption Laws[N]	(O) Gun Laws Grade (A=strongest)
Alabama	N	N	N	N	N	N[M1]	Y	F
Alaska	N	N	N	N	N	N[M2]	Y	F
Arizona	N	N	N	N	N	N[M2]	Y	F
Arkansas	N	N	N	N	N	N[M1]	Y	F
California	Y[I1,I2,I3,I4,I5,I6]	Y[Ia1]	Y[J1]	Y[K1,K1a]	Y[L1,L2,L4]	Y[M3]	N[N3]	A-
Colorado	N	Y[Ia6]	N	N	Y[L5]	N[M1]	Y[N2]	C-
Connecticut	Y[I1,I2,I3,I4,I5,I6]	Y[Ia7]	Y[J2]	N	Y[L1,L3]	Y[M3]	N[N3]	A-
Delaware	N	N	N	N	Y[L5]	Y[M3]	Y	B
Florida	N	N	N	N	Y[L1,L3]	N[M1]	Y	F
Georgia	N	N	N	N	Y[L5]	N[M1]	Y	F
Hawaii	Y[I2,I4,I5,I9]	Y[Ia2]	N	N	Y[L1,L2,L4]	Y[M3]	N	B+
Idaho	N	N	N	N	N	N[M2]	Y	F
Illinois	N	N	N	N	Y[L1,L3]	N[M1]	Y	B+
Indiana	N	N	N	N	Y[L5]	N[M1]	Y[N4]	D-
Iowa	N	N	N	N	Y[L1,L3]	N[M1]	Y	C-
Kansas	N	N	N	N	N	N[M2]	Y	F

(continued)

Table 5.1 (continued)

STATE	(I) Restrictions on Assault Weapons	(Ia) Restrictions on High-Capacity Magazines	(J) Ballistic Fingerprinting[J]	(K) One Gun Per Month Law[K]	(L) CAP Law[L]	(M) "May-Issue" Concealed Carry Law	(N) Preemption Laws[N]	(O) Gun Laws Grade (A=strongest)
Kentucky	N	N	N	N	Y[L5]	N[M1]	Y	F
Louisiana	N	N	N	N	N	N[M1]	Y	F
Maine	N	N	N	N	N	N[M2]	Y	F
Maryland	Y[I1,I4,I5,I8,I10]	Y[Ia1]	N	Y[K2]	Y[L1,L2]	Y	Y[N1]	A-
Massachusetts	Y[I1,I2,I7]	Y[Ia4]	N	N	Y[L1,L2,L4]	Y[M3]	N[N3]	A-
Michigan	N	N	N	N	N	N[M1]	Y	C
Minnesota	Y[I11]	N	N	N	Y[L1,L2]	N[M1]	Y[N1]	C
Mississippi	N	N	N	N	Y[L5]	N[M1]	Y	F
Missouri	N	N	N	N	Y[L5]	N[M1]	Y	F
Montana	N	N	N	N	N	N[M1]	Y	F
Nebraska	N	N	N	N	N	N[M1]	N[N6]	D
Nevada	N	N	N	N	Y[L5]	N[M1]	Y[N1]	F
New Hampshire	N	N	N	N	Y[L1,L3]	Y[M3]	Y	D
New Jersey	Y[I1,I2,I3,I4,I7]	Y[Ia5]	N	Y[K3]	Y[L1,L2]	Y[M3]	N[N3]	A-
New Mexico	N	N	N	N	N	N[M1]	Y	F
New York	Y[I2,I3,I4,I5]	Y[Ia2]	N	Y[K4]	N	Y[M3]	N[N3]	A-
North Carolina	N	N	N	N	Y[L1,L3]	N[M1]	Y	F

State						Grade
North Dakota	N	N	N	N[M1]	Y	F
Ohio	N	N	N	N[M1]	Y	D
Oklahoma	N	N	Y[L5]	N[M1]	Y[N1]	F
Oregon	N	N	N	N[M1]	Y	C
Pennsylvania	N	N	N	N[M1]	Y	C
Rhode Island	N	N	Y[L1,L3]	Y[M3]	Y	B+
South Carolina	N	N	N	N[M1]	Y	F
South Dakota	N	N	N	N[M1]	Y	F
Tennessee	N	N	Y[L5]	N[M1]	Y	F
Texas	N	N	Y[L1,L2]	N[M1]	Y[N1]	F
Utah	N	N	Y[L5]	N[M1]	Y	F
Vermont	N	N	N	N[M2]	Y	F
Virginia	Y[I12]	N	Y[L5]	N[M1]	Y	D
Washington	N	N	N	N[M1]	Y	B-
West Virginia	N	N	N	N[M2]	Y	D-
Wisconsin	N	N	Y[L5]	N[M1,M4]	Y	D
Wyoming	N	N	N	N[M2]	Y	F

(A) NICS Background Check

[A1] States for which the FBI conducts NICS background checks for all firearms transactions.

[A2] States that act as the point of contact (POC) for all firearms transactions.

(continued)

Table 5.1 *(continued)*

[A3] Permit POC for handguns, while the FBI does background checks for long guns.

[A4] Florida Department of Law Enforcement for all firearms, except licensees may contact the FBI for certain pawn transactions.

[A5] Maryland State Police do checks for handguns and assault weapons, while the FBI does so for long guns and pawn redemptions.

[A6] Chief law enforcement officer for handguns without concealed pistol license (CPL); FBI for long guns and handguns with CPL.

[A7] New Hampshire Department of Safety for handguns; FBI for long guns.

From: FBI, National Instant Criminal Background Check System: Participation Map. https://www.fbi.gov/about-us/cjis/nics/general-information/participation-map (accessed July 13, 2016).

(B) State Waiting Period

[B] Some states have their own waiting periods to obtain a permit to purchase and/or for actual purchase.

[B1] Ten-day waiting period for any firearm; sales, transfers, and loans of handguns must be made through a dealer or through a sheriff's office; transfers of a long gun to a person's parent, child, or grandparent are exempt from the waiting period. Persons who are screened and cleared through the Personal Firearms Eligibility Check are still subject to the 10-day waiting period and background check provisions; a permit is required to acquire another handgun before 30 days have elapsed following the acquisition of a handgun; Must have Handgun Safety Certificate receipt, which is valid for five years.

[B2] A certificate of eligibility is required for handgun purchases; a hunting license or a permit to carry exempts the holder for long gun purchasers; a certificate of eligibility or a carry permit is required to obtain a handgun and a carry permit is required to transport a handgun outside your home. To receive certificate of eligibility, you must complete a handgun safety course approved by the Commissioner of Public Safety. These certificates negate previous required hunting licenses and 14-day waiting periods. However, a long gun transaction is not complete until the issuance of an authorization number from the Department of Emergency Services and Public Protection.

[B3] Three-day waiting period for handguns; the waiting period does not apply to a person holding a valid permit or license to carry a firearm.

[B4] Purchase permits are required for all firearms; no permit can be issued earlier than 14 days after the date of the application. Purchaser must have completed an approved handgun safety course.

[B5] Three-day waiting period to purchase a handgun, one-day waiting period for a long gun; a Firearm Owner's Identification Card is required to possess or purchase a firearm, which must be issued to qualified applicants within 30 days, and is valid for 5 years.

B6 A purchase permit is required for handguns, and is valid for one year. Three-day waiting period to obtain purchase permit.

B7 Seven-day waiting period for handguns and assault weapons; purchasers of regulated firearms must undergo background checks performed by the state police, either through a dealer or directly through the state police; a permit is required to acquire another firearm before 30 days have elapsed following the acquisition of a handgun; must complete an approved handgun safety course.

B8 Firearms and feeding devices for firearms are divided into classes. Depending on the class, a firearm identification card (FID) or class A license or class B license is required to possess, purchase, or carry a firearm, ammunition thereof, or firearm-feeding device, or "large-capacity feeding device." Licensing agencies are required to notify applicants of their FID status within 40 days.

B9 A handgun purchaser must obtain a license to purchase from local law enforcement, and within 10 days present the license and handgun to obtain a certificate of inspection; a person must correctly answer 70 percent of the questions on a basic safety review questionnaire in order to obtain a license to purchase.

B10 Seven-day waiting period for any handgun or semiautomatic military-style assault weapon; a handgun purchaser must obtain a license to purchase from local law enforcement, and within 10 days present the license and handgun to obtain a certificate of inspection; a handgun transfer or carrying permit, or a seven-day waiting period and handgun transfer report, is required to purchase handguns or "assault weapons" from a dealer. A permit is valid for one year; a transfer report for 30 days.

B11 A certificate is required to purchase a handgun. Two-day waiting period to obtain purchase certificate.

B12 Firearm owners must possess a FID, which must be issued to qualified applicants within 30 days. To purchase a handgun, a purchase permit, which must be issued within 30 days to qualified applicants and is valid for 90 days, is required. Seven-day waiting period to provide the permit prior to purchase of handgun. An FID is required to purchase long guns.

B13 Purchase, possession, and/or carrying of a handgun requires a single license, which includes any restrictions made upon the bearer. This license can take up to six months to process and obtain; the license may take longer following advanced written notice to the gun owner. New York City also requires a license for long guns; some counties require a handgun safety training course to receive a license.

B14 To purchase a handgun, a license or permit is required, which must be issued to qualified applicants within 30 days. Persons with a right-to-carry license are exempt.

B15 No private sales. All handgun purchases must go through a licensed dealer or the county sheriff.

(continued)

307

Table 5.1 *(continued)*

B16 Seven-day waiting period for all guns: private sales can be made through a dealer or the seller, which must follow the same guidelines as a sale from a dealer; must receive a state-issued handgun safety card.

B17 Five-day waiting period for handguns; the waiting period is waived for those with a concealed carry license. May be extended by police to 30 days in some circumstances. An individual not holding a driver's license must wait for 60 days.

From: The Law Center to Prevent Gun Violence, *Waiting Periods Policy Summary.* http://www.smartgunlaws.org/waiting-periods-policy-summary/ (accessed March 2, 2016); National Rifle Association, *State Gun Laws.* https://www.nraila.org/gun-laws/state-gun-laws/ (accessed March 2, 2016).

(C) Registration Laws

C Registration law requires a record of the transfer of ownership of a specific handgun.

C1 A person moving into California has 60 days to file a registration form with the Department of Justice; for "assault weapon" registration, California had two dates by which assault weapons had to be registered or possession after such date would be considered a felony: March 31, 1992, for the named make and model firearms banned in the 1989 legislation, and December 31, 2000, for the firearms meeting the definition of "assault weapons" in the 1999 legislation.

C2 "Assault weapon" registration: those firearms banned by specific make and model in the 1993 law had to be registered by July 1, 1994, or possession would be considered a felony. State law requires registration of additional guns in this category.

C3 Must register any firearm(s) brought into the state within five days of arrival of the person or firearm(s), whichever occurs later. Handguns purchased from licensed dealers must be registered within five days.

C4 Must get Firearm Owner's Identification Card after receiving driver's license.

C5 Must register for handguns and assault pistols only; exempted for active duty/retired military personnel with identification cards or active/retired law enforcement officials. Comprehensive background checks and training are required.

C6 An FID is required to possess or carry a firearm, ammunition, or firearm-feeding device. Exemptions include temporary handgun holdings, possession by a chartered veterans' organization, and the use of a rifle or shotgun for hunting or target shooting. New residents of Massachusetts and residents returning after absences of less than 180 consecutive days who already possess a handgun are also exempt.

C7 Must register handguns with the city chief of police or the county sheriff of their residential locality.

C8 In certain cities or counties.

C9 A record of handgun transfers must be made available for law enforcement. Any "assault weapon" not registered, licensed, or rendered inoperable pursuant to a state police certificate by May 1, 1991, is considered contraband.

C10 Must register for handguns; registration required for long guns in New York City only. "Assault weapons" must be registered with the state police before April 15, 2014.

C11 Local authorities maintain the right to provide a list of permitees to law enforcement.

C12 Must register fully automatic firearms (machine guns) with the Department of State Police within 24 hours of acquisition.

C13 Dealers must provide record of purchases to law enforcement.

From: National Rifle Association, *State Gun Laws*. https://www.nraila.org/gun-laws/state-gun-laws/ (accessed March 4, 2016).

(D) Permit to Purchase Required

D1 California-approved safety training required; all firearms transactions, including private transactions and sales at gun shows, must go through a licensed firearms dealer. Permit for handgun purchase is required; a permit is required to acquire another handgun before 30 days have elapsed following the acquisition of a handgun; must have Handgun Safety Certificate receipt, which is valid for five years.

D2 Connecticut requires a permit for handgun purchase; a certificate of eligibility or a carry permit is required to obtain a handgun or long gun, and a carry permit is required to transport a handgun outside your home; to receive certificate of eligibility, must complete a handgun safety course approved by the Commissioner of Public Safety.

D3 Hawaii requires a purchase permit for all firearms; must have completed an approved handgun safety course.

D4 Illinois requires a purchase permit for all firearms; a Firearm Owner's Identification Card is required to possess or purchase a firearm and must be issued to qualified applicants within 30 days, and is valid for five years.

D5 Iowa requires a purchase permit for handguns, and is valid for one year.

D6 Maryland requires a permit for handgun purchase; a permit is required to acquire another handgun before 30 days have elapsed following the acquisition of a handgun; must complete an approved handgun safety course.

D7 Massachusetts requires a purchase permit for all firearms. Firearms and feeding devices for firearms are divided into classes. Depending on the class, an FID or class A license or class B license is required to possess, purchase, or carry a firearm, ammunition thereof, or firearm feeding device, or a "large capacity feeding device."

(continued)

Table 5.1 *(continued)*

D8 Michigan requires a safety training course; permit for handgun purchase is required for private transactions done through federally licensed firearms dealers; however, a sales record must be made with the FFL number. A handgun purchaser must obtain a license to purchase from local law enforcement, and present the license and handgun, within 10 days, to obtain a certificate of inspection. A person must correctly answer 70 percent of the questions on a basic safety review questionnaire in order to obtain a license to purchase.

D9 Minnesota requires a permit for all firearms purchases; a handgun transfer or carrying permit, or a seven-day waiting period and handgun transfer report, is required to purchase handguns or "assault weapons" from a dealer. A permit is valid for one year, a transfer report for 30 days.

D10 Nebraska requires a permit for handgun purchase unless purchased through a federally licensed firearms dealer.

D11 New Jersey requires a permit for all firearms purchases; firearm owners must possess an FID, which must be issued to qualified applicants within 30 days.

D12 New York requires an approved safety training course; permit for handgun purchase is required for long gun purchase is required for purchases in New York City; purchase, possession, and/or carrying of a handgun requires a single license, which includes any restrictions made upon the bearer. New York City also requires a license for long guns. Some counties require a handgun safety training course to receive a license.

D13 North Carolina requires a permit to purchase a handgun, which must be issued to qualified applicants within 30 days. Persons with a right-to-carry license are exempt.

D14 Pennsylvania requires all handgun purchases to go through a licensed dealer or the county sheriff.

D15 Rhode Island requires an approved safety training course; permit for handgun purchase is required; must receive a state-issued handgun safety card.

From: National Rifle Association Institute for Legislative Action, *State Gun Laws*. https://www.nraila.org/gun-laws/state-gun-laws/ (accessed March 5, 2016).

(E) Juvenile Possession Laws

E Federal law prohibits possession of handguns for those under 18 (except under certain circumstances, namely hunting, ranching, and target shooting); a federally licensed firearms dealer cannot sell a handgun to anyone under the age of 21, though a private seller can to those aged 18–20; otherwise state law dictates possession of long guns for juveniles, and for handguns for those aged 18–20.

E1 Must be 16 years old for long guns.

E2 Must be 21 years old for handgun.

E3 Must be 18 years old for long guns.

E4 Must be 21 for handguns, and 18 for long guns.

E5 Must be 21 years old for all firearms.

E6 Must be 16 years old for long guns; can be 14 or 15 years old if in possession of a firearms safety certificate.

E7 Must be 14 years old for long guns.

E8 Must be 19 years old for handguns.

E9 Must be 21 years old for handguns and 16 for long guns.

E10 Must be 18 years old for long guns. Only applies to guns of a specific length. It does not encompass all long guns.

E11 Must be 18 years old for handgun.

From: Law Center to Prevent Gun Violence, *Minimum Age to Purchase and Possess Firearms Policy Summary*. http://smartgunlaws.org/minimum-age-to-purchase-possess-firearms-policy-summary/ (accessed March 12, 2016).

(F) Juvenile Sales Laws

F Note that some states appear to violate federal law, where the state's minimum age for purchases from licensed dealers is below the federal minimum of 18 for long guns and 21 for handguns.

F1 Must be 18 years old for all firearms.

F2 Must be 21 for handguns and 18 for long guns.

F2a Massachusetts's minimum age for the purchase of large-capacity rifles and shotguns is 21.

F3 Must be 21 years old for all firearms.

F4 Must be 18 for handguns, 16 for long guns.

F5 Must be 18 for handguns; no minimum age for long guns.

(continued)

Table 5.1 *(continued)*

F6 Must be 21 for handguns; no minimum age for long guns.

F7 Must be 16 for all firearms.

From: Law Center to Prevent Gun Violence, *Minimum Age to Purchase and Possess Firearms Policy Summary.* http://smartgunlaws.org/minimum-age-to-purchase-possess-firearms-policy-summary/ (accessed March 12, 2016).

(G) Record of Sale

G Federal firearm licensees) are required to maintain records of the acquisition and sale of firearms indefinitely. The dealer must record, "in bound form," the purchase or other acquisition of a firearm not later than the close of the next business day following the purchase or acquisition. The dealer must similarly record the sale or other disposition of a firearm not later than seven days following the date of such transaction and retain Form 4473, the Firearms Transaction Record. When a firearms business is discontinued, these records are delivered to the successor or, if none exists, to the attorney general. With very limited exceptions, records of firearm sales are not maintained at the federal level. The NFA branch of ATF does maintain a limited registry of machine guns, short-barreled shotguns or rifles, and silencers, known as the National Firearms Registration and Transfer Record.

G1 Sellers are required to retain records of handgun sales permanently; state retains seller-reported information on handgun sales.

G2 Sellers are required to retain records of all firearm sales for three years; state retains seller-reported information on handgun sales.

G3 Sellers are required to retain records of all handgun sales (unspecified length of retention).

G4 Sellers are required to retain records of all firearm sales for five years (except pistols and revolvers, which must have records kept for six years); state retains seller-reported information on all firearm sales.

G5 Sellers are required to retain information on all firearm sales for five years.

G6 Sellers are required to retain records on handguns (unspecified length of retention); to retain records of all firearm sales for 10 years.

G7 Sellers are required to retain records of all firearm sales (unspecified length of retention).

G8 Sellers are required to retain records of "regulated firearms" and handgun sales for three years; state retains dealer-reported information on "regulated firearms" sales.

G9 Sellers are required to retain records of all firearm sales (unspecified length of retention); state retains seller-reported information on all firearms sales.

312

G10 Seller must retain records of all firearm sales (unspecified period of retention); state retains seller-reported information on handgun sales.

G11 Sellers are required to retain records of all handgun sales (unspecified length of retention); state retains dealer-reported information on all firearms sales.

G12 Sellers required to retain records of "handguns, assault weapons, and rifles and shotguns of certain dimensions" (unspecified length of retention); state retains seller-reported information on "handguns, assault weapons, and rifles and shotguns of certain dimensions."

G13 Sellers required to retain records of all firearms sales for 20 years; private sellers are also required to retain records of "handguns and certain rifles and shotguns" for 20 years; state retains seller-reported information on "handguns and certain rifles and shotguns."

G14 Sellers are required to retain records of all firearms sales for six years.

G15 Sellers are required to retain records of handgun sales for six years.

G16 Sellers are required to retain records of handgun sales for six years; state retains seller-reported information on handgun sales.

From: Law Center to Prevent Gun Violence, *Maintaining Records & Reporting Gun Sales Policy Summary*. http://smartgunlaws.org/maintaining-gun-sales-background-check-records-policy-summary/ (accessed March 14, 2016).

(H) Secondary Sales Law

H Some states prohibit secondary sales or require that such sales be registered or routed through a licensed firearms dealer.

H1 Prior to any firearm transfer, a licensed dealer or law enforcement agency must conduct a background check on the prospective firearm transferee; all transfers must be processed through licensed dealers; all firearm transfers are subject to recordkeeping and sales reporting requirements for licensed dealers (because all transfers are processed through a licensed dealer); handgun sales must to reported to law enforcement.

H2 A background check through a licensed dealer is required prior to any firearms transfer; purchasers are subjected to a similar background check if neither the seller nor the buyer is a licensed dealer. Exemptions include concealed handgun permit holders.

H3 Purchasers must obtain a license or permit before purchasing a firearm from any seller; a background check through a licensed dealer or law enforcement is required to complete the permit acquisition and purchase. All transfers must be reported to state and local law enforcement.

H4 Background checks are required for transfers or sales conducted at gun shows. Sellers required are to retain records of handgun sales for 10 years; state retains seller-reported information on handgun sales.

(continued)

Table 5.1 *(continued)*

[H5] Purchasers must obtain a permit before purchasing a handgun from a private seller; a background check is required to complete the permit acquisition and handgun purchase.

[H6] A background check is required on every prospective transferee of "regulated firearms" (handguns and assault weapons), which may be conducted by a licensed dealer or a designated law enforcement agency.

[H7] Sellers are required to retain records of handgun sales permanently; state retains seller-reported information on handgun sales.

[H8] Private sellers are not required to conduct background checks on purchasers, but they *may* request a background check of the purchaser; the seller must make the request to the relevant state agency, which must process the request.

[H9] Purchaser must complete a background check through a licensed dealer prior to point of transfer; sellers required to retain records of firearms sales permanently; state retains seller-reported information on firearms sales.

[H10] All handgun sales must be completed by licensed dealers; all handgun transfers are subject to recordkeeping and sales reporting requirements for licensed dealers (because all transfers are processed through a licensed dealer); handgun sales must be reported to law enforcement.

[H11] Prior to any firearm transfer, a licensed dealer, or law enforcement agency, must conduct a background check on the prospective firearm transferee; all sellers must obtain a completed application form from the prospective purchaser and submit the form to law enforcement for the purposes of conducting a background check.

From: Law Center to Prevent Gun Violence, *Universal Background Checks & the "Private" Sale Loophole Policy Summary.* http://smartgunlaws.org/universal-gun-background-checks-policy-summary/ (accessed March 14, 2016).

(I) Restrictions on Assault Weapons

[I1] States that include a list of assault weapons banned by name.

[I2] States that provide a generic feature definition of assault weapon.

[I3] States that use a one-feature test to determine if a firearm is an assault weapon.

[I4] States that require registration of grandfathered weapons.

[I5] States that generally prohibit the transfer of grandfathered weapons.

[I6] States that limit the places a grandfathered weapon may be possessed.

314

[7] States that require a license for possession.

[8] Includes assault pistols.

[9] Assault pistols only.

[10] Rather than the traditional one-feature test to determine if a firearm is an assault weapon, Maryland uses its own two-feature test. In addition to its ban on assault pistols, Maryland also regulates the sale of other assault weapons, defined to include a list of specified firearms or their copies. Assault weapons are defined as "regulated firearms" under state law, and transfers are subject to various regulations, including requiring enhanced background checks on purchasers, requiring dealers to obtain a state license, and requiring private transfers to be processed through licensed dealers or a law enforcement agency. In addition, purchasers (1) must be aged 21 or older; (2) are subject to a seven-day waiting period; and (3) are limited to one assault weapon in any 30-day period.

[11] Minnesota prohibits the possession of "semiautomatic military-style assault weapons" by persons under 18 years of age, as well as other prohibited persons, and imposes additional restrictions on transfers through firearms dealers.

[12] Virginia limits the knowing and intentional possession and transportation of certain semiautomatic "assault firearms" to citizens and permanent residents aged 18 and older. These weapons may not be carried, loaded, in public places in certain cities and counties. Virginia also imposes a general ban on the importation, sale, possession, and transfer of the "Striker 12" and semiautomatic folding stock shotguns of like kind, but does not refer to them as "assault firearms."

From: Law Center to Prevent Gun Violence, *Assault Weapons Policy Summary*. http://smartgunlaws.org/assault-weapons-policy-summary/ (accessed March 16, 2016).

(Ia) Restrictions on High-Capacity Magazines

[Ia1] Size limit: 11 or more. Ban on the manufacture and sale of high-capacity magazines.

[Ia2] Size limit: 11 or more. Ban on the manufacture, sale, and possession of high-capacity magazines.

[Ia3] Size limit: 21 or more. Ban on the manufacture and sale of high-capacity magazines.

[Ia4] Size limit: 11 or more. Ban on the sale and possession of high-capacity magazines; pre-owned high-capacity magazines are "grandfathered in" and allowed to be possessed.

[Ia5] Size limit: 16 or more. Ban on the manufacture, sale, and possession of high-capacity magazines.

(continued)

Table 5.1 *(continued)*

Ia6 Size limit: 16 or more. Ban on the sale, transfer, and possession of high-capacity magazines; pre-owned high-capacity magazines are "grandfathered in" and allowed to be possessed.

Ia7 Size limit: 11 or more. Ban on distribution, importation, sale, and possession of high-capacity magazines; pre-owned high-capacity magazines must be registered.

From: Law Center to Prevent Gun Violence, *Large Capacity Ammunition Magazines Policy Summary.* http://smartgunlaws.org/large-capacity-ammunition-magazines-policy-summary/ (accessed March 30, 2016).

(J) Ballistic Fingerprinting

J All firearms leave unique markings on the bullets and shell casings they fire. Ballistic identification (sometimes called ballistic "fingerprinting") laws make it possible to link bullets and shell casings recovered at crime scenes to the firearm that fired them by requiring gun manufacturers to test-fire the firearms they produce. Images of the unique ballistic markings left on bullets and shell casings by each weapon are then stored in a database so that law enforcement can later determine whether a particular gun fired a particular bullet. Ballistic identification systems can identify the make, model, and serial number of the gun from which a bullet or cartridge case was fired without recovering the gun itself.

J1 With legislation passed in 2007, California became the first state to require the use of handgun microstamping. On October 13, 2007, Governor Arnold Schwarzenegger signed into law the Crime-Gun Identification Act, which requires all new semiautomatic handguns manufactured or sold in California after January 1, 2010, to be etched with a microscopic array of characters that identify the make, model, and serial number of the firearm. These characters would be transferred to each cartridge case when the handgun is fired, thereby enabling law enforcement to match a cartridge case found at a crime scene to the gun that fired it and, ultimately, through an existing database maintained by the California Department of Justice, to the gun's owner.

J2 Connecticut requires that the Division of Scientific Services ("Division") of the Connecticut Department of Public Safety establish a firearm evidence databank. The databank is a computer-based system that scans a "test-fire" from a handgun and stores an image of the test-fire in a manner suitable for retrieval and comparison to other test-fires and to other evidence in a criminal investigation. All handguns recovered by the police through a criminal investigation, as found property, or for destruction must be submitted to the Division's laboratory for collection of a test-fire. Police departments are also required to submit test-fires from all handguns issued to employees.

From: Law Center to Prevent Gun Violence, *Microstamping & Ballistic Identification Policy Summary.* http://smartgunlaws.org/microstamping-ballistic-identification-policy-summary/ (accessed March 30, 2016).

(K) One-Gun-per-Month Law

K One-gun-a-month laws prohibit the purchase of more than one handgun per person in any 30-day period.

K1 California law prohibits any person from purchasing more than one handgun within any 30-day period. In addition, a licensed firearms dealer may not deliver a handgun to any person following notification from the California Department of Justice that the purchaser has applied to acquire a handgun within the preceding 30-day period. Finally, firearms dealers must conspicuously post in their licensed premises a warning, in block letters at least one inch in height, notifying purchasers of these restrictions. Because all firearm transfers must be conducted through licensed dealers in California, the restriction on multiple handgun sales necessarily also applies to private sellers.

K1a Los Angeles, California's ordinance provides that no person shall submit an application to a firearms dealer to purchase a handgun within 30 days of making a prior application for the purchase of a handgun within the state of California. It also prohibits firearms dealers from transferring the title of any handgun to any person whom the dealer knows has applied to purchase more than one handgun within the state within a 30-day period prior thereto. The Los Angeles ordinance was enacted in 1999. Later that year, the state of California adopted its one handgun-a-month law, effective January 1, 2000.

K2 Maryland prohibits any person from purchasing more than one handgun or assault weapon within a 30-day period. Under limited circumstances, a person may be approved by the secretary of the Maryland State Police to purchase multiple handguns or assault weapons in a 30-day period.

K3 New Jersey recently enacted a law that prohibits individuals from purchasing more than one handgun in a 30-day period and prohibits dealers from selling more than one handgun to the same person in a 30-day period. Two laws adopted in 2010 amend provisions of New Jersey's one-handgun-a-month law: One new law exempts from the one-handgun-a-month law any person who: (1) purchases from a person who obtained the handguns through inheritance or intestacy; (2) is a collector of handguns and has a legitimate reason or justification to purchase or otherwise receive multiple handguns; or (3) participates in lawfully sanctioned handgun shooting competitions and has a legitimate reason or justification to obtain multiple handguns. The other new law clarifies that certain transfers of handguns are not subject to the one-handgun-a-month limitation, including transfers between or to dealers and manufacturers.

K4 New York City limits sales of handguns, rifles, and shotguns, prohibiting dealers from selling more than one handgun, rifle, or shotgun to any one person as part of the same transaction. In addition, no dealer may sell a handgun, rifle, or shotgun to a person if he or she knows or should know that the person has purchased a firearm within the prior 90 days. New York City also provides that no person may acquire more than one handgun in a 90-day period, and that no person may acquire more than one rifle or shotgun in a 90-day period.

From: Law Center to Prevent Gun Violence, *Sales of Multiple Guns Policy Summary*. http://smartgunlaws.org/multiple-purchases-sales-of-firearms-policy-summary/ (accessed March 30, 2016).

317

(continued)

Table 5.1 *(continued)*

(L) CAP ("Child Access Protection") Law

L Also known as safe gun storage laws, CAP laws require gun owners to store their firearms in a manner that would prevent children and mentally ill or incompetent individuals from gaining unauthorized access.

L1 State laws based on negligent storage.

L2 States imposing criminal liability for allowing a child to gain access to the firearm, regardless of whether the child uses the firearm or causes injury.

L3 States imposing criminal liability only if a child uses or possesses the firearm.

L4 States imposing criminal liability for negligent storage of unloaded firearms.

L5 State laws prohibiting intentional, knowing, or reckless provision of firearms to minors. State laws vary on which firearms (handguns, loaded firearms, etc.) are prohibited from intentional, knowing, or reckless provision.

From: Law Center to Prevent Gun Violence, *Child Access Prevention Policy Summary.* http://smartgunlaws.org/child-access-prevention-policy-summary/ (accessed March 31, 2016).

(M) "May-Issue" Concealed Carry Law

M "May-issue" laws allow for a federally qualified individual to obtain a concealed weapon permit, but local authorities have some discretion (and may require letters of reference, a statement from the applicant on why a permit is needed, and/or more extensive background checking).

M1 "Shall-issue" states do not allow for local authority discretion; if the applicant passes a federal background check, and in some states a short gun-safety course, a concealed carry permit must be issued.

M2 State allows the right to carry a concealed weapon without a permit. State also has "permit to carry" systems to establish reciprocity with other states.

M3 State requires a showing of "good cause" for issuance of a concealed weapons permit; individual must have a valid reason for wanting to carry a concealed firearm.

M4 Wisconsin: "If a person satisfies the training requirement and passes a background check, the Department of Justice (DOJ) shall issue a permit to the applicant. Wisconsin residents, who wish to lawfully carry a concealed firearm, must have a WI license to carry. The carry license shall be issued by the DOJ to (1) residents of the state who are at least 21 years old; (2) not prohibited from possessing a firearm under federal or state law; (3) has satisfied the training requirement; and (4) paid the maximum $50 fee."

From: Law Center to Prevent Gun Violence, *Concealed Weapons Permitting Policy Summary.* http://smartgunlaws.org/concealed-weapons-permitting-policy-summary/ (accessed April 15, 2016).

(N) Preemption Laws

[N] Preemption restrictions arise from either state statues or judicial rulings; a "Y" (yes) denotes that the restrictions severely limit or outright prohibit local jurisdictions from enacting any gun control regulations at all, or, in some cases, any that are in conflict with state-level equivalents—especially if they would be stricter than those of the state.

[N1] Local municipalities may regulate one or more aspects of firearms or ammunition.

[N2] Municipalities may prohibit open carry in government buildings if such prohibition is clearly posted.

[N3] Preemption through judicial ruling.

[N4] Except Gary and East Chicago and local laws enacted before January 1994.

[N5] California expressly preempts local governments from regulating in the areas of registration or licensing of firearms; manufacture, sale, or possession of imitation firearms; and licensing or permitting with respect to the purchase, ownership, possession, or carrying of a concealable firearm in the home or place of business. However, judicial rulings have given localities authority in regulating ammunition and registration.

[N6] According to the attorney general of Nebraska, a 2010 law that prohibits "cities and villages" from regulating ownership, possession, or transportation of a concealed handgun invalidated Omaha's handgun registration requirement. However, outside of the context of concealed handgun permit holders, there are no laws expressly limiting local authority to regulate firearms or ammunition.

From: Law Center to Prevent Gun Violence, *Local Authority to Regulate Firearms Policy Summary*. http://smartgunlaws.org/local-authority-to-regulate-firearms-policy-summary/ (accessed April 15, 2016); National Rifle Association of America, Institute for Legislative Action, *State Gun Laws*. https://www.nraila.org/gun-laws/state-gun-laws/ (accessed July 13, 2016).

(O) Law Center to Prevent Gun Violence Letter Grade for Strength of State Gun Laws (A=Strongest . . . through . . . F=Weakest)

From: Law Center to Prevent Gun Violence, *2015 Gun Law State Scorecard*. gunlawscorecard.org/ (accessed July 12, 2016).

Selected Documents

The Second Amendment (1791)

The 27 words of the Second Amendment are at the heart of much of the contemporary gun debate. Two important points set the stage for the controversy over its interpretation: (1) In all of the peer nations of the United States (industrialized democracies like those of Western Europe), and, indeed, in all but one of the developing nations of the world (Yemen), gun ownership is generally regarded a privilege for ordinary citizens and not *a right. (2) However, the phrasing of the amendment is not entirely clear whether the guaranteed right is* only *for the collective right of each individual state to arm its own militia for self-defense, or the guaranteed right of* both *the individual states* and *of its individual citizens to arm for self-defense.*

A well regulated Militia, being necessary to the security of a free State, the right of the people to keep and bear Arms, shall not be infringed.

Source: U.S. Constitution, National Archives.

District of Columbia v. Heller (2008)

With a few exceptions—in United States v. Cruikshank *(1876),* Presser v. Illinois *(1886),* Miller v. Texas *(1894), and* United States v. Miller *(1939)—the U.S. Supreme Court had a long history of declining to hear appeals cases involving the Second Amendment. Except in the cases of* United States v. Emerson *(2001) and* Parker v. District of Columbia *(2007), dozens of lower federal district court and circuit court of appeal decisions had emphasized the first part of the amendment—that it protected the collective right of the state to arm "a well-regulated militia" to ensure "the security of a free State." The amendment was not intended to protect the right of an individual but of the individual states to maintain active, organized militias—which in the modern era are tantamount to their respective National Guard units. Thus, because of its declining to hear Second Amendment cases, the collective-right interpretation of the lower federal court system had all of the appearances of the Supreme Court agreeing with it.*

For many years, however, some legal scholars had contended that the Second Amendment also guaranteed the right of an individual to defend him- or herself with a firearm. These scholars emphasized the second half of the amendment—that "the right of the people to keep and bear Arms shall not be infringed." As modern history turned out, these scholars, all of whom have been extolled by gun rights proponents (not surprisingly!), won the war of interpretations in the related landmark decisions of the Supreme Court in District of Columbia v. Heller *(2008) and* McDonald v. City of Chicago *(2010).*

In the Heller *case, the Court explicitly ruled that on federal property, such as the District of Columbia, the government could not ban a law-abiding individual the right to own a handgun for legal purposes, including for self-defense—because a ban would be in violation of the Second Amendment's guarantee of this right. In the* McDonald *case, the Court "incorporated" the amendment to apply to the individual states, and thus the city of Chicago could not restrict handgun possession to a law-abiding citizen for self-defense. Both decisions are long (in the official bound copies,* Heller *is 153 pages, and* McDonald *is 202 pages!), but the essence of each is captured in the preamble "syllabus" to the decision. The syllabus is not officially part of the opinion, but is published by the Court to help the average person understand what is at stake in the case, the final decision rendered, and the reasoning behind the decision. The* Heller *syllabus is presented here, and the reader is encouraged to peruse the* McDonald *syllabus online (https://www.law.cornell.edu/supct/html/08-1521 .ZS.html).*

Because the cases were so narrowly decided (both by 5–4 votes), the reader is also encouraged to peruse the powerful and articulate dissenting opinions of Justice John Paul Stevens (for Heller: *https://www.law.cornell.edu/supct/html/07-290.ZD.html; and for* McDonald: *https://www.law.cornell.edu/supct/html/08-1521.ZD .html).*

District of Columbia law bans handgun possession by making it a crime to carry an unregistered firearm and prohibiting the registration of handguns; provides separately that no person may carry an unlicensed handgun, but authorizes the police chief to issue 1-year licenses; and requires residents to keep lawfully owned firearms unloaded and dissembled or bound by a trigger-lock or similar device. Respondent Heller, a D.C. special policeman, applied to register a handgun he wished to keep at home, but the District refused. He filed this suit seeking, on Second Amendment grounds, to enjoin the city from enforcing the bar on handgun registration, the licensing requirement insofar as it prohibits carrying an unlicensed firearm in the home, and the trigger-lock requirement insofar as it prohibits the use of functional firearms in the home. The District Court dismissed the suit, but the D.C. Circuit reversed, holding that the Second Amendment protects an individual's right to possess firearms and that the city's total ban on handguns, as well as its requirement that firearms in the home be kept nonfunctional even when necessary for self-defense, violated that right.

Held:

1. The Second Amendment protects an individual right to possess a firearm unconnected with service in a militia, and to use that arm for traditionally lawful purposes, such as self-defense within the home. Pp. 2–53.

   (a) The Amendment's prefatory clause announces a purpose, but does not limit or expand the scope of the second part, the operative clause. The operative clause's text and history demonstrate that it connotes an individual right to keep and bear arms. Pp. 2–22.

(b) The prefatory clause comports with the Court's interpretation of the operative clause. The "militia" comprised all males physically capable of acting in concert for the common defense. The Antifederalists feared that the Federal Government would disarm the people in order to disable this citizens' militia, enabling a politicized standing army or a select militia to rule. The response was to deny Congress power to abridge the ancient right of individuals to keep and bear arms, so that the ideal of a citizens' militia would be preserved. Pp. 22–28.

(c) The Court's interpretation is confirmed by analogous arms-bearing rights in state constitutions that preceded and immediately followed the Second Amendment. Pp. 28–30.

(d) The Second Amendment's drafting history, while of dubious interpretive worth, reveals three state Second Amendment proposals that unequivocally referred to an individual right to bear arms. Pp. 30–32.

(e) Interpretation of the Second Amendment by scholars, courts and legislators, from immediately after its ratification through the late 19th century also supports the Court's conclusion. Pp. 32–47.

(f) None of the Court's precedents forecloses the Court's interpretation. Neither *United States v. Cruikshank*, 92 U.S. 542, nor *Presser v. Illinois*, 116 U.S. 252, refutes the individual-rights interpretation. *United States v. Miller*, 307 U.S. 174, does not limit the right to keep and bear arms to militia purposes, but rather limits the type of weapon to which the right applies to those used by the militia, i.e., those in common use for lawful purposes. Pp. 47–54.

2. Like most rights, the Second Amendment right is not unlimited. It is not a right to keep and carry any weapon

whatsoever in any manner whatsoever and for whatever purpose: For example, concealed weapons prohibitions have been upheld under the Amendment or state analogues. The Court's opinion should not be taken to cast doubt on longstanding prohibitions on the possession of firearms by felons and the mentally ill, or laws forbidding the carrying of firearms in sensitive places such as schools and government buildings, or laws imposing conditions and qualifications on the commercial sale of arms. Miller's holding that the sorts of weapons protected are those "in common use at the time" finds support in the historical tradition of prohibiting the carrying of dangerous and unusual weapons. Pp. 54–56.

3. The handgun ban and the trigger-lock requirement (as applied to self-defense) violate the Second Amendment. The District's total ban on handgun possession in the home amounts to a prohibition on an entire class of "arms" that Americans overwhelmingly choose for the lawful purpose of self-defense. Under any of the standards of scrutiny the Court has applied to enumerated constitutional rights, this prohibition—in the place where the importance of the lawful defense of self, family, and property is most acute—would fail constitutional muster. Similarly, the requirement that any lawful firearm in the home be disassembled or bound by a trigger-lock makes it impossible for citizens to use arms for the core lawful purpose of self-defense and is hence unconstitutional. Because Heller conceded at oral argument that the D.C. licensing law is permissible if it is not enforced arbitrarily and capriciously, the Court assumes that a license will satisfy his prayer for relief and does not address the licensing requirement. Assuming he is not disqualified from exercising Second Amendment rights, the District must permit Heller to register his handgun and must issue him a license to carry it in the home. Pp. 56–64.

478 F. 3d 370, affirmed.

Scalia, J., delivered the opinion of the Court, in which Roberts, C.J., and Kennedy, Thomas, and Alito, JJ., joined. Stevens, J., filed a dissenting opinion, in which Souter, Ginsburg, and Breyer, JJ., joined. Breyer, J., filed a dissenting opinion, in which Stevens, Souter, and Ginsburg, JJ., joined (https://www .law.cornell.edu/supct/html/07-290.ZS.html).

Source: *District of Columbia v. Heller*, 554 U.S. 570 (2008)

Introduction

The literature on guns in American society is enormous. The print and nonprint sources listed in this chapter represent some of the better known and more influential in the field. They are slanted toward peer-reviewed academic journals, scholarly book presses, and the websites of government agencies and larger advocacy organizations. It is important to keep in mind that even "dispassionate" scholars often find it hard to conceal their predispositions; as such, the reader should stay alert to their pro- or anti-gun inclinations and biases. Academicians, government researchers, and popular writers alike generally begin their studies with either a pro- or anti-gun perspective and then proceed to line up the evidence correspondingly—ignoring or discounting or minimizing any findings that do not fit the given perspective.

Massachusetts Attorney General Maura Healey, top center, responds to questions from reporters while standing behind a table covered with seized guns during a news conference at the federal courthouse in Boston in June of 2016. Law enforcement officials say more than 60 alleged gang members from Boston and other cities in eastern Massachusetts have been charged with drug, weapons and racketeering violations. Community-based policing efforts that target known gang members and illegal gun owners have generally been very successful in reducing gun violence since the U.S. Department of Justice began funding such efforts in 1991. (AP Photo/ Steven Senne)

Sources are categorized by selected key topics that are entwined with the contemporary gun debate in the United States. For each topic a relatively small number of references are given. Scholars and general readers alike can easily become overwhelmed by the volume of studies available in print and on the web, and each topical list could have easily extended into dozens, if not hundreds. However, the law of diminishing returns applies, and the number and importance of fresh ideas and data shrink quickly as one moves beyond the top handful of sources.

Gun Violence: The United States vs. Other Economically Developed Nations

Altheimer, Irshad. 2010. "An Exploratory Analysis of Guns and Violent Crime in a Cross-National Sample of Cities." *Southwest Journal of Criminal Justice* 6: 204–227.

> Altheimer finds strong, independent effects of gun prevalence on assault, gun assault, robbery, and gun robbery rates—even after controlling for unemployment, family disruption, age structure, the sex ratio, and the percentage of residents who go out nightly. More guns equates to more violent crime.

Gunpolicy.org. 2016. *Armed Violence and Gun Laws, Country by Country.* http://www.gunpolicy.org/firearms/home. http://www.gunpolicy.org/documents/5360-global-civilian-small-arms-stockpiles.

> The University of Sydney's GunPolicy.org website is the best single source for international data on gun prevalence, gun violence, and gun control laws.

Hemenway, David, and Matthew Miller. 2000. "Firearm Availability and Homicide Rates across 26 High-Income Countries." *Journal of Trauma* 49: 985–988.

> Hemenway and Miller, strong proponents of the public health perspective as the key way to approach problem of

gun violence, show a strong connection between cross-national firearms availability and violent gun deaths.

Kates, Don B., and Gary Kleck. 2001. *Armed: New Perspectives on Gun Control.* Amherst, NY: Prometheus Books.
Criminologist Gary Kleck and legal scholar Don B. Kates Jr. are well-known authors associated with the gun rights side of the contemporary debate over gun control. Both are highly critical of cross-national comparisons of gun availability, gun control laws, and the prevalence of gun violence, which usually reveal the United States as an outcast nation. Compared with other economically developed democracies, the United States has very high rates of gun ownership and gun violence. Gun control advocates see the correlation of these rates as causal, but Kates and Kleck argue otherwise. Rather than guns and their control being the root problems, unchecked criminal behavior and cross-cultural differences can account for the correlation.

Killias, Martin. 1993. "International Correlations between Gun Ownership and Rates of Homicide and Suicide." *Canadian Medical Association Journal* 148: 1721–1725.
Killias argues for strong links between cross-national homicide/suicide rates and gun availability.

Kleck, Gary. 1991. *Point Blank: Guns and Violence in America.* Hawthorne, NY Aldine de Gruyter.

Kleck, Gary. 1997. *Targeting Guns: Firearms and Their Control.* Hawthorne, NY: Aldine de Gruyter.
Criminologist Gary Kleck became famous with gun rights advocates after he published these two groundbreaking books. After reviewing a wide variety of evidence regarding the alleged evils of guns—in crime and suicide—Kleck concludes that blame is misplaced. He also observes that

guns are used as often for "good" purposes as bad ones, in that guns are often used for defensive purposes in warding off a criminal attack.

Kopel, David B. 1992a. *Gun Control in Great Britain: Saving Lives or Constricting Liberty?* Chicago: Office of International Criminal Justice, University of Illinois.

Kopel, David B. 1992b. *The Samurai, the Mountie, and the Cowboy: Should America Adopt the Gun Controls of Other Democracies?* Buffalo, NY: Prometheus Books.

Kopel, David B., ed. 1995. *Guns: Who Should Have Them?* Amherst, NY: Prometheus Books.

A strong gun rights proponent, Kopel does comparative analyses of gun violence in the United States, Great Britain, Canada, Japan, and other industrialized democracies in these three books—all of which lead him to the fundamental conclusion that the key explanation of a nation's violence should be sought in its culture, not in gun availability nor in gun control legislation.

Krug, Etienne G., Kenneth E. Powell, and Linda Dahlberg. 1998. "Firearm-Related Deaths in the United States and 35 Other High- and Upper-Middle-Income Countries." *International Journal of Epidemiology* 27: 214–221.

Krug, Etienne G., James A. Mercy, Linda L. Dahlberg, and Kenneth E. Powell. 1998. "Firearm- and Non-Firearm-Related Homicide among Children: An International Comparison." *Homicide Studies* 2: 83–95.

In this article and the one immediately above, Krug and his colleagues demonstrate a strong link between cross-national firearms availability and gun violence, showing how it is especially devastating to children.

Parker, Sarah. 2001. *Small Arms Survey 2011, States of Security—Balancing Act: Regulation of Civilian Firearm Possession*. Geneva, Switzerland: Small Arms Survey, Graduate Institute of International and Development Studies. http://www.smallarmssurvey.org/fileadmin/docs/A-Yearbook/2011/en/Small-Arms-Survey-2011-Chapter-09-EN.pdf.

This is an excellent survey of international gun laws, sampling both developed and developing nations— including how these laws have been affected by mass shootings.

United Nations. 1999. *United Nations International Study on Firearm Regulation*. Vienna, Austria: Crime Prevention and Criminal Justice Division, United Nations Office.

Although somewhat dated, the cross-national comparisons of international firearms laws are still generally accurate and valid.

United Nations. 2016a. *Statistics on Crime*. http://www.unodc.org/unodc/en/data-and-analysis/statistics/crime.html.

United Nations. 2016b. *Global Study on Homicide: UNODC Homicide Statistics 2013*. http://www.unodc.org/gsh/en/data.html.

With this report and the one immediately above, the United Nations Office on Drugs and Crime provides the homicide, assault, and other data typically used as dependent variables in cross-national studies of the impacts of gun prevalence and gun laws on criminal violence.

Van Dijk, Jan J. et al. 2007 (and before). *International Crime Victims Survey*. Turin, Italy: United Nations Interregional Crime and Justice Research Institute.

Van Dijk and his colleagues provide rich data on international criminal victimization dating back to 1989; the data and associated reports are available at http://www.unicri.it/services/library_documentation/publications/icvs/publications/.

Zimring, Franklin E., and Gordon Hawkins. *Crime Is Not the Problem: Lethal Violence in America.* New York: Oxford University Press.

> Criminologists Zimring and Hawkins acknowledge that many developed nations have serious crime problems, but they conclude that the United States stands out regarding its high *murder* rate, which they attribute to its relatively high prevalence of handguns compared to its peer nations.

The Second Amendment

Cornell, Saul. 2006. *A Well Regulated Militia: The Founding Fathers and the Origins of Gun Control in America.* New York: Oxford University Press.

> Cornell emphasizes that the contemporary debate over gun control has ignored the language and culture of the Founding Fathers, and that when these are taken into account both the "individual-right" and the "collective-right" interpretations are found wanting. Rather, it was civic duty to be borne by all free men—to be prepared to fight with the state militia should they be called on to do so.

Cornell, Saul, and Nathan Kozuskanich, eds. 2013. *The Second Amendment on Trial: Critical Essays on* District of Columbia v. Heller. Amherst: University of Massachusetts Press.

> A thoughtful collection of critical essays, plus friend-of-the-court briefs, on the landmark 2008 U.S. Supreme Court decision in *District of Columbia v. Heller.*

District of Columbia v. Heller. 2008. https://www.supreme court.gov/opinions/07pdf/07-290.pdf.

> In this landmark case, the Supreme Court ruled that the "Second Amendment protects an individual right to possess a firearm unconnected with service in a militia, and to use that arm for traditionally lawful purposes, such as self-defense within the home."

Freedman, Warren. 1989. *The Privilege to Keep and Bear Arms: The Second Amendment and Its Interpretation.* Westport, CT: Praeger.

The author deconstructs the Second Amendment phrase by phrase, relating each part to its historical roots and related court decisions. He comes down on the collective-right side of the debate over the amendment.

Halbrook. Stephen P. 1989. *A Right to Bear Arms: State and Federal Bills of Rights and Constitutional Guarantees.* Westport, CT: Greenwood Press.

Halbrook's historical and legal analysis leads him to come down strongly on the side of those interpreting the Second Amendment as guaranteeing an individual right to own firearms—and to do so with the minimum of legal encumbrances.

Jones, Jeffrey. 2008. *Americans in Agreement with Supreme Court on Gun Rights.* Princeton, NJ: Gallup. http://www.gall up.com/poll/108394/americans-agreement-supreme-court-gun-rights.aspx.

After the landmark 2008 *District of Columbia v. Heller* decision of the U.S. Supreme Court, the Gallup poll asked a national probability sample of U.S. adults if the amendment "guarantees the rights of Americans to own guns, or . . . only guarantees members of state militias such as National Guard units the right to own guns"; 73 percent responded that it gives gun ownership rights to individual Americans—however, 89 percent of the respondents also agreed that legal restrictions on guns should be at least as strong or stronger as they are currently.

Malcolm, Joyce Lee. 1994. *To Keep and Bear Arms: The Origins of an Anglo-American Right.* Cambridge, MA: Harvard University Press.

The author concludes that the Second Amendment guarantees an individual right to bear arms, and she carefully traces this right back to its origins in 17th-century English society and politics.

McDonald v. City of Chicago. 2010. https://www.supremecourt .gov/opinions/09pdf/08-1521.pdf.
    In the second most momentous decision of U.S. Supreme Court in the area of gun rights; the Court affirmed the validity of the 2008 *Heller* decision and declared that the Second Amendment guarantees the right of the individual to own a firearm for legal purposes, including self-defense, in all 50 states.

Uviller, H. Richard, and William G. Merkel. 2003. *The Militia and the Right to Arms, Or, How the Second Amendment Fell Silent*. Durham, NC: Duke University Press.
    The authors view the Second Amendment as giving individuals in the early part of U.S. history—or rather *selected* individuals (able-bodied, free white men)—the right to bear arms, but only to fulfill their duty of serving in the state militia. Because state militias have long since disappeared, the amendment is, at worst, irrelevant to the modern debate and, at best, no barrier to the enactment of strict gun regulations.

Waldman, Michael. 2014. *The Second Amendment: A Biography*. New York: Simon & Schuster.
    This history of the Second Amendment is one of the most important scholarly narratives on the legal and cultural battles over its meaning. Waldman shows how constitutional "originalism" (reading the Constitution as it was originally intended by its crafters) is untenable because the world that the amendment was written in, and for, is long gone.

Winkler, Adam. 2013. *Gunfight: The Battle over the Right to Bear Arms in America*. New York: W.W. Norton.

This book is an in-depth examination of the landmark *District of Columbia v. Heller* case, using it as a springboard to discuss the contentious history of the gun rights debate.

Public Opinion

Gallup. 2016. *Guns.* Princeton, NJ: The Gallup Organization. http://www.gallup.com/poll/1645/guns.aspx?version=print.
A wide variety of contemporary and historical data on gun ownership and public opinions regarding gun control, politics, and violence.

National Opinion Research Center. 1972–2016. *General Social Survey (GSS).* Chicago: National Opinion Research Center. http://gss.norc.org/.
The GSS is one of the most important sources of information available on U.S. attitudes and behavior regarding guns and gun laws. Importantly, the National Opinion Research Center provides GSS raw data in readily downloadable formats. Analyses of selected GSS items reveal steadily declining rates of household gun ownership and hunting, and consistently strong support for gun control.

Pew Research Center. 2016. *Gun Control.* Washington, DC: Pew Research Center. http://www.pewresearch.org/topics/gun-control/.
The center is an excellent source of contemporary and historical public opinion data on gun culture and politics. Dozens of reports are organized by year, staring in 2007.

Smith, Tom, and Jaesok Son. 2015. *Trends in Gun Ownership in the United States, 1972–2014.* Chicago: National Opinion Research Center. http://www.norc.org/pdfs/GSSReports/GSS_Trends in Gun Ownership_US_1972-2014.pdf.
The authors provide straightforward analyses of trends in gun ownership and attitudes toward gun control—and

they include breakdowns by a variety of social background characteristics (e.g., by gender, race, and region).

The Role of Politics

Carter, Gregg Lee. 1997. *The Gun Control Movement*. New York: Twayne.

> The birth and rise of Handgun Control, Inc. (now the Brady Campaign), is detailed, including its struggles to get two of the most significant pieces of gun legislation passed in the past three decades—the 1993 Brady Act and the 1994 federal Assault Weapons Ban.

Carter, Gregg Lee, ed. 2012. *Guns in American Society: An Encyclopedia of History, Politics, Culture, and the Law*, Vols. 1–3. Santa Barbara, CA: ABC-CLIO.

> A massive three-volume contribution to the gun debate that includes dozens of entries on the often nuanced and complex relationships among the passage of gun laws, the lobbying of gun groups, and the American political system.

Goss, Kristin. 2008. *Disarmed: The Missing Movement for Gun Control in America*. Princeton, NJ: Princeton University Press.

> Goss's analytical narrative shows how the lack of success of the gun control movement is not only due to the National Rifle Association (NRA) and the gun rights lobby, but also due to the inability of the movement itself to articulate a clear message and to mobilize public support.

Institute for Legislative Action, National Rifle Association. 2016. *Legal and Legislation Articles*. https://www.nraila.org/legal-legislation/.

> The institute provides a wealth of reports on the premier gun rights organization's attempts to influence state and national political activities regarding gun control.

Riestenberg, Jay. 2015. *Whose Government? Whose Voice?* http://www.commoncause.org/research-reports/whose-government-whose-voice/whose-government-whose-voice.pdf.

Published by the liberal advocacy group Common Cause, the book by Riestenberg and his colleagues offers an empirical analysis of the detrimental impacts of the U.S. Supreme Court's 2010 decision in *Citizens United v. Federal Election Commission* on American politics. The decision ultimately allowed corporations, labor unions, and associations like the NRA to make indirect donations channeled to candidates through independent political groups. The decision has greatly increased the NRA's ability to influence the campaign process.

Spitzer, Robert J. 2015. *The Politics of Gun Control*, 6th ed. Boulder, CO: Paradigm Publishers.

This classic work analyzes the nature of U.S. politics to demonstrate how one-issue organizations like the NRA can have enormous impact on legislation. The author believes national regulation would reduce gun violence, but such regulation is stymied by polarized gun politics where gun rights advocates see all attempts at gun control as disguises for the ultimate aim of gun confiscation.

Spitzer, Robert J. 2015. *Guns across America: Reconciling Gun Rules and Rights.* New York: Oxford University Press.

Spitzer embellishes his well-known *The Politics of Gun Control* with further analyses of how the American political system is too easily swayed by the gun rights lobby, and that how the lobby's depiction of country's history—that in its past gun rights were unfettered by burdensome gun laws—is seriously flawed.

Wilson, Harry L. 2006. *Guns, Gun Control, and Elections: The Politics and Policy of Firearms.* Lanham, MD: Rowman & Littlefield.

The author shows the complex relationships of politicians, political parties, and interest groups as they intersect to affect gun legislation at both state and national levels.

Wilson, Harry L. 2015. *The Triumph of the Gun-Rights Argument: Why the Gun Control Debate Is Over*. Santa Barbara, CA: Praeger.
Wilson shows how the well-organized approach of gun rights groups has overpowered the efforts of gun control advocacy groups in shaping both public opinion and state and national legislation on gun regulations.

Gun Control and Gun Violence: The Public Health Approach

Center for Gun Policy and Research. 2016. *Center Publications*. Baltimore, MD: Bloomberg School of Public Health, Johns Hopkins University. http://www.jhsph.edu/research/centers-and-institutes/johns-hopkins-center-for-gun-policy-and-research/publications/.
A series of public health reports analyzing gun violence that date back to 2000.

Cook, Philip J., and Kristin A. Goss. 2014. *The Gun Debate: What Everyone Needs to Know*. New York: Oxford University Press.
A wide-ranging examination of key issues in the contemporary gun debate, which emphasizes a public health perspective on the costs and possible preventions of gun violence in the contemporary United States.

Cook, Philip J., and Jens Ludwig. 2002. *Gun Violence: The Real Costs*. New York: Oxford University Press.
An excellent introduction to the hidden costs of gun violence—from lost employment time and productivity to acute and long-term medical expenses.

Harvard Injury Control Research Center (HICRC). 2016. *Firearms Research.* https://www.hsph.harvard.edu/hicrc/fire arms-research/.
  The HICRC provides a wealth of recent studies on the effects of gun control and gun prevalence on firearms injuries and deaths (accidental, homicides, suicides) from the public health perspective.

Hemenway, David. 2004. *Private Guns, Public Health.* Ann Arbor: University of Michigan Press.
  The best single source detailing the public health approach to gun violence, which includes the national and cross-national evidence for the efficacy of this approach.

Kates, Don B., Jr., John K. Lattimer, and James Boen. 1997. "Sagecraft: Bias and Mendacity in the Public Health Literature." In *The Great American Gun Debate: Essays on Firearms and Violence*, ed. Don B. Kates Jr. and Gary Kleck, 123–147. San Francisco: Pacific Research Institute for Public Policy.
  A somewhat dated article, but its theme of gun rights scholars and advocates maintaining a generally highly negatively view of public health researchers' analyses of gun violence data has not changed.

National Center for Injury Prevention and Control. 2016. *Web-Based Injury Statistics Query and Reporting System (WISQARS).* Atlanta: Centers for Disease Control and Prevention, U.S. Department of Health and Human Service. http://www.cdc.gov/injury/wisqars/.
  Historical and recent raw data on firearms fatalities, injuries, and accidents. The data extraction program takes only a few minutes to learn, and ordinary users can generate sophisticated reports with very little practice.

Violence Prevention Research Program. 2016. *Publications, Editorials, and Commentaries.* Davis: University of California,

Davis. http://www.ucdmc.ucdavis.edu/vprp/research/Publica
tions.html.
    A continually updated series of public health reports on
    gun violence, many authored by Magdalena Cerdá and
    Garen Wintemute.

Webster, Daniel W., and Jon S. Vernick, eds. 2014. *Reducing
Gun Violence in America: Informing Policy with Evidence and
Analysis*. Baltimore: Johns Hopkins University Press.
    A wide variety of articles on the public health impacts
    of gun violence and on the effectiveness of selected gun
    control measures.

Gun Control and Gun Violence: The Law Enforcement Approach

Braga, Anthony A., et al. 2001. "Problem-Oriented Policing,
Deterrence, and Youth Violence: An Evaluation of Boston's
Operation Ceasefire." *Journal of Research in Crime and Delin-
quency* 38: 195–225.
    The Boston Gun Project and similar efforts to reduce gun
    violence can and do work if properly managed, as revealed
    in this empirical assessment.

City of New York. 2009. *Gun Show Undercover: Report on Illegal Sales at Gun Shows*. http://everytownresearch.org/docu
ments/2015/04/gun-show-undercover.pdf.

City of New York. 2011. *Point, Click, Fire: An Investigation of
Illegal Online Gun Sales*. http://everytownresearch.org/docu
ments/2015/04/point-click-fire.pdf.
    These two major studies conclude that illegal gun sales
    can be reduced if the Bureau of Alcohol, Tobacco, Fire-
    arms and Explosives (ATF) increases its monitoring of
    unregulated firearms sales at gun shows and online.

Everytown for Gun Safety. 2015. *Business as Usual: How Unlicensed High-Volume Gun Sellers Fuel the Criminal Market and How the President Can Stop Them.* http://everytownresearch .org/documents/2015/11/business-as-usual.pdf.

> A detailed account on how unlicensed dealers evade federal surveillance from the ATF by avoiding licensing. The researchers conclude that increased scrutiny by local, state, and federal law enforcement, as well as increased prosecutions of violators, can reduce illegal trade in firearms—with many guns obtained in this trade being used in the commission of violent crimes.

National Research Council. 2005. *Firearms and Violence: A Critical Review.* Washington, DC: National Academies Press.

> An intensive review of measures to reduce gun violence, with a detailed assessment of the relatively effective approaches of community-oriented policing and of enhanced sentencing for those convicted of firearm-related crimes.

Pierce, Glenn L., et al. 2004. "Characteristics and Dynamics of Illegal Firearms Markets: Implications for a Supply-Side Enforcement Strategy." *Justice Quarterly* 21: 391–422.

Pierce, Glenn L., Anthony A. Braga, and Garen J. Wintemute. 2015. "Impact of California Firearms Sales Laws and Dealer Regulations on the Illegal Diversion of Guns." *Injury Prevention* 21: 179–184.

> In this article and the one immediately above, Pierce and his colleagues conclude from their analyses of crime–gun trace data that cracking down on corrupt gun dealers can reduce gun violence by cutting the supply of new guns ending up in the hands of street criminals. Each new generation of felons must be armed, and many of their guns actually come from federally licensed firearms dealers.

President's Task Force on 21st Century Policing. 2015. *Final Report of the President's Task Force on 21st Century Policing.* Washington, DC: Office of Community Oriented Policing Services. http://www.cops.usdoj.gov/pdf/taskforce/taskforce_ finalreport.pdf.

> Community policing emphasizes direct contact between neighborhood police officers and neighborhood residents to create trust and ultimately the ability to "coproduce" public safety. Although not directed specifically to gun violence, the report speaks to how community-oriented policing can reduce all types of criminal violence, including that which is gun-related.

Schildkraut, Jaclyn, and H. Jaymi Elsass. 2016. *Mass Shootings: Media, Myths, and Realities.* Santa Barbara, CA: Praeger.

> Although representing only tiny fraction of the gun homicides, active-shooter mass-shootings have captured public attention like no other kind of murder. The authors detail the measures that can reduce the number of—and the harm created by—mass shootings, with a heavy focus on *capable guardianship* of target populations (involving the training and tactics of law enforcement and of the guardians of target populations, e.g., teachers, security personnel, and other staff).

U.S. Department of Justice. 1999. *Promising Strategies to Reduce Gun Violence.* Washington, DC: U.S. Department of Justice. http://www.ojjdp.gov/pubs/gun_violence/173950.pdf.

U.S. Department of Justice. 2002. *Gun Violence Reduction: National Integrated Firearms Violence Reduction Strategy.* Washington, DC: U.S. Department of Justice. https://www .justice.gov/archive/opd/gunviolence.htm.

> Although somewhat dated, the findings and recommendations of these two reports on the potential for selected law enforcement practices for reducing gun violence are as salient today as they were when first published.

Defensive Gun Use

Ayres, Ian, and John D. Donohue III. 2003. "Shooting Down the More Guns, Less Crime Hypothesis." *Stanford Law Review* 55: 1193–1312.

> John R. Lott's "more guns, less crime" thesis (see below) is not confirmed in this highly analytical, statistical tour-de-force article; if anything, the authors conclude that more guns lead to more crime.

Hemenway, David, and Sara J. Solnick. 2015. "The Epidemiology of Self-Defense Gun Use: Evidence from the National Crime Victimization Surveys 2007–2011." *Preventive Medicine* 79: 22–27.

> An analysis of five years of the National Crime Victimization Survey reveals no support for the benefits of defensive gun use in fending off criminal attack compared to other forms of self-defense (e.g., yelling, running, hiding, hitting, or kicking). The typical incident of defensive gun use involves a rural male away from home—against another male who has a gun.

Kleck, Gary, and Marc Gertz. 1995. "Armed Resistance to Crime: The Prevalence and Nature of Self-Defense with a Gun." *Journal of Criminal Law and Criminology* 86: 150–187.

> Gun rights advocates contest public health researchers' estimates of the costs of gun violence to the United States because such estimates ignore the *savings* incurred from the *defensive* use of guns by law-abiding citizens to fend off criminal attacks. These advocates point to the findings of the Kleck and Gertz's study as proof of reality of defensive gun use (as many as 2.5 million uses per year). "More guns" in the hands of ordinary citizens translates into "less crime," and less of all its associated costs to the judicial and healthcare systems.

Lambert, Tim. 2004. *Do More Guns Cause Less Crime?* https://web.archive.org/web/20140528141856/http:/www.cse.unsw.edu.au/~lambert/guns/lott/lott.pdf.

A strong empirical and theoretical attack on John Lott's "more guns, less crime thesis."

Lott, John R., Jr. 2010. *More Guns, Less Crime: Understanding Crime and Gun-Control Laws*, 3rd ed. Chicago: University of Chicago Press.

The thesis of Lott's controversial book is in its title.

#DisarmHate

UNITED STATES
CONGRESS

ORY JAMES CONNELL
AGE 21

The following chronology presents the long and broad range of watershed events that have shaped the contemporary gun debate in American society. The details and social impacts of many of these events are discussed in greater detail in earlier chapters.

1787–1791   The place of militias in the new nation is one of a myriad of issues during the U.S. Constitutional Convention's deliberations in 1787. States' rights advocates emphasize that citizens in new republics should fear standing armies at all costs. After prolonged debates, the First Congress passes the Second Amendment. States' rights advocates want certainty that federal power will not be used to annul state sovereignty—and they see state militias as essential to this goal. As ratified in 1791, the Second Amendment declares: "A well regulated Militia, being necessary to the security of a free State, the right of the people to keep and bear Arms, shall not be infringed."

Rep. John Lewis (GA-05), center, speaks at an event on the steps of the U.S. Capitol Building for an evening of remembrance honoring the victims and survivors of the mass shooting that took place at the Pulse nightclub in Orlando, Florida, on June 12, 2016. With 49 killed, the shooting was the worst in U.S. history, and sparked many attempts by gun control advocates in Congress to move forward legislation that requires universal background checks and denies gun sales to those on the FBI's Terror Watchlist. All such attempts, thus far, have failed. (Paul Morigi/AP Images for Human Rights Campaign)

1792–1794   On May 1 and 8, 1792, President George Washington signs the First and Second Militia Acts of 1792, which set a minimum standard for the federal militia. The acts require free, able-bodied, 18- to 45-year-old white men to enroll in the militia. Each militiaman is required to supply his own gun, powder, ammunition, shot-pouch, powder horn, and knapsack and to "appear so armed, accoutered, and provided, when called out to exercise or into service."

Washington uses the act to muster the militia and put down the "Whiskey Rebellion" of August 1794. The Rebellion is in protest to a tax the first U.S. Congress had placed on distilled spirits to raise money to pay down the national debt. The rebels are Pennsylvania farmers who earn extra income by distilling their surplus grain into whiskey. Many believe the tax is unfair and violates a key reason for the Revolutionary War from which the United States had been born—"taxation without local representation."

1865–1866   In the post–Civil War South, *Black Codes* are enacted in Alabama, Arkansas, Florida, Georgia, Louisiana, Mississippi, North Carolina, South Carolina, Tennessee, and Texas. These statutes deprive African Americans of many basic rights, including the right to own and carry firearms. For example, a Mississippi law dictates that "no freedman, free Negro, or mulatto not in the military service of the United States government, and not licensed so to do by the board of police of his or her county, shall keep or carry firearms of any kind, or ammunition, dirk, or Bowie knife." Such laws contribute to keeping African Americans servile.

1871   The National Rifle Association is founded. In its early years, it is a small shooting association sponsoring rifle matches and sharpshooter classes. But over the course of the next century, it will evolve into a powerful political force in U.S. politics—developing a working philosophy that virtually all new gun control regulations should be resisted, existing ones being more than sufficient, if enforced.

1876   In *United States v. Cruikshank*, the U.S. Supreme Court renders its first major decision on the Second Amendment. The Court rules that the Second Amendment is a guarantee against federal infringement of a preexisting right that "is found wherever civilization exists." However, the Second Amendment right is not one of the "privileges or immunities of citizens of the United States." In short, the decision supports the contention that of gun control advocates that the Second Amendment should not pose a barrier to the enactment of strict gun laws.

1886   The U.S. Supreme Court addresses the Second Amendment for a second time in *Presser v. Illinois*. Herman Presser, the leader of a German American labor group called the *Lehr und Wehr Verein* (the "Learning and Defense Club"), is arrested for parading the group through downtown Chicago while carrying a sword, and while club members were carrying unloaded rifles. He is accused of conducting an "armed military drill," which could legally be done only with a license, under Illinois statutes in force at the time. Presser appeals, invoking the Second Amendment in his defense. The Supreme Court rules against him, citing the 1876 *United States v. Cruikshank* decision discussed earlier. Again, the Court contends that the Second Amendment does not directly apply to the individual states, and is not made applicable to them by the privileges or immunities clause of the Fourteenth Amendment.

1903   Congress passes the Militia Act of 1903, also known as the Dick Act (named after the Ohio congressman who sponsors the legislation, Rep. Charles Dick, himself a National Guard officer). The act separates the organized militia, to be known as the "National Guard" of the state, from the "unorganized militia" (which, in actuality, has not existed for decades). It provides federal support for state governments to arm, train, and drill the guards.

1911   New York State passes the Sullivan Law, requiring a license for both the purchase and carry of handguns. Such licenses are rarely issued for carrying. However, gun rights advocates point out that it has little effect on violent crime and is motivated, at heart, by xenophobic fears within the mainstream leadership of New York, who want to keep firearms out of the hands of Italian and other recent immigrants.

1916   Congress passes the National Defense Act, increasing federal support for the state National Guard units, and also further subsumes them under national military rules, organization, and authority. They operate under a dual enlistment system, whereby a guard member is simultaneously part of the relevant *state* National Guard and the *U.S.* National Guard.

1927   Congress passes the Mailing of Firearms Act of 1927, also known as the Miller Act, prohibiting sending concealable firearms through the U.S. Post Office. The law is easy to skirt until the passage of the Gun Control Act of 1968, because mailers can legally send guns via private mail delivery companies such as UPS (United Parcel Service).

1929   The Saint Valentine's Day Massacre in Chicago shocks the nation. Four members of Al Capone's gang, two dressed as police officers, ruthlessly mow down seven members of a rival Chicago gang using Thompson submachine guns. The murders prompt several gun control proposals in Congress, two of which eventually pass (the National Firearms Act of 1934 and the Federal Firearms Act of 1938).

1934   The first major federal gun control legislation is passed as the National Firearms Act. It mandates all persons engaged in the business of selling gangster-type weapons—machine guns, sawed-off shotguns, and silencers—and all owners of these to register with the collector of internal revenue and pay applicable taxes for the firearm transfer. Because criminals are unlikely to register their weapons, the effect is to give law enforcement authorities a new reason to arrest gangsters (possession of an unregistered weapon). Lawful trade in these weapons is also dramatically reduced due to the hefty taxes.

1938 The second major federal gun control legislation is passed as the Federal Firearms Act. It imposes the first federal limitations on the sale of ordinary firearms. It requires manufacturers, dealers, and importers of guns and handgun ammunition to obtain a federal firearms license. Dealers must maintain records of the names and addresses of persons to whom firearms are sold. Gun sales to persons convicted of violent felonies are prohibited.

1939 In *United States v. Miller*, the U.S. Supreme Court makes its third major ruling bearing on the Second Amendment. The Court rules that the federal government has the right, which it exercised in the National Firearms Act of 1934, to control the transfer of (and in effect, to require the registration of) certain firearms. In this particular case, the sawed-off shotgun, a favorite weapon of gangsters, is deemed unprotected by the Second Amendment. However, gun rights advocates point out that in its *Miller* ruling, the Supreme Court noted that the writers of the Constitution clearly intended that the states had both the right and the duty to maintain militias and that "when called for service, these men were expected to appear bearing arms supplied by themselves. . . . This implied the general obligation of all adult male inhabitants to possess arms."

1961 An amendment to the Federal Aviation Act of 1958— by Public Law 87–197 of 1961—bars individuals from bringing on board a passenger aircraft any concealed firearm (except in the form of check-in luggage).

1963 Using a false name, Lee Harvey Oswald buys an imported Italian military rifle for less than $20 from a mail-order dealer in Chicago. He uses it to assassinate President John F. Kennedy. The ease with which he has obtained the weapon stuns many Americans, and soon there are numerous bills brought before Congress to regulate the gun market, though it will take more violence, as it unfolds in the mid-1960s, before any of these bills are passed into law.

1965 The Texas Tower shooting shocks the nation. On August 1, former Marine sharpshooter Charles Whitman climbs the clock tower on the University of Texas campus in Austin with seven firearms. He methodically kills 15 people and wounds 31 others.

The Texas Tower massacre and its immediate aftermath are played out many times over the next five decades: An active-shooter, mass-murder shooting—that is not gang- or drug-related—shocks the nation and sparks national legislative proposals to control guns; within a few months, however, emotions die down and almost all of the proposals fail enactment. Legislation does occur at the state level, but in states that are controlled by Republicans the legislation supports increased gun rights and decreased gun regulation.

1968 The assassinations of Reverend Martin Luther King Jr. and Senator Robert F. Kennedy, as do the urban riots exploding in hundreds of urban areas since 1965, increase national attention on gun violence and, according to many observers, the need for stronger gun control. Congress is finally motivated to pass twin bills containing serious gun control measures—the Omnibus Crime Control and Safe Streets Act of 1968 and the Gun Control Act of 1968 (GCA). More recent federal gun laws, including the 1993 Brady Law and the 1994 federal Assault Weapons Ban, are enacted as amendments to the GCA statutes (or, less often, to the 1934 National Firearms Act).

The GCA creates nine categories of individuals that are to be prohibited from buying or possessing firearms (e.g., convicted felons), and it places severe restrictions on the importation of firearms and on the sale of guns and ammunition across state lines.

The GCA leads to the creation of the Bureau of Alcohol, Tobacco, Firearms and Explosives (ATF)—upgraded from its previous status as a division—within the Department of the Treasury (and moved to the Deparment of Justice in 2003).

The ATF is the key federal agency assigned to effectuate gun control, but its advocates complain that it is hampered by lack of funding and by restrictions placed on it by the gun rights–leaning Congresses of the 1986 and of the post-1994 era.

1972 The Consumer Product Safety Commission is created to "protect against unreasonable risks of injuries associated with consumer products." However, firearms are excluded from the commission's oversight. Congress further clarifies its intent with a follow-up piece of legislation, the Firearms Safety and Consumer Protection Act of 1976, which excludes ammunition from regulations by the Consumer Product Safety Commission. Gun control advocates rue these exclusions.

1973–1974 From October 1973 through April 1974, the Zebra Killings in the San Francisco area captivate the public's attention and eventually strengthen the gun control movement both locally and nationally. The label given to the killings is attributed to the fact that the killers are black and the victims are white. Fourteen people are murdered and seven wounded during the five-month killing spree.

The Zebra killing of college student Nick Shields leads his father, Pete Shields, to become a gun control activist. Shields leaves an executive position with DuPont to become executive director of a new advocacy group, Handgun Control, Inc. (HCI). A victim of gun violence, Mark Borinsky had founded HCI in 1974 with the original name of the National Council to Control Handguns. Under Shields's leadership, HCI develops into the premier organizational advocate for strengthening gun control in the United States (it is renamed the Brady Campaign to Prevent Gun Violence in 2001).

1977 The "Revolt at Cincinnati" occurs at the annual meeting of the National Rifle Association. It is a watershed event that will change the organization from one largely dedicated to promoting the sporting uses of firearms to one largely dedicated to fighting any and all forms of gun control.

1980   On the evening of December 8, Mark David Chapman uses a Charter Arms .38 caliber revolver to gun down John Lennon in New York City. Lennon's murder stokes national interest in gun control and the membership of still-fledgling HCI (renamed the Brady Campaign to Prevent Gun Violence in 2001) rockets from 5,000 to 80,000 contributing members in a matter of weeks.

In *Lewis v. United States*, the Supreme Court upholds a provision of the Gun Control Act of 1968; in a footnote, it states that "restrictions on the use of firearms are neither based upon constitutionally suspect criteria, nor do they trench upon any constitutionally protected liberties," and cites the 1939 *United States v. Miller* case for support.

1981   John Hinckley uses a cheap handgun in March to wound President Ronald Reagan and his press secretary, James Brady, as well as Secret Service agent Timothy McCarthy and local police officer Thomas Delahanty. The assassination attempt results in a boon for HCI and the gun control movement. The event motivates Sarah Brady, James Brady's wife, to dedicate herself to the gun control movement; she joins HCI, takes on leadership roles, and eventually becomes its president.

The assassination attempt also moves Congress to renew its discussions on gun control, and encourages its support of legislation that eventually will be enacted in the late 1980s and early 1990s.

1986   The Firearms Owners' Protection Act (FOPA)—known also as the McClure-Volkmer Act—is passed against the protests of gun control advocates. FOPA curtails many of the more stringent provisions of the Gun Control Act of 1968.

The Law Enforcement Officers Protection Act is signed into law. It bans so-called cop killer handgun bullets—or more accurately, bullets with very dense cores made from certain metals—that are capable of piercing some bullet-resistant vests and other body armor. Amended in 1994, the statute defines "armor piercing ammunition" as a handgun bullet "constructed entirely" from "tungsten alloys, steel, iron, brass, bronze, beryllium copper, or depleted uranium." or with a jacket having a weight greater than one-quarter of the projectile's total weight.

1988   The Undetectable Firearms Act is passed. It bans the manufacture, importation, possession, receipt, and transfer of "plastic guns"—those with less than 3.7 ounces of metal, which could potentially defeat metal detectors. At the time, it is a symbolic victory for the gun control movement, as commercially manufactured guns have always met this standard; but with the invention of 3-D printing in the early 2000s, the act becomes more salient and is renewed in 2003 and again in 2013.

1989   On January 17, Patrick Purdy enters a Stockton, California, schoolyard and fires 105 rounds from a semiautomatic assault rifle, killing 5 children and wounding 29 others. The slaughter mobilizes public and political support for gun control throughout the nation. California responds quickly and enacts the Roberti-Roos Assault Weapons Control Act of 1989. Over the next few years, six other states follow with legislation restricting the sale of assault weapons (Connecticut, Hawaii, Maryland, Massachusetts, New Jersey, and New York).

At the federal level, President George H.W. Bush, even though a member of the NRA and a gun rights proponent during his election campaign, responds in March of 1989 by placing a temporary ban on the importation of assault rifles and selected similar weapons. Several bills are introduced in Congress to outlaw or restrict assault pistols, rifles, and shotguns. President Bill Clinton eventually pushes one of these through Congress as part of the Violent Crime Control and Enforcement Act of 1994 (see below).

1991   The Killeen, Texas, massacre unfolds on the afternoon of October 16, 1991, when George Hennard Jr. plows his truck into Luby's Cafeteria. Repeatedly firing and then reloading two handguns, he slaughters 23 people and wounds 21 others.

Two of Hennard's victims are the parents of Suzanna Gratia. Gratia normally travels with a handgun for self-protection, but keeps it in her car to be in compliance with Texas law, which in 1991 does not allow ordinary citizens to carry concealed weapons. She testifies ruefully at a public hearing that she might have been able to save her parents if she had had her gun in her purse: "I had a perfect shot at him. It would have been clear. I had a place to prop my hand. The guy was not even aware of what we were doing. I'm not saying that I could have saved anybody in there, but I would have had a chance."

Gratia's testimony becomes instrumental in changing the political climate in Texas and many other states regarding right-to-carry laws; indeed, Texas and a dozen other states soon adopt such law. (Note, that as of 2016, 34 states are classified as "shall-issue"—allowing an ordinary citizen to readily obtain a permit to carry a concealed handgun).

The U.S. Department of Justice, working in conjunction with state and local authorities and coordinating key law enforcement groups (the ATF, FBI, and Drug Enforcement Administration), develops Project Triggerlock. Over the years, Triggerlock is expanded and reformulated—to accommodate the unique circumstances of various metropolitan areas— under dozens of guises in hundreds of local and regional jurisdictions (program titles include Project Exile, Operation Ceasefire, Project Felon, Project Safe Neighborhoods, Triggerlock II, and many others). These programs use federal firearm statutes—for example, those barring the possession of firearms by high-risk individuals, including convicted felons, drug dealers, and domestic abusers—to prosecute gun-carrying offenders in *federal* ("U.S. District") courts, where conviction rates are typically much higher and penalties much stiffer than in state and local courts. The programs often contain media campaigns to increase public awareness of gun crime and its ramifications, including the death and maiming of innocent victims, the financial losses suffered by the community, and the stern penalties gun-carrying criminals will face when turned over to the federal judicial system. Sometimes the programs incorporate a "carrot" approach—for example, increasing funding for school and community development agencies, especially those that seek to take teens and young adults off the streets through recreational, educational, and job-placement programs.

1993–1994   On July 1, 1993, Gian Luigi Ferri, a disgruntled former client, enters the law office of Pettit and Martin at 101 California Street in San Francisco. Armed with three handguns, two of them TEC-DC9 assault pistols, he kills eight people and wounds another six in the law office and in neighboring offices. The police quickly arrive and corner him in a stairwell, where he commits suicide. Although California had banned the sale of assault weapons after the Stockton schoolyard massacre of 1989, Ferri easily obtains his at a gun show and pawn shop in Nevada.

The massacre sparks outcries for strong gun controls and contributes to the passage of the 1994 federal Assault Weapons Ban.

On November 30, 1993, President Clinton signs the Brady Handgun Violence Prevention Act, requiring a five-government-business-day waiting period for the purchase of a handgun. The waiting period allows time for at least a minimal background check of the prospective buyer; it also allows for a "cooling-off" period to minimize impulse purchases that might lead to suicide or criminal violence. Five years after its enactment, the five-day waiting period sunsets by its own terms and is replaced by the National Instant Criminal Background Check System (NICS), which allows background checking for both handgun and long-gun sales (rifles and shotguns).

The Gun-Free Schools Act of 1994 requires that any state receiving federal education funds "shall have in effect a State law requiring local educational agencies to expel from school for a period of not less than one year a student who is determined to have brought a weapon to a school."

Enacted under Title XI as part of the Violent Crime Control and Law Enforcement Act of 1994, the federal "Assault Weapons Ban" prohibits for 10 years the future manufacture and transfer of 19 named assault weapons, and approximately 200 firearms covered by the law's generic definition of an "assault weapon." It also bans large-capacity ammunition feeding devices ("magazines")—those that can hold more than 10 rounds. The ban does not apply to assault weapons or magazines already in circulation.

The first modern gun court is created in Providence, Rhode Island, in September 1994 (note that Chicago had created one in the 1930s to handle an onslaught of gun crime in that era). Before its existence, the average time for the disposition of a gun case—via a plea bargain or the start of a trial—is 518 days, with a conviction rate of 67 percent. After the court is created, the maximum time for the disposition of a gun case falls to 126 days, while the conviction rate rises to 87 percent. These impressive results encourage the creation of gun courts in other cities, with high-profile courts appearing in Birmingham, Detroit, Indianapolis, Minneapolis, New York City, Philadelphia, Seattle, and Washington, D.C.

1996 The Lautenberg Amendment to the Gun Control Act of 1968, also called the Domestic Violence Offender Gun Ban, expands prohibition of gun purchase, ownership, or possession to include persons convicted of domestic violence misdemeanor offenses. The amendment strengthens the existing regulation that prevents gun possession by a person under a court order that restrains him or her "from harassing, stalking, or threatening an intimate partner or child of such intimate partner" (per the "Wellstone Amendment" in the Violent Crime Control and Law Enforcement Act of 1994).

1999 On April 20, in Littleton, Colorado, two Columbine High School students kill 12 fellow students, one teacher, and then themselves. A wave of schoolyard shootings follow in the next several years and spark dozens of state and federal legislative proposals to tighten up gun laws, none of which are enacted at the federal level.

2000   Many seasoned political observers credit the power of the NRA and the gun rights movement for George W. Bush's victory over Al Gore in the 2000 presidential election. More particularly, Gore loses in his home state of Tennessee, Bill Clinton's home state of Arkansas, and the normally strongly Democratic state of West Virginia. A win in any of one of these would have given the presidency to Gore. The NRA had strongly targeted these states, railing against Gore for his generally strong support of gun control legislation, both existing (e.g., the Brady Act and the Assault Weapons Ban) and proposed (e.g., handgun licensing, closing the "gun show loophole," and opposing protections for gun dealers and manufacturers against civil liability suits).

2001   On September 11, 2001, the United States suffers the worst terrorist attack in its history, with nearly 3,000 people dying on a single day. Over the next decade, attempts are made to strengthen gun control via legislation aimed at antiterrorism, but all fail. Most contentious is that being on the FBI's Terrorist Screening Center's watch list does not prevent an individual (if otherwise qualified, e.g., not being a convicted felon) from legally buying a firearm. If anything, the 9/11 attack enhances public attitudes toward self-defense and gun rights legislation—including the Arming Pilots against Terrorism Act (2002), allowing airline pilots to carry firearms on passenger flights.

2002   John Allen Muhammad and John Lee Malvo use a Bushmaster assault rifle in October to murder ten people and injure three others in the Washington, D.C., area. The shooting spree prompts gun control advocates to call for the creation of a national ballistic fingerprinting database, in which all firearms would have digital images of their shell casing and (in the case of rifles and handguns) bullet markings on file. They contend that such a database would have led law enforcement authorities to identify the snipers much sooner. These advocates also contend that the shooting spree is strong evidence for strengthening and extending the federal ban on assault weapons. No federal legislation is passed in either regard.

2004 Tucked away in an omnibus spending package approved by both houses of Congress in January are provisions reducing the length of time the Department of Justice can maintain background check records on firearm sales: from 90 days to 24 hours. Records are kept on file to ensure that if an individual prohibited from buying guns (e.g., a convicted felon) is inadvertently allowed to make such a purchase, the mistake can be corrected. Gun control advocates complain that requiring these records to be destroyed within 24 hours makes it nearly impossible for the Justice Department to correct errors, and the end result will be the arming of more criminals. The change in recordkeeping is pushed by Todd Tiahrt (R-KS), and becomes known as the "Tiahrt amendment."

Despite the protests of gun control advocates, the 1994 federal Assault Weapons Ban, originally enacted to last for 10 years, is allowed to expire in September.

In another federal legislative response to the 9/11 terrorist attack, the Law Enforcement Officers Safety Act of 2004 is signed into law. It allows current and retired, qualified law enforcement offices to carry concealed firearms throughout the country without a concealed carry permit, with very few restrictions.

In the 2004 presidential election, John Kerry loses the hotly contested state of Ohio. Had he triumphed, he would have won the Electoral College. Gun rights observers contend that Kerry's association with the gun control movement cost him several hundred thousand Ohio votes—and he loses by 120,000.

The 2004 election reveals how elections increasingly favor the gun rights camp. Politicians favoring gun control (mainly Democrats) begin to mute their cries for more regulation—in part, because they fear public challenges from the NRA (if not its outright wherewithal to make them lose in the next election), and, in part, because they see efforts in this area as wasted.

2005–2006   Congress passes the Protection of Lawful Commerce in Arms Act of 2005. The act prohibits civil liability actions against manufacturers, distributors, dealers, and importers of firearms or ammunition products, and their trade associations, for any harm caused by the criminal or unlawful misuse of firearms or ammunition. The act does not exempt those in the gun industry breaking the law or selling defective weapons or ammunition. However, gun control advocates see this legislation as a major setback. Although civil lawsuits are not won in the courtroom, they have the potential for yielding out-of-court settlements that promote reform in the gun industry.

Hurricane Katrina devastates the Gulf Coast states of Mississippi and Louisiana on August 29, 2005. Severe flooding in New Orleans breaks down the public safety system, and government responses, at all levels (federal, state, local), are inadequate. In reaction to looting and criminal assaults, some area residents arm themselves—but on September 8, city officials announce a ban on possession of firearms and instruct law enforcement to confiscate all guns they come across. Local and state police join in the effort, as does the National Guard. Gun rights advocates, and many in the gun control camp, are outraged, and numerous lawsuits and modifications to state laws ensue over the next year. In 2006, the Robert T. Stafford Disaster Relief and Emergency Assistance Act is signed into federal law, banning the disaster-related confiscation of guns. Many states, including Louisiana, enact similar legislation.

2007   On the morning of April 16, Virginia Tech student Seung-hui Cho uses two semiautomatic pistols to slay a total of 32 students and faculty. Before authorities can stop the carnage, he turns one of his guns on himself—ending the worst case of mass murder in U.S. history at the time.

The shock of the Virginia Tech massacre is magnified when it is discovered that despite Cho's lifelong history of mental illness, he had obtained his firearms *legally* in the preceding months. Gun control proponents use the tragedy to bemoan the inadequacy of current U.S. gun regulations, while gun rights proponents note that had Cho's adjudicated mental illness been properly registered with the federal government, he would have failed a background check and never been sold the guns he used in the massacre.

In a rare display of cooperation (albeit motivated for different reasons), the major gun control organization in the nation, the Brady Campaign, and the major gun rights organization, the NRA, work with congressional representatives to fashion the NICS Improvement Act of 2007—intended to improve the quality and quantity of criminal, mental health, and related data used by the NICS—with which federally licensed firearms retailers check the backgrounds of prospective gun buyers. More hardline groups on both sides of the gun issue (e.g., the Gun Owners of America and the Coalition to Stop Gun Violence) are disappointed by the final legislation. But many on both sides of the gun debate extol the act's carrot-and-stick approach toward getting the states to improve and then to submit their relevant computerized data to the NICS system in a timely manner, while enhancing the ability of prospective gun buyers previously judged as ineligible because of having been placed under a court order related to mental illness to seek relief. On December 17, 2007, the NICS Improvement Act is passed with strong bipartisan support, and signed into law (PL 110–180) by President George W. Bush on January 8, 2008.

Another consequence of the Virginia Tech massacre is the invigoration of the gun rights movement to allow college students and employees who have government permits to carry licensed concealed handguns everywhere else in the state to bring their weapons to campus, and to carry them concealed in accordance with state law. Founded on the evening of the massacre, Students for Concealed Carry grows to more than 40,000 members by 2016—at which time five states allow concealed carry allowed on their college campuses, and another five allow concealed carry but with restrictions being permitted by individual institutions on the locations where concealed carry is allowed.

2008–2010   In June 2008, in a landmark 5–4 decision in *District of Columbia v. Heller*, the U.S. Supreme Court holds that the district's ban on handgun possession in the home and its prohibition against rendering any lawful firearm in the home operable for the purposes of immediate self-defense violates the Second Amendment. The Court holds that the Second Amendment protects an individual right to possess a firearm unconnected with service in a militia and to use that firearm for traditionally lawful purposes, such as self-defense within the home.

In a follow-up 5–4 vote in June 2010, the sharply divided Court extends its ruling to include the 50 U.S. states and their municipalities in *McDonald v. City of Chicago*. The majority— Justices Alito, Roberts, Scalia, and Kennedy basing their decision on the due process clause of the Fourteenth Amendment, and Justice Thomas on the basis of the amendment's privileges or immunities clause—holds that the Fourteenth Amendment makes the Second Amendment applicable to state and local governments, as it does for most of the rest of the Bill of Rights.

Both decisions are watershed victories for the gun rights movement, though gun control activists note that the Supreme Court acknowledges in both cases that the individual-right interpretation does not mean that the right is unlimited—and that reasonable gun control regulations, including the major ones in effect at the time, are allowable.

2011   On January 8, a mentally ill gunman severely wounds U.S. congresswoman Gabrielle Giffords and kills six others at a political rally in Tucson, Arizona—including federal district court judge John Roll and nine-year-old Christina Taylor-Green. Giffords and her husband are motivated to found what becomes a major gun control advocacy group, Americans for Responsible Solutions.

In February, a secret ATF operation, "Fast and Furious," is exposed for having gone wrong and is heavily criticized in the media. The program allows selected "straw buyers"—those believed to be supplying Mexican drug cartels with weapons—to purchase assault-style and other firearms at U.S. retailers along the border; the intent is to follow the buyers and to document their handing over of the weapons to drug cartel members. However, many of the weapons are lost track of, some are smuggled into Mexico, and two are eventually recovered at the scene of a shootout where a U.S. Border Patrol agent is killed. When U.S. attorney general Eric Holder is asked about details of the operation, he claims ignorance of many of them—and almost immediately, the NRA starts a national petition to have him fired.

On June 2, Florida governor Rick Scott signs HB-155 into law. The legislation bars physicians from asking routine questions about firearms ownership and storage, as well as recording any such information they might receive in interviews with patients. More broadly, HB-155 reflects the long-held distrust of scholars and activists associated with the gun rights camp of public health research showing harmful outcomes of gun ownership, gun carrying, and having guns in the home—and at the same time giving no credibility to the benefits of guns in personal self-defense.

2012–2013   Horrific mass shootings in Aurora, Colorado (12 killed at the midnight opening of the Batman movie *Dark Knight Rises*; 6/20/2012), and Newtown, Connecticut (26 killed, including 20 first graders, at Sandy Hook Elementary School; 12/14/2012), motivate a rare bipartisan legislative proposal to create a federal universal background checking system. The legislation, proposed by Democratic senator Joe Manchin of West Virginia and Republican senator Pat Toomey of Pennsylvania, fails passage on April 13, 2013.

One bipartisan gun control proposal does pass, however, when on December 9, 2013, the Undetectable Firearms Act of 1988, which had already been renewed in 1998 and 2003, is once again renewed for a 10-year period. Not unnoticed by those who closely follow the contemporary American gun debate, the renewal of the plastic weapons ban is done by voice vote in the Senate—meaning no individual senator's vote is recorded. It is assumed by these observers that senators preferred the voice vote so as not to face criticism from strong proponents on either side of the debate in the upcoming 2014 midterm elections.

In an attempt to do something to reduce gun violence at a national level, President Barack Obama issues 23 executive actions on January 16, 2013—including requiring federal agencies to increase their efforts to supply the federal background check system with more complete data; improving incentives for states to supply more and better data to this system; and directing the Centers for Disease Control and Prevention to research the causes of gun violence. Although applauded by gun control proponents, few observers believe the executive actions will have any real effects on the problem of gun violence.

2015   The 2013 Machin-Toomey legislation is again proposed after the horrific mass shooting of 14 attendees of a holiday party in December of 2015 in San Bernardino, California. And, again, the legislation fails.

2016   The U.S. experiences the worst mass shooting in its history, as 49 are murdered and 53 injured at the Pulse nightclub in Orlando, Florida, in the early morning hours of June 12, 2016. Strong gun control legislation—on universal background checks and denying the sale of guns to those on the FBI's Terrorist Watchlist—is immediately proposed in the U.S. Senate, but fails passage. The House of Representatives refuses to hear any legislative proposals related to gun control, and in protest, on June 22, 2016, 170 Democratic Representatives lead an historic "sit-in" that lasts more than 24 hours. All to no avail.

Public attitudes in support of strong gun control laws begin to strengthen, for example, the Gallup Poll tracking of gun control with the question "In general, do you feel that the laws covering the sale of firearms should be made more strict, less strict, or kept as they are now?" reveals that those favoring more strict laws has increased from 44 percent in 2010 to 55 percent by 2016. In contrast to federal elections between 2002 and 2014, and reflective of this change in public opinion, Hillary Clinton brings gun violence and gun control to her political campaign and promises to work toward stronger gun control legislation if elected in November. Her defeat, however, almost assures that no new federal gun control legislation will be passed until at least 2020 (with the chances of passage being serious only if the Democrats win the presidency and both Houses of Congress).

The vocabulary commonly used in the gun debate is unfamiliar to many observers, even those who have grown up in a gun culture—where hunting or sport shooting or training in self-defense are common pursuits. This chapter offers brief definitions of some of this vocabulary.

active-shooter   A shooter actively engaged in killing or attempting to kill people in a confined and populated area, with the weapon of choice often being a semiautomatic handgun or rifle equipped with a large-capacity ammunition magazine. Although active-shooter incidents frequently take place in private homes and domestic settings, they are also commonly seen in public settings such as schools, workplaces, or shopping areas.

AK-47   A military rifle that can be fired in both automatic (continuous fire) or semiautomatic modes, it is one of the most widely used guns in the world. Since the late 1950s, it has seen many derivatives that shoot only as semiautomatics, even though they have the look and feel of the original AK-47, including having a high-capacity, detachable ammunition magazine that typically holds 20 or 30 rounds—but can handle an ammunition casket or drum of 60 or 100 rounds. Although the AK-47 and its derivatives are characterized by gun control advocates as *assault rifles*, the traditional definition of this term only includes guns that can fire in a fully automatic mode (like a machine gun).

ammunition   A combination of a projectile or projectiles (bullet in the case of rifles and handguns; pellets in the case of shotguns), powder, and an igniter into a single unit—called a *cartridge* for rifle and handgun ammunition, and a *shell* for shotguns.

AR-15   A smaller competitor of the Russian designed AK-47 carbine, it is lighter and more accurate than the AK-47 but fires a smaller round (most commonly, a .223). It is one of the most popular firearms purchased in the contemporary U.S. gun market (with an estimated 9 million in circulation in 2016). Gun manufacturers and gun rights proponents balk at the label "assault rifle" for the civilian versions of the AK-47 and AR-15. Regarding the latter, some gun control advocates have mistakenly understood "AR" as standing for "assault rifle" or "automatic rifle." However, it refers to ArmaLite—the original name of the firearm when it was created in the 1950s by the Fairchild-ArmaLite corporation. The corporation sold its AR-15 platform to Colt Manufacturing Company in 1959. Like the AK-47, the Colt platform has evolved into many clones in the civilian market. Gun manufacturers and gun rights activists prefer to call weapons like the AR-15 "modern sporting rifles," "tactical rifles," or simply "black guns."

assault rifle   The Department of Defense defines an "assault rifle" as a medium-caliber military rifle capable of "selective fire." That is, it is capable of being fired semiautomatically or fully automatically. Although the AK-47 and the AR-15 and their derivatives are characterized by gun control advocates as *assault rifles*, the traditional definition of this term only includes guns that are capable of being fired in a fully automatic mode (like a machine gun).

State and federal legislation aimed at regulating AK-47 and AR-15 platforms do not agree with gun rights groups' complaints that it is impossible to give a generic, operational definition of an "assault rifle." Instead, this legislation is based on the contention that certain characteristics differentiate military-style from civilian-style (for use in hunting and target shooting) rifles. Among the characteristics that define an assault rifle are a more compact design, a barrel less than 20 inches in length, extensive use of plastics in construction, lighter in weight (less than 10 pounds when unloaded), a pistol grip or thumbhole stock, a folding or telescoping grip, a barrel shroud, a threaded barrel for adding a silencer or flash suppressor, and the ability to receive a large-capacity ammunition magazine (that holds greater than the traditional 5–10 rounds; a high-capacity ammunition magazine typically holds 20–30 rounds, but can come in ammunition cartons or drums with as many as 100 rounds).

assault weapon   A firearm developed for military use as a light machine gun, but capable of firing in semiautomatic or fully automatic mode. The most common assault firearm is a carbine (short-barreled rifle), but there are also shotgun and handgun forms. A semiautomatic fires one bullet with each trigger pull, while a fully automatic weapon fires continuously when the trigger is pulled and not released.

automatic weapon   A fully automatic weapon fires continuously when the trigger is pulled and not released. Automatic weapons may be handguns, shotguns, rifles, or machine guns. Although not illegal to own or buy in the Unites States, fully automatic weapons are highly regulated by a special tax, license, registration, and transfer system.

background check   An inspection of criminal, mental health, and selected other aspects of the personal history of a prospective purchaser of a firearm. Federally licensed firearm dealers (typically retailers, pawnbrokers, and home-business operators) are required to have a potential gun purchaser complete ATF Form 4473, which is then matched against computerized records maintained by the state or federal government to ensure that the purchaser is not in a prohibited category of firearm possession according to federal law. Among other key pieces of information collected, this form asks the purchaser to attest that he or she: is not buying the firearm for another person; is not under indictment for a felony; has never been convicted of a felony (and if the crime involves domestic violence, of even a misdemeanor); is not a fugitive, unlawful drug user, or under a domestic violence restraining order; and has never been committed to a mental institution nor has ever been determined as mentally incompetent or as a danger to him- or herself by a lawful authority—such as court or board of medical examiners.

breech   The rear of the barrel of a firearm, which in modern guns is the point of entry for a cartridge when a gun is being loaded.

caliber   The diameter of a bullet (the projectile portion of a cartridge) of a rifle or handgun. Depending on which country a gun and its ammunition are manufactured, the diameter is expressed in hundredths (in the United States) or thousandths (in the United Kingdom) of an inch, or in millimeters (Europe, Asia, and elsewhere). Thus, for example, a U.S.-made .50 caliber handgun shoots ammunition with a bullet diameter of half inch.

carbine   A short-barreled rifle that has become popular in civilian use as an AK-47 or AR-15, or as a clone of one of these. A barrel under 20 inches long reduces size and weight, thus making the gun easier to handle compared to a traditional rifle with long barrel (22–26 inches). A common length for an AR-15 is 16 inches.

cartridge   A single round of rifle or handgun ammunition that combines a projectile (bullet), powder, and an igniter into a single unit.

case, or casing   The container used for the powder, igniter, and a portion of the projectile (bullet) of a cartridge. The casings for handguns and rifles are usually brass, whereas the casings (or shells) for shotguns are paper or plastic.

castle doctrine   A castle doctrine law allows for the use of deadly force with no duty to retreat if defending oneself at home. It is more restrictive than the *related stand-your-ground* law, which has a similar allowance but is not restricted to being on one's property.

clip   An ammunition clip holds cartridges for loading into a magazine and is sometimes used as a synonym for "magazine," though technically it is not a spring-based ammunition holder and loader (the operational definition of a common type of magazine). In short, a clip feeds a magazine, while a magazine feeds a semi- or fully automatic firearm.

concealed weapons laws   Laws adopted by most states in the 1800s and early 1900s banning the carrying of concealed weapons, including handguns and other firearms. Such laws have become an important part of the gun control debate since the late 1980s, when gun rights proponents pushed to remove permit-granting discretion from local police chiefs and sheriffs and to allow issuance of permits to those passing a standard federal background check (and in some cases, a gun safety course). At present, all 50 states allow concealed carry, with most requiring a readily obtainable "shall-issue" concealed carry license (or permit).

defensive gun use   Considered by gun rights activists to be one of the major "good" effects of gun possession—that is, its usefulness in defending against criminal attack. Defensive gun use normally does not involve the actual firing of the weapon—but more commonly the potential victim simply saying "I have a gun," or, in some cases, brandishing the weapon.

federally licensed firearms dealer (a.k.a. federal firearms licensee, or FFL)   All civilian sales of new firearms in the United States are made through federally licensed firearms dealers, regulated by the federal Gun Control Act of 1968. Retail dealers range from individuals selling guns from their homes to large chain stores such as Wal-Mart. Retailers get most of their guns from wholesale distributors, who are also federally licensed. Nevertheless, a large percentage of all gun sales each year are bought in the so-called secondary market—such as flea markets, gun shows, the Internet, and private transactions between individuals—which allow for the easy evasion of federal gun control laws. FFLs are required to maintain detailed paper records of firearms transactions, and are subject to periodic inspection by the ATF. (Note that some states impose their own licensing requirements on gun dealers.)

gun rights advocate/proponent   Individuals believing that the Second Amendment guarantees the right of the individual to keep and bear firearms. Their major fear is that gun control regulations will snowball to the point where gun ownership is banned outright. Although many gun rights proponents agree with certain limited forms of gun control, the major organizations representing the "rights of gun owners" in the political area—such as the National Rifle Association and the Gun Owners of America—resist almost all forms of gun control, no matter how much they are supported by public opinion.

gun show   An exposition where an organizer rents a facility and sells booth or table space to people selling guns. Gun shows appeal to hunters, target shooters, collectors, and those interested in self-defense. Many of the dealers at gun shows are licensed by the federal government and thus submit all prospective purchasers to a computerized background check to make sure they are legal buyers (e.g., do not have a felony conviction). However, many other sellers are unlicensed and do not conduct any background checking. Gun control proponents have labeled the latter situation the "gun show loophole," and closing this loophole has become one of their major aims. Although federal legislation has been proposed many times to close this loophole, none has been passed into law. Gun rights advocates contend that such legislation would increase costs for law-abiding citizens and do little to prevent criminals and others barred from possession (such as minors) from acquiring guns.

handgun   A short firearm that can be held and fired with one hand. The two main types are revolvers and semiautomatic pistols, the latter of which now dominates the market. Handguns make up about one-third of the privately owned firearms in the United States and are present in about one-quarter of households. Most owners cite self-defense as their primary reason for owning a handgun. Other reasons for handgun ownership include target shooting and job-related needs. A relatively small number of people also collect handguns or hunt with them.

high-capacity magazine   An ammunition holder and loader that holds more than 10 or 15 cartridges (federal law has used the 10-round maximum definition; state laws use either 10 or 15 rounds). High-capacity magazines are a controversial part of the modern gun control debate. Traditionally (and by law in many jurisdictions), hunters' ammunition magazines were nondetachable and held no more than five or six cartridges. Gun control advocates contend that high-capacity magazines are a favorite of gang members and of active-shooter, mass-murders and have no legitimate purposes. On the other hand, gun rights proponents maintain that such magazines are legitimate for sporting purposes other than hunting, as well as for self-defense.

iron pipeline   An iron pipeline is the systematic transportation of firearms bought in a state where gun control regulations are lax to states with stricter gun control regulations, where the weapons are then sold in the private market—often illegally (e.g., to known felons or drug abusers).

licensing   A method that governments use to regulate behavior by the granting of permission to engage in a particular activity. Gun licensing applies to gun manufacturers, gun dealers, and gun owners. Proponents of licensing justify it on the basis that it can help to prevent selected categories of individuals from obtaining guns—including criminals, children, and those considered mentally incompetent. It is also justified as a means to promote competency in gun use and safety on the part of gun owners. Retail and wholesale gun dealers, as well as gun and ammunition manufacturers, are required to have a federal license. Attempts to enact a national system of licensing for gun owners are a critical goal of gun control advocates, but all of their attempts to bring this about have failed. However, the District of Columbia and 14 U.S. states currently require a prospective gun buyer to obtain a license for buying a handgun, and the District of Columbia and 6 states add this requirement even for the purchase of a "long gun" (rifle or shotgun).

long gun A gun that is normally fired from the shoulder. Rifles and shotguns are the two primary types of long guns.

magazine A spring-loaded cartridge container that can be either built into a firearm or detachable. High-capacity magazines hold 10 or more cartridges and are a controversial part of the modern gun control debate.

mass murder The FBI defines a mass murder as one involving at least four homicide victims. Most mass murders are drug- or gang-related. A special subcategory of mass murders are those deemed "active-shooter mass-murders"; these are nongang- and nondrug-related (classic examples would be the mass shooting in December 2012 at Sandy Hook Elementary School in Newtown, Connecticut, and the mass shooting at the Pulse nightclub in June 2016 in Orlando, Florida).

militia A citizens' group organized to defend the community or state, whether against outside attack, rebellion, or the threats of a tyrannical government. All 13 of the original colonies had a colony-wide militia, in addition to many local militias within each colony. By the early 20th century, state and local militias were replaced by the U.S. military and the National Guard. In the modern era, militia groups have most often been associated with strong sentiments against the federal government, which is perceived as a tyranny.

modern sporting rifle A semiautomatic carbine (short-barreled rifle)—also known as a "tactical rifle" or "black gun"—that has become increasingly popular in the U.S. gun market. The two most common platforms are the modified (semiautomatic only) AK-47 and the AR-15. They have gained notoriety as a common weapon used in active-shooter, mass-shootings; and gun control activists refer to them as military-style "assault rifles."

open carry laws   State laws that allow ordinary citizens to carry their weapons openly. Laws vary by state; for example, some require a permit or limit the open carry to long guns, but currently 45 states have some version of legal open carry.

preemption laws   Laws in 45 states, many legislatively enacted and others created through judicial rulings, that prevent local governments from passing firearms laws stricter than those of the state.

purchase permit   The requirement that an individual obtain a permit (or license) before purchasing a firearm. A license is only granted after a criminal background check has been performed and a specified waiting period (ranging from three days to several months) has been satisfied. Currently, the District of Columbia and 14 U.S. states require a prospective gun buyer to obtain a license before buying a handgun, while the District of Columbia and 6 states add this requirement even for the purchase of a "long gun" (rifle or shotgun).

registration laws   Registration laws require that individuals possessing a firearm record that fact with law enforcement officials (at the local, state, or national level). Registration laws also cover the transfer of a firearm from one person to another (e.g., through purchase). Currently the District of Columbia and 11 states have some form of mandated gun registration. Except for the outright government confiscation of their firearms, the biggest fear of gun rights proponents is a computerized, national registration system—which could potentially allow a government gone tyrannical to identify and disarm gun owners.

revolver   A handgun holding five to nine rounds (usually six) in chambers bored in a rotating cylinder located at the breech of the barrel. Before each shot is fired, the cylinder is rotated to bring the next chamber in line with the barrel for firing. Cylinder rotation is accomplished by cocking the hammer. This can be done manually, or, in double-action revolvers, merely by pulling the trigger.

rifle   A shoulder-fired gun with a long barrel. It differs from shotguns and muskets in that the inside of the barrel has spiral-shaped grooves (usually three) running the length of the barrel. The grooves, or rifling, in the barrel impart a spin on the bullet that keeps it moving on a straighter path for longer distances than would be the case if it were shot from a smoothed bore gun (such as a musket or shotgun).

rifling   In modern handguns and rifles, a cartridge (which consists of a bullet mounted in a brass case with gunpowder and a primer) is inserted in the firing chamber at the breech, or rear end of the barrel. When the trigger is pulled, the firing pin is allowed to strike the primer, igniting the powder, which propels the bullet down the barrel. The barrel is "rifled" with spiral grooves running its entire length to make the bullet spin. This prevents the bullet from tumbling in flight, increasing accuracy over longer distances.

right-to-carry laws   Laws allowing for the average citizen to acquire, relatively easily, a concealed weapons permit to carry a handgun. The usual requirements are passing a federal background check (revealing, e.g., no felony convictions or domestic violence abuse incidents) and a training course in gun safety and operation. All 50 states allow right-to-carry, though in 9 states local law enforcement is given some discretion in issuing a concealed weapons permit (e.g., by conducting a more extensive background check than the instant check provided by the National Instant Criminal Background Check System).

semiautomatic   A gun that fires with each pull of the trigger without the shooter having to manually insert a cartridge into the chamber. After each shot, the spent shell is automatically ejected and a new cartridge is automatically loaded into the chamber for immediate firing. Rifles, shotguns, and handguns all have semiautomatic versions. Semiautomatics increase the firing rate compared with their bolt action, lever action, and revolver counterparts.

sentence enhancement laws   An approach to controlling gun violence whereby those using guns in the commission of crimes are given stiffer prison sentences (a longer sentence, usually with a reduced possibility of parole).

shall-issue law   The definition of shall-issue law is the same as right-to-carry law. "Shall-issue" implies that local or state law enforcement agencies do not have the *discretion* to issue a concealed weapons permit for an ordinary citizen to carry a handgun. If a citizen passes a federal background check and, in some cases, a firearms safety course, the relevant agency *must* issue a permit.

shotgun   A long gun developed for bird hunting. Unlike the other type of long gun, the rifle, the inside of a shotgun barrel is smooth—and thus incapable of throwing objects very far (targets are usually less than one hundred yards away) or very accurately. The loss of accuracy is made up for by the large number of pellets contained in a shotgun shell. The pellets spray out in a large circular pattern (up to three feet in diameter; note that many birds can be taken down when hit by only a few pellets). Shotguns are a preferred weapon for self-defense, because the shooter does not have to aim that well to hit an attacker.

stand-your-ground law   A stand-your-ground law allows for the use of deadly force with no duty to retreat if defending oneself at home or in a public place where one is legally allowed to be. It is less restrictive than related *castle-doctrine* law, which has a similar allowance but is limited to self-defense on one's property.

straw purchaser   An acquaintance or relative without a criminal record purchasing a gun on behalf of someone barred from possessing a firearm—such as a juvenile or convicted felon.

trigger lock A device designed to prevent the accidental discharge of a firearm. The simplest of these is a combination or key lock that fits over the trigger area (called a "clamshell" lock); a related type is the cable lock, which is strung through the barrel or trigger guard. Since 1999, the U.S. Department of Justice, in conjunction with the National Shooting Sports Foundation, has funded the distribution of millions of cable and related trigger locks through their Project ChildSafe program. More sophisticated trigger locks use "smart gun" technology that makes the weapon inoperable until the lock is released by a signal from a special ring or bracelet worn by the owner, or until the owner's finger or palm print is matched.

waiting periods A legally mandated delay between the time a gun is purchased and the time the purchaser may take possession of it (sometimes called a "cooling-off" period). Waiting periods provide authorities with the opportunity to conduct a criminal and mental competency background check of the prospective purchaser and allow for a cooling-off period—in case the individual is buying the gun on impulse (to commit a crime or suicide). The 1993 Brady Handgun Violence Prevention Act imposed a five-business-day waiting period for handgun purchases but was replaced by a computerized "instant" background checking system in 1998. However, the District of Columbia and 16 states maintain waiting periods, ranging from three days to several months, especially for the purchase of handguns.

About the Author

Gregg Lee Carter is professor of sociology at Bryant University in Smithfield, Rhode Island. He earned his PhD degree in sociology at Columbia University. He has authored or edited 24 books, including *Guns in American Society: An Encyclopedia of History, Politics, Culture, and the Law*, 2nd ed. (ABC-CLIO, 2012; first edition 2002), *Gun Control in the United States: A Reference Handbook* (ABC-CLIO, 2006), and *The Gun Control Movement* (1997).

His writings on gun control and contemporary social issues have also appeared in more than a dozen academic journals.